TURNING
THE TIDE

DECISIVE BATTLES OF
THE SECOND WORLD WAR

TURNING THE TIDE

DECISIVE BATTLES OF THE SECOND WORLD WAR

Nigel Cawthorne

ARCTURUS

Arcturus Publishing
1–7 Shand Street, London SE1 2ES

Published in association with

W. Foulsham & Co. Ltd

The Publishing House, Bennetts Close, Cippenham,
Slough, Berkshire SL1 5AP

ISBN 0-572-02841-5

Printed in China

Edited by Paul Whittle
Cover & book design by Alex Ingr
Maps by Alex Ingr and Simon Towey
Cover images ©Robert Hunt Library

CONTENTS

INTRODUCTION

A LTHOUGH THE SECOND WORLD WAR has been over for nearly 60 years and most of those who took part in it are no longer with us, the war remains a topic of enduring fascination. How was it that the world could be drawn into such madness, which consumed the lives of some fifteen million servicemen and women, and between twenty and forty-five million civilians? And how was it that the efficient and well-equipped armies of ruthless warlike states, who seemed initially unstoppable, could be defeated by a coalition of nations who had no desire to go to war?

The origins of the Second World War can be found in the First World War. As an ally of Britain, France and America, Italy had been on the winning side in 1918, but it did not do as well out of the peace settlement as it expected. In the period of economic instability that followed the war, the political agitator Benito Mussolini seized power. In 1922, he became the first Fascist dictator, promising his people a return to the glories of imperial Rome. His new empire did not stretch very far though. In 1935–36, he seized Abyssinia (now called Ethiopia) and in 1939 he occupied Albania.

After the First World War, many former members of the German army, including the Austrian corporal Adolf Hitler, were disaffected. They felt that they had been defeated not on the battlefield, but by Communist agitation at home, a feeling encouraged by the Dolchstoss legend (the 'stab-in-the-back'). Many prominent German Communists at that time were Jewish. Those who opposed them played on the long tradition of anti-Semitism in Germany. The $33 billion in reparations demanded by the victors in the First World War at the Versailles Conference of 1919 bankrupted Germany and brought political infighting to the streets. The result was the rise to power of the Nazi Party and its demagogic leader Adolf Hitler, who became Chancellor in 1933. In 1936, he signed an agreement with Mussolini, forming an anti-Communist 'Axis'.

Hitler made no secret of his ambitions. In his political mani-festo, *Mein Kampf* ('My Struggle') published in two volumes in 1925 and 1927, he makes no attempt to hide his anti-Semitism. He also makes clear that he intends to make Germany a mighty empire on the Continent with its borders extending to include European Russia, where the Slav peoples would be dominated by the Teutonic master race.

Hitler made his first gains by diplomacy, arguing for the return of territory taken from Germany by the Versailles agreement. He got the Saarland back from France in 1935, reoccupied the Rhineland in 1936, against the advice of his generals, and took his native Austria into his Third Reich in 1938. (The First Reich – or realm – had been the Holy Roman Empire from 1157 to 1806; the Second Reich was the German Empire under the Prussian Hohenzollerns from 1871 to 1918.) After the *Anschluss* (joining) with Austria, Hitler demanded the Sudetenland, part of Czechoslovakia, and threatened war. A peace conference in Munich in September 1938 dismembered Czechoslovakia, giving Hitler the territory he wanted. In March 1939, however, he seized the rest of Czechoslovakia. What Hitler really wanted was to go to war. He had progressively defied the Versailles agreement that had also disarmed Germany. He rearmed and soon had a powerful army, air force and navy. The Western Allies, particularly Britain and France, had suffered huge losses in the First World War and they had no desire to go to war with Germany again. Their armed forces were ill-prepared for a modern war so they had little choice but to appease the demands of the dictator.

Japan had also been on the winning side in the First World War and, again, was disappointed in the territorial gains it was award-ed in the peace settlement. However, the Versailles Conference awarded Japan former German concessions in China. The Japanese had long coveted an Empire like the ones Britain, France and the Netherlands had established in the Far East. In 1910, it had annexed Korea and, during the First World War, had established a toehold in Manchuria. In 1931, the Japanese consolidated their hold on Manchuria and, when the Chinese objected, fire-bombed Shanghai. The Chinese appealed to the League of Nations, which found in China's favour. Japan promptly withdrew from the League. When China was further weakened by the fall of the last Emperor of the Manchu Dynasty, Japan swallowed up Mongolia and parts of China's Hebei province.

Up until this time, the Japanese military had been constrained by a civilian government at home. But in 1936, the military seized power in Tokyo and signed the anti-Communist 'Axis' pact with Nazi Germany and Fascist Italy. In 1937, the Japanese commanders in Manchuria decided to 'solve the Chinese question once and for all' and launched a full-scale invasion. The United States insisted that Japan be 'quarantined' for this aggression.

On 23 August 1939, the staunchly anti-Communist Hitler signed a Non-Aggression Pact with the leader of the Soviet Union – Communist Russia and its satellites – Joseph Stalin. Everything was set for a war that would engulf the whole world.

Over the six years of war that followed, there were hundreds of battles. Unfortunately there is not the space to cover them all here. Indeed whole campaigns are missing, such as the heroic fight by British and Dominion troops against the Japanese in Burma. It has also not been possible to include such decisive action as the Battle of the Atlantic, which maintained the British lifeline from America against German submarines and warships, or the RAF and USAAF – the United States Army Air Force, as the American air force was then known – bombing campaign against Germany. But these actions went on day-after-day for years and are not battles in the conventional sense.

However, the decisive battles we have picked here do cover the main scenes of action. Taken together, they explain how the war progressed and how the use of improved technology, the harnessing of industrial might, the development of well co-ordinated combined operations and the willingness of individuals to sacrifice their own lives for what they thought to be right finally brought victory to the Allies.

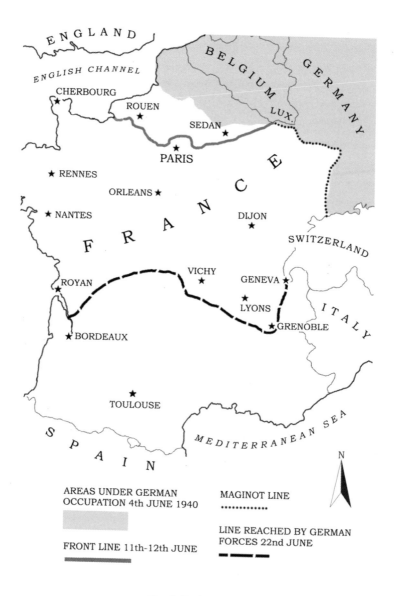

ENGLAND

ENGLISH CHANNEL

BELGIUM

GERMANY

CHERBOURG ★

ROUEN ★

LUX.

SEDAN ★

PARIS ★

F R A N C E

★ RENNES

ORLEANS ★

★ NANTES

DIJON ★

SWITZERLAND

ROYAN ★

VICHY ★

GENEVA ★

LYONS ★

ITALY

★ BORDEAUX

GRENOBLE ★

TOULOUSE ★

S P A I N

MEDITERRANEAN SEA

N

AREAS UNDER GERMAN
OCCUPATION 4th JUNE 1940

MAGINOT LINE
••••••••••••

LINE REACHED BY GERMAN
FORCES 22nd JUNE

FRONT LINE 11th-12th JUNE

*The fall of France
June 1940*

1

WESTERN EUROPE

THE ROAD TO DUNKIRK

THE SECOND WORLD WAR began on 1 September 1939. At dawn, a huge German army rolled across the 1,250-mile Polish border. Immediately Britain and France ordered a general mobilisation. Their ambassadors in Berlin delivered identical messages to the German Foreign Ministry saying that if Germany did not withdraw her troops from Poland, Britain and France would 'fulfil their obligations to Poland without hesitation'. France had had a military treaty with Poland since 1921 and Britain had pledged its assistance to Poland, if its independence was threatened, on 31 March 1939, marking an end to the policy of appeasement.

Britain had given Germany a deadline for her withdrawal from Poland – 0900 on 3 September. Two hours later, Prime Minister Neville Chamberlain declared war. At midday, the French ambassador in Berlin called the German Foreign Minister Joachim von Ribbentrop who told him that Germany refused to halt her invasion of Poland. France declared war at 1700.

The fifty-five German armoured and motorised divisions that rolled over the Polish border on 1 September faced just seventeen infantry divisions, three infantry brigades and six cavalry brigades. Poland had only mobilised on 31 August and thirteen divisions were still moving to their concentration areas, with another nine mustering in their barracks. While the Germans had modern arms and equipment, a large part of the Polish weaponry dated from the 1920s and fast-moving German Panzers (tanks) were charged by cavalry wielding lances. Against the Polish Air Force's 842 obsolescent planes, the Luftwaffe – the German airforce – could put 4,700 modern aircraft in the air. German planes devastated Polish road, railways, bridges and power stations, and terror-bombed the cities.

There was little Britain and France could do to help Poland. The French Army had been prepared for defence not attack and there were no British forces on the Continent until the first part of the British Expeditionary Force took its place in the line at Lille, in France, on 3 October – one month after Britain had declared war.

Nevertheless the French did attack Germany on 7 September in Operation Saar. It was a disaster. To avoid violating Belgian neutrality, the French had to attack along the frontier between the Rhine and the Moselle which had been drawn up after the defeat of Napoleon at Waterloo with the specific aim of discouraging French aggression. The Germans held the high ground and salients into French territory. The Germans had booby-trapped houses and laid cleverly sited fields of anti-tank and anti-personnel mines. The French were completely defensive. They did not possess any mine detectors. Beyond the border was the Siegfried Line, a German defensive wall built during the 1930s. To attack it, the French had to bring their own artillery within range of the German batteries, which were well defended inside concrete casemates. French 155mm shells made little impression and the heavier 220mm and 280mm shells were not fitted with delayed action fuses which would have let them penetrate the casemates before exploding. Although French fire was rapid and accurate, many of their shells, which were of the First World War vintage, failed to explode.

In Poland, however, the Germans were demonstrating the effectiveness of their new tactic of Blitzkrieg – 'lightning war'. Armoured columns would race across the flat Polish landscape with any defensive action being annihilated by dive-bombers. By 8 September, a German armoured corps was in the outskirts of the

Polish capital Warsaw, having advanced 140 miles in seven days. The attack had been so swift that, by 10 September, Polish defence had been reduced to pockets of isolated troops.

By 13 September, the French decided that the Battle of Poland had been lost and the French advance into the Saarland, which was making no significant progress, was told to halt. French casualties were twenty-seven killed, twenty-eight missing and twenty-two wounded. They had also lost nine fighters and eighteen reconnaissance planes, out of an air force that was already significantly under strength.

Then on 17 September, Soviet forces entered Poland from the east. The country was to be partitioned by Hitler and Stalin under a secret protocol that accompanied their Non-Aggression Pact. On the morning of 18 September, the Polish government and high command crossed the Rumanian frontier into exile and formal resistance was over. The Warsaw garrison held out against the Germans until 28 September, while terror-bombings and artillery barrages reduced parts of the city to rubble. The Germans set the city's flour mills ablaze and destroyed the water supply with no regard for the civilian population. The last serious body of the Polish Army held out until 5 October, though some guerrilla fighting went on into the winter. By then, Poland, as an independent state, had been ceased to exist. The Germans took a total of 700,000 prisoners. The Soviets took 217,000. The officers were murdered in the Katyn Forest. Many of the rest died from maltreatment. About 80,000 Polish soldiers escaped over the Rumanian frontier and continued the fight against Germany from France and Britain. It is not known how many Poles were killed, wounded, or missing. The cost to the Germans was 45,000 casualties.

On 27 September 1939, before the Germans had even taken Warsaw, Hitler told his generals that an offensive should be launched immediately against France. Hitler had wanted to defeat

France, particularly, to erase the humiliation of Germany's defeat in the First World War. The attack should come as soon as possible as the Western Allies were then ill-prepared for war and could only get stronger. Plans were laid to launch an attack between 20 and 25 October.

However, Hitler was still prepared to make peace. In a speech to the Reichstag – the German Parliament – on 5 October, he proposed a peace agreement on the basis of the partition of Poland, along the lines of that agreed in a new treaty signed with Stalin in Moscow on 28 September. Britain and France declined, so on 9 October Hitler told his army, navy and air force to begin preparations. The initial attack, like that in the First World War, would be through Belgium, but it would also violate Dutch territory in what was known as the 'Maastricht Appendix'. The head of the Luftwaffe, *Reichsmarschall* Herman Göring, feared that the Dutch government might retaliate by allowing the British Royal Air Force to use their airbases to bomb Germany, so the plan was altered to take in the invasion of the Netherlands.

Britain and France watched the German build-up on the borders of Holland and Belgium with growing disquiet, but heavy rain that autumn meant that Hitler had to postpone the attack no fewer than thirteen times. Due to the lack of action that period became known as the Phoney War.

Before the Battle of France got underway Hitler's attention turned to the north. Initially he had intended to respect Norway's neutrality, but rumours leaked of British designs on Norway. Winston Churchill, then First Lord of the Admiralty, planned to lay mines in Norwegian waters to stop the export of Swedish iron ore from Gällivare to Germany through the Norwegian port of Narvik. The British Cabinet also authorised Churchill to prepare a landing at Narvik.

Hitler feared that, if the British took Norway, they would cut

German ports off from the Atlantic and threaten Germany itself through the Baltic. However, an argument between the French and the British delayed the beginning of mine-laying operations from 5 April until 8 April. On 9 April, with the connivance of the leader of the Norwegian Fascist Party, Vidkun Quisling, Hitler invaded, deploying paratroopers for the first time in warfare. Quisling was rewarded by becoming 'minister president' under a German commissioner. That same day, the German Army – the *Wehrmacht* – overran Denmark. However Sweden managed to maintain its neutral status throughout the Second World War.

The British and French responded by sending in troops of their own to Norway. Despite setbacks elsewhere, on 27 May, the Allies eventually took Narvik after fierce German resistance. But by this time, the Battle of France had begun and, ten days after taking Narvik, the 25,000 Allied troops there were evacuated. For the rest of the war, some 300,000 German troops were stationed in Norway. This guaranteed Germany its supply of Swedish iron ore and gave them naval and air bases for their struggle against the British.

Although the French were ill-equipped to attack, it had been thought that they were more than ready to defend themselves. In 1939 France had a standing army of 800,000 men which was thought to be the most powerful in Europe at the time. During the 1930s, the French had also built the Maginot Line, a line of fortifications that ran along France's border with Germany from the Swiss frontier to the Belgian border south of the Ardennes Forest. Its giant pillboxes, underground supply depots, fortified communications facilities and heavy guns pointing eastwards were designed to discourage German aggression. With forty-one divisions manning it, it seemed invincible. However, there were no fortifications along the border with Belgium, though it was defended by thirty-nine divisions.

The Dutch Army had ten divisions and ten smaller formations, a conscript army of over 400,000 men. But the Netherlands had managed to stay out of the First World War, so they had no experience of modern warfare. On 10 May, the Germans attacked with just seven divisions. Again they used paratroopers who captured vital bridges at Rotterdam, Moerdijk, and Dordrecht. They also landed at the airfields around The Hague, but were repulsed. At the same time, the German 9th Panzer Division raced across the country to link up with their airborne troops. On 11 May the Dutch defenders fell back to Breda, along with the French Seventh Army which had sped 140 miles across Belgium to assist them. By midday on 12 May German tanks were in the suburbs of Rotterdam. The Dutch retreated into the 'Fortress of Holland', the area north of the Maas and Waal rivers, to protect Amsterdam and Utrecht. But with few planes and few anti-aircraft guns, the Dutch had no defence against German air attacks. Queen Wilhelmina and her government escaped to England on 13 May, where she was later joined by the Norwegian king Haakon VII and his government. The Germans threatened to bomb Rotterdam and Utrecht if resistance continued and, on 14 May, Holland capitulated – though Rotterdam was bombed anyway due to a mix-up in German communications.

But the attack on Holland was a diversion. The main attack would come through Belgium. On 10 May German paratroops landed in gliders on the top of the fortress of Eben Emael, to the north of Liège, and on bridges over the Albert Canal, which runs from Maastricht to Antwerp and was the Belgians' forward line of defence. Although the invaders had only four army corps and one armoured corps, along with five hundred airborne troops, at their disposal, air attacks and terror-bombing quickly took their toll on the defenders. On 11 May, the Belgian line collapse and German tanks swept through to take Liège from the rear. The Belgian army retreated to a defensive line along the River Dyle, where they were joined by British and French troops. Two tank divisions staged a set piece battle to check the German advance. The Dyle Line might have held, but by 15 May it had been outflanked and had to be abandoned.

However, the setbacks in Norway, Holland and Belgium brought with them one benefit which may well have been decisive. On the evening of 10 May, the architect of the policy of appeasement, British Prime Minister Neville Chamberlain, resigned and was succeeded by Churchill, who formed a national government.

The British and the French had imagined that the main German attack would come through Liège and Namur as it had in the First World War. The plain there was perfect tank country. Instead, using a plan developed by General Erich von Manstein, the German main offensive came on a narrow front through the dense and hilly Ardennes Forest, which the French thought was impassable to tanks. Again on 10 May, Field Marshal Gerd von Rundstedt threw 1,500,000 men and over 1,500 tanks – two-thirds of Germany's forces in the west and nearly three-quarters of its tanks – against the weakest part of the front, which was defended by just twelve infantry divisions and four cavalry divisions mounted on horses. The attack was brilliantly organised. A thrust through Luxembourg took just three hours to cover the thirty miles to the Belgian border. Another thrust through the forest itself sent the armoured divisions down the narrow lanes. It reached France in less than three days, crossing the border on the evening of 12 May. The infantry followed, using pathways through the woods, travelling so fast that they reached the River Meuse just a day behind the armour. The French had not expected an advance in this area and the defences there were rudimentary. There were no fortifications in that sector and the French forces there had few anti-aircraft or anti-tank guns to take on the German dive-bombers or armoured columns; the French cavalry divisions which rode in on horseback to reinforce the sector were forced to retreat to the Semois River on 11 May.

On 13 May, after the French defenders on the south bank had

been devastated by waves of dive-bombers, German infantry crossed the Meuse on rafts and in rubber dinghies at Sedan – the site of France's defeat in the Franco-Prussian War in 1870. The French had just a handful of aircraft aloft, while the German thrust was supported by a thousand. The next day, German tanks crossed the river and, on 15 May, they broke through what remained of the French defences. It was estimated that the Germans could be in Paris in two days. Instead, the Germans turned westwards towards the Channel. The following day, the German spearhead covered almost fifty miles of open country. The advance was so fast that even the German High Command were worried that it was vulnerable but, when it was joined by a diversionary German force that had come through Liège, French resistance collapsed. Facing almost no opposition, the Germans reached Amiens on 19 May. German tanks entered Abbeville on 20 May and on 22 May they turned northwards towards Dunkirk and Calais. The French and British suddenly found that had been fighting the wrong war. They imagined that the German advance would sweep across Belgium to the coast and turn southwards, as it had in the First World War. Instead it swept southwards into France, then swept around in an arc to the north. This move was known as the *Sichelschitt* (sickle stroke). It broke all communication between Allied forces north and south of this 'Panzer corridor' and the French and British forces that had advanced into Belgium were now threatened with encirclement. As early as 19 May the British commander, Viscount Gort, had considered withdrawing the British Expeditionary Force (BEF) by sea, but the British government wanted action, for the sake of the alliance with France. Gort gave it to them. On 21 May, he launched an attack southwards from Arras against the Germans' right flank in an attempt to break through to the French forces to the south. This kind of counter-attack was just what the German High Command had feared.

By that time, the head of the German column had swept through Boulogne and Calais. Dunkirk was now the only Channel port left in Allied hands that the BEF could withdraw through. The Allies had set up their final defence line along the Canal d'Aire outside Dunkirk. On 24 May, the Germans were crossing the canal, ready to make their final push to take the town when Hitler ordered them to halt their advance. News of the counter-attack at Arras was confused and it seemed that the British were a genuine threat.

The German dive-bombers had virtually had the skies to themselves up to this point, but as they approached the coast found themselves under attack from RAF fighters based in England. Nevertheless, Göring promised Hitler that he could finish off the Dunkirk bridgehead with his Luftwaffe alone.

As it was, Gort did not have the armour to break through the Panzer corridor. He was running short of supplies and ammunition and, on 25 May, he ordered the BEF to fall back on Dunkirk. The British government now decided that they had to save what could be saved. On 19 May, Churchill had ordered Admiral Bertram Ramsay to prepare for an evacuation. Already the call had gone out for small boats. Now the race was on to evacuate the troops before Dunkirk fell to the Germans. Operation Dynamo, as the evacuation was called, began on 26 May. With the British in Belgium withdrawing towards Dunkirk, the Belgian Army were left to face the Germans alone. On 27 May, they broke. The following day, King Leopold surrendered unconditionally. Rather than go into exile, he remained a German prisoner for the rest of the war.

As Gort no longer posed a threat, Hitler ordered that the advance on Dunkirk be resumed. But the hiatus had allowed the British to consolidate their defences. When the order came to advance again, the Germans met considerable resistance. Almost immediately Hitler ordered the German armour to stop. Hitler and Von Rundstedt agreed that it would be best to reserve the Panzers for use against the remaining French army under General Maxime Weygand to the south.

With resistance in Belgium over, the Luftwaffe began bombing the harbour at Dunkirk, putting it out of action. However, the RAF's air cover prevented Göring fulfilling his boast that he could destroy what was left of the BEF on the beaches at Dunkirk with his planes. The harbour's bomb-damaged breakwater was still serviceable and allowed many of the troops to be taken off by larger craft. The rest were picked up directly from a ten-mile stretch of beach, where they mustered, by small craft largely manned by amateur sailors. In all 848 British, French and Belgian ships of all sizes – from destroyers to private motor cruisers – joined the operation. In the eight days of Operation *Dynamo*, some 340,000 men, two-thirds of them British, were rescued. But almost all their equipment was abandoned and, of the forty-one destroyers participating in the evacuation, six were sunk and nineteen others damaged.

Another 220,000 Allied troops were rescued by British ships from Cherbourg, Saint-Malo, Brest, and Saint-Nazaire in north-western France, bringing the total of Allied troops evacuated to about 560,000. But in three weeks the German army had taken more than a million men prisoner, while sustaining some 60,000 casualties itself.

Although the action at Dunkirk was actually a withdrawal, it was hailed as a victory by the British. In the long run, it proved decisive. The bulk of Britain's most experienced troops had been saved. Controversy still rages about why Hitler stayed his hand and allowed the British Army to get away. It may have been one of the several key mistakes he made during the Second World War, though some believe that Hitler still wanted to make peace with Britain and thought that this might be more easily achieved if the British Army was not forced into a humiliating surrender.

Although the BEF was now safely back in Britain, the Battle of

France was not over. The French had lost thirty divisions so far, but General Weygand could still muster forty-nine divisions, along with another seventeen who were still holding the Maginot Line. But the Germans had 140 divisions at their disposal, including ten divisions of tanks. On 5 June the Wehrmacht started pushing southwards from their positions on the Somme. The French held them for two days, but on 7 June Panzers under Major-General Erwin Rommel, the 'Desert Fox', broke through south-westwards toward Rouen. Two days after that they crossed the Seine. That same day, 9 June, the Germans broke through to the south-east, then made a dash for the Swiss border, cutting off the French forces still holding the Maginot Line. To all intents and purposes, the Battle of France was lost.

When Hitler attacked Poland, Italy had not been prepared to go to war and, for some time, the British had hoped that Italy might be persuaded to join the Allied side, as it had in the First World War, or at least remain neutral. However, on 22 May 1940, Mussolini had signed a military alliance with Hitler, known as the Pact of Steel. Plainly, if Mussolini wanted to benefit from this alliance it would be best if he did not let Hitler win his war against the western democracies single-handedly. On 10 June 1940, Mussolini declared war on France and Great Britain. Some thirty Italian divisions massed on the French frontier, though the attack was delayed until 20 June. Even then the Italians made little progress against local defence and made no contribution of strategic importance.

As the Germans advanced, the French government under Paul Reynaud had left Paris for Cangé, near Tours. There, on 12 June, he received news from General Weygand that the Battle of France was lost. Reynaud wanted to continue the war from the French possessions in North Africa, but his cabinet was split.

On 14 June 1940, the Germans entered Paris and drove on rapidly south. The French government had to flee southwards from Tours to Bordeaux to stay ahead of the advance. The French Army was now split into a dozen fragments and Weygand pressed for an armistice. Reynaud's position was untenable and he resigned on 16 June. He was replaced by his deputy the elderly Marshal Philippe Pétain, who was France's most honoured soldier in the First World War and hero of the Battle of Verdun. That same day, General Charles de Gaulle, then under-secretary for defence in Reynaud's administration, arrived in London. That night, Pétain's government requested an armistice. While the two sides discussed terms, the German advance continued until it had swallowed two-thirds of the country. On 22 June 1940, the representatives of Germany and France met at Compiègne. This had been the site of the headquarters of the invading German Army in the First World War and the armistice ending the war in 1918 had been signed in a railway carriage there. The carriage had been preserved as a monument. Hitler came to Compiègne personally to watch the new armistice being signed in that same carriage. The carriage was then taken back to Germany. It was destroyed in April 1945 to prevent it falling into Allied hands.

The 1940 armistice divided France into two zones. Northern France, from the Swiss border to the Channel and a western strip down the Atlantic coast to the Spanish border, was to be held under German military occupation. The rump of the country and its overseas possessions were to be left in the hands of a collaborationist government under Pétain based at Vichy. Later, when its overseas possessions were lost, the Vichy government became a mere puppet. However on 18 June, de Gaulle began broadcasting appeals for France to continue the war from London, where he organised the Free French Forces. On 2 August 1940, he was tried in absentia by a French military court and sentenced to death.

Although the Battle of France had been decisively lost, there was one last action. Britain – with its Empire – now stood alone. Sea power was all important and the British government decided that it could not risk the French Navy, which was technically under the control of Vichy, falling into German hands. Britain seized all French ships in ports under its control, but the French still had a considerable fleet at its naval base at Mers-el-Kébir in Algeria. On 3 July 1940, British ships appeared off the Algerian coast. When the French fleet refused to join the Allies, the British opened fire, putting the fleet out of action. In protest the Vichy government broke diplomatic relations with the British. The ships that survived were later destroyed by the Germans to prevent them falling into Allied hands.

THE BATTLE OF BRITAIN

'What General Weygand called the "Battle of France" is over. I expect the "Battle of Britain" to begin,' Churchill told a hushed House of Commons on 18 June 1940. With France out of the way, Hitler once again sought to make peace, keeping the Continent for himself and leaving Britain its overseas Empire. But as Britain showed no willingness to come to terms, Hitler began to prepare for battle once again.

The enemy, he knew, was in no position to resist him. In Great Britain and Northern Ireland, there were just twenty-nine divisions – including two Canadian divisions – and eight independent brigades, six of which were armoured. They were outnumbered four to one. What is more, the British were poorly equipped. On 8 June, they had just seventy-two tanks. This number was to increase to 200 by August and 438 by September but – as events in North Africa would later show – they were already obsolescent.

In June, the British Home Forces had just 420 field guns and 163 heavy guns with 200 and 150 rounds respectively. The British two-pounder (40mm) guns – of which they had just fifty-four – were of little use against tanks. What was needed was 75mm guns, which had proved their worth as tank-killers in the Battle of France. Fortunately, the United States allowed the British to take over arms contracts that the French had signed. Orders included 900 75mm guns with 1,000 shells each, along with 500,000 rifles. The British had to pay cash for these and transport them to Britain themselves. The British Merchant Navy did this without a single loss to U-boats.

For nearly a month after the fall of France, Hitler dallied, hoping that the British would settle. Then on 16 July 1940, he signed Führer Directive No. 16, authorising Operation *Sealion* – the invasion of England. The month had not been wasted by the British. They had stepped up armament production and prepared their defences. And the delay gave them cause for optimism. It was estimated that the Germans would need at least two months to prepare for the invasion. That meant it could not come earlier than 16 September, when rougher autumn weather would be starting in the Channel. This could prove decisive.

On 19 July Hitler addressed the Reichstag, saying that he saw no reason for further bloodshed and, again, offering to come to terms with the British. London made no response, so the preparations for Operation Sealion went ahead. However, the German schedule was much quicker than the British anticipated. D-Day was set at 25 August. The invasion force would consist of forty-one divisions, six armoured and three motorised, along with two divisions of airborne troops. The Sixteenth Army would land between Ramsgate and Hastings, while the Ninth would land between Brighton and Littlehampton, with a detachment taking the Isle of Wight. This force under Von Rundstedt would head for a line running from Gravesend through Reigate to Portsmouth. Soon after, the Sixth Army, which was mustered on the Cherbourg Peninsula, would land on the Dorset coast between Weymouth and Lyme Regis. It would strike towards Bristol with a detachment taking Devon. At that same moment, the Ninth Army would break through the

British defences on the North Downs, cross the River Thames at Reading and encircle London from the west.

There was a problem though. The commander of the German Navy (*Kriegsmarine*) Grand-Admiral Erich Raeder, pointed out that, even if he requisitioned every available vessel from the fishing fleets and inland waterways – which would have devastating effects on food supplies and war production – he could not land the first wave of thirteen divisions, even if their numbers were considerably reduced. Besides, the Royal Navy was still a considerable fighting force and Raeder did not think he would be able to give the invasion fleet sufficient protection. So the attack on Devon was dropped from the plan and in the invasion force reduced to twenty-seven divisions.

The Germans did not have a battle fleet large enough to give the troops landing on the English beaches the necessary artillery support and the Luftwaffe would not be able to provide total coverage either. So huge batteries were built along the French coast from Sangatte to Boulogne which would pound the invasion beaches. To provide the assault force support when they got ashore, the Germans developed submarine tanks. These were regular Panzers that had been waterproofed and fitted with a flexible snorkel so that the engine would run, and the occupants could breath. They would be dropped offshore by special landing craft, sink to the bottom in 25-30 feet of water, then drive up onto the beaches. Experiments off the island of Sylt in the North Sea showed that the submarine Panzers worked perfectly. Even so, the German land forces would need the support of dive-bombers and, as a preliminary, massive Stuka attacks would be needed to destroy the British coastal defences. To do that, the Germans would need air superiority.

On 1 August 1940, Hitler signed Führer Directive No. 17, ordering the Luftwaffe to smash the RAF as quickly as they could. They were to take the RAF on in the air and attack their ground facilities and supply centres. They were to bomb aircraft factories and factories producing anti-aircraft guns. They were also to attack the ports which brought in vital supplies – though leaving intact the Channel ports which would be needed in the invasion. British cities, though, were not to be terror-bombed without the express order of Hitler himself.

The Germans deployed three air fleets against Britain. They flew from Norway and Denmark, Belgium and Holland, and Northern France. Between them they had 2,442 aircraft – 969 heavy bombers, 336 dive-bombers, 869 single-engined fighters and 268 twin-engined fighters.

Although the RAF fighter force – some 620 aircraft – was considerably smaller than the Germans' 1,137, the British had not been sitting on their hands. Fighter production had risen from 157 a month in January 1940 to 496 in July. The RAF did however have a shortage of trained pilots. There were only 1,134 in all, but they could draw on the pilots of Coastal Command and the Fleet Air Arm. They also formed four Polish and one Czech squadron, whose pilots had escaped from Eastern Europe.

The RAF's Hurricanes and Spitfires were much faster and more manoeuvrable than the twin-engined Messerschmitt Bf 110 'destroyer' – which was also known as 'Göring's folly'. On the other hand, the single-seated Messerschmitt Bf 109E was faster than the Mark I Hurricane and about as fast as the Mark I and II Spitfires that were just appearing in front-line squadrons. The Bf 109 could also climb faster than the British fighters, though the British planes were more manoeuvrable. With eight machine-guns, they could out-shoot their German adversaries and it is generally reckoned that the Spitfire, though in short supply, was unrivalled as an interceptor at that time.

German heavy bombers were vulnerable to attack from both Hurricanes and Spitfires, particularly in daylight, and did not have the bomb-carrying capacity to deliver a knock-out blow. Their effectiveness was also blunted by the lack of an overall strategy. Sometimes they would attack airfields, sometimes factories, sometimes ports. British fighters also found that German dive-bombers could be shot down easily, and German fighters could only give them partial protection as they were fighting at the limit of their flying range.

The British had other advantages. Since 1938, the British had the most advanced radar defence network in the world, which stretched from Land's End to the Shetland Islands. Incoming German planes could be detected in time for commanders to get their fighters airborne, so they were not caught and destroyed on the ground. With this radar information, control centres could direct the fighters by radio to intercept the enemy, often taking the Germans by surprise.

As the battle was fought over home soil, the British could recover their downed pilots, while if a German aircraft was shot down both the plane and crew were lost. For example, on 15 August 1940, seventy German planes were shot down and all their crews were either killed or taken prisoner. That same day, twenty-eight Hurricanes and Spitfires were also lost, but over half their pilots eventually returned to their squadrons.

Although there had been preliminary attacks in June and July, the air war began in earnest on 8 August with the Germans sending up to 1,500 aircraft a day to bomb the British airfields and radar stations. In fighting, on 8, 11, 12, and 13 August, the RAF lost eighty-eight planes, while the Luftwaffe lost 145 aircraft. Between 13 and 17 August, the RAF lost 184, against the Luftwaffe's 255. The battle was becoming so expensive that Göring withdrew *Luftflotte V* flying from Norway and Denmark, along with his Stuka dive-bombers. However, in late August the Luftwaffe were close to winning the battle. Essential British airfields were pitted with bomb craters. The RAF's effectiveness was further curtailed by bomb damage to its radar stations and operations centres which were, unfortunately, sited on airfields. Aircraft were being destroyed on the ground and it was becoming difficult to co-ordinate formations in the air.

Aircraft losses began to turn in Germany's favour. Between 24 August and 6 September, the Luftwaffe lost 378 planes, against the RAF's 262. Although this appears to give the British an advantage of forty-five per cent, the German losses included both bombers and fighters. The British were losing all-important fighters and their experienced pilots. Fighter Command had less than a thousand pilots. All of them were in action several times a day and desperately in need of rest. With fifteen to twenty pilots killed or wounded every day, Fighter Command was reaching its last gasp.

Salvation came by glorious accident. Late in the evening of 24 August, a German plane accidentally bombed non-military targets in London. Churchill immediately ordered a retaliatory attack on Berlin. The next night, eighty-one twin-engined bombers took off for the German capital. Only twenty-nine planes made it. The others got lost on the way. Eight men were killed and twenty-eight wounded. The damage to Berlin was slight, but Hitler had promised the German people that such a thing would never happen. Infuriated, he abandoned the 1 August Directive and ordered the terror-bombing of London. Britain's capital was about to get the same treatment as Warsaw and Rotterdam.

The German bombing campaign that followed became known as the Blitz, – 'lightning'. It began on 7 September when 330 tonnes of bombs were dropped on London. The terror-bombing campaign was later extended to Liverpool, Coventry and other cities. Although the population suffered terribly from these attacks, the switch of the Luftwaffe's objective gave Fighter Command the breathing space to recover. Between 7 and 30 September, the RAF downed 380 German aircraft for the loss of 178 of their own. The

German air offensive reached a peak on Sunday 15 September with a series of attacks during which British air defences claimed to have downed 185 German planes. The figure was later dropped to fifty-six. But it hardly mattered. The British had defeated the Germans in the air and were shooting down bombers faster that German factories could produce them. By 31 October the Germans had lost 1,733 planes against Britain's 1,379, and Fighter Command had only lost 414 men. So Churchill was not exaggerating when he told the House of Commons on 20 August 1940, 'Never in the field of human conflict has so much been owed by so many to so few'. It was a view he repeated when he wrote his History of The Second World War.

Even so, Hitler continued his preparations for Operation Sealion. The troops of the Ninth and Sixteenth Armies gathered at their embarkation points. An invasion fleet comprising 2,500 transports, tugs, lighters, barges and fishing boats were assembled in ports from Le Havre to Rotterdam. These came under attack from the RAF's Bomber Command. Losses were less than ten per cent, but the craft still had to be replaced. The mine-laying and mine-sweeping programmes designed to secure invasion lanes across the Channel went ahead but, because the Luftwaffe had not gained the upper hand in the air, they were disrupted by attacks by Coastal Command.

On 11 September, Hitler announced his intention to begin the countdown to Sealion on 14 September – and the landings would begin at dawn on 24 September. But on 14 September, he postponed the decision for another three days – 27 September being the last day the tides were favourable. The strong winds and high seas that could be expected in the Channel from October onwards would make an invasion impossible. On 17 September, Hitler ordered that Sealion be postponed and on 19 September, the invasion fleet was dispersed to protect it from further bombing. Hitler ordered that it should be dispersed in such a way that it could be rapidly reassembled, but this was never to happen. Although daylight raids on British cities continued until the end of the month, German losses continued at such a rate that, at the beginning of October, the Luftwaffe turned to night bombing, which was much less effective militarily. The Blitz continued sporadically until the end of October. By then it was recognised that the Battle of Britain was over.

Victory for the Luftwaffe in the air would inevitably have led to the invasion and occupation of Britain. Fighter Command had denied the Germans the air superiority they needed. They had created the conditions for Britain's survival, for the continuation of the war and for the eventual defeat of Nazi Germany.

No one knew this at the time, of course. Britain merely felt that it was safe for one more winter. During the following months, the Luftwaffe continued its Blitz with night-time bombing raids on Britain's biggest cities. By February 1941 the bombing offensive had eased, but in March and April it was stepped up again. Some 10,000 sorties were flown, with the bombing concentrated on the East End of London. However, the Luftwaffe never turned its attention back to British airfields. By the time suitable weather for a fresh invasion came the following spring, Hitler had turned his eyes eastwards and was planning his attack on Soviet Russia which began with Operation *Barbarossa* in August 1941.

THE INVASION OF CRETE

In preparation for his attack on the Soviet Union, Hitler began drawing other central European countries – Hungary, Rumania, Slovakia, Bulgaria, Yugoslavia – into the Axis. Following Germany's huge gains in the west, Italy began to find itself very much the junior partner in the Pact of Steel. Mussolini wanted to make some territorial gains of his own. So without informing Hitler, he sent

155,000 men across the border from Albania, which Italy had invaded in 1939, into Greece. The Italian invasion was a disaster. Mussolini's seven divisions were halted by a handful of Greeks, who pushed the Italians back until, by mid-December, the Greeks occupied one-third of Albania.

The British rallied to the defence of Greece, sending men and planes to airbases on the mainland near Athens. This put them within striking distance of the Rumanian oilfields at Ploesti which were vital to Germany's attack on Russia. So Hitler had no option but to help Mussolini out. In March, there was a coup d'état against the pro-Axis regime in Belgrade, so the Germans decided to invade Yugoslavia with Italian support, and sweep through into Greece. They made a lightning thrust through the Balkans, forcing the British to evacuate their forces from mainland Greece, though 20,000 remained as prisoners of war. By 11 May, the whole of Greece and the Aegean islands, with the exception of Crete, were in German hands.

However, the British wanted to hold Crete. It was just 500 miles from Alexandria and 200 miles from Tobruk. The bastion of British resistance in North Africa, Tobruk had to be supplied by sea and would be in great danger if the Germans had the airfields at Heraklion, Réthimnon and Máleme on Crete.

The Germans needed Crete as well, but not just to starve out Tobruk. From the airbases there, the RAF were still in striking distance of the Rumanian oilfields. With the attack on the Soviet Union about to deprive Hitler of Russian oil – albeit temporarily, if all went well – he could not afford to be without a supply from Rumania. On 25 April 1940, in Führer Directive No. 28, Hitler ordered the invasion of Crete.

A plan was drawn up to attack the island using an airborne division and three infantry regiments from the 5th and 6th Mountain Divisions which would be landed by a hastily requisitioned flotilla, comprising sixty-three motorised sailing ships and seven small steamers. This would be protected by two destroyers and twelve motor torpedo boats from the Italian Navy.

Defending the island were 41,500 men, 10,300 of whom were Greek. There were 17,000 British troops and a large ANZAC force, comprising 7,700 New Zealanders and 6,500 Australians who had escaped from mainland Greece. On the way, they had abandoned much of their equipment. They had only sixty-eight anti-aircraft guns, which were far too few to defend an island 162 miles from end to end. They were also short of field guns, infantry weapons, ammunition, vehicles, entrenching tools, barbed wire, blankets and mess tins. They were led by General Bernard Freyberg, a hero of Gallipoli who had been wounded twenty-seven times during the First World War. But he was the seventh British commander on the islands in six months, and he had been given just three weeks to prepare the island's defences.

On 1 May, the RAF had thirty-five operational aircraft on Crete. By 19 May, after incessant bombing by the Luftwaffe, they had only four Hurricanes and three Gladiators left. These were sent to Egypt for safekeeping, but the airstrips were only obstructed rather than put out of action as it was intended that they be used again as soon as possible.

The Battle of Crete began on 20 May. The Germans had an air fleet of 500 transport planes and seventy-two gliders, supported by 500 bombers and fighters. At 0715 German gliders carrying elements of the 5th Mountain Division landed to the west and south of Máleme airfield. Soon after more landed on Hill 107, overlooking the airfield, but a third company which aimed to take the nearby Tavronitis Bridge landed among New Zealand troops. Although they took heavy casualties, they managed to take the bridge and hold it.

Then the paratroop drop began. The 3rd Battalion of the 7th Parachute Division were supposed to drop around the airfield but, again, they landed among the New Zealanders and, within three-quarters of an hour, 400 of the 600 paratroopers were dead. The 4th Battalion dropped west of Tavronitis and found themselves under attack from a band of civilians whom they quickly subdued, while the 2nd Battalion landed among Greek troops and armed civilians who butchered them. Only thirteen of the 2nd Battalion were still alive when they surrendered.

The 3rd Parachute Regiment dropped south of the nearby town of Canea, while the 2nd Company of the *Luftlande Sturmregiment* landed in fifteen gliders to the north-west. They were to take the anti-aircraft batteries there, but soon discovered that the guns were dummies. The Northumberland Hussars in the area were real enough, though, and the 136 men who landed had soon sustained 108 casualties. But the 1st Company, landing to the south-east, managed to spike the anti-aircraft battery there, before striking out to join up with other troops landing in the area.

The 3rd Parachute Regiment found itself widely dispersed. One company, carrying heavy mortars, dropped into a reservoir. Some men were drowned and all their equipment was lost. The survivors found themselves under fierce attack from the New Zealand and Greek troops in the area. However, they managed to take the village of Agia and set up their regimental HQ there. The divisional staff then flew in, but the glider carrying the divisional commander split its tow rope and crashed into the island of Aegina.

On the ground, things looked bleak for the Germans. Few of their objectives had been secured and the landing force was broken up into pockets, which were pinned down by the New Zealanders. A second wave of landings around the airfields at Réthimnon and Heraklion was due that afternoon. But the planes deploying them had to be refuelled on the mainland by hand which delayed them. Taking off from dirt strips in Greece also kicked up clouds of dust, so the planes carrying the airborne troops had to be despatched in discrete groups. This meant that the men were land-ed in small bands, often widely scattered, and preliminary attacks by bombers and fighters had alerted the defenders. One of the bat-talions landing around Réthimnon found itself among Australian troops. The paratroopers were pinned down in the drop zones and unable to reach their weapons containers. The two other groups landing there dug in, in defensive positions. This meant there were three discrete pockets of Germans around the airfield.

The troops dropped about Heraklion were even more widely scattered and found themselves under fire from the British troops who were holding the town. So the second wave was even more unsuccessful than the first. None of its objectives were taken. Some 1,800 of the 3,000 men who had been dropped were dead and the survivors were in no shape to mount an offensive action.

While the defenders had overwhelming superiority in men, armour and artillery, Freyberg took a generally pessimistic view of the situation. There were no counter-attacks that night that might have disrupted the enemy and finished it off as a fighting force. In the morning, the commander of the 22nd New Zealand Battalion mistakenly thought his forward positions had been overrun and ordered a withdrawal from Hill 107. In the confusion, the New Zealanders really were overrun and the Germans took the vital hill. Shortly after, another 550 paratroops were dropped and, with these reinforcements, the Germans captured the airfield. The Germans began to fly in ammunition, though incoming planes were sub-jected to withering machine-gun fire.

Reinforcements began landing at 1600. Artillery fire wrecked some of the transports. Others were damaged in collisions on the small airfield, but most of the troops got out safely. By 1800, there were another 1,000 German troops on the ground. The New Zealanders planned a quick counter-attack. But by the time they had mustered their troops, the Germans had landed in enough strength to hold on to the airfield.

The Germans also managed to strengthen their positions around Heraklion. They had begun house-to-house fighting in the outskirts, when the Greek commander came forward to surrender the town. The British commander knew nothing of this and counterattacked, but was unable to dislodge the Germans.

The Royal Navy caught the first flotilla of German sea-borne troops as they came in sight of Máleme and sank it. Over 500 officers and men of the 100th Mountain Regiment drowned and it was destroyed as a fighting force. But before the Royal Navy could sink the second flotilla in the Mediterranean, it came under air attack. German Stukas sank two cruisers and four destroyers, while the battleship HMS *Warspite* and the aircraft-carrier HMS *Formidable* were so badly damaged they had to be sent to the United States for repairs. Even so, the second flotilla of German troops was taken back to Piraeus, rather than risk further loss of life.

That night the New Zealanders tried to counter-attack again at Máleme to prevent any more reinforcements being landed, but to the east of the airfield they ran into the remnants of the 3rd Battalion of the 7th Parachute Division who had been so badly mauled on the first day. Individual paratroopers scattered across the rough ground put up such a fight that they slowed the New Zealanders' advance considerably. By dawn the ANZACs were far from their objective and German fighters and dive-bombers forced them to withdraw.

On 22 May, more Germans landed and Major-General Ringer flew in to take command. He divided his men into three *Kampfgruppen* (battle groups) which were to push outwards at dawn the next day. One group moved north towards the sea and found themselves up against armed civilians, including women and children. The Cretan Resistance was particularly savage, torturing and mutilating any German who fell into their hands. A second Kampfgruppe moved into the mountains to the east, but were halted by the New Zealanders at the village of Modi. After fierce fighting, the New Zealanders were outflanked and they were forced to withdraw. This took their artillery out of range of the airstrip and the Germans could now land more reinforcements without coming under fire. Now the Germans brought in their artillery.

On 24 May, there were heavy German air attacks on the towns of Canea and Galatas and new battle groupings were drawn up. The Germans marched fifty miles in a flanking movement to cut the main road from Canea and Réthimnon, and they joined up with the paratroopers who had been cut off south-east of Canea since their drop on 20 May.

On 25 May, the Germans made a concerted attack on the key village of Galatas. The New Zealanders were ousted but, in a bitter counter-attack, retook the village. By then their numbers were so depleted, they knew they could not hold it so, that night, they withdrew. Now Canea lay within the Germans' grasp.

Under attack from the skies and with the Royal Navy unable to prevent further landings, Freyberg called for an evacuation on 27 May. Despite the danger, Admiral Andrew Cunningham, commander in chief in the Mediterranean, ordered the Royal Navy to go in and evacuate Freyberg and his men. When one of his aides pointed out this put his ships in great danger, Cunningham replied, 'It takes the Navy three years to build a ship. It would take 300 years to rebuild a tradition'.

The evacuation of Crete began on the night of 28 May. Altogether some 8,800 British, 4,704 New Zealanders and 3,164 Australians were brought out of the small port of Sphakia on the southern shore of the island and taken to Alexandria. Some 1,464 were wounded. Another 11,835 had been taken prisoner. On board the cruiser HMS *Orion*, Vice-Admiral Pridham-Wippell's flagship, a single German bomb killed 260 men and wounded 280. The Royal Navy lost, in all, 2,011 officers and men.

The Germans lost 3,714 killed and missing, along with 2,494 wounded. Eight days fighting on Crete had cost the Germans more than the entire Balkan campaign. After Crete, Hitler forbade any further large-scale use of paratroops and plans to invade Cyprus and, later, Malta were abandoned.

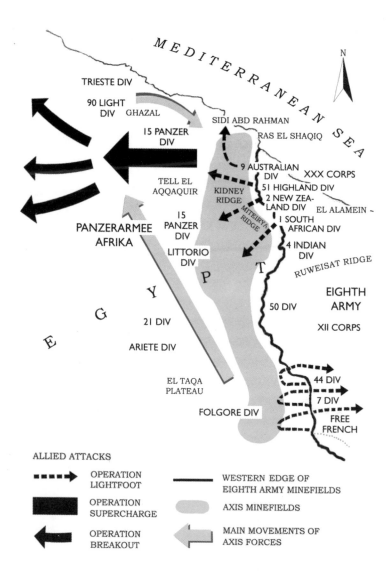

The Alamein battles
October–November 1942

2

NORTH AFRICA

THE SIEGE OF TOBRUK

THE FALL OF FRANCE worried Mussolini. He feared that Hitler would make peace with the British and any pact between Britain and Germany would thwart his territorial ambitions in the Mediterranean. The armistice particularly was a disappointment. Mussolini coveted the French possessions in North Africa, but they remained in the hands of the Vichy government.

Italy already had one possession in North Africa – Libya, which it had invaded in 1911. By the outbreak of the Second World War, some 150,000 Italian colonists lived there. So when the British rejected Hitler's peace overtures, Mussolini turned his attention to Egypt, which had been in British hands since 1882. He ordered Marshal Graziani to launch an offensive eastwards against the British troops in Egypt who were under the command of General Sir Archibald Wavell. On 13 September 1940, the Italian Tenth Army took the small border port of Sollum. They then advanced a further fifty miles into Egypt and occupied the British base at Sidi Barrani on 16 September. Six weeks later the British Western Desert Force under Lieutenant-General Richard O'Connor started a 'five day raid' which pushed the Italians back across the border on 10 December. Reinforced by Australians, the Western Desert Force continued the advance and took the small port of Tobruk in northeast Libya on 21 January 1941. By the time the Italians surrendered on 7 February, the British had driven them back 500 miles, taking over 130,000 prisoners, along with 400 tanks and 1,290 guns.

Meeting no further resistance, the Western Desert Force could have gone on to take Tripoli, but their supply lines were already over-stretched and Churchill wanted to divert men and resources to Greece.

Again Hitler came to Mussolini's aid. On 6 February, he sent Rommel and his Afrika Korps to Tripoli. On 24 March, Rommel attacked at El Agheila, capturing O'Connor and pushing the British column back the way it had come. However, Wavell decided to hold Tobruk while the rest of the British force retreated into Egypt to regroup. As Tobruk had fallen so effortlessly on 21 January, its fortifications were largely intact. Its strongpoints, which were laid out in alternating rows, were protected by three-foot-thick concrete which offered protection against 150mm guns, the heaviest the Afrika Korps had at the time. It had an anti-tank ditch, camou-flaged planks and sand, and the perimeter defences described an arc twenty-eight miles long round the port and reached nine miles inland. This was to be defended by the 9th Australian Division, reinforced by a brigade of the 7th and the Sikhs of the 18th Cavalry Regiment. Major-General Leslie Morshead, commander of the 9th, told his men, 'There will be no Dunkirk here. If we have to get out, we will fight our way out. No surrender and no retreat'.

The artillery support was supplied by the Australian Royal Artillery and Royal Horse Artillery. Although their 25-pounder field guns were not designed as anti-tank weapons, they were very effective against Rommel's Panzers, bearing in mind that the stan-dard anti-tank gun was the two-pounder. Tobruk was also defended by anti-aircraft batteries with seventy-five guns between them and, in the early days of the siege, four Hurricanes were stationed there, but these were soon either shot down or withdrawn.

On 10 April, Rommel reached Tobruk and sent a motorised detachment to storm the town, but it was repulsed by heavy gun-fire which killed its commander. On the night of 13 April, an infantry battalion of the Afrika Korps' 5th Light Division made its way through a minefield and across the anti-tank ditch. A counter-attack destroyed the infantry battalion and Jack Edmondson, an Australian defender who went on fighting even though he was fatally wounded, was posthumously awarded the Victoria Cross in the action. Meanwhile, elements of the Afrika Korps had bypassed Tobruk and had reached the Egyptian border. From now on, the 22,000 men at Tobruk would have to be supplied by sea.

This was a dangerous business as the Luftwaffe had complete air superiority. However, the anti-aircraft gunners managed to keep the harbour open. The heavy batteries were armed with British 3.7-inch guns, which produced shrapnel, while light anti-aircraft batteries used Bofors 40mm and captured Italian 20mm and 40mm Breda guns which fired tracer shells that exploded on impact. Between them, they would throw up a barrage at a predetermined height. But the German pilots got wise to this and started hanging back to see what height the barrage had been fixed at before start-ing their bombing runs. So the barrage was then spread more thinly over varying heights to make it more difficult to penetrate. The Luftwaffe's response was to begin dive-bombing the sites of the heavy guns, so the light anti-aircraft batteries with their rapid-fire tracer were moved in closer to protect them.

Just before dawn on 14 April the Panzers attacked for the first time. They came on the left of the road that led south to El Adem. Thirty-eight tanks broke through the two lines of the zig-zagged perimeter defences and headed for the town. Three miles on they hit the second line of defence – the Blue Line. There they met point-blank fire from British 25-pounders. The Germans' artillery support and machine-gunners had been held up by the Australian infantry who had stayed in position when the tanks broke through. In the face of the 25-pounders, the Panzers had no choice but to retreat. As they did so British tanks and Australian anti-tank guns pummelled their flanks. The routed Germans left behind seventeen tanks. Twelve aircraft had been shot down, 110 men killed and 254 captured. It was the first time that Hitler's Panzers had tasted defeat.

Rommel realised that Tobruk could only be taken with an all-out attack, but he lacked the resources. Even the 15th Panzer Division, which was on its way, had suffered significant losses when the convoy carrying it was attacked on its way to Libya. By then operations in the Balkans and, later, the Soviet Union starved Rommel of the tanks and men he needed to take Tobruk, and the stand-off there went on to become the longest siege in British history.

For the next two weeks, Rommel bided his time and brought up more forces. By the end of the month, he had some 400 German and Italian tanks against the defenders' thirty-one. On the evening of 30 April, he threw his men at Hill 209, known as Ras el Medauur, near the water-tower on the south-west corner of the perimeter. Twenty-two Stukas began dive-bombing the Australian positions at 1915 hours and an artillery barrage opened up at 2000. This cut the telephone lines and neutralised the front-line defences.

Under cover of the bombardment, the Germans blew gaps in the wire and cleared paths through the minefield. By 2115 a German machine-gun battalion a mile inside the perimeter opened fire on the reserve company. The Australians began a counter-attack, but with poor communication they could not find the beleaguered perimeter posts in the darkness. By the following morning it was clear the Germans had punched a hole through the outer defences a-mile-and-a-half wide, capturing seven perimeter posts and taking more than 100 prisoners. However, the Australians had put up such determined resistance that they had taken the momentum out of the German attack.

Soon after 0800, the Germans advanced again with forty tanks but were stopped by a minefield. Heavy shelling forced them to retreat, though a dust storm covered their withdrawal. Rommel tried a diversionary tactic with some twenty tanks to draw in the Allied armour, but Morshead was reluctant to commit his tanks, preferring to let mines and artillery shells do their work before risking his precious armoured reserve. Repeated air attacks failed to knock out the Allied artillery and by 0900 the German attack had petered out.

As they could make no further progress forwards, Rommel's Panzers and their infantry support attacked the posts at either side of the mouth of the German bridgehead. One fell at noon, but the heavy shelling prevented the Panzers co-ordinating with their supporting infantry and their attempts to take the other post failed. However, twenty-five light Panzers got beyond the perimeter posts and ran around the southern edge of the minefield. They were shelled all the way but, by 0915, they had reached Post R12 three miles east of Hill 209. There they were halted by fourteen cruiser tanks. Rommel sent in another nine tanks. A sporadic tank battle broke out but, though the German tanks outnumbered those of the British, the Panzers withdrew after losing three of their number.

The German tanks refuelled and, that afternoon, began a new attack. Again they were met by accurate British shelling. The Australians in the perimeter posts, armed only with Bren guns and rifles, put up fierce resistance. Two heavy Panzers tried to blast one post into surrender from seventy-five yards, but the German infantry was repeatedly beaten back. By dusk half the defenders were wounded. In the twilight, the Germans attacked again with tanks and flame-throwers and they took the post at 1930. A second post fell the next morning.

Having abandoned any attempt to drive forward directly on the harbour, Rommel continued to push inside the perimeter in the south-east until the bridgehead cleared the southern minefield. But he was stopped by a counter-attack against Hill 209 that evening. Impeded by the fading light and the dust kicked up by enemy shelling, the Australians advanced for more than a mile before they met resistance from anti-tank and machine-gun emplacements. By then they had lost the cover of their artillery barrage. Lacking the machine-guns they needed, the men withdrew. They had not retaken Hill 209, but they had forced the enemy onto the defensive and stopped the Germans getting around a vital minefield.

A sandstorm on 2 May halted the German advance, giving the defenders time to lay new minefields, bring up fresh infantry and strengthen their positions. The artillery continued to pummel the German positions and, when the storm cleared the next day, the Germans did not resume their offensive. The garrison had lost just five tanks, while out of the eighty-one German tanks Rommel started the battle with only thirty-five were in action – though, of the forty-six lost, only twelve were completely destroyed. However, the Panzers had suffered their second defeat and their morale was shaken. On the other hand, the Germans had made a breach in the defences and held a large salient.

Morshead planned to do something about that. He would send two battalions to attack the shoulders of the salient, retake the lost posts and cut off the enemy spearhead. At the same time, a third battalion would make deep raids into enemy territory. The problem was that as the Germans held Hill 209, they could see the Australians as they assembled. This gave them ample warning of the attack. After dark the Australians advanced under an artillery barrage. The Germans fought back with heavy machine-gun fire. Flares lit up the sky and German mortar and artillery fire brought the Australian advance on the northern flank to a standstill. On the southern flank, they retook one post and attacked another but could not take it. The other attacks pushed the German outposts back more than half a mile. The Germans had lost 1,700 men, compared to the garrisons' casualties of 797 – 59 killed, 355 wounded and 383 missing. However, the German High Command grew alarmed at the losses and ordered Rommel not to attack again.

Morshead was jubilant. 'The actions before Tobruk in April and May are the first in which armoured formations of the German Army have been defied and defeated,' he said.

Churchill was also impressed. He sent a telegram which read, 'The whole Empire is watching your steadfast and spirited defence of this important outpost of Egypt with gratitude and admiration.'

Wavell's message to Morshead struck a more practical note. It read, 'Your magnificent defence is upsetting enemy's plans for attack on Egypt and giving us time to build up force for counter offensive. You could *not* repeat *not* be doing better service.'

The Nazi radio propagandist William Joyce – a US citizen hanged for treason after the war, and known in Britain as 'Lord Haw Haw' because of his sneering voice – crowed that the garrison were 'caught like rats in a trap'. A German newspaper then dubbed the British defenders the 'Rats of Tobruk', a name they embraced.

From the Allied point of view, Tobruk was psychologically important because it showed, for the first time, that the Germans could be stopped. The Panzers were not invincible. The German Blitzkrieg could be defeated by minefields, artillery fire and infantry who stood their ground. Even the terror-bombers could be thwarted by dedicated anti-aircraft gunners. It also gave a vital fillip to British prestige in the Arab world. Strategically, if Tobruk had fallen, Rommel would have rolled on through Egypt, to take the Suez Canal and the oilfields in the Persian Gulf, and cut the British Empire in two. As it was Britain had time to recover from the disasters of Greece and Crete. In Egypt, British forces could regroup, while fresh American aid arrived via Britain.

The defence of Tobruk also kept Turkey – a German ally in the First World War – out of the war. That prevented Hitler from using

Turkey as a southern springboard for his attack on the Soviet Union and delayed his attack on Russia by at least a month. As winter is considered to be Russia's greatest general, this may have been crucial.

The greatest measure of the defenders of Tobruk's success was the fact that it took three battalions of Rommel's best troops and four Italian divisions to hold the salient around Hill 209. Playing on this, Morshead maintained a strategy of aggressive night patrolling to dominate no man's land and undermine the enemy's morale. Meanwhile, although short of tanks, the British kept up harassing attacks on Rommel's forces on the Egyptian frontier to keep him from regrouping his whole force and turning it on Tobruk.

With the evacuation of Greece, fifty tanks were diverted to Egypt. Wavell quickly organised Operation Brevity to relieve Tobruk. On 15 May 1941 the British took the Halfaya Pass on the way to Sollum. But they were forced to withdraw on 17 May and the Germans retook the pass.

On the night of 15 May the Germans launched an attack on three perimeter posts at Tobruk. It was thought that all three were lost, but when one was recaptured it was found that the other two had held out, although desperately short of ammunition. Once they were resupplied, the Australians found they were on a roll and tried to recapture more of their outposts. A smoke-screen was laid to prevent observation from Hill 209 and supporting fire came from thirty-nine British guns, while machine-gunners from the Northumberland Fusiliers swept into the disputed area. But the Germans laid their own smoke-screen and barrage. In the dust and smoke the British tanks lost their way. However the Australian infantry carried on alone through intense fire to take two posts. But the Germans were too well established, holding not only the concrete posts but also intermediate positions that could provide flanking fire. Without the corresponding posts in the zig-zag defence, they could not be held. So the Australians withdrew.

By June the two sides were consolidating their defensive positions. In the salient, the Germans had fallen back to defensive line behind the positions they held on 3 May. By 26 June the Australians had been able to advance their line 1,000 yards, reducing its length from over five miles to under four. This allowed the Australians to take one battalion out of the line and hold it in reserve. On the other hand, the German line was more closely packed. The Germans had also mined no man's land, preventing any further Australian advances.

Wavell made a second attempt to relieve Tobruk, starting on 15 June. This was beaten back by the 15th Panzer Division and Wavell was replaced as Commander-in-Chief in the Middle-East by General Sir Claude Auchinleck on 1 July.

The Australians had held out in Tobruk for over three months. The heat, dust, flies, sand and the poor food was affecting fighting ability and the Australian government asked that they be withdrawn. The bulk were evacuated in the late summer and replaced by the British 17th Division under Major-General Scobie, supported by the 1st Polish Carpathian Brigade and a Czechoslovak Battalion. However, some Australians, along with the original British forces, stayed on.

While Rommel planned a new attack, General Auchinleck began organising Operation Crusader, a third attempt to relieve Tobruk, and formed the Eighth Army under General Sir Alan Cunningham. Cunningham's plan was to send XXX Corps across the Libyan border to the south and deploy it at a place called Gabr Saleh. He expected Rommel and his Panzers to seize the opportunity for a tank battle, which Cunningham believed the better equipped and more numerous British and South African forces would win. Meanwhile, XIII Corps would overrun the frontier positions on the coast and push up the coast road towards Tobruk while Rommel was being crushed in the desert. The danger was that there would be a large gap between the two columns where the British would be vulnerable. So another column was drawn up between them, but it drew its strength from XXX Corps, considerably weakening the force that was supposed to take on Rommel.

Crusader got underway on 18 November in torrential rain. Unfortunately Rommel had plans of his own. He was readying himself to take Tobruk, so instead of moving to meet XXX Corps at Gabr Saleh he kept his armour around Gambut on the coast road. But worse was to befall Cunningham. The Eighth Army's operational plans, brought to the front by a careless British officer, fell into enemy hands. As Rommel failed to meet XXX Corps at Gabr Saleh, the British pressed on. But on 19 November, fifty of their new Crusader tanks were destroyed when they tried to take Bir el Gubi to the south of Tobruk. Another column pushed on towards Tobruk, but were met with a counter-attack by the Afrika Korps at Sidi Rezegh, which destroyed much of their armour. Rommel could have wiped out the whole of XXX Corps if he had followed up the next day. Instead, he took a gamble. With 100 tanks he made a dash across the desert to the Egyptian border with the intention of cutting off the entire Eighth Army and attacking it from the rear.

The reverses took a terrible toll on Cunningham, who wanted to withdraw. Believing that Rommel's bold move was an act of desperation, Auchinleck urged him on. But the strain was too much for Cunningham, and Auchinleck had to replace him with his own deputy chief of staff, Major-General Neil Methuen Ritchie, on 26 November. However, it was Auchinleck who was now really in command.

In a letter home, Rommel described his 'dash to the wire' as a great success. In fact, he had made little impression on the 4th Indian Division who held the rear, nor did he deprive the Eighth

Army of its supplies. Worse, his radio had broken down and he had left his Panzer group without orders for four days.

While XXX Corps had been decimated to the south, XIII Corps had had an easier time of it running along the coast road. The New Zealand Division broke through. On 25 November, Scobie received a telegram telling him that the New Zealanders would make another attack on Sidi Rezegh the next day. At the same time, the garrison was to attempt to break out. They did this among fierce fighting. At 1300 hours they saw tanks on the horizon. Suddenly three red rockets burst in the sky. It was the Eighth Army's recognition signal. Tobruk had been relieved at last. But not for long. In the absence of Rommel, the 21st Panzer Division, which had been on the Egyptian border, was ordered to retreat. Rommel confirmed this order when he reappeared at his headquarters on 27 November. A confused battle followed with the New Zealand Division was cut in two, with one half thrown back to Tobruk. In the mêlée, the commander of the 21st Panzer Division, General von Ravenstein, was captured.

Meanwhile, Auchinleck reinforced and reorganised XXX Corps and threw it back into battle. Rommel now had few tanks left and he was told that he was not going to be resupplied until the latter part of December, so he withdrew his forces attacking Tobruk from the east on 5 December. The following day, a final counter-attack failed and he ordered a general retreat, leaving behind an Italian division with orders to hold out as long as possible. Short of food and ammunition, the Italians surrendered on 17 January.

The Siege of Tobruk lasted 242 days from 10 April to 7 December 1941, fifty-five days longer than the siege of Mafeking in the Boer War. It was the first defeat of German land forces in the Second World War.

THE DRIVE ON GAZALA

After the relief of Tobruk, Rommel was driven back to El Agheila, where the British advance had first halted in February 1941. With the attack on Pearl Harbor in December 1941 and Japan's rapid advance on Britain's colonies in the Far East, the Allies turned their attention there, starving the desert forces of supplies. However, during his retreat from Tobruk, Rommel had been supplied with new tanks. In January 1942 a convoy arrived in Tripoli carrying more reinforcements. Soon the Afrika Korps had 111 tanks with twenty-eight more in reserve, while the Italians had eighty-nine.

Rommel quickly counter-attacked, destroying nearly half of the British armour. In the swift reversal, the Desert Fox captured huge quantities of supplies as, once again, he made a dash eastwards. By 6 February, he had pushed the British back to Gazala, just 30 miles west of Tobruk. There the British had constructed a continuous minefield running from the town of Gazala on the Mediterranean coast thirty miles southwards to Bir Hacheim in the desert. Another minefield ran from Bir Hacheim to Bir Harmat fifteen miles to the north-east. A further belt of mines five miles south of the Aslag Ridge joined the two. This area in between the Aslag Ridge and the Gazala Line was known as the 'Cauldron' and would be critical in the outcome of the battle.

The British retreated behind this line, hoping to build up their strength for a new offensive. However, Rommel was ready first. The problem with any defensive line in the North African campaign was that it necessarily had an open flank at the desert end. On 26 May 1942, Rommel began an attack that aimed to sweep around the southern end of the Gazala Line and seize Tobruk in just three days.

Rommel's Panzers destroyed the 3rd and 7th Indian Motor Brigades south-east of Bir Hacheim, then turned north. The Italians kept up the pressure on the front of the line, while the 15th and

21st Panzers drove up towards the coast behind the Gazala Line to attack the defenders from the rear and the 19th Light Division headed for Tobruk itself.

But this was not the walk-over Rommel had planned. The British 4th Armoured Brigade struck back with its new American Grant tanks which were equipped with 75mm guns. The 15th Panzer Division lost 100 tanks on the first day of battle and a counter-attack by the 2nd Armoured Brigade forced them onto the defensive near Bir Harmat. The 21st Panzers were halted ten miles north west of 'Knightsbridge', the British 1st Armoured Division's desert stronghold. And the 19th Light Division were stopped at El Adem, just outside the defensive perimeter at Tobruk.

Rommel's forces were short of fuel and ammunition and danger-ously dispersed, so he pulled them back to the Cauldron, which was protected on three sides by British minefields. There they could be resupplied after the Italian X Corps cut two lanes through the Gazala Line itself. This meant that Rommel's supply lines were no longer vulnerable to disruption by the strong British forces to the south.

However, the northern supply route was under fire from the British 150th Brigade, supported by the First Army Tank Brigade, at Got el Ualeb. Rommel had to take this stronghold. Infantry, tanks and new six-pounder anti-tank guns were brought up, until the British force was greatly outnumbered. They put up stubborn resistance but were eventually forced to surrender. The Germans took 101 tanks, 124 guns and over 3,000 prisoners.

To the north of the Line, the Italians attacked, but were held off by the South Africans who were deeply entrenched. On 4 June General Ritchie then launched Operation Aberdeen to crush the enemy in the Cauldron. It was a failure. It had been planned for 2 June, when Rommel was held with his back to the minefield, before the Italians had broken through and while the 150th Brigade were still a fighting force. Now the situation had changed dramatically.

Ritchie tried to seize the initiative again on 7 June. The South Africans in the northern sector were to attack the Italian positions. However, the Italians were as well dug-in as the British and they too had laid minefields. These had to be cleared first. This limited the size of the South African attack and it was never large enough to overwhelm the defenders.

With supply lines to the west, the Cauldron was now a huge salient in the Gazala Line and the Free French holding Bir Hacheim to the south were practically cut off. Not only could this salient be defended from the British, it could also be used to launch an attack. On the night of 1 June, the Italian Trieste Division from the west and the 19th Light Division from the north attacked Bir Hacheim. Despite heavy bombardment by the Luftwaffe, the French put up fierce resistance for eleven days, then surrendered after one of the bravest defensive actions of the desert war. After the fall of Bir Hacheim, Ritchie had to turn his defensive line so it faced south rather than east. He now had a defensive position only fifteen miles wide, and his back to the sea.

Rommel regrouped his forces at Bir Hacheim. On 12 June he made a push on El Adem, crushing four armoured brigades on the way. Between them they lost 185 cruiser and fifty infantry tanks. The next day he smashed the British armour at Acroma to the rear of the northern sector of the Gazala Line. By 14 June, the British only had fifty cruiser and twenty infantry tanks left. Retreat was inevitable.

This time Auchinleck wanted to abandon Tobruk, but he was ordered by Churchill to hold it. So he told Ritchie to hold an outer defensive line. However, Auchinleck assumed that Ritchie would have at his disposal the two divisions that were still holding the northern half of Gazala Line. What he did not know was that Ritchie had already ordered the British 15th Division and the 1st South African Division to head back to Egypt. As it was, their direct line of retreat had already been cut by Rommel and they had to break out westward through the Gazala Line then sweep southwards through the desert. As a result, Ritchie simply did not have the manpower to hold the line. Knightsbridge was evacuated. On 18 June, the Afrika Korps cut the road to the east of Tobruk and the fortress was under siege again. Once again the Afrika Korps bypassed Tobruk and dashed on eastwards, forcing the RAF to withdraw from Gambut and denying the besieged garrison any air support.

On 15 June, Major-General Klopper of 2nd South African Division became commander of the garrison at Tobruk, while Rommel dusted off his plan to attack the south-east section of the defensive perimeter. This was what he had intended to do in November 1941 before he was beaten to the punch by Operation *Crusader*.

Shortly before 0520 on 20 June, the Luftwaffe pummelled the line between posts R58 and R63, which effectively neutralised the Mahratta Light Infantry who were holding that sector. By 0830 the 15th Panzer Division had crossed the anti-tank ditch. With the 21st Panzer, it drove for 'King's Cross', a key intersection inside the perimeter. A counter-attack was delayed by a dispute between the British commanders. At 0930, the 22nd Army Tank Brigade went in, but it was repulsed and by 1330 King's Cross was in enemy hands. While 21st Panzer headed towards the port, 15th Panzer drove along the Pilastrino Ridge to the west. By dusk, only isolated pockets of resistance were holding out. Major-General Klopper had been forced to move his headquarters. He had lost all his tanks and half his guns. The situation was desperate.

Early next morning it was decided that any troops that still had transport should be evacuated. Few could get out as, by then, most of the vehicles were in German hands. Klopper wanted to fight on, but realised that the casualties he would sustain would not justify any possible gain. He did his best to destroy the port facilities and the remaining stock of petrol. Then, soon after 0630, he surrendered. Some 32,200 prisoners were taken, including 19,000 British, 10,000 South Africans and 2,500 Indians, along with a large quantity of stores.

Winston Churchill was in Washington when he heard the news. It was a national disaster. Throughout 1941 the small garrison at Tobruk's defiance of the might of the German Army had been a beacon of hope. Now that beacon had been extinguished. Hitler, on the other hand, was delighted and promoted Rommel to the rank of Field Marshal.

EL ALAMEIN

With Rommel's victory on the Gazala Line and the eventual fall of Tobruk, the Axis shelved its plan for an airborne invasion of Malta and Rommel captured enough stores to push on into Egypt before the British had time to regroup.

The Allies thought that they could delay Rommel's advance with a line of fortification Ritchie had built running south along the Egyptian border from Sollum to Sidi Omar. But this suffered from the same tactical weakness as the Gazala Line – the desert flank remained open. Rommel swept around it on 24 June, advancing over 100 miles in one day. However, realising that the line could not be held, the Eighth Army had already fallen back to Mersa Matruh, 120 miles east of the frontier. The situation was now desperate. The Luftwaffe were already in range of Alexandria. And if the Eighth Army failed to hold back Rommel there was nothing to stop him taking both Egypt and the oilfields of the Persian Gulf, and going on to attack the beleaguered Russians' southern flank.

Ritchie intended to make one final stand at Mersa Matruh, but Auchinleck realised that a defensive line there would suffer exactly the same weaknesses as the ones at Gazala and Sollum. So on 25 June he sacked Ritchie and took personal command of Eighth Army. The following day he issued new orders. There would be no new line at Mersa Matruh. Instead, he intended to keep his all troop formations fluid. Mobile columns would strike at the enemy from all sides. To that end he reorganised into brigade battle-groups made up of artillery – always the Western Desert Force's strength – supported by armour and infantry.

On 27 June, the Axis caught up with the Allies again. There were a series of punishing skirmishes with units of the British forces being bypassed, cut off and having to break out eastwards. Eventually, they fell back on a line at El Alamein, just 60 miles from Alexandria. There Auchinleck blocked any further advance.

What was different about Auchinleck's line at El Alamein and from that at Gazala, 350 miles to the west, was that the El Alamein line did not have an open flank to the south. It ended at the Qattara Depression, 7,000 square miles of salt lakes and marshes impassable to tanks and other heavy military vehicles. The German spearhead reached the El Alamein line on 30 June. It was manned by Australians who had been the original 'desert rats' of Tobruk, along with British, South African, New Zealand and Indian troops who had fallen back across the desert. And at El Alamein, critically, they would be supported by the RAF.

Having come so far, so fast, the Afrika Korps was now exhausted. And it was at the end of a very long supply line. Its first assaults failed to break through, so it halted to build up its forces, and began to lay minefields. Throughout July 1942, assault was met with counter-stroke, with neither side giving way.

On 13 July, Rommel launched his newly re-equipped Afrika Korps into what became known as the First Battle of El Alamein. Again the Panzers were halted and, that night, Auchinleck counter-attacked. Indians and New Zealanders overwhelmed two Italian divisions and held a counter-strike by the Panzers.

The battle became a war of attrition, leaving some 10,000 dead. Rommel quickly used up all the supplies that he had taken at

Tobruk. He had been reinforced with 260 tanks but, after the fall of Tobruk, Roosevelt had sent 100 self-propelled guns and 300 Sherman tanks. The Shermans were armed with 75mm guns that at last gave the British a tank to rival the Mark III and Mark IV Panzers.

Although Auchinleck had stopped Rommel's advance, he had not thrown him back and, on 4 August, Churchill arrived in Cairo to see what could be done. Auchinleck told him that he intended to delay any offensive until September to give the new reinforcements that he had just received time to acclimatise. Churchill sacked him and appointed Sir Harold Alexander Commander-in-Chief in the Middle East. Command of the Eighth Army was given to General Bernard Montgomery, who took over on 13 August. Montgomery quickly reorganised the Eighth Army again so that it fought in divisions with units giving each other mutual support.

The Eighth Army was expecting Rommel to go on the offensive at some time around the full moon on 26 August. It was anticipated that he would attack, as usual, to the south of the line, aiming to break through, surround the Eighth Army within a matter of hours and rush on to take Cairo. The spot he would choose for his attack was defended only by a minefield. But Montgomery had spotted the weakness in his defences too. Behind it he prepared positions so that any attacking force would have to run the gauntlet between six-pounder anti-tank guns and dug-in tanks.

Rommel's long supply lines meant that he had problems obtaining fuel. This delayed the attack until 31 August, giving the Allies more time to prepare. He had been hoping that his attack would take the British by surprise. But two hours before the attacking force – 200 Panzers, 243 Italian medium tanks and thirty-eight light tanks – set off, it came under attack by the RAF. Troops advancing in front of the tanks to lift the British mines came under heavy fire from well dug-in troops. More air strikes were called in.

The commander of the Africa Korps was badly wounded and the commander of the 21st Panzer Division was killed.

Rommel narrowed the front. His column made its way through two minefields, but was stopped by a third. The Panzers also found that they could only make slow progress on the soft sand. Casualties were heavy and the stalled column came under heavy artillery fire. But then a sand storm blew up, grounding the RAF and hampering the artillery.

On 1 September the storm lifted and the Panzers continued their advance. British armour drove them back. They tried another offensive in the afternoon but were beaten back again. Montgomery tightened a ring of steel around the Afrika Korps. It tried to break out and failed, sustaining heavy casualties. Meanwhile it was being bombed day and night. By the afternoon of 3 September, Rommel's men were in retreat. Montgomery now aimed to go on the offensive, but he did not feel that his reinforcements were sufficiently welded together to give chase. As it was he let the Germans hold on to a strong point between the two minefields at the end of the El Alamein line.

On 7 September, he broke off the battle and began making new preparations. He had worked out a plan of deception to keep the enemy's strength at the south end of the line. He deployed a dummy pipeline, dummy supply dumps and dummy vehicles in that sector. Radio traffic was stepped up in the southern part of the line to suggest that an attack would be launched from there early in November.

The real attack would be launched further north. The guns and tanks massed there were moved in at night and camouflaged carefully. Slit trenches were dug out into the desert for the infantry to attack from. These too were camouflaged to prevent German aerial reconnaissance knowing the British intentions. As the six-week period of preparation grew to a close, the RAF stepped up its attacks on enemy airfields, effectively grounding the Luftwaffe by 23 October – the night of the attack.

Montgomery had abandoned the conventional wisdom of desert warfare. He would not attack to the south and try to turn the flank. Nor would he take on the enemy's armour, then deal with the infantry later. He would begin by sending a diversionary force against the armour in the south to make Rommel think that the main thrust would come there. Meanwhile there would be a massive bombardment, first of the artillery positions in the north, then the infantry positions there. Montgomery's infantry would then infiltrate down their slit trenches to take on German troops still dazed from the bombardment. There would inevitably be vicious hand-to-hand fighting, but Montgomery reckoned his men would get the best of it. Then the armour would pour through the hole made by the infantry, systematically finish off the German infantry, then get into position at the rear to take on any remaining armour on ground of his own choosing. Even if he could not destroy the Panzers completely, without infantry they could not hold ground and would have to retreat.

There was a full moon on the night of 23 October. This was vital as thousands of mines would have to be lifted to make a hole in the enemy's defences. The minefields were 5,000 to 9,000 yards in depth and strengthened with booby-trap bombs and barbed wire. At 2140 the Second Battle of El Alamein began, when more than 1,000 guns along the whole line opened fire simultaneously on the German artillery. Twenty minutes later they switched their aim to the enemy's forward positions. As a huge curtain of dust and smoke rose over the enemy, the British infantry moved in with fixed bayonets to the skirl of the pipers.

The Germans resisted valiantly, but by 0530 the next morning two corridors had been opened and the armour began moving down them. Then things began to go wrong. The infantry still had not made it all the way through the minefields when they were met with fierce resistance. This left the armour dangerously exposed. By dusk the following day, one column of armour had made it through. But the 10th Armoured Division was still in the middle of the minefields and taking shelter behind the Miteiriya Ridge. Its commander, General Lumsden, had always been critical of Montgomery's plan. He thought it was suicide to send tanks through narrow corridors in minefields where there was heavy anti-tank artillery, well dug in. If one tank was hit, those behind it could not move and would be sitting ducks.

Lumsden was summoned to Montgomery's HQ and explained his position. Montgomery then called Brigadier Alec Gatehouse who was commanding the spearhead and ordered him to send the 10th Armoured Division over the ridge. Gatehouse refused to waste his division in such a reckless fashion. After a robust exchange of views, Montgomery ordered him to send one regiment over the ridge, instead of the entire division. Of the forty-nine tanks of the Staffordshire Yeomanry that went over, only fifteen limped back. Gatehouse had been right.

Nevertheless, the advance continued and by the morning of 25 October two armoured columns had reached the enemy's positions. But the situation on the battlefield had grown confused. The Germans made a number of bloody counter-attacks. One, on the vital salient known as Kidney Ridge, was led by Rommel himself. All were repulsed. Gradually things turned in Britain's favour. On 27 October the 1st Armoured Division alone knocked out fifty German tanks and repeated sorties by the RAF broke up the Panzer formations.

With the two armies locked in fierce fighting, it became apparent to Rommel that everything depended on which side would be exhausted first. However, Montgomery had been skilfully pulling units out of the line to build up a force that could deliver a knock-out punch. Those that remained were told to adopt a defensive posture, but to use aggressive patrolling and artillery fire to give the impression that the advance was continuing.

On the night of 28 August, the 9th Australian Division drove a wedge down the coastal road. This was what Rommel was hoping for. If the British attempted to move around him to the north, he could cut their forces in two. So he moved his Panzers to the north. However, Montgomery did not follow up with a major attack down the coast. Instead he sent the 2nd New Zealand Division against a weak point in the German line which was defended by the Italians.

The battle was reaching its climax. Rommel told his commanders that they must fight to the death, although shortage of fuel meant that he was already considering withdrawing. Then on the night of 30 October, he thought he had got lucky. The Australians got up out of their trenches and moved forward against fierce resistance. This would inevitably exhaust the tenacious Australians. But a force of Panzergrenadiers found themselves surrounded in a fortified position known as Thompson's Post. The Panzers attacked repeatedly in an attempt to relieve them. After three days of fighting, they managed to get through to the survivors.

Meanwhile, the full weight of Montgomery's remaining forces was thrown against a 4,000-yard stretch of the front, in Operation Supercharge. At 0100 on 2 November, two British infantry brigades moved through the New Zealanders' lines and attacked. They were followed by 123 tanks of the 9th Armoured Brigade. Their objective was to destroy the anti-tank screen, especially the lethal 88mm guns. Montgomery told its commander, Brigadier John Currie, 'I am prepared to accept one hundred per cent casualties'. Currie led the attack personally.

The tanks, which were followed by infantry with bayonets fixed, ran over mines. As the sun came up, they were hit by dug-in German anti-tank guns. All but nineteen of the 9th Armoured

Brigade's tanks were knocked out and 230 of Currie's 400 men were killed. However, the attack succeeded in its objective. Through the new corridor it had created plunged the 1st Armoured Division. When Rommel realised that he had been tricked, he sent formations of Panzers south. The following day anti-tank guns were moved into position, but by that time the British had expanded their salient to the south and were pushing relentlessly westwards. A tank battle ensued, but the German and Italian tanks was held in check by the RAF and artillery fire. After two hours, the German counter-attack petered out. That afternoon, Rommel tried again, throwing an Italian armoured division into the fray. But more and more British reinforcements were pouring through the gap and fanning out behind it.

The Afrika Korps was down to just thirty-five tanks when Rommel decided to withdraw. But then he got an order from Hitler, telling him to hold the position to the last man.

'There will be no retreat, not so much as a millimetre,' read the Führer's message. 'Victory or death.'

Rommel knew that to hold his current position would be suicidal. But then, it would also be suicidal to disobey Hitler. When General von Thoma, head of the Afrika Korps, asked for permission to retreat, Rommel refused to give it, but he turned a blind eye when Von Thoma pulled back anyway. Von Thoma was captured soon after and did not have to face Hitler's wrath. After twelve days of fighting, the Axis forces were now in full retreat. Fuel was low and there were only enough vehicles for the Germans to get away. The hapless Italians were abandoned and surrendered by the thousand.

Brigadier Gatehouse wanted the 10th Armoured Division to give pursuit. He was sure that he could outrun them in forty-eight hours and destroy them. But Montgomery was more cautious. Rommel had already shown that he could suddenly mount a counter-attack that could turn a rout into a new offensive. The retreating column was bombed and strafed by the RAF, and the 8th Armoured Brigade managed to head off a German column taking a large number of prisoners, tanks and lorries. Other units also gave pursuit, but a downpour on 7 November turned the road into a quagmire and the Afrika Korps got away. It left 10,000 men behind it. Another 20,000 Italians had been captured. And 20,000 had been killed or wounded. On the battlefield there were 450 knocked-out tanks, along with seventy-five abandoned by the Italians due to lack of fuel. Over 1,000 enemy guns had been destroyed or abandoned.

During the Battle of Alamein, the British Eighth Army sustained 13,500 casualties. Some 500 British tanks had been knocked out, though 350 of those could be repaired, and 100 guns were lost. In Britain, the church bells had been silent for years as they were to act as an invasion alarm. Churchill ordered that they be rung out in celebration. Speaking of the victory at El Alamein at the Mansion House in the City of London on 10 November 1942, he said memorably, 'Now is not the end. It is not even the beginning of the end. But it is, perhaps, the end of the beginning'.

For Britain, the Battle of Alamein was a turning point. For three years, the British had been battered in Europe, in the Atlantic and in the Far East.

'After Alamein,' wrote Churchill with some justification, 'we never had a defeat.'

OPERATION TORCH

America had joined the war after the Japanese attacked Pearl Harbor on 7 December 1941 (see Chapter Four: The Pacific War). On 11 December, Hitler had declared war on the United States, and the US declared war on Germany and Italy. Now the sides were drawn up. The strategy agreed between Britain and America was that they should take on Hitler before dealing with the Japanese.

The US would maintain only defensive operations in the Pacific while the bulk of its effort would go into defeating the Axis powers. As soon as the US joined the war, the American military had wanted to launch an amphibious assault on the coast of France. But after two years of fighting, the British were more cautious and persuaded the US to join in the fight in an area of the world where they had already had some success – North Africa.

On 8 November 1942, with Rommel in full retreat from El Alamein, a 117,000 Anglo-American task force under General Dwight D. Eisenhower was to land in French North Africa. Some 45,000 men under Major-General George S. Patton would sail directly from the US and seize Casablanca and the Atlantic coast of Morocco. Another 39,000 US troops under Major-General Lloyd R. Fredendall would sail from Scotland and take the Mediterranean port of Oran in Algeria, while a 33,000-man Anglo-American force under Major-General Charles Ryder would take the port of Algiers itself. This was to be code-named Operation *Torch*.

The situation in French North Africa was far from clear and no one knew what the reaction to the invasion would be. Officially, the French forces in North Africa were loyal to the collaborationist government in Vichy, though many in the military had sympathies with General de Gaulle and the Free French. However, there was still a lot of bitterness about the Royal Navy's attack on the French Fleet in the port of Mers-el-Kebir in July 1940, which killed more than 1,200 French sailors.

Three weeks before the invasion a small team of officers under Major-General Mark Clark was landed secretly near Algiers. There they had talks with sympathetic French officers. These were inconclusive, but Clark's team made contact with General Henri Giraud, an officer sympathetic to the Allied cause and not tarnished by any association with Vichy. They offered Giraud Anglo-American support if he would take command of the French forces in North

Africa. They also contacted Admiral Jean Darlan who, by chance, was in Algiers visiting his sick son. Darlan was Pétain's deputy and Commander-in-Chief of all French forces under the control of Vichy. Darlan was equivocal so, as the landings went ahead, no one could be sure what resistance they would meet.

Operation Torch had been planned hastily. The men were poorly trained for their task and the American forces were new to war. The amphibious landings went ahead on 8 November in high seas and losses in landing craft were heavy. If they had met determined French resistance, the operation could easily have turned into a disaster. As it was, after the fall of Algiers, Darlan was persuaded to order all French forces to cease fire. But this came too late to prevent heavy fighting at Oran, where the French fought bitterly for two days before surrendering to Major-General Terry Allen's US 1st Infantry Division. The Axis powers took Darlan's cease-fire as a violation of the armistice Pétain had signed and invaded unoccupied France. The remains of the French Fleet in Toulon then scuttled its ships. Giraud then became Commander-in-Chief of the French forces in North Africa. Darlan was shot by a young anti-Vichy fanatic on 24 December.

While General Patton's troops remained in Morocco training, the rest of the Allied forces turned east towards the western border of Tunisia, while Rommel's Afrika Korps was retreating towards its eastern border. With Libya lost, Hitler was determined to hold on to the key ports of Tunis and Bizerte. The Luftwaffe attacked Eisenhower's forces on land, while U-boats sank Allied supply ships at sea.

The British First Army, under Lieutenant-General Kenneth Anderson, was to lead the assault on Tunis, which was 500 miles east of Algiers. Transporting fuel, food and ammunition all that way down the primitive road network of northern Algeria proved to be a logistical nightmare. When Anderson arrived at the

Tunisian border he found it strongly defended and his first assault was repulsed. The major threat came from the Luftwaffe in Tunisia which had been strengthened to 445 aircraft earlier that month. The nearest Allied all-weather airbase was at Bône, 120 miles from the front lines. The Luftwaffe's nearest airbase was just five miles from the battlefield.

By the end of November 1942, the Axis forces in Tunisia had grown to around 25,000 men. These included fresh reserve units from Germany, Italy and France, along with reinforcements that had been destined for the Afrika Korps. Organised by General Walther Nehring, a former commander of the Afrika Korps who was convalescing after being wounded, the troops were supported by seventy Panzers – twenty of which were armed with the new 88mm guns. This was already a formidable force. But Field Marshal Albert Kesselring, Commander-in-Chief in the Mediterranean, was convinced that it was vital to block General Anderson's advance on Tunis and sent three more divisions.

In December, Anderson made a second attempt to take Tunis, but the Allied forces were inexperienced. Neither the British First Army nor the US II Corps had been tried in battle. Added to this was the difficulty of fighting as a coalition, which the Allies had by no means yet perfected. The Allied air force could not give them the close air support the Luftwaffe gave to their men. Anderson's men were still fighting as reinforced brigades as the British had in Libya and Egypt under Auchinleck. However, a joint British-French-American force reached Longstop Hill overlooking the Gulf of Tunis in December. The battle there lasted four days, until a powerful counter-attack supported by tanks on Christmas Day brought the Allies to a halt. Casualties were high on both sides, but any attempt to take Tunis would now have to be postponed. From the end of December to March, the rains come to North Africa, turning the parched landscape into a sea of mud.

The Allied forces would have to sit out the cold Tunisian winter at the end of long, tenuous supply lines. If aircraft strayed off their make-shift runways, or trucks left the road they would sink irretrievably into the mud. There was friction between the Allies with plenty of bar-room brawls between British and American troops. Eisenhower decided to put a stop to this. When one of his senior officers called his counterpart a 'British bastard', Eisenhower bellowed, 'There are no British, American or French bastards in this headquarters. There are certainly bastards aplenty and I am looking at one.'

Part of the friction came from the fact that the British Army, which had a fighting tradition centuries old, rubbed up against a peace-time American Army suddenly thrust into global war. The British found the inexperienced Americans brash and boastful, while the Americans found the British professionalism and sangfroid patronising. Anderson particularly came in for criticism, not least from Montgomery who said that he was no better than 'a good plain cook'. Even Field Marshal Alan Brooke, Chief of the Imperial General Staff, lamented the quality of his army and corps commanders, mourning the loss of so many good men in the First World War. It has to be said that the Americans were not a lot better. General Mark Clark was mistrusted by fellow Americans as being an intriguer who issued contradictory orders. And Eisenhower discovered that Fredendall held not only Anderson and the French in disdain, he also viewed Major-General Orlando W. Ward, commander of the 1st Armored Division, with outright contempt.

Against this ill-suited bunch, Hitler pitched the experienced Colonel-General Jürgen von Arnim. He was moved from the Eastern Front to take command of the Fifth Panzer Army and the defence of Tunisia. Von Arnim had more than 100,000 veteran German troops under his command and, by January 1943, he had all the mountain passes around Tunis under Axis control. Meanwhile, Eisenhower's planners developed Operation Satin. This was a plan for American and French forces, at the 250-mile-long southern front they now occupied, to punch their way through a mountain range called the Eastern Dorsal to the coast, south of Tunis, thereby cutting Von Arnim's forces off from Rommel's retreating army. When this was raised at the conference between Churchill and Roosevelt in Casablanca, Morocco, in January 1943, the British condemned the plan on the grounds that the inexperienced Allied troops would stand no chance against the veteran Panzer divisions that opposed them. Satin was shelved.

When Montgomery reached Tripoli in late January 1943, he decided that his troops must rest and essential repair work must be done on his armour before he tackled Rommel again. As a result, Rommel halted when he reached the Tunisian border and established the formidable Mareth Line there. He knew that he could not defeat Montgomery's veteran Eighth Army. But if he could hold them with minimal troops at the Mareth Line, he could launch an attack on the inexperienced and ill-supplied troops to his rear. With his Panzers he would destroy the untested and understrength American II Corps, then push along another mountain range called the Western Dorsal to the coast near Bône, knocking out the Allied airfield.

However, Rommel did not have the Panzers to pull this off. He did not get on with Von Arnim, a Prussian aristocrat who did not trust Rommel's flair, and Von Arnim would not go along with this daring plan. However, Von Arnim would support a more limited attack to strengthen his position on the Eastern Dorsal. On 14 February, German dive-bombers attacked the American forces guarding the town of Sidi Bou Zid in the Faid Pass. Then the tanks and infantry of the 10th Panzer quickly overran them, inflicting huge losses. The 21st Panzers attacked from the south through the

Maizila Pass. By noon the defenders of Sidi Bou Zid had been routed. The Americans quickly counter-attacked with a force of light tanks and infantry on half-tracks. This has been compared to the charge of the Light Brigade. The Americans lost over 2,000 of which 1,400 were taken prisoner, including Patton's son-in-law, Lieutenant Colonel John Waters. Only 300 got out. Some ninety-four tanks were lost along with sixty half-tracks and twenty-six self-propelled guns. But Von Armin would not give Rommel the support he needed to follow up on this success.

It was only on 19 February that Rommel got the authority to proceed. Even then Von Armin withheld part of the 10th Panzer and some newly arrived Tiger tanks. Rommel's forces were under strength when they began their attack on the Kasserine Pass in a rain storm. This was held by Task Force Stark, who occupied the high ground on either side of the pass. It was not taken until the following day. The British then fought a brilliant delaying action as Task Force Stark withdrew along the road to Thala, where the advance was halted. Although Rommel had won another tactical victory at the Kasserine Pass, it was a strategic failure. Allied reinforcements were on their way. He had lengthened his supply lines and his flanks were now open to attack. And it would only be a matter of time before Montgomery turned up at the Mareth Line. Rommel called off the offensive on 22 February.

In early March, Rommel advanced again – this time towards Medenine and Montgomery's advancing forces. By this time Montgomery knew Rommel well. At the first hint of the attack, he turned the 2nd New Zealand Division, two other infantry brigades and two armoured brigades, and positioned them along a line 43,000 yards long at right angles to Rommel's line of attack. Rommel found himself attacking across open terrain against 810 medium, field and anti-tank guns, including many of the new 17-pounder anti-tank guns in use for the first time. Salvoes of concentrated fire knocked out fifty-two tanks and inflicted 640 casualties before the Germans retreated. The British lost one Sherman tank and 130 men. Again Montgomery expressly forbade his men to pursue the fleeing enemy who disappeared behind the Matmata mountains. Two days later, Rommel – now out of favour with Hitler – left Africa and his command was ceded to Von Arnim.

Another British victory did nothing to help American morale. So far the Americans had sustained 6,000 casualties with nothing to show for it. Their equipment was no match for the Germans'. The British contended that their gung-ho attitude was no more than bravado, while in their intercepted communications the Germans were openly contemptuous. General Alexander, who was brought in as overall commander of ground forces, despaired that, from private to general, the Americans 'simply did not know their jobs as soldiers' and 'lacked the will to fight' – though he told Eisenhower, diplomatically, that once they had overcome their inexperience they would match any soldiers in the world. Chief of the Imperial General Staff Field Marshal Alan Brooke feared that the American forces would be 'quite useless' in the European theatre of war. Only Rommel had any time for them. He saw that their tactical defence of the Kasserine Pass was superb. He also knew that America's industrial might would mean it would soon be out-producing Germany with equipment equal to anything the Wehrmacht had. For the moment, though, the American forces' main problem was leadership.

Eisenhower was still a very inexperienced general and he had not tackled the personality problems in his own chain of command. The stridently anti-British attitudes of General Fredendall were causing problems, but Eisenhower felt he could not replace him as he was a favourite of General George C. Marshall, then the US Army Chief of Staff in Washington. Instead he called in veteran cavalry officer Major-General Ernest Harmon from the 2nd Armored

Division in Morocco and sent him to Fredendall's II Corps HQ. These were sixty-five miles behind the lines and housed in an enormous underground bunker that it had taken 200 combat engineers three weeks to build. When Harmon arrived there at 0200 on 23 February, a nervous Fredendall asked him if he thought the corps headquarters should be moved. Harmon thought that this was a strange question to ask in the middle of the night when he had had no time to assess the situation and he said, simply, 'Hell, no'.

Fredendall then took to his bed for a day and Harmon effectively took over command. The first thing he did was visit the British in Thala, who were still holding off the 10th Panzers. He immediately countermanded Anderson's order to withdraw the US artillery and sent his men into battle.

'I figured if I won the battle I would be forgiven,' Harmon said. 'If I lost, the hell with it anyway.'

Harmon then sent a report to Eisenhower saying that Fredendall was unfit to command. He told Patton that Fredendall was a moral and physical coward. Eisenhower dismissed Fredendall. However, the Army were afraid of the adverse effect dismissing the officer in charge of the first US ground troops in combat against the Axis might have on American public opinion. So it was made out that he was being transferred home because of his invaluable expertise in training. He arrived back in the US to a hero's welcome and was later promoted.

Eisenhower offered Fredendall's command to Harmon, but Harmon refused it on the grounds that he could not take over from a commander whose relief he had recommended. Instead Harmon suggested that Patton be brought in to command II Corps. He was joined by Major-General Omar N. Bradley, first as an observer, then – when Patton refused to have 'one of Ike's goddam spies' in his command – as his deputy. Although the two men could hardly have been more dissimilar – Patton was volatile and outspoken, while Bradley hated theatrics and any kind of profanity – they instinctively got on. Patton began reorganising II Corps along the lines of Montgomery's Eighth Army, while Alexander streamlined the overall command structure.

As the Germans withdrew through the Kasserine Pass and down the Eastern Dorsal, they were harassed by the planes of the Northwest African Tactical Air Force, now commanded by Air Marshal Arthur Coningham who had previously led the Desert Air Force which had done such an effective job supporting Montgomery.

With the Germans now on the retreat in the west, Alexander planned for his ground forces to tie up with the Eighth Army, which was massing to drive through the Gabes' Gap – a narrow corridor between salt lakes of Chott el Fedjadj and the sea – and punch its way through the Mareth Line. Then the 18th Army Group, as the combined command was known, would bottle the Axis forces up in northern Tunisia, while the Allied air forces and navies would deny them any possibility of escape or reinforcement.

In preparation, Alexander asserted his authority and made it clear that the British attitude of professionalism should take over from American amateurism. British officers set up training programmes, so the inexperienced troops could be toughened up before they were thrown into battle. Even so, in battle, British formations would be used ahead of American ones. This destroyed Eisenhower's strategy of building a truly equal alliance. However unpopular his policy was, Alexander enjoyed the respect of the American commanders in Tunisia. However unpalatable the truth might be, they knew that their troops were going to have to improve their performance before they won the respect of the British. Fortunately, in Patton, Bradley, Harmon and others they had the officers who could inspire their men to deliver just that result.

Ten days after he took command Patton was ordered to stage a diversionary attack to draw troops away from the Mareth Line. Alexander wanted him to take back the ground the Americans had lost the previous month and take the airfield at Gafsa, which would be used as a supply base when Montgomery broke through. Patton had other plans. He intended to push on past Gafsa and reach the coast at Gabes, cutting the Axis forces in two. Patton had brought a whole new attitude with him to II Corps.

'Gentlemen, tomorrow we attack,' he told his commanders. 'If we are not victorious, let no one come back alive.'

Despite heavy rains, on the night of 16 March, Patton's 1st Infantry Division took Gafsa. Von Arnim reacted as Alexander had predicted and sent the 10th Panzers to defend the pass at El Guettar, and Maknassy Pass which led from the Eastern Dorsal to the sea. The 10th Panzer arrived at the Maknassy Pass on 22 March, just as the 1st Armored Division got there. General Ward, commanding, realised that they had already exceeded Alexander's orders. He was also fearful of the Luftwaffe, who were flying from bases nearby, so he stopped to regroup. Patton was furious and replaced Ward with Harmon.

The following day an armoured battle group of the 10th Panzers, supported by artillery, infantry and Stukas, advanced across an open plain along the road that led from Gabes to Gafsa to the east of El Guettar. They were ambushed by tank destroyers, massed artillery and 1st Infantry Division who lay in wait in the hills flanking the road. By the time they withdrew in disarray, the Germans had lost thirty-two tanks and large numbers of infantrymen.

By the standard of the war, the Battle of El Guettar was small engagement, but to the Americans it was a decisive battle. They had shown the Germans – and the British too – that they could fight. Naturally Patton then wanted bigger fish to fry.

'Let me meet Rommel in a tank,' he said, 'and I'll shoot it out with the son-of-a-bitch.'

Unfortunately, Rommel was back in Germany by then.

While Patton was making his thrust down the Eastern Dorsal, Montgomery launched his offensive against the Mareth Line on 19 March. He used the same tactics as Rommel, sending Freyberg's New Zealand Corps around the south end of the line. They would go through the Tebega Gap in the Matmata Hills and attack the line from the rear, while XXX Corps attacked the line from the front across Wadi Zigaou. But the winter weather favoured the defenders. The wadi, which was normally dry, was full of water. The tanks that got across were subjected to a fierce counter-attack by the 15th Panzers, which took a fearful toll on them and their supporting troops. After twenty-four hours, Montgomery called off the frontal assault. He now had to depend on Freyberg and sent the British 1st Armoured Division, under Lieutenant-General Brian Horrocks, to reinforce him. The 4th Indian Division, under Major-General Francis Tuker, was also to swing to the south on a shorter route to attack a section of the Mareth Line weakened by the withdrawal of the 164th Light Division which had been sent to reinforce the 21st Panzer at the Tebega Gap. Freyberg had been halted by this formidable force but, with Horrocks reinforcing him and an all-out attack by the Desert Air Force, he broke through after nine days fighting. The Axis forces fell back through Gabes, but turned to fight again at Wadi Akarit ten miles further on. After another furious battle which cost the British 1,300 casualties, the remains of the German and Italian forces fell back to Endifaville, just fifty miles short of Tunis.

An attempt was made to cut off the fleeing forces by a provisional British corps commanded by Lieutenant-General John Crocker. They were ordered to break out of the Eastern Dorsal at Fondouk, cutting the line of retreat at Sousse. The American 34th Division under Major-General Charles Ryder was to take the pass at Fondouk in a frontal attack. Ryder planned to encircle the enemy but was overruled by Crocker. The assault failed, costing the 34th heavy casualties. Crocker blamed Ryder and ordered the 34th to be withdrawn for retraining.

Bradley feared that this would damage American morale. He had been at West Point with Ryder and knew that he was a good tactician. With Patton, who had now been designated American invasion commander for Sicily, he opposed the withdrawal of 34th Division and Alexander overruled Crocker. Nevertheless, the Americans were getting fed up with the contempt in which they were still held by the British. Patton struck back, blaming poor close air support for the shortcomings of II Corps. Air Marshal Coningham responded by saying that II Corps was not battle-worthy. In an attempt to heal the rift, Eisenhower ordered Coningham to apologise personally to Patton.

By this time the Axis forces were confined to a small enclave at the tip of the Tunisian peninsula, but it was clear to the Allies that they would not give up without a fight. Alexander drew up Operation Strike, his plan to finish them off. But once again he gave the Americans only a minor role. Marshall wrote to Eisenhower from Washington, complaining. He pointed out that the American press were saying that the 34th Division had already ruined the British chances of trapping the remains of the Afrika Korps. Bradley also put pressure on Eisenhower, who persuaded Alexander to change his plan and let II Corps take Bizerte.

Key to the success of the attack was a German strongpoint called Hill 609. Bradley assigned Ryder's 34th Division to the task.

'Get me that hill and no one will ever again doubt the toughness of your division,' he told Ryder.

The result was one of the most ferocious actions in the entire campaign. For five days the 34th battled to take the surrounding high points. They finally took Hill 609 with a combined assault using tanks and infantry. Then they successfully fought off a series of bloody counter-attacks. After that, Harmon restored the 1st Armored Division's tarnished glory with a thrust through the German defences on the road to Mateur. This broke the back of Bizerte's defences and cut off the Axis forces' only escape route. Von Arnim was determined to fight on, but Hitler turned a deaf ear to his requests for more ammunition and supplies. By then, the remains of the Axis forces were encircled on the plain of Tunis and on 12 May Von Arnim surrendered along with 250,000 crack troops – at a time when tens of thousands more were being wasted on the Eastern Front.

Overall Allied loses between 12 November 1942 and 13 May 1943 were 70,341. The French had lost 16,180; the British 35,940. The Americans had lost 18,221, including 2,715 killed. But Tunisia had been the American proving ground. Bradley said, 'In Africa we learned to crawl, to walk, to run.'

The British did not recognise how far the US forces had improved in so short a time and the bitterness and rivalry between the two Allied armies continued. But between them the Allies were now masters of North Africa. To their north lay what Churchill called 'the soft underbelly of Europe'. From North Africa they could attack in Greece, the Balkans, Italy or the South of France. They chose to take Sicily, and then fight their way up the Italian peninsula.

Operation Barbarossa
June 1942

3

THE RUSSIAN FRONT

OPERATION BARBAROSSA

HITLER WAS AN AVOWED anti-Communist. When he came to power in 1933, Joseph Stalin, leader of Communist Russia and its satellites, collectively known as the Union of Soviet Socialist Republics, was concerned about Hitler's rush to rearm Germany, fearing a German military expansion in the east. After the Munich Agreement of 1938 ceded Czech territory to Germany in an attempt to buy peace, Britain and France sought to establish an alliance with the USSR to encircle the German Reich. But Stalin believed that such an alliance would have guaranteed a Nazi attack on the Soviet Union and sought to make a pact with Germany instead.

On 3 May 1939, Stalin fired Soviet Commissar of Foreign Affairs Maksim Litvinov, an advocate of an alliance with the western powers and a Jew, and replaced him with Vyacheslav Molotov, who began negotiations with the Nazi foreign minister Joachim von Ribbentrop. On 23 August 1939, in Stalin's presence, Molotov and Von Ribbentrop signed what is known variously as the Nazi-Soviet Non-Aggression Pact, the German-Soviet Treaty of Non-Aggression, the Hitler-Stalin Pact or the Molotov-Ribbentrop Pact. The pact not only came as a surprise to Britain and France, but also to the Soviet people who had been subjected to years of anti-Nazi propaganda. Now Nazi Germany was a trusted friend.

However, the Molotov-Ribbentrop Pact contained a number of secret protocols which divided Eastern Europe into German and Soviet spheres of influence. Poland would be divided between the two, while Finland, Estonia, Latvia, Lithuania and Bessarabia (now divided between Ukraine and Moldova) would be ceded to the USSR. On 1 September 1939, Germany invaded Poland, starting the Second World War. Soviet troops invaded from the east on 17 September, meeting the advancing Germans near Brest-Litovsk two days later. The German Blitzkrieg had progressed so quickly that the Germans had already moved into areas that were to be in the Soviet sphere. The dividing line between the German and Soviet zones was altered a little in Germany's favour and the partition came into effect on 29 September. According to Molotov, Nazi-Soviet co-operation was now 'cemented in blood'.

While Hitler had honoured the secret protocols, for now, he had no intention of honouring the Non-Aggression Pact itself. In his political treatise Mein Kampf, written in the 1920s, Hitler said that the destruction of Communism was one of his primary goals. He also wanted Russian territory as far as the Volga River as *Lebensraum* (living space) for the German people. The Slavs who lived there, regarded as sub-human under the Nazi ideology, would provide slave labour for Hitler's 'Thousand Year Reich'. After the failure of Operation Sealion and defeat in the Battle of Britain, Hitler believed that a swift invasion of Russia would be such an awesome demonstration of German military might that it would keep America out of the war and force Britain to sue for peace.

In February 1941, British intelligence learned that Germany planned to invade the USSR that spring. The US picked up similar information. Both informed Moscow. But Stalin refused to believe it and he assured the Soviet people that Germany intended to live up to the Non-Aggression Pact.

Then seemingly out of the blue, the German ambassador in Moscow went to see Molotov and, at 0530 on 22 June 1941, he delivered a declaration of war. The reason – or excuse – was 'gross and repeated violations' of the Molotov-Ribbentrop Pact. A huge

German army was already pouring across a 1,900-mile front from the Baltic to the Black Sea. Even though the Soviets had been tipped off, the Germans achieved total surprise. Stalin had believed it when he had been told that the Axis forces massing on his borders were there for military manoeuvres.

In Operation *Barbarossa*, named for the 12th-century German founder of the First Reich, Hitler threw some 180 divisions into Russia – more that 3,000,000 German troops, supported by thirty Rumanian and Finnish divisions. There were nineteen Panzer divisions with 3,000 tanks; 2,500 aircraft were involved along with 7,000 artillery pieces. The German forces were divided into three army groups. Army Group North, commanded by Field Marshal Wilhelm von Leeb; Army Group Centre, commanded by Field Marshal Fedor von Bock; and Army Group South, commanded by Field Marshal Gerd von Rundstedt. The plan was to destroy all Soviet resistance in lightning advances on Leningrad (St Petersburg), Moscow and Kiev.

'We have only to kick in the door,' said Hitler to Rundstedt, 'and the whole rotten structure will come crashing down.'

When told of the invasion, it was said that Stalin had a 'nervous collapse'. He did not speak for eleven days. However, the Soviet Union was hardly defenceless in the face of this attack. Stalin had twice or maybe even three times the number of tanks and aircraft the Germans had and, while many of the aircraft were obsolete, the Russians' heavy tanks, the KV series, were superior to any the Germans threw against them, while the Russian T-34 medium tank was arguably the best of the war.

In one of his more lucid moments Hitler also said, 'At the beginning of each campaign one pushes a door into a dark, unseen room. One can never know what is hiding inside.'

In the Barbarossa campaign, what was hiding inside was the vast manpower that Stalin could call on. German intelligence estimated correctly that Stalin had about 150 divisions in the western USSR, and reckoned that he might be able to muster fifty more. In fact by the middle of August, Stalin had brought up 200 fresh divisions, dwarfing the German onslaught. However, they were badly led as many of their best generals had been killed during the 1930s when Stalin had purged the Soviet Red Army of supposed anti-Communist elements.

The Germans were also better trained and, after the campaign in the west, more experienced. They also had the element of surprise on their side and, as they made their advance into Russia, they attacked in places where they would have decisive superiority. The Russians were poorly deployed to meet the attack and their defensive positions were quickly overrun. In the Baltic states and areas of the Ukraine and Belorussia which had been under Soviet Communist rule since 1917, the Germans were greeted as liberators. Even the Jews of Kiev welcomed the Germans, as they had been well treated by the Germans who had invaded the Ukraine in the the First World War. But within days 100,000 Ukrainian Jews had been massacred at Baby Yar, a large ravine to the north of the city. SS death squads also sought out Soviet Commissars for execution and Slavs were summarily killed.

Army Group North began its advance from East Prussia. It was to sweep through the Baltic states, then advance towards Leningrad. Hitler believed that, with the capture of Leningrad, Army Group Centre would be able to move on Moscow. Although Army Group North was the weakest of the three army groups and faced the most powerful opposition, it made the most rapid progress. Despite the swampy, forested terrain and unpaved roads, by 26 June Army Group North had already taken Lithuania and was well into Latvia.

One of the major obstacles the Germans faced on their way to Leningrad was the Dvina River. But on 26 June, the 8th Panzer

Division and the 56th Panzer Corps seized the road and rail bridges over the Dvina at Dvinsk (now Daugavopils) and went on to seize the city before the Red Army was able to reduce it to rubble. After five hours of street fighting the Germans had crushed all resistance. Three days later Army Group North had captured Riga, the capital of Latvia, then halted to regroup.

On 3 July, Stalin had rallied sufficiently to make a radio address to the Russian people. He called on their nationalism and reminded them of the fate of Napoleon and Kaiser Wilhelm who had invaded their country in the the First World War. Both had been toppled from power by their military adventures. He told Soviet citizens in the territories already occupied by the Germans to form partisan groups. He also announced a 'scorched earth' policy, like the one that had been used against Napoleon's invasion of Russia in 1812. The Germans, Stalin said, must be not be allowed to take 'a single engine, or a single railway truck, and not a pound of bread nor a pint of oil'. The Soviet economy was turned over to war production. Entire factories were moved eastwards, out the reach of the Germans, and began turning out tanks and aircraft at an astonishing rate.

Far from scaring the British into surrender, Operation Barbarossa gave them new heart. At last, they had a powerful ally – one corner of the grand alliance Churchill intended to build to defeat Hitler. Both Britain and the US began supplying the Soviet Union, via the Arctic Ocean to the northern Russian port of Archangel and through Persia (Iran) which Britain and the USSR jointly occupied.

On 2 July, Army Group North had resumed its offensive. The Red Army had hopes of stopping the German advance at Pskov on the border of Estonia, the most northerly of the Baltic states, but by 8 July the German armour had broken through. Sixteenth Army took Opochka and moved on toward Lake Ilmen, south of

Leningrad, while in the west Eighteenth Army took Tallin, the capital of Estonia, on the Gulf of Finland.

Army Group North then advanced towards the Luga River where the Red Army hoped, once again, to stop them. But the Germans simply split their corps either side of the Soviet concentration and crossed the river in full strength on 15 July. Army Group North was now poised to make a thrust towards Leningrad. The Red Army had had no time to fortify the approaches to the city. However, the German High Command told Army Group North to stop to regroup and shore up their supply lines.

When Army Group North got underway again the following month, Eighteenth Army took Narva on the Gulf of Finland and Sixteenth Army seized Novgorod on the north side of Lake Ilmen on 16 August, and 4th Panzer Group reached Krasnógvardeisk, 21 miles from Leningrad, on 20 July.

Russia had seized parts of Finland under secret protocols of the Molotov-Ribbentrop Pact. But after Barbarossa began, the Finns seized the opportunity to side with Germany. On 10 July, they began their offensive to take back the lands they had lost. By 16 August, they had advanced approximately sixty miles along the western shore of Lake Ladoga. This cut Leningrad off from the north, but the Finns stopped at the Russo-Finnish border and could not be persuaded to advance any further.

As the Germans closed on Leningrad from the south, the Red Army suddenly mounted a counter-attack. This gave the population of the city enough time to dig anti-tank trenches and build a defensive perimeter. By 9 September the Germans had pushed the Red Army back until they were within artillery range of Leningrad. They also began bombing the city. German tanks broke through the last fortified line, but they could make little headway in the narrow streets where tanks are particularly vulnerable. It was then decided that the Panzers would be more use in the south, so they were withdrawn. But the German infantry and artillery remained to besiege the city.

One million of the city's inhabitants had already been evacuated. The remaining two million were now completely cut off with the Finns to the north and the Germans to the south. A siege began that lasted 900 days. During that time, Leningrad's only lifeline was across Lake Ladoga, by barge in the summer and by truck and sled across the ice in the winter. When the siege was finally lifted on 19 January 1944, some 200,000 civilians had been killed by the German bombardment and at least 630,000 had perished of starvation and disease.

In the first weeks of Operation Barbarossa, Army Group South quickly overtook most of the Ukraine, giving Hitler the benefit of its summer harvest. When Stalin ordered a counter-attack in the south-west, Hitler reacted by sending both Rumanian and more German forces into the southern front, and a massive struggle ensued between the German and Russian armoured divisions. By the end of the first week, the Soviets' twenty-four divisions were looking decidedly threadbare. Army Group South hit at any weak spots they found in the Soviet lines and, by 11 July, the German army was ten miles from Kiev. Stalin did not want to lose his hold on the Dnieper River. But on 31 August, the German army crossed the river and pounded the Russian flanks. Although the Russians were taking heavy losses, Stalin refused his generals' request to pull out of Kiev and replaced his commander. Then as the losses mounted, Stalin made a snap decision to pull out. It was too late. On 20 September, the Fifth Army and its Russian armoured column were encircled and captured. Some 520,000 prisoners were taken.

Army Group Centre, under Field Marshal Fedor von Bock, was the strongest of the three army groups. It consisted of Fourth and Ninth Armies as well as 2nd and 3rd Panzer Groups, later re-designated as Panzer Armies, and it was supported by 2nd Air Fleet under Field Marshal Albert Kesselring. Its Panzer and motorised formations burst out from the area north of Warsaw on 22 June, tore huge holes in the Soviet defences and smashed the Soviet forces in Belorussia. Its primary task was to guard Army Group North's right flank as it swept through the Baltic states towards Leningrad. Hitler had decreed that only after Leningrad had been captured should Army Group Centre advance on Moscow.

Its Panzer spearheads reached Minsk, capital of Belorussia on 29 June, encircling four Soviet Armies and taking 287,000 prisoners. On 16 July, the German pincers reached Smolensk, just 260 miles from Moscow, surrounding another large Russian force and taking a further 300,000 prisoners. By the end of July the Germans controlled an area of Soviet territory more than twice the size of France.

By early August, Army Group Centre had covered two-thirds of the distance to Moscow. Feeling that the Red Army could not successfully resist a German advance upon the Soviet capital, Von Bock urged the High Command to let him push on to Moscow. But Hitler insisted that taking Kiev and Leningrad were the priority. His aim was to prevent the bulk of the Red Army escaping eastwards into the depths of Russia and he diverted Army Group Centre's forces northwards and southwards to assist. The result was the encirclement of the huge Russian force at Kiev, yielding another 665,000 prisoners.

With Kiev now taken and Army Group North menacing Leningrad, Hitler gave Von Bock permission to resume his march on Moscow in Operation Typhoon. But Army Group Centre was not able to regroup and renew the offensive until 2 October, which gave the Russians the chance to prepare defensive positions and bring up reinforcements. Once it had regrouped, Army Group Centre quickly made deep thrusts into the Russian lines. Using its superior mobility it encircled large pockets of Red Army troops at Vyazma and

Bryansk. The Vyazma pocket yielded 663,000 prisoners; Bryansk another 100,000. By then the Russians only had 824 tanks left on the Western Front, no air support, and all their massed armies had been lost. All that was left were a few divisions of defeated men and some improvised workers' battalions. The road to Moscow was now open. Foreign diplomats were evacuated from the city and the embalmed body of Lenin, the founder of the Soviet Union, had been removed from his tomb in Red Square for safe-keeping.

Stalin was about to flee the city, then changed his mind. He imposed martial law and recalled Marshal Georgii Zhukov, his ablest general, from Leningrad to command the defence of Moscow. The Germans were also experiencing severe problems and hardships. The troops were exhausted. The Soviets' scorched earth policy had destroyed any housing that could be used as a billet and their equipment was wearing out. Every advance stretched the German supply lines and, at night, the Russians would attack the German guards and destroy their supplies.

The diversion of some of Army Group Centre's strength to Kiev and the time it had taken to regroup had delayed its advance. It was now October and the weather was changing. Whenever it rained, the roads turned into a sea of mud and the advance slowed to six miles a day. The German Panzers to the north of Moscow, under General Hoth, could not make a rapid attack in formation through the dense forest there. However, General Guderian's force could attack from the south across the open country there. But Zhukov had stationed his last independent tank force, the 4th Armoured Brigade, to the south. They were well trained and equipped with T-34 tanks, which had armour that could not be penetrated by the German artillery. Fourth Armoured stopped the German advance almost within sight of Moscow.

Hoth continued to push forward though. The Russians responded with Katyusha rockets, whose multiple launchers were nicknamed

'Stalin organs' by the Germans, and the Soviet Air Force was airborne again. But Hoth pushed on and, by 12 November, he was in a position to attack the city. By then though, Zhukov had 1,700 tanks and 1,500 aircraft to defend Moscow, along with fresh troops brought in from Siberia.

The Germans launched their final thrust on Moscow on 15 November. They moved rapidly, at first, as the roads were now frozen and the 7th Panzer Division reached the Moscow-Volga canal, just 20 miles from Moscow. On 4 December 1941, the Soviets began a counter-attack. Army Group Centre was forced back in spite of Hitler's insistence that they hold their positions regardless of the cost. But the situation was hopeless. The weather had closed in. Blizzards and snowdrifts hampered the movement of supplies and the scorched earth policy meant that the Germans could not support themselves from the land. The German Army was not prepared for the brutal Russian winter. Hitler had been so confident of a quick victory he had not provided him men with winter clothing. Soon almost everyone was suffering from frostbite. The German equipment was not built to withstand the freezing temperatures either. Oil froze in the tanks' engines. Packing grease in the artillery froze and automatic firing mechanisms seized up.

Hitler blamed his generals. He fired them and took over as Commander-in-Chief himself. But there was nothing he could do about the weather. That winter was the coldest for 140 years. It was so cold that boiling soup ladled out from German field kitchens froze within minutes. Axe-shafts splintered when meat was being hacked up and butter had to be cut with a saw. By the end of the year 100,000 cases of frostbite had been reported and over 14,000 were so serious that a limb had to be amputated. Then on 7 January, Stalin ordered another offensive. Using the last of his reserves, Zhukov pushed the Germans back and, by the end of January, the front stabilised some 40 miles west of Moscow. Operation Typhoon had been thwarted and the city had been saved.

However, Army Group Centre held a position at Rzhev, a hundred miles west of Moscow, until March 1943 when Hitler finally allowed it to withdraw. Hitler did not try to take Moscow again. Instead he sought to defeat Russia in the south, concentrating his strength on the battle for Stalingrad, a battle which would prove to be a turning point in Hitler's war in Russia.

STALINGRAD

During the winter of 1941, despite the privations of his men on the Eastern Front, Hitler was not down-hearted. Most of the Soviet Union's European territory was now in his hands and, by February 1942, the Soviet's winter counter-attack had petered out. Now Hitler began to make plans to crush the Red Army once and for all. The renewed campaign would attack Stalingrad (now Volgograd), a city that stretched some 30 miles along the Volga, 600 miles south-east of Moscow. It was a huge new industrial city and was paraded as one of the great achievements of the Soviet system. It also bore the name of the Soviet Union's leader, who had organised its defences against the White Russians in the civil war that followed the founding of the Soviet state. Stalin realised that the city must be held at all costs. If it fell, so would he.

For Hitler, too, Stalingrad was important. It was a symbol of Communism and had to be crushed. It was also an important centre for mass production of armaments. Once it had been taken, his victorious army would head up the Volga to encircle Moscow, while another second army would move south-east to take the oilfields of the Caucasus and threaten Turkey and Persia.

Army Group Centre was then split into two groups, under the overall control of Field Marshal von Bock. Army Group B, under General Freiherr von Weichs, was much the stronger of the two. It comprised Fourth Panzer Army under Hoth, Second Army, and the powerful Sixth Army, under General Friedrich Paulus, supported by other crack infantry and Panzer divisions. By comparison Army Group A was practically a reserve force. It had the crack First Panzer Army under Field Marshal Ewald von Kleist, which was going to take the oilfields of the Caucasus, and Seventeenth Infantry Army. But the numbers were made up with Italian, Rumanian and Hungarian troops. Altogether there were now twenty-five Panzer divisions compared with nineteen the year before. However, the war was very different now. The Wehrmacht no longer seemed to be invincible and Hitler was no longer infallible. German soldiers now feared being posted to the Eastern Front. The brutal treatment of the civilians there – including mass shooting, burnings, the summary execution of prisoners and the deliberate starvation of men, women and children – was sure to invite retribution.

In the spring of 1942, Stalin made a counter-attack in the Kerch Peninsula in the Crimea. This was crushed and the Germans took 100,000 prisoners. Two fresh Siberian divisions sent to relieve Leningrad were encircled. Then 600 Russian tanks, two-thirds of their force, punched through the Rumanian Sixth Army to take Kharkov. But then the trap closed. Von Kleist crushed the southern flank of the Soviet advance on 18 May, while Paulus swept down from the north the following day. The Soviets lost nearly a quarter of a million men, along with all their tanks. Now the stage was set for Hitler's summer offensive.

On 28 June, on a wide front stretching from Kursk to Rostov, the Panzers went roaring across the open steppes. The dust pall they kicked up could be seen for forty miles and it was soon joined by smoke from burning villages. There were no significant forces to oppose them as the reserves were still being held back for the defence of Moscow. The Red Army put up a fight at the industrial town of Voronezh. When Von Bock attempted to crush them rather than bypass them and continue the offensive, Hitler sacked him. Army Group A, led by Von Kleist's Panzers, then crossed the River Don and headed southwards towards the oilfields, while Army Group B headed for Stalingrad.

While Army Group A progressed quickly and were almost in sight of the oil derricks of the Caucasian field by 9 August, Fourth and Sixth Armies with 330,000 of Germany's finest soldiers advanced more slowly over the 200 miles to Stalingrad and became strung out. As they massed to mount an assault, Stalin made the decision to commit the Moscow reserve to the defence of Stalingrad and the desperate race to get them there began. Between 25 and 29 August, Paulus's Sixth Army made a ferocious attempt to storm the city before reinforcements could arrive. Meeting stiff opposition, Paulus asked Hoth's Fourth Panzer Army for help. It attacked from the south, forcing the Soviet Sixty-Fourth Army, which was defending the southern part of city, to extend its flank to meet the threat. The Soviet front was now eighty miles long, but only fifty miles wide. Paulus threw his entire Sixth Army, now supported by the Fourth Army Corps, against it. On 22 August, German troops penetrated the northern suburbs and on the next day reached the Volga, within mortar range of a vital railway bridge. The Soviet Sixty-Second Army in the northern sector were now outflanked. The Luftwaffe was then called in to deliver an all-out night bombardment. The idea was to demoralise the defenders and cause panic among the citizens. Much of the civilian population fled to the other side of the Volga and the authorities began evacuating the largest factories. When Stalin heard of this, he stopped the evacuations. The result was that the factories themselves became centres of resistance. Workers in the tractor factory continued producing new tanks and armoured cars until the Germans were on their doorstep. Then they would sling ammunition belts over their overalls, pick up grenades, rifles and anti-tank weapons, and take up their positions in the firing-points or bunkers with their comrades from the Red Army, while the remaining women, children and the elderly hid in cellars, sewers and caves in the cliffs above the Volga.

Despite fierce fighting following the terror-bombing, the German advance in the north of the city was halted. In the south Hoth's Panzers pushed the Sixty-Fourth Army back, but failed to penetrate the line. And once they entered the heart of the ruined city, their advance too ground to a halt.

For Hitler, Stalingrad was going to be where the war was won or lost. His summoned his commanders to his new forward head-quarters at Vinnitsa over 500 miles away in the Ukraine. The drive up the Volga was vital to the success of his Russian campaign, he told them. New Hungarian and Rumanian armies were brought in to protect the left flank along the Don and three new infantry divisions were sent to reinforce Sixth Army. Stalin, too, believed that the war would be won or lost at Stalingrad. He moved in a new team of commanders headed by Zhukov.

The Germans were the masters of the Blitzkrieg. They were not used to slow, grinding, man-to-man fighting through the rubble of a ruined city. The Russians, by contrast, quickly learned to adapt their tactics to the new situation and every move the Germans made cost them dearly. After weeks of ceaseless fighting against crack German troops, the Red Army still held a nine-mile strip along the banks of the Volga. A series of gentle curves in the Volga and a number of small islands prevented German ground troops bombarding all the river crossings with artillery and mortar fire. Nor did the Luftwaffe bomb them or the Soviet artillery on the other bank. Instead, they continued to throw everything they had against the Soviet enclave on the west bank.

On 12 September, Hitler authorised a new offensive. The following day, Paulus sent in three Panzer divisions backed by eight divisions of infantry. Against them, the Soviets had forty tanks, all but nineteen immobile. The Sixty-Second Army had been reduced to just three infantry divisions, the remnants of four others and two battle-damaged tank brigades. And there were no reserves as every man had already been thrown into the battle. However, the Soviet headquarters were on the spot. General Vasili Chuikov had made the dangerous crossing of the Volga and had set up his command post in a dug-out, by the river near Puskin Street bridge. With their backs to the river Chuikov inspired his men with the words, 'There is no land across the Volga'. For those who did not get the message, there were firing squads to deal with the deserters. Hundreds were shot.

The Germans flung themselves at the middle of the Russian line and, on the afternoon of 14 September, they broke through and seized Mamaye Hill. From the high ground there, they could concentrate artillery fire on the vital ferry link from Krasnaya Sloboda. The 76th Infantry Division overwhelmed the defenders at a ruined hospital in the middle of the Soviet line. Victory now seemed certain and many Germans got drunk on looted vodka. The only resistance now seem to be snipers.

Chuikov then threw his nineteen tanks in and the battle resumed. That night the fighting came within 200 yards of Chuikov's headquarters and staff officers joined in. But the Germans still pushed forward and the vital central landing stage came under machine-gun fire from close range. On the night of 14 September, Russian Guardsmen had to scramble ashore under fire. There was no possibility of them counter-attacking as a coherent division, and they were soon dispersed among the ruins in isolated pockets with no intercommunication.

The street fighting had also broken up the German formations. They now fought through the devastated streets in small battle groups comprising three or four Panzers and a company of German infantrymen, which had to laboriously clear each pocket individually. Russian riflemen and machine-gunners hid in ruined buildings, craters and behind mountains of rubble. They hid until the Panzers had gone by, then attacked the infantry. The Panzers then found themselves attacked by roving T-34s, or they ran into anti-tank guns or dug-in tanks. In the narrow streets, the Panzers were very vulnerable both to grenades dropped from directly above and to anti-tank guns which the Russians had a plentiful supply of, while their armour-piercing shells made a comparatively small hole in a building, most of which had been destroyed anyway. The battle hinged on house-to-house combat fought with bullet, grenade, bayonet and flame-thrower.

The Germans found that it took a whole day and numerous casualties to take 200 yards. Even then the Russians reappeared at night, knocking holes in attic walls so that they could reoccupy buildings over the heads of the Germans. Even so, victory seemed near. A German salient ran down the Tsarita tributary to the Volga itself. They had almost complete control of much of the city. And the landing stages and most of the river crossings were within range of their guns. The Russians' only lifeline lay to the north where the ferries were out of range.

But it did not seem to matter how much of the city the Germans occupied. The Russians would not give up. The remains of the 92nd Infantry Brigade formed isolated pockets of resistance across the south of the city. The grain elevators there, though bombed and blasted, still stood defiant. At all levels from top to bottom, they were occupied by pockets of Guardsmen and Russian Marines who repelled wave after wave of attackers. Their stout resistance brought the German assault inexorably to a halt.

For the Germans, two months of fighting for a narrow strip of the ruined city of Stalingrad was a propaganda disaster. The German people were told that the Russians were throwing wave after wave of men into the battle and were exhausting their reserves. In fact, the opposite was true. During September and October, the Germans threw no fewer than nineteen newly formed armoured brigades and twenty-seven infantry divisions into the battle. In that same period, only five Soviet divisions crossed the Volga. Zhukov sent only the bare minimum needed to hold off the Germans, so that he could build up strength for a counter-attack.

Around this time a crucial change was made in the Red Army. Since the Red Army was formed in the wake of the 1917 Revolution, its officers, many of whom came from the former Imperial Army, had been stripped of their badges of rank and their every move was watched over by political commissars attached to each unit. Now old-fashioned gold-braided epaulettes were distributed. Old regimental traditions were revived. Political interference ceased and soldiers were told that they were fighting for Mother Russia, not for the Communist party.

While Russian spirits received a boost, German morale sagged. Russian artillery fire grew steadily heavier. Meanwhile the nights began to draw in. The skies became grey, the weather chilly and the Germans began to fear that they would be spending another winter in Russia. Quickly Paulus planned a fourth all-out offensive. This time he was determined to score a great victory as he had heard that Hitler was considering promoting him to Chief of the High Command and Hitler had also publicly promised that Stalingrad would fall 'very shortly'.

Forty thousand Russians now held a strip of the city barely ten miles long. At its widest it reached a mile and a quarter inland from the west bank of the Volga, at its narrowest 500 yards. But the Russians defending it were hardened troops who knew every cellar, sewer, crater and ruin of this wasteland. They watched German advances through periscopes and cut them down with machine-gun fire. Snipers stalked the cratered streets, or lay camouflaged and silent for hours on end awaiting their prey. Against them were pitched veteran German troops, who were demoralised by the losses they had taken, or raw recruits, who could be in no way prepared for the horrors they were about to face.

On 4 October, the Germans were about to launch their offensive when the Russians counter-attacked in the area around the tractor factory. This threw the Germans off balance. Although little ground was lost, it cost them many casualties. The Luftwaffe sent in 800 dive-bombers and the German artillery pounded the city mercilessly. Occasionally a pet dog, escaping from a bombed building, would race through the inferno, leap into the river and swim to freedom on the other side. After a five-hour bombardment, which shattered glass deep below ground and killed sixty-one men in Chuikov's headquarters, the German attack eventually went ahead.

On 14 October, two new armoured divisions and five infantry divisions pushed forward on a front just three miles wide. They found themselves lured into special killing grounds the Russians had prepared, where houses and sometimes whole blocks or squares had been heavily mined. Combat became so close that the Germans would occupy one half of a shattered building, while the Russians occupied the other. When the Russians prepared a building as a stronghold they would destroy the stairs so that the Germans would have to fight for each floor independently. And when it came down to hand to hand fighting, it was usually the Russians who came off best. If they lost a building, the survivors would be sent back with the first counter-attack to retake it. That day, 14 October, according to Chuikov, was 'the bloodiest and most ferocious day of the whole battle'.

By sheer weight of numbers, the Germans pushed forward towards the tractor factory. The Soviets reinforced it with 2,300 men. After an entire day, the Germans had taken just one block. But although they took enormous casualties the tractor factory eventually ended up in German hands and the Soviet forces were pushed back so close to the Volga that boats bringing supplies across the river came under heavy machine-gun fire.

Next door to the tractor factory, the ruined Red October factory looked as if it might fall too. But at the last moment a Siberian division was put in. Its men were told to fight to the death. They dug in among shattered concrete, twisted girders, heaps of coal and wrecked railway wagons. Behind them were the icy waters of the Volga – there was nowhere to retreat to.

Unable to shift the Siberians, the Germans bombarded them with mortars, artillery and dive-bombers. But the Siberians had dug a series of interconnecting trenches, dug-outs and strong points in the frozen ground around the factory. When the barrage was lifted and the German armour and infantry went in they found themselves under blistering attack. After forty-eight hours of continuous fighting, hardly a man was left of the leading Siberian regiment. But the German offensive had been halted.

For the next two weeks, the onslaught on the Red October factory continued. The Germans made 117 separate attacks – twenty-three on one single day. But backed by artillery from across the river directed by observation posts hidden in the ruins, the Siberian division held out.

'Imagine Stalingrad,' wrote a German veteran, 'eighty days and nights of hand-to-hand fighting. The streets are no longer measured in metres, but in corpses. Stalingrad is no longer a town. By day it is an enormous cloud of burning, blinding smoke. It is a vast furnace lit by the reflection of the flames.'

Paulus's offensive was at a standstill. The defenders of the city were unyielding and he had no more men to throw against them. For the moment there was a stalemate, but winter was on its way. Then Sixth Army received reinforcements in the form of a number of battalions of Pioneers, front-line engineering and sapper troops. These would be used in the vanguard of a new offensive along a front just 400 yards wide. Instead of fighting from house to house, they would move through the sewers, cellars and tunnels under the city.

The offensive began on 11 November with a bombardment that turned what remained of the city into rubble. The first rush of fresh troops took the Germans through the last 300 yards under the city to the bank of the Volga. But when they reached it, the Russians emerged from their hiding places behind them, cutting them off. The German advance troops were trapped. But surrender was not an option. They were far past the point where prisoners were taken. The attack collapsed into sporadic pockets of desperate, hand-to-hand combat in hidden caverns under the rubble. On both sides men fought with unmitigated savagery. The troops were filthy, smelly, unshaven and red-eyed. They were high on vodka and benzedrene. No sane, sober man could fight in such conditions. After four days, only Russians were left. Then a terrible silence fell over Stalingrad – the silence of death.

But at first light on 19 November, the air was full of sound again. Two hundred Russians guns opened fire to the north of the city. The next day, hundreds more opened up to the south. While the Germans had been exhausting their forces fighting inside the city, Zhukov had been busy building up a new army. He had massed 900 brand new T-34 tanks, 115 regiments of the dreaded Katyusha multi-rocket launchers, 230 artillery regiments and 500,000 infantrymen.

Two spearheads attacked the northern and southern tips of the German forces. The German flanks were turned fifty miles north and fifty miles south of Stalingrad and the Red Army rushed forward to encircle the German forces inside the city. This took the Germans completely by surprise. Paulus had imagined that the Russian reserves were drained and the German High Command was bracing itself for a new Russian winter offensive against Army

Group Centre at Rzhev. The flanks of Paulus's Army were held by Rumanian troops who were ill-equipped and had little stomach for fighting. As far as they were concerned, this was Germany's war.

The Germans never knew what had hit them. They found it impossible to judge the scale or direction of the offensive. Paulus sent Panzers to the north, but they could not stem the tide there. Twenty miles to the rear of the main German forces besieging Stalingrad was the town of Kalach and its bridge across the Don, a vital link in Paulus's supply line. Demolition charges had already been placed so that the bridge could be blown if the Russians threatened to take it. But on 23 November the Russians took the Germans by surprise by turning up in a captured Panzer. They machine-gunned the guards and removed the demolition charges.

Meanwhile, the Russians' southern pincer had smashed through the German lines and turned northwards, and the two spearheads met at Kalach that evening. They had encircled 250,000 Germans and made the most decisive breakthrough on the Eastern Front. They had defeated an Italian army, a Hungarian army, and a Romanian army, and had taken 65,000 prisoners. Three days later the Russians had thirty-four divisions across the Don and were breaking out to the north. Some armoured columns stayed behind to trouble Paulus's rear, while Russian infantry moved around the Germans and dug in. More than a thousand anti-tank guns were deployed to prevent a German break-out and the Germans menacing Stalingrad were bombarded by heavy artillery from the other side of the Volga.

Hitler told Paulus to hold his ground until 'Fortress Stalingrad' was relieved. Göring told Hitler that his Luftwaffe could fly in 500 tonnes of stores a day. Paulus was not wholly convinced and, knowing that the winter was imminent, he prepared a force of 130 tanks and 57,000 men for a break-out. Hitler countermanded this. He had not given up on Stalingrad and ordered General Erich von

Manstein, author of the attack through the Ardennes, to collect up the remaining Axis forces in the region and relieve Paulus.

Reinforcements were rushed to Manstein from Army Group Centre at Rzhev and Army Group A in the Caucasus. The attack began on 11 December and was led by Hoth and his Fourth Panzer Army. Following them was a convoy of trucks carrying 3,000 tonnes of supplies. They would make their attack from the south-west and punch their way into the city where Paulus was still holding his position. The ground was frozen, which made the going better for the Panzers, and the heavy snow made them difficult to spot. The Russians in Stalingrad were also having a hard time and ice floes coming down the Volga menaced their ferries.

But the Russians also knew how to turn the snow to their advantage. The winter sky denied the German's air reconnaissance. As Hoth made progress towards Stalingrad, he did not notice Russians hidden behind the snow in the gullies that criss-crossed the landscape. At dusk and dawn, T-34s would emerge and attack the infantry's trucks and the supply convoy following the Panzers. The German armour would then have to halt, turn around and deal with them. This slowed the German advance. However, on 17 December, Hoth reached the Aksay River, thirty-five miles from Stalingrad, where Zhukov had sent 130 tanks and two infantry divisions to meet him.

The powerful 48th Panzer Corps was planning an attack to relieve Stalingrad from the north-east. But 450 Russian T-34s suddenly came rumbling across the ice of the Don, smashing the Italian, Rumanian and Hungarian armies in that sector and pushing on towards Voronezh. The 48th were so busy containing this thrust that a counter-thrust towards Stalingrad was out of the question.

To the south, Hoth was in trouble with his north-eastern flank crumbling along its entire 200-mile length. Manstein now realised that the only hope for the quarter-of-a-million Germans in Fortress

Stalingrad was for Paulus and Hoth to attack at the same place on either side of the Russian line simultaneously. Paulus refused to try to break out, saying that Hitler had ordered him to stay where he was. There was to be no retreat from Stalingrad. Besides, his ill-fed troops were not physically strong enough to make the attack and they only had the fuel to go twenty miles, only just enough to reach the Russian lines. Göring was still promising that he would supply them and Hitler wanted Paulus's army in position for a new offensive next spring.

On 19 December, Hoth crossed the Aksay and, two days later, Manstein talked to Hitler, telling him that it was vital for Sixth Army to attempt to break out to meet him. But Hitler backed Paulus. Manstein had no choice but to recall Hoth. He had lost 300 tanks and 16,000 men in the failed attempt to relieve Paulus. With Hoth pulling back, Army Group A also had to withdraw as it risked being cut off in the Caucasus.

The Sixth Army was now left to its fate. It was fanciful to believe that it could hold its position all winter. The infantry were running short of ammunition. The maximum allocation was thirty bullets a day. The Russians now had the 250,000 beleaguered Germans surrounded by 500,000 men and 2,000 guns. Meanwhile the retreating German forces were being chased out of southern Russia by a new Soviet offensive.

In an effort to free up more manpower, the Soviets offered Paulus the chance to surrender on 8 January on the best possible terms. There would be food for the hungry, medical care for the wounded, guaranteed repatriation for everyone at the end of the war and the officers would even be allowed to keep their weapons. But Hitler had taken personal charge of Fortress Stalingrad from his bunker in Poland and refused these terms. Instead he promoted Paulus to the rank of Field Marshal and told him to fight on.

It had been estimated that the remains of Sixth Army could be sustained on 550 tonnes of supplies a day – fifty less than Göring, at his most optimistic, had promised. The Luftwaffe had 225 Junkers Ju 52s available for the task. The nearest airfields were then an hour-and-a-half's flying time away and it was assumed that each plane could make one flight a day. In fact, there were rarely more than eighty Junkers serviceable on any one day. Two squadrons of converted Heinkel 111 bombers were brought in, but they could only carry one-and-a-half tons of supplies each. Then as the Russians advanced, Sixth Army had to be supplied from airfields even further away. As the weather closed in, supply by air grew erratic. The Soviets massed anti-aircraft guns along the flight paths and Sixth Army could then only be resupplied at night. In all, 536 German transport planes were shot down and the average supply drop fell to 60 tons a night. The bread ration was cut to one slice a day and one kilogram of potatoes had to feed fifteen men. The horses of the Rumanian cavalry were eaten. Dogs, cats, crows, rats, anything the soldiers could find in the ruins were consumed. The only drinking water came from melted snow.

As the tightening Russian noose forced them to retreat, the Germans found that they were too weak to dig new defences. They slept with their heads on pillows of snow. Frostbite was endemic. Any wound meant death almost inevitably. Even if the wounded man's comrades were strong enough to carry him to the first aid post, there were few medical supplies left and little the doctors could do. Suicide was so common that Paulus had to issue a special order declaring it dishonourable. Even so, when the rumour circulated that the Russians were taking no prisoners, everyone kept one last bullet for themselves.

On 10 January, the Russians began their final attack. The perimeter shrank by the hour. By 24 January, the Germans were forced back behind the line the Russians had held on 13 September. The command structure collapsed. Medical posts and make-shift hospitals were full of wounded men begging their comrades to kill them. The airstrips – their only lines of supply – were taken and the remnants of Sixth Army were forced back into the ruined factories, the cellars and the sewers of the city. But still Hitler would not surrender.

Finally, on 30 January, Paulus's command post was overrun and he was captured. Two days later resistance was at an end. In all, 91,000 frozen and hungry men, including twenty-four generals, were captured. As they were marched away a Soviet colonel pointed at the rubble that was Stalingrad and shouted angrily at a group of German prisoners, 'That's how Berlin is going to look.' Two entire German armies were wiped out including their reserves. Some 300,000 trained men had been lost. They were irreplaceable. The battle had been a bloodbath. In the last stages alone, 147,200 Germans and 46,700 Russians had been killed.

Stalingrad was the decisive battle on the Eastern Front. It humiliated what was once thought to be an invincible German army. On 5 February 1943, the Red Army newspaper *Red Star* wrote:

What was destroyed at Stalingrad was the flower of the German Wehrmacht. Hitler was particularly proud of the Sixth Army and its great striking power. Under Von Reichmann it was the first to invade Belgium. It entered Paris. It took part in the invasion of Yugoslavia and Greece. Before the war it had taken part in the occupation of Czechoslovakia. In 1942 it broke through from Kharkov to Stalingrad.

Now it was no more. This was a terrible blow to German morale. With the destruction of the Sixth Army at Stalingrad, the German offensive in Russia was over. The tide had turned and the Red Army would eventually push the Wehrmacht all the way back to Berlin and beyond.

In captivity, the tide turned for Paulus too. Once one of Hitler's favourites, he agitated against the Führer among German prison-ers of war. If they did not make peace, he warned, the whole of Germany would be turned into one 'gigantic Stalingrad'. He joined the Soviet-backed 'Free Germany Movement', broadcasting appeals to the Wehrmacht to give up the fight. After the war, he testified at the International Military Tribunal at Nuremberg. After his release in 1953, he settled in East Germany and died in Dresden in 1957.

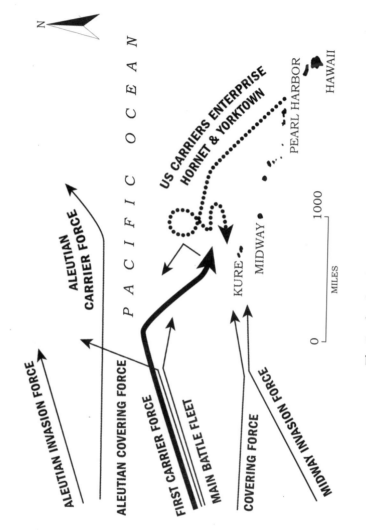

The Battle of Midway, 3–7 June 1942

4

THE PACIFIC WAR

PEARL HARBOR

AT 0753 ON SUNDAY 7 December 1941, 181 Japanese warplanes attacked the US Pacific Fleet as it lay at anchor in Pearl Harbor, the great American naval base on Oahu in the Hawaiian Islands. Forty minutes later, a second wave of 170 planes staged a second attack. There had been no formal declaration, but the United States was now at war.

Although the attack at Pearl Harbor was a surprise, a war between the United States and Japan had not been entirely unexpected. In the early 20th century Japan had risen to be a great naval power, beating the great Russian Imperial Fleet in the Russo-Japanese War of 1904–05. In the 1930s, militarists gained the upper hand in the government. Already the Japanese held Korea and Manchuria and, in 1937, they attacked China. To add to their growing possessions on the mainland, they aimed to take over the British, French and Dutch colonies in the Far East, along with the Philippines which was under US control, and establish what Japan called a 'Greater East Asia Co-Prosperity Sphere' – in other words, a Japanese empire.

Washington backed Chiang Kai-shek, the Chinese nationalist leader who was resisting the Japanese onslaught, and imposed sanctions on Japan. The Japanese joined the Axis and signed the Tripartite Pact with the Germans and Italy on 27 September 1940. Just as America wanted no part of the war in Europe, it was equally reluctant to go to war in the Far East. But diplomatic talks between America and Japan got nowhere.

When Hitler attacked the Soviet Union in June 1941, he had invited Japan to join the war and seize Russia's eastern seaboard. But Japan decided to benefit from the German attack, rather than aid it. Operation Barbarossa effectively neutralised Russia as an enemy in the Far East and it presented the Japanese with the opportunity to attack to the south and seize the European colonies there – provided any threat from the United States could be neutralised as well.

On 20 November 1941, America received an ultimatum from the Japanese government, saying that the US must withdraw its support from the Chinese government, lift its trade embargo and supply Japan with the one vital commodity it lacked – oil.

The US could not comply. Any concession to the Japanese would mean that China would fall, along with British possessions in the Far East. Without its Empire, Britain would fall, leaving the whole of Europe, Africa, and Asia to the Axis. America would then be surrounded on all sides by hostile dictatorships.

On 26 November, Washington sent a reply to the Japanese ultimatum that simply outlined the principles of self-determination once more. The US knew that this would not be acceptable to the Japanese, but it did not know that the Japanese fleet had already sailed. For Japan there was no time to lose. The Germans seemed on the brink of victory in Europe. In that case, they would soon arrive in the Far East to seize their enemies' colonies as spoils of war. If Japan was to have its empire, it had to strike straight away – at Pearl Harbor.

The man who had drawn up the plan for the attack on Pearl Harbor was the Commander-in-Chief of the Japanese Imperial Navy, Admiral Isoroku Yamamoto. He was opposed to a war with the United States. He believed that Japan could not win such a war. It could not invade and hold such a vast country. And as naval attaché to Washington, he had seen the industrial might of America first hand. Asked about Japan's chances of victory, Yamamoto replied, 'If I am told to fight regardless of the consequences, I shall run wild for the first six months or a year, but I have absolutely no confidence about the second and third years.'

However, the Japanese government gambled that six months was enough. In that time, its forces could sweep through Southeast Asia, seize the oilfields of Indonesia and enough raw materials to supply its industry for a prolonged war.

The Japanese Navy had realised that aircraft carriers, not battle-ships, would be the crucial weapon in a war in the Pacific. They had built a carrier fleet and equipped it with dive-bombers, torpedo bombers and fighters that were the best in the world. Yamamoto's plan was to knock out the US Pacific Fleet at Pearl Harbor in an attack so swift that it would have no time to react. He knew that the element of surprise would be on his side. The received wisdom was that making a surprise attack nearly 4,000 miles from its home port without being detected was impossible. The Americans also thought that their fleet was safe at Pearl Harbor. Although the British had destroyed the Italian fleet with torpedo planes at Taranto in November 1940, it was thought that Pearl was too shallow to launch torpedo attacks. The anchorage was only twelve metres deep and an airborne torpedo sank to twenty metres before beginning its run. In Pearl Harbor torpedoes, it was thought, would bury themselves harmlessly in the mud. But the Japanese simply added wooden fins to their torpedoes, which gave them extra buoyancy. It also helped them run straight and, during practice in Kagoshima Bay in south-ern Kyushu, the strike rate rose to seventy per cent.

While increasingly hostile diplomatic traffic was exchanged between Washington and Tokyo, Yamamoto secretly massed an armada under Vice-Admiral Chuichi Nagumo in the Kurile Islands to the north-east of Japan. There were six huge aircraft carriers –

the *Akagi, Kaga, Hiryu, Soryu, Shokaku* and *Zuikaku* – carrying 423 warplanes between them. They set sail on 26 November in two columns of three, flanked by the heavy cruisers *Chikuma* and *Tone*, while the battleships *Hiei* and *Kirishima* brought up the rear. The light cruiser *Abukuma* and nine destroyers were also deployed to protect the convoy. The strike force sailed slowly eastwards at 13 knots so that the oilers, the vital refuelling ships, could keep up. Meanwhile, radio traffic was generated so that it would appear that they were still in their home ports.

The fleet took a northerly route, staying out of the shipping lanes, and maintained radio silence. It arrived in position north-east of the Hawaiian Islands on 6 December. That day the government in Tokyo began sending a long message to the Japanese embassy in Washington, D.C. This brought any further negotiations to a con-clusion, though it fell short of a declaration of war. It was to be delivered to the Secretary of State Cordell Hull the following morn-ing, before the attack. However, delay in decoding such a long letter meant that it was not delivered until after the first wave of Japanese planes had gone in and the second were on their way.

On the night of 6 December, two Japanese submarines sailed close to the coast of Oahu to deploy five two-man midget sub-marines, which were also to attack the Pacific Fleet. At 0342 hours, the minesweeper USS *Condor* spotted the periscope of a midget submarine just outside Pearl Harbor's anti-submarine nets. She summoned the destroyer USS *Ward* who began searching the area. The contact was reported, but submarine sightings were not uncommon.

By this time it was known that the Japanese fleet had sailed. But no one knew where it was. Some historians have claimed that President Roosevelt knew where and when the attack was coming. Although he had won the 1940 Presidential election on the promise of keeping America out of the war, his growing support of Britain –

and, later, the Soviet Union – indicates that he felt America would be dragged into the war sooner or later. After the attack on Pearl Harbor, there was no doubt in the minds of the American people that they should go to war. Crucially, the Pacific Fleet's aircraft carriers were not in port. When it sailed, the Japanese fleet thought that all six US aircraft carriers were in Pearl Harbor. Five had been, but the *Hornet* and the *Yorktown*, had been transferred to the Atlantic, while the *Saratoga* had been pulled back to protect America's West Coast. And on 28 November, the *Enterprise* and the *Lexington* set sail westwards to deliver planes to Wake Island and Midway.

An accusing finger has also been pointed at Churchill, whose strategy from the beginning had been to get the United States into the war. Not only had the British broken the German Enigma codes, they were also reading the Japanese equivalent called Purple. The Americans had also broken Purple but, not being on a war footing, they did not have the manpower to decode the amount of material they were intercepting. Churchill read all intercepted messages, while Roosevelt was considered a security risk and was not shown raw intelligence data. So Churchill would have had a better idea of what was going on in the Japanese mind. He repeatedly told Roosevelt that the first attack would be on Singapore. To maintain this fiction, he reinforced the garrison there with Australians, even though a recent assessment of its defences showed that it could not be held. This deceit cost the British 130,000 fighting men, captured when Singapore fell to the Japanese in February 1942.

At 0550 on the morning of 7 December the Japanese carriers turned into the wind. Japanese pilots assembled on deck and tied around their heads ceremonial hachimaki scarves carrying the Japanese characters meaning 'Certain Victory'. The ships' crews were allowed time off from their duties to witness this historic moment. Conditions were far from perfect. The wind was gusting and the sea was high, but only one of the 183 planes in the first wave was lost on take-off. Another developed engine trouble and had to turn back. But by 0620, forty-nine bombers, fifty-one dive-bombers, forty torpedo planes, and forty-one Zero fighters were heading to Oahu, while the second wave was being marshalled on the flight deck.

At 0630, just off Oahu, the USS *Antares*, a supply ship, spotted another submarine. The *Ward* closed in, put a shell through its conning tower, then finished it off with depth charges. In the battle of Pearl Harbor, it was first blood to America.

At 0700, Commander Fuchida, the attack force flight leader, picked up music from a Hawaiian radio station and locked onto it. Five minutes later, two American radar operators in the newly established US military radar station on the north of Oahu spotted a blip. This indicated that a group of more than fifty planes was bearing down on them. They reported what they had seen, but were told that a flight of American B-17s were expected from the mainland that morning.

The Japanese planes stayed above a thick layer of cloud, out of sight. Below, Oahu was quiet and sleepy. The Japanese had deliberately chosen a Sunday morning to attack. Few navy men were on deck. Most were still in their bunks sleeping off their shore leave the night before. The ships were moored close together, making them an easy target. No smoke was coming from their stacks and none were ready to sail. Of the 300 planes based at the airfields on the island, only three were airborne, with those on the ground parked in close formation. With a large Japanese population on the islands, there was a fear of sabotage and the planes were easier to guard when they were close together. They also made a better target.

At 0753, Fuchida sent the famous radio message 'Tora, Tora, Tora' – 'Tiger, Tiger, Tiger' – which meant that the Americans had been taken completely by surprise. And the Japanese planes went in for the kill.

When the first bomb dropped, those Americans who heard it assumed it had been dropped by accident by one of their own planes. It was only when a dive-bomber blew up a hangar at the Ford Island Command Center that Commander Logan Ramsey realised that the island was under attack. Frantically, he sent the radio message, 'Air raid, Pearl Harbor. This is no drill.'

By 0755, the Pacific Fleet and the surrounding airfields were under full-scale attack. For the next two hours, bombs rained down and torpedoes sliced through the unprotected hulls of the US Navy's prize battleships. Amid the explosions gunners managed to return fire, but they were hampered by firing from capsizing decks and a shortage of ammunition. To prevent sabotage, it had been kept in the locked storage boxes. Meanwhile, Japanese planes bombed and strafed American airfields against virtually no opposition.

The havoc the Japanese wrought was immense. The battleship USS *Arizona* blew up and was completely destroyed. The *Oklahoma* capsized. The *California*, *Nevada* and *West Virginia* sank at their moorings. Three other battleships, three cruisers, three destroyers, and several other vessels also suffered damage. Some 169 aircraft were completely destroyed and 150 damaged, mainly on the ground. Some 2,403 Americans were killed, including sixty-eight civilians. Another 1,176 were wounded.

The Japanese lost between twenty-nine and sixty planes – some sacrificed in kamikaze suicide attacks. Another ten or fifteen got back to their carriers, but were so badly damaged they were pushed overboard to make room for incoming planes. Around another forty were damaged but repairable. All five midget submarines had been lost, along with one, perhaps two, fleet submarines and fewer than a hundred men. It seemed an overwhelming victory. However, a fatal mistake had been made. Despite the pleadings of Fuchida, Admiral Nagumo had refused to send in a third wave of planes already fuelled, loaded with bombs and waiting on the flight decks. With the defences at Pearl now crippled, a third or fourth wave could have finished off the battleships, destroyed some of the lighter shipping and put the airfields out of action. An attack on the US Navy fuel depot would have sent America's complete naval strategy for the Pacific up in smoke.

However, to pick up incoming planes, the Japanese fleet had sailed to within 190 miles of the island and was now vulnerable. Nagumo did not know where the US carrier fleet was but, by now, it would be looking for them. He had fulfilled his mission. According to the damage reports he had been receiving, the US Pacific fleet would be out of action for at least six months, which was all that was required. Why risk turning a victory into a defeat? So Nagumo's flagship, the *Akagi*, hoisted the signal flag ordering a withdrawal to the north-west. Below decks, the disappointed pilots said, 'Now we can live to be a hundred.'

The following day, President Roosevelt addressed a joint session of Congress:

Yesterday, December 7, 1941 – a day which will live in infamy – the United States of America was suddenly and deliberately attacked by the naval and air forces of the Empire of Japan. The United States was at peace with that nation and, at the solicitation of Japan, was still in conversation with its government and its emperor looking toward the maintenance of peace in the Pacific. Indeed, one hour after Japanese air squadrons had commenced bombing in Oahu, the Japanese ambassador to the United States and his colleague delivered to the Secretary of State a formal reply to a recent American message. While it stated that it seemed useless to continue the existing diplomatic negotiations, it contained no threat or hint of armed attack.

In fact the Japanese had never been concerned about the niceties of a declaration of war. On 7 February 1904, Admiral Heihachiro Togo's fleet had won a great victory when it attacked the Russian fleet in the harbour of Port Arthur in Manchuria without declaring war. That had been the first attack of Asian people on Europeans, and the first significant use of torpedoes, in modern warfare. After the attack on Pearl Harbor, the Japanese government maintained that an Imperial proclamation declaring war had been released at 0900 Tokyo time, but it was later admitted that it had not been signed by the Emperor until 1145.

Pearl Harbor was not the only target that came under attack by the Japanese on 'the day of infamy'. President Roosevelt went on to list for Congress what else had happened on that day:

Yesterday the Japanese government also launched an attack against Malaya. Last night Japanese forces attacked Hong Kong. Last night Japanese forces attacked Guam. Last night Japanese forces attacked the Philippine Islands. Last night the Japanese attacked Wake Island. This morning the Japanese attacked Midway Island. I ask that Congress declare that since the unprovoked and dastardly attack by Japan on Sunday, December 7th, a state of war has existed between the United States and the Japanese Empire.

The Senate passed the resolution 82 to 0; the House of Representatives by 388 to 1 – the only vote against coming from Representative Jeanette Rankin of Montana, who had also voted against US entry into the First World War. And at 1610 that afternoon, 8 December, President Roosevelt signed the declaration of war. That same day, Britain also declared war on Japan.

But although the attack on Pearl Harbor had been a crushing defeat for the US, within it were the seeds of victory. It had awoken the sleeping giant. For Americans, isolationism was over. The country was now at war and the American people rallied to the cause. Although the West Coast was now vulnerable to attack, the situation in the Pacific was far from hopeless. The carrier fleet was unscathed. And, while the rest of the fleet had been sunk, the vital oil storage facility and the naval dockyard at Pearl Harbor remained intact. Indeed, all of the ships sunk by the Japanese that day – with the exception of the *Arizona* and the *Oklahoma* – were repaired and returned to service.

In Tokyo, initial misgivings had turned to jubilation. At first, people did not know what to make of an attack on America, a country they had long sought to emulate. But the attacks on Hong Kong and Singapore were particularly gratifying, as Britain was seen as Japan's real enemy in the Far East. The following day, the Japanese occupied Bangkok and landed on Tarawa and Makin in the Gilbert Islands. Then on 10 December Britain's two most powerful warships east of Suez – the ultra-modern 35,000-ton battleship *Prince of Wales* and the 32,000-tonne battle cruiser *Repulse* – steaming to the defence of Singapore, had been sunk in the Gulf of Siam. That same day, the Japanese landed on Camiguin Island and at Gonzaga and Aparri on the main Philippine island of Luzon. An American destroyer, two submarines, and a minesweeper had been damaged.

What was the purpose of these unprovoked attacks? 'To assure the stability of eastern Asia and to contribute to world peace,' an Imperial Japanese spokesman said.

On 11 December 1941, Hitler made another blunder – perhaps the biggest blunder of the war. He declared war on the United States. He was not obliged to do that under the Tripartite Pact, just as Japan had failed to declare war on the Soviet Union. Although the American people were eager to get their own back on the Japanese, Roosevelt was by no means assured of getting a declaration of war on the Axis powers through Congress. As it was, America returned the compliment and declared war on Germany and Italy.

Now the sides were drawn.

Roosevelt already had an agreement with Churchill that, apart from defensive actions in the Pacific, they would pursue the war in Europe first. But the American public were baying for blood. The commander of the Pacific Fleet, Admiral Husband E. Kimmel, and the garrison commander General Walter C. Short were relieved of duty, though subsequent reports found them guilty of errors of judgement rather than dereliction of duty. Admiral Chester W. Nimitz replaced Kimmel and began rebuilding his fleet.

The three carriers that had been out to sea when the Japanese had attacked – USS *Lexington*, *Saratoga* and *Enterprise* – along with five others – the *Langley*, *Ranger*, *Wasp*, *Hornet* and *Yorktown* – would be the backbone of the US fleet that fought the Pacific war. There would be some twenty battles with the Imperial Japanese Navy. Five of them would be fought between aircraft carriers and four would be fought within a six-month period in 1942 that would decide the outcome of the war in the Pacific.

THE BATTLE OF THE CORAL SEA

In the months following Pearl Harbor, nothing could stop the Japanese advance. They overran the Philippines, the East Indies, Guam and Wake Island. By mid-April, they held most of the South Pacific. Their next objective was to take Tulagi to the north of Guadalcanal in the British Solomon Islands and Port Moresby on New Guinea. Then they would cut the supply route between America and Australia, in preparation for the invasion of Australia itself. An invasion force assembled at Truk in the Carolines. On 30 April, it sailed for Rabaul in northern New Britain, where Vice-Admiral Shigeyoshi Inouye was mustering a separate naval force as part of his intricate plan. The Japanese now occupied much of the area and Inouye's ships would be supported by 140 land-based aircraft.

Australia was a British dominion whose soldiers were fighting fiercely in North Africa. It was also a long-time friend of America's, and Nimitz rallied to its defence. He sent Task Force 17, under the command of Rear-Admiral Frank J. Fletcher, to the Coral Sea. His flagship was the *Yorktown*, which had been transferred back from the Atlantic after the attack on Pearl Harbor. It was accompanied by the *Lexington*, a converted cruiser, under Rear-Admiral Aubrey W. Fitch. These two carriers were escorted by seven cruisers and a screen of destroyers. They carried three types of plane. They had thirty-six Douglas TBD-1 Devastators, which were the first all-metal monoplanes to be carried by the US Navy. Designed in 1934, they were slow and had a poor rate of climb and a limited range, and carried a torpedo which tended towards the unreliable. The bomber force comprised seventy-two Douglas SBD-2 Dauntless dive-bombers which were already considered obsolete. Fighter support was provided by thirty-six Grumman F4F-3 Wildcats.

Fletcher's ships would meet Rear-Admiral Takagi's main strike force which comprised two of the aircraft carriers that had attacked Pearl Harbor, the *Shokaku* and the *Zuikaku*, two cruisers and a screen of destroyers. They carried forty-two Mitsubishi A6M5 Zero fighters, forty-two Aichi D3A Val dive-bombers and forty-one Nakajima B5N torpedo planes. Although the Japanese planes were superior to anything the Americans had at this point in the war, Fletcher had more dive-bombers. The American carriers also had radar and the *Yorktown's* planes carried IFF – Identification, Friend or Foe – equipment. The Japanese possessed neither of these innovations.

Takagi's strike force set off from the Carolines and swung to the east to stay out of the range of US reconnaissance planes for as long as possible. On 3 May, a small force landed on Tulagi and, by 1100, the island was in Japanese hands. It was here that Fletcher decided to strike back. At 0630 on 4 May twenty-eight Dauntless dive-bombers and twelve Devastators took off from the *Yorktown*.

At 0815 they were over the island. The first two strikes sunk a destroyer, three minesweepers and a patrol boat. A third sank four landing barges and five Kawanishi H6K Mavis flying-boats. Returning to the *Yorktown* at 1632, they had lost one Devastator, downed over the target, and two Wildcats which had strayed off course on their return to the carrier and crash-landed on Guadalcanal. Their pilots were recovered later.

Meanwhile Takagi's strike force had headed west towards the Coral Sea but, due to bad weather, US reconnaissance planes could not find it. A Japanese flying-boat spotted the US fleet, but was shot down by Wildcats.

The New Guinea invasion force set off from Rabaul with six Japanese Army transports, five Navy transports and a destroyer escort, under the command of Rear-Admiral Kajioka in his flagship *Yubari*. It rendezvoused with a support group under Rear-Admiral Marushige off the island of Bougainville and headed south towards the Jomard Passage, which would take it into the Coral Sea.

The fleets then began to sight each other. The *Yorktown* and the *Lexington* were spotted by a Japanese flying-boat, though the report did not reach Takagi until 18 hours later. Meanwhile the *Shoho*, which was supporting the invasion force, was spotted by USAAF B-17Es on 6 May. However, they did not spot Takagi's strike force due to the bad weather. That evening the two fleets were with seventy miles of each other, though they did not know it. Later they both changed course and the gap widened again.

There was another Allied force in the area. Under the command of Rear-Admiral Crace of the Royal Navy, it comprised two Australian cruisers, one American cruiser and a destroyer escort. On 7 May, Fletcher told Crace to close the southern end of the Jomard Passage, while Fletcher himself closed in from the southeast. At 0815, US reconnaissance planes reported seeing 'two carriers and four heavy cruisers' approaching the Louisiade Archipelago, north of the Jomard Passage. Fletcher thought that this was the main force and, between 0926 and 1030, ninety-three planes were sent off to attack it, leaving only forty-seven with the fleet. When the spotter plane returned, it became clear that there had been an error in encoding. It had only seen two heavy cruisers and two destroyers. But soon after 1100, Lieutenant-Commander Hamilton, leading *Lexington's* squadrons, spotted the *Shoho* and its escort of four cruisers and a destroyer off Misima Island in the Louisiades. Despite its powerful escort, the first wave of American planes blew five aircraft over the side of the *Shoho*. Successive waves hit the carrier with six torpedoes and thirteen bombs, leaving it listing and on fire. It sank at 1135 with 600 of its 800 hands. Six American planes had been lost.

The invasion force now had no air cover and halted north of the Louisiades until the Jomard Passage was cleared. That afternoon, Crace's fleet was attacked by waves of land-based torpedo bombers, but they failed to sink any of the Allied ships. Meanwhile reconnaissance planes from Takagi's strike force had mistakenly reported that they had located Fletcher's carriers. They launched over sixty sorties and sank the USS *Sims*, a destroyer, and the oil tanker USS *Neosho*. At 1630, fifteen torpedo planes and twelve dive-bombers were launched with instructions to seek out Fletcher's force and destroy it. But the weather closed in and, without radar, the Japanese planes had little chance of finding the American fleet. However, the American fleet picked up the bomber force on radar and the *Lexington* sent up its Wildcats. They shot down nine bombers, losing two fighters in the process.

The Japanese torpedo squadron did not find the fleet either and gave up the search. They dumped their torpedoes in the sea and headed back to their carriers. But they had been closer to the American fleet than they had realised. At 1900, three of the

Japanese planes spotted an Aldis lamp sending out morse code from the *Yorktown*, but got clean away. At 1720, another Japanese plane was not so lucky and was shot down. A further 11 planes failed to find their carriers and crashed into the sea in the darkness. And, of the original twenty-seven, only six planes returned safely to their carriers.

Unable to clear Crace's force from the Jomard Passage, the invasion force withdrew, leaving Fletcher and Takagi to fight it out in the Battle of the Coral Sea – the first sea battle in history in which the opposing ships neither saw nor engaged each other. That night, the two fleets deliberately sailed away from one another, neither willing to risk a night engagement. Next morning, while the skies over Takagi's fleet remained overcast, Fletcher's fleet was bathed in sunshine. At around 0600 both sent out reconnaissance planes. Even though the weather gave the Japanese the advantage, at 0815 one of the *Lexington's* Dauntlesses dived through the clouds and saw ships. As it went in for a closer look, the plane was rocked by a shell exploding near its left wing-tip and it quickly climbed back into the clouds. The Japanese fleet was 175 miles north-east of the American position. Its position was radioed back. At 0850, twenty-four dive-bombers and two fighters took off from the rolling deck of the *Yorktown*. They were followed by nine torpedo planes escorted by four fighters. Ten minutes later, the *Lexington* started sending a flight consisting of twenty-two dive-bombers, eleven torpedo planes and nine fighters. By 0925 all the planes were away.

The Japanese had also spotted the American fleet and, while the American planes headed for the Japanese fleet, fifty-one bombers and eighteen fighters were going the other way. At 1030, the American dive-bombers saw the *Zuikaku* and the *Shokaku* eight miles ahead and pulled up to hide in the clouds until the slower torpedo planes caught up. Then, as the *Shokaku* appeared from under the cloud cover, they attacked. Seeing them coming, the

Japanese sent up fighters, which downed three of the Dauntlesses. This disrupted the American attack, and only two of their bombs hit the ship. One damaged the flight deck enough to prevent any more fighters taking off. The other started a fire in a machine shop. But the *Shokaku* still responded to the helm and weaved violently. As a result, all the torpedoes either missed or failed to go off.

The *Lexington's* dive-bombers failed to find the carriers. They ran low on fuel and had to return to the 'Lady Lex'. But the torpedo planes and their fighter escort continued the search and spotted the enemy fifteen miles out. They were immediately attacked by Japanese Zeros who drove off the Wildcats. The low-flying Devastators managed to release their torpedoes but, again, none of them hit. However, by this time, the *Shokaku* was on fire and out of action. One hundred and eight of its crew had been killed, but it had not been hit below the waterline. It limped back to Truk, while most of its planes transferred to the *Zuikaku*, which had briefly emerged from the murk only to disappear again.

The American fleet had no such protection. Above it the skies were clear and it had little fighter cover. The Wildcats were low on fuel and, even though the bandits had been spotted on radar sixty-eight miles out, they were badly positioned for a fight. Only three Wildcats spotted the Japanese planes as they started their attack at 1055 and they were at 10,000 feet and did not have the fuel to climb up to meet the Vals who began their dive from 18,000 feet. Twelve other Dauntlesses, having been trained to expect a low-level attack, patrolled at 2,000 feet three miles outside the destroyer screen. The Japanese torpedo planes and their fighter escort flew over them at 6,000 feet, only to drop to release height inside the ring of destroyers. Nevertheless the Dauntlesses reacted quickly and managed to down two Kates before they could release their torpedoes. They also managed to shoot down two Zeros, a Val and two more Kates for the loss of four Dauntlesses.

The *Yorktown* managed to dodge the eight torpedoes launched at her port quarter and everything the dive-bombers threw at her. But, five minutes later, when a second wave of Japanese planes arrived an 800-pound bomb went through her flight deck and exploded three decks down, killing sixty-six American sailors. Black smoke streamed from the gaping hole in her deck. She was on fire but still afloat.

The Japanese pilots then turned their attention to the *Lexington*. They attacked both bows, dropping their torpedoes at between 50 and 200 feet, 1,000 yards out. Two hit and all three boiler rooms were flooded. Two dive-bombers also scored hits and the *Lexington* was listing badly when they turned for home. Although both American carriers had been hit, the returning planes could still land on them.

But the jubilant Japanese pilots returning to the *Shokaku* found they had to ditch in the sea. This left the Japanese fleet with only nine planes, while the Americans still had twelve fighters and thirty-seven attack aircraft. At that point in the battle, the Japanese had lost eighty planes and some 900 men; the Americans sixty-six planes and 543 men. But worse was to come. Fuel was escaping and vapour built up inside the damaged *Lexington*. At 1247, a spark from a generator ignited it and the ship was rocked by a massive explosion. A second internal explosion tore through her again at 1445. The fires on board got out of control and, at 1710, the crew abandoned ship. At 1956, a destroyer put her out of her misery with five torpedoes and the *Lexington* went to her watery grave.

THE BATTLE OF MIDWAY

The outcome of the Battle of the Coral Sea had been indecisive. However, the Japanese were forced to cancel their sea-borne invasion of Port Moresby. But it did not ruin their appetite for a fight. Yamamoto went back on the offensive. He planned to take Midway

Island, 1,300 miles north-west of Oahu. From there, he would be able to mount further attacks on Pearl Harbor, denying America a navy base west of San Francisco. This was a response to the 'Doolittle' raid, where Lieutenant-Colonel Jimmy Doolittle led a force of sixteen B-25s from the USS *Hornet* on a bombing raid on Tokyo on 18 April 1942. As it was, the *Hornet* could not get close enough to Japan for Doolittle's planes to land back on the carrier, and they had to fly on to airstrips in China. But Yamamoto wanted to push the Japanese naval perimeter back so that no American aircraft carrier could get in range of the imperial capital again.

As the US now employed enough code breakers to read all the Purple intercepts they collected, Admiral Nimitz knew what to expect. Yamamoto's plan was to stage a diversionary attack on the Aleutians, the chain of islands belonging to the US that run out into the Pacific from the coast of Alaska. They would invade and occupy two of the inhabited islands – Attu and Kiska – and intern the people there. Such a humiliation would force America to react. To make sure that America sent sufficient of its strength northwards, Yamamoto would also have to commit capital ships, including the aircraft carrier *Junyo* and the light carrier *Rjujo* which would have been useful at Midway.

Admiral Nagumo, the victor of Pearl Harbor, would lead the attack on Midway with four of the carriers that had been there that day – the *Akagi, Kaga, Hiryu* and the *Soryu* – while the light carrier *Zuiho* would be part of a central covering force, that could help out either in the Aleutians or at Midway. They would face the *Enterprise* and the *Hornet*, along with the rapidly refitted *Yorktown* which was ready to put to sea again after only three days in the all-important navy yard at Pearl. Its fighter compliment had been increased from eighteen to twenty-seven as it was carrying the new F4F-4 Wildcats, which had folding wings allowing the carrier to accommodate the extra planes, and six machine-guns instead of four. Her pilots were the survivors from the *Yorktown* and the *Lexington*, who now had combat experience.

On 30 May, Admiral Fletcher sailed north-westwards to meet up with the two cruisers and five destroyers surviving from Task Force 17. They then joined up with Task Force 16, under Admiral Raymond Spruance on board the *Enterprise*. On Midway, the USAAF stationed four squadrons of Flying Fortresses and some B-26 Marauders, while the Marine Corps had nineteen Dauntless dive-bombers, seven F4F-3 Wildcats, seventeen Vought SB2U-3 Vindicators (or 'Wind Indicators' as the Marines called them), twenty-one obsolete Brewster F2A-3 Buffaloes and six new Grumman TBF-1 Avenger three-man torpedo bombers.

Yamamoto himself led the main Japanese force from the battle-ship *Yamoto* and sent Nagumo's carrier strike force towards Midway from the north-west, while the minesweepers, transports and supply ships of the invasion force approached further to the south. The invasion fleet was spotted by a US Catalina reconnaissance flying-boat 700 miles west of Midway on 3 June. At 1230, nine Flying Fortresses took off. Four hours later they found the invasion force 570 miles to the west. Short of fuel they dropped their bombs amid heavy anti-aircraft fire, but hit nothing. However, at dawn the following morning, four Catalinas from Midway torpedoed a tanker.

At 0415 hours, fifteen Flying Fortresses were on their way to bomb the invasion fleet again, when they got word that another fleet – complete with carriers – was approaching Midway and was then only 145 miles away. Fifteen minutes later, ten Dauntless scouts were airborne, searching for the carriers to the north of the island. At the same time, thirty-six Val dive-bombers, thirty-six Kate torpedo-bombers carrying 1,770-pound bombs and thirty-six Zeros took off from Nagumo's carriers. They headed for Midway, intending to soften up its defences for the invasion which was scheduled two days later. Once the strike force was airborne, more Kates were hoisted up to the flight deck, armed with torpedoes to attack shipping. At the same time, spotter planes were despatched to hunt for the US fleet. Here America got lucky. One of the two float-planes launched from the cruiser *Tone* was delayed for half an hour, when the catapult malfunctioned. It was headed for the search sector where the fleet was.

At 0534, a Navy flying-boat reported to Midway that there was a Japanese carrier fleet, 250 miles away to the east. The *Yorktown* also picked up the message and Fletcher told Spruance to take the *Enterprise* and the *Hornet* to attack the Japanese carriers. Radar operators on Midway spotted 108 Japanese planes heading for the island at 0553. They warned the flying-boats and Flying Fortresses to stay away while the seven Wildcats and twenty-one Buffaloes of the island's defence force went to take on the attackers. They managed to shoot down four Japanese bombers and damage several others before they were overwhelmed by the nimble Zeros. In the ensuing dogfights, three Wildcats and thirteen Buffaloes were shot down. Seven more were damaged beyond repair. Of the twenty-eight US planes, only five survived intact – and one of those had not even been involved in the engagement as it had engine trouble and had to turn back. They had managed to down just two Zeros. A further three Japanese planes were downed by ack-ack fire over Midway.

While this disastrous dogfight had been going on, six Grumman Avengers and four Marauders headed off to attack the Japanese fleet. As they attacked at low-level, seventeen Zeros pounced on them from 3,000 feet. The unprotected bombers were easy prey and turned back. Two of the B-26s made it back to Midway, where they crash-landed. The Avengers managed to loose their torpedoes, but furious fire from the Zeros and the fleet shot down five of them. Only one Avenger, badly damaged and with a wounded radio operator and a dead gunner on board, made it back to Midway.

However, this attack convinced Admiral Nagumo and the strike force commander Lieutenant Joichi Tomonaga that a second wave of bombers needed to be sent against Midway, so the Kates were lowered from the flight deck to be rearmed with bombs. This was a time-consuming process. At 0728, the *Tone's* second float-plane had finally located the 'ten enemy surface ships' around 240 miles from Midway. Nagumo waited, weighing up the information. Then, at 0813, he ordered that the Kates' torpedoes be replaced. Then a report came, saying that the ships were only cruisers and destroyers – not carriers – and posed no imminent threat as they were well out of range, so arming the Kates with bombs could resume.

It was then that Midway's bomber force, fifteen USAAF Flying Fortresses and sixteen Marine Corps Dauntless dive-bombers, arrived. The Flying Fortresses dropped their bombs from 20,000 feet. But when the pluming sea subsided, the Japanese carriers were still intact. As the Flying Fortresses turned for home, Nagumo could see that the pilots of his eighteen airborne Zeros were wary of these heavily armed bombers. They needed reinforcing. He ordered the thirty-six Zeros intending to escort the Kates to take off in time to intercept the Dauntlesses as they came in. The Zeros fell on the American dive-bombers, whose inexperienced pilots were bringing them in too low. these Dauntlesses being land-based, their pilots had not been trained to attack shipping, and posed no threat to the Japanese fleet. Only a handful got close enough to release their bombs. Just eight of the sixteen made it back to Midway and they were riddled with shrapnel and bullet holes.

Then Nagumo got the bad news. The *Tone's* float-plane now reported that the ten American ships they were shadowing were a vanguard for the carrier force which was following in the rear. They were streaming south-east and were now just 200 miles away – well within range. And carrier aircrew were trained to attack enemy ships. Nagumo's second-wave attack aircraft were still below decks being rearmed. His fighters were getting low on fuel and ammunition, and his first wave force was expected back any minute. Rather than muster what planes he had that were ready to go, Nagumo decide to retire to the north until his fighters were refuelled and his first wave recovered. Then he would send a properly armed force into the attack.

Admiral Spruance coolly assessed the situation and realised that he had the upper hand. If he bided his time, he could attack the Japanese carriers when they were at their most vulnerable – when their decks were full of returning aircraft. His timing was immaculate and, within a few minutes of the last Japanese plane arriving back from Midway putting down, Nagumo's destroyer screen reported American planes approaching.

The timing may have been immaculate, but the tactics were not. Broken cloud along the route had scattered the American formations. Nagumo's change of course meant that the Japanese carriers were not where they were thought to be. Some planes grew short of fuel as they searched for the fleet and had to return. Others lost their fighter escort and ten Wildcats ditched in the sea. But, piecemeal, the US squadrons found their target.

The first into the attack were fifteen obsolete Devastators. They came skimming in at 300 feet but, unescorted, they were no match for the fifty Zeros that attacked them. Fourteen were blown out of the skies before they got near enough to release their torpedoes. But the last one, piloted by Ensign George H. Gay, who was wounded in the leg and arm and carried a dead gunner, pressed on. He managed to loose his torpedo, before he skimmed over the deck of the carrier and crashed in the sea. The torpedo missed its mark, but Gay managed to get out of his plane before it sank and he kept himself afloat with his rubber seat cushion which had floated clear. When night fell and he was no longer in danger of being strafed by Zeros, he inflated his dinghy. The next day he was picked up by a

US Navy Catalina.

The Japanese sailors were still cheering, when fourteen more Devastators from the *Enterprise* arrived and began attacking the Kaga from the starboard. At the same time, twelve more Devastators from the *Yorktown* turned up and attacked the *Soryu*. They were accompanied by seventeen Dauntlesses and six Wildcats. These drew some of the Zeros away from the Devastators. Even so, eleven of the *Enterprise's* torpedo planes were downed.

With the support of the six Wildcats, the *Yorktown's* Devastators were within three miles of their target before they were attacked. Almost immediately one Wildcat was downed and two others so badly damaged that they had to break off. The remaining three could do little to help the torpedo planes other than try to draw some of the Zeros off. And they too were soon forced to break off and return to the *Yorktown*.

As well as being attacked by the Zeros, the cumbersome Devastators drew withering fire from the Japanese ships. Some of them managed to release their torpedoes before they were blasted from the skies. Again not one of the torpedoes hit their targets, but two passed within fifty feet of the *Kaga*.

However, these three suicidal attacks had served to keep the Zeros at low altitudes and some were landing to refuel when the Dauntlesses came in. They saw below them an unforgettable sight – four Japanese carriers completely unprotected. Three dive-bombers from the *Yorktown* peeled off and attacked. One bomb hit the *Akagi* amidships, ripping through the hangar deck and exploding among the stored torpedoes, carelessly stowed bombs and refuelling tanks, setting off secondary explosions. A second set the planes on the flight deck ablaze. The stern was shattered, the rudder useless and, as the huge ship lurched drunkenly around, Nagumo's officers begged a stunned admiral to abandon the blazing hulk.

Then a squadron of Dauntlesses from the *Enterprise* turned up and directed their attentions to the unprotected *Kaga*. The carrier took four direct hits. Three bombs hit the planes that were being prepared for take-off, setting them ablaze. The fourth hit a petrol tank on deck. Burning gasoline engulfed the bridge, killing the captain and the staff officers and putting the ship out of action.

The *Yorktown's* dive-bombers regrouped and attacked the *Soryu*. In minutes, she was a raging inferno. All three carriers stayed afloat while they burnt. But they had to be abandoned and were later sunk by Japanese or American torpedoes. However, the *Hiryu* had escaped and its air group, now augmented by twenty-three Zeros seeking refuge from their blazing carriers, still posed a threat, and Yamamoto had not yet abandoned his plan to invade Midway. Thinking there was only one American carrier in the area, he steamed on towards the island. The rest of the task force was to join up with his battleships and bombard the island's defences before the Japanese invasion force, standing by 500 miles away, went ashore.

In the attack on the *Akagi*, *Kaga* and *Soryu*, seven Dauntlesses had been lost, while eight Zeros had been shot down. However, eleven more Dauntlesses had been ditched when they ran out of fuel on the way back to their ships. Fletcher knew that his fleet was still in danger. He ordered the remaining Dauntlesses aloft to search for the *Hiryu*, while twelve Wildcats flew a defensive patrol around the *Yorktown*. What Fletcher did not know was that a reconnaissance plane from the *Soryu* had already spotted the *Yorktown*, and eighteen Vals and six Zeros from the *Hiryu* were on their way. At midday, they were picked by the *Yorktown's* radar about forty-six miles out. The Wildcats intercepted them 15 miles out and shot down four Zeros and seven Vals. The surviving bombers broke away and attacked the *Yorktown*. Six more were shot down – two by anti-aircraft fire from the American cruisers. However, before it broke up, one of them managed to lob a bomb through the *Yorktown's* flight deck, causing a fire in the hangar below. A second bomb knocked out the engine room; while a third caused a fire that threatened the forward ammunition stores and petrol tanks. Despite severe loss of life, the crew managed to get the fires under control.

While the *Yorktown's* Wildcats refuelled and rearmed on the *Enterprise*, engineers on board the *Yorktown* managed to get her underway again and Captain Elliot Buckmaster ran up a huge new Stars and Stripes. As it fluttered defiantly above the wrecked ship, a second wave of Japanese planes came screaming low over the horizon. This time there were ten Kate torpedo planes, escorted by six Zeros. The Wildcats managed to down three Zeros, at a cost of four F4Fs. Five Kates were also downed in the curtain of fire put up by the cruisers. But four torpedoes were launched within a range of 500 yards. Two hit the *Yorktown* below the waterline. They knocked out all power, lights and communications, and the great ship listed to port. Fearing a further wave, Buckmaster gave the order to abandon ship at 1500.

Revenge was not long in coming. An American scout-plane had already spotted the *Hiryu*. Fourteen Dauntlesses from the *Enterprise*, along with ten transferred from the *Yorktown*, set off to attack the remaining Japanese carrier. They were followed by six-teen more dive-bombers from the *Hornet*. As they neared the *Hiryu*, they were intercepted by thirteen Zeros who shot down three Dauntlesses as they dived. Nevertheless, four bombs pierced the *Hiryu's* flight deck, causing uncontrollable fires. When the planes from the *Hornet* arrived, they turned their attention to a battleship and a cruiser in the carrier's escort. Some Flying Fortresses en route from Hawaii to Midway also joined in, to little effect. Some of the Zeros attacked the B17s, but the fighters were soon out of fuel and ditched in the sea. That night, more bombers set out from Midway to try and discover what had happened to the *Hiryu*, but could not find it and flew back to their base guided by the fires still burning on Midway.

The loss of the *Hiryu* still did not put paid to Yamamoto's plan to invade Midway. However, he knew his invasion force would be vulnerable to the land-bombers. To have any chance of carrying off the invasion, they would have to attack that night. But then came the news that two of the cruisers he had designated to bombard the island could not make it before nightfall. Then he learned that there were other American carriers in the area and bowed to the inevitable. At 0255 on 5 June, he issued an order, saying, 'The occupation of Midway is cancelled.'

His admirals were mortified. Some would rather lose the entire fleet than lose face.

'How can we apologise to His Majesty for this defeat?' asked one.

'Leave that to me,' said Yamamoto. 'I am the only one who must apologise to His Majesty.'

The *Hiryu* was finally abandoned and sunk by Japanese torpedoes. But the defenders of Midway did not know this and went on searching. Yamamoto had already turned for home and was out of range, but a dozen dive-bombers put the *Mikuma* and the *Mogami*, two heavy cruisers, out of action. The *Mikuma* was badly damaged, not by a bomb, but by the Dauntless of Captain Richard E. Fleming hitting the rear gun turret. Gasoline from the aircraft seeped into the engine room and ignited, killing the entire engine room crew.

The last victim of the Battle of Midway was the *Yorktown*. Now unable to sail under her own steam, she was being towed back to Pearl Harbor by a minesweeper when, soon after dawn on 6 June, a Japanese submarine torpedoed her again and sunk one of her destroyer escorts, the *Hannan*. The *Yorktown* stayed afloat until the early hours of 7 June, when she suddenly rolled over and plunged to the bottom of the Pacific.

The Battle of Midway was the decisive battle in the Pacific war. America had had its revenge on the carriers whose planes had attacked Pearl Harbor. The Japanese Imperial Navy which, before Midway, matched the strength of the US Navy was now a shadow of its former self. Although Japanese pilots had beaten their American adversaries, who had lost eighty-five out of 195 aircraft, in the air, most of their elite fliers were dead. But crucially the Japanese shipyards could not hope to replace the carriers they had lost. The US was already turning out new carriers in large numbers and its aircraft factories were producing more powerful planes to put on them. With Midway, the Japanese expansion across the Pacific had reached its height. But as the Japanese Imperial Navy turned for home, they left hundreds of small islands occupied by Japanese troops, which it would take a bloody campaign of island-hopping to clear.

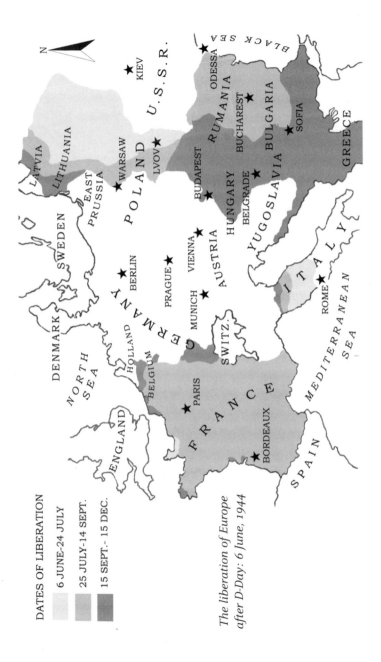

DATES OF LIBERATION

6 JUNE-24 JULY

25 JULY-14 SEPT.

15 SEPT.-15 DEC.

*The liberation of Europe
after D-Day: 6 June, 1944*

N

KIEV

U.S.S.R.

LATVIA

LITHUANIA

EAST PRUSSIA

WARSAW

POLAND

LVOV

ODESSA

BLACK SEA

RUMANIA

BUCHAREST

BULGARIA

SOFIA

BUDAPEST

HUNGARY

BELGRADE

YUGOSLAVIA

GREECE

SWEDEN

VIENNA

AUSTRIA

BERLIN

PRAGUE

MUNICH

GERMANY

SWITZ.

ITALY

ROME

MEDITERRANEAN SEA

DENMARK

NORTH SEA

HOLLAND

BELGIUM

PARIS

FRANCE

BORDEAUX

SPAIN

ENGLAND

134

5

VICTORY IN EUROPE

OPERATION OVERLORD

SINCE THE SOVIET UNION had come into the war it had been urging Britain to begin a second front in western Europe. And when the US entered the war, they wanted to make an attack on the Germans in France as soon as possible. The British were more circumspect. Having been in the war longer that their new allies, the British felt that it would be foolish to risk everything in one reckless operation. Many of the British commanders had experienced the carnage of the the First World War and were afraid of throwing men against enemy lines in a frontal assault – inevitable when making an amphibious assault against a fortified coastline. As First Lord of the Admiralty in the First World War Churchill himself had been responsible for the disastrous amphibious assault at Gallipoli in the Dardanelles where 250,000 men, largely Australians and New Zealanders, were lost before the 83,000 survivors could be evacuated. Britain's worst fears were realised when 5,000 Canadians, 1,000 British and 50 US Rangers staged a disastrous raid on the Channel port of Dieppe in August 1942 – 2,600 men were lost. The American Army was still untested, so President Roosevelt was persuaded to join the war in North Africa.

When this was brought to a successful conclusion, Churchill proposed an attack on the 'soft underbelly of Europe'. On 10 July 1943 an Anglo-American force landed on Sicily. Italian resistance collapsed and on 25 July Mussolini fell from power and was arrested. The German forces, under Field Marshal Kesselring, were then evacuated from Sicily and prepared to defend the Italian mainland.

On 2 September, a small Allied force landed on the 'heel' of Italy and quickly captured the ports of Taranto and Brindisi. On 3 September Montgomery's Eighth Army crossed the Strait of Messina and landed on the 'toe' of Italy, meeting little resistance. That day, the new Italian government agreed to change sides and its capitulation was announced on 8 September. The following day, the combined US–British Fifth Army under General Mark Clark landed at Salerno on the 'shin'. This was where Kesselring had expected the attack to come. The situation was precarious for six days, but the Fifth Army eventually broke out, taking Naples on 1 October.

On 13 October 1943, Italy declared war on Germany. This was not unexpected and Kesselring had already consolidated his hold on central and northern Italy. And he held the Allies at the Gustav Line, a defensive line that ran right across the narrow peninsula of Italy some sixty miles south of Rome. To get round this, the Allies landed 50,000 men north of the Gustav Line at Anzio. At first they met with little resistance, but instead of driving directly on Rome, the landing force stopped to consolidate the beachhead. Kesselring quickly counter-attacked, nearly pushing the Allies back into the sea.

The main Allied force was held up by the German defenders at Monte Cassino, a mountain-top monastery pivotal in the Gustav Line. The Eighth Army was then switched from the Adriatic side of the peninsula to the western flank. On the night of 11 May 1944, the Allies managed to breach the Gustav Line to the west of Monte Cassino, which was outflanked and fell to the Polish Corps of the Eighth Army on 18 May. On 26 May, the main Allied force joined up with the beachhead at Anzio and on 5 June 1944 the Allies drove into Rome.

However, progress on such a narrow front up the Italian peninsula was bound to be slow. It did little to divert German strength from the Russian front. By this time the Red Army was making good progress against the Wehrmacht. By sheer weight of numbers it would eventually overwhelm the German army and overrun Germany. Even if the Allies pushed Kesselring all the way to the Alps it would have been impossible to cross them before the Red Army had swept right across Germany and, perhaps, taken the rest of western Europe as many people feared. By the spring of 1944 a landing in France, politically, was vital.

The delay in staging an amphibious assault across the English Channel gave the Germans time to fortify the coastline. They built what they called the 'Atlantic Wall' down the west coast of Europe from the Arctic Circle to the Pyrenees. By the time of the invasion 12,247 of the planned 15,000 fortifications had been completed, along with 943 along the Mediterranean coast. Half-a-million beach obstacles had been deployed and 6.5 million mines had been laid.

The huge extent of the wall was partly due to a campaign of misinformation called Operation *Fortitude* which the British used to feed the Germans the idea that an landing might come anywhere at any time. To defend his empire against attack from the west, Hitler would have to spread his forces thinly.

At the beginning of the war, the British had arrested every German spy in Britain and turned many of them, so that they could be used to feed false information back to their spymasters in Hamburg and Berlin. False information was also conveyed by radio traffic that the Germans intercepted. The British had also broken the German Enigma code, so they could see whether their deception was working. On occasions, the British even fed the Germans information that the invasion would come in the South of France or Norway, through the Balkans or in the Black Sea. This meant Hitler had to disperse his troops to the four corners of his empire.

However the major thrust of Fortitude was to convince him that the Western Allies would take the most direct route. They would take the shortest Channel crossing at the Straits of Dover to the Pas de Calais. It would be easy for them to support the landings with air and artillery cover from England there. And it would give them the shortest route to Paris and Germany itself. This deception was reinforced by the invention of the First US Army Group, or FUSAG. This was a non-existent army, apparently mustered in Kent, ready for embarkation at Dover. Radio traffic poured out of Kent and setbuilders from theatres and film studios were employed to mock up tanks and landing craft that would look like the real thing in German aerial reconnaissance photographs. One badly-wounded prisoner of war, a Panzer officer who was being returned to Germany, actually saw FUSAG with his own eyes – though the tanks and trucks he saw were not in Kent at all but in Hampshire, ready for embarkation at the southern ports. He was also introduced to General Patton, who German intelligence had been led to believe was commanding officer of FUSAG. Hitler became so convinced that FUSAG existed and that this was where the attack would come that he kept his mighty Fifteenth Army in the Pas de Calais and his Panzers east of the Seine for seven weeks after the Allies had landed on the beaches in Normandy.

The Calvados coast in Normandy was chosen as the site of the landings because it had a number of wide flat beaches close enough together that the forces landing on them could quickly join up and form a single bridgehead. It was poorly defended. The fortifications there, and in other places, had been built by slave labourers who had weakened them with deliberate sabotage. Many of the defenders were Russians, Poles or other Eastern Europeans who had little motivation to fight against the Americans or the British. What Germans there were, were largely either to old to fight on the Russian front, too young or had been wounded there.

The other advantage of the Calvados coast was that it did not have a major port. The conventional wisdom was that, for an invasion to succeed, the landing force would have to seize a port to get men and materiel ashore quickly enough to defend against a counter-attack that would aim to push them back into the sea. This was another reason why Hitler and his High Command were so convinced that the attack would come in the Pas de Calais, where there were three ports – Calais, Boulogne and Dunkirk. But the raid on Dieppe had taught the British that an attack on a heavily defended port was not a good idea. Even if a landing force managed to take it, the Germans placed demolition charges in the harbour facilities in all the ports they occupied. Once these had been set off they could render the port useless and the invasion would inevitably fail. Instead British planners came up with an ingenious solution – the Allies would bring their own. Two prefabricated 'Mulberry' harbours would be built in sections which would then be towed across the Channel and assembled at the landing beaches. The Americans laughed when they first heard the idea, but began to take it very seriously when they realised that landing in an area that had no existing port would give the invasion force the element of surprise.

The Allies' plans were well advanced when, in November 1943, Hitler sent his most trusted and most able commander, Field Marshal Erwin Rommel, to take charge of the Atlantic Wall. He found it wanting, especially in Normandy and began strengthening it, for example, supervising the laying of over four million mines in little more than four months. Then, with just a week to go before the Allied landings, the battle-hardened 352nd Infantry Division, direct from the Russian Front, were posted to man the defences along what was to become Omaha Beach.

During the late spring of 1944, southern England had become one huge parking lot for tanks, trucks and aeroplanes. There were weapons and ammunition dumps in country lanes and village pubs were full of soldiers from every part of the English-speaking world, along with Poles, Czechs, Hungarians, Free French and Jews from Germany, Austria and all parts of Nazi-occupied Europe. In all more than six million people were involved in the D-Day landings. Twenty US divisions, fourteen British, three Canadian, one French and one Polish division were billeted in southern England, along with hundreds of thousands of other men who belonged to special forces, headquarters' units, communication staff and corps personnel. Then suddenly, as this huge force made its way to the embarkation ports, silently at night, these men simply disappeared.

In the ports and waiting out to sea were 138 battleships, cruisers and destroyers who would bombard the French coast. They were accompanied by 279 escorts, 287 minesweepers, four line-layers, two submarines, 495 motor boats, 310 landing ships and 3,817 landing craft and barges for the initial assault. Another 410 landing craft would join them as part of the ferry service to get more personnel and equipment ashore after the beachhead had been secured. A further 423 ships, including tugs, would be involved in the construction of the Mulberry harbours and the laying of the PLUTO (Petroleum Line Under The Ocean) pipeline, that would pump petrol under the Channel, and the telephone cables that would connect the commanders on the ground to SHAEF (Supreme Headquarters, Allied Expeditionary Force) in London. Another 1,260 merchant ships would also be involved in supplying the landing force, making a total of over 7,000 vessels.

Some 10,000 aircraft were also deployed in Operation *Overlord*. They would bomb key fortifications, drop paratroopers, tow gliders carrying airborne troops, attack enemy formations and protect the airspace above the beaches.

For political reasons the head of the invasion force had to be an American and Churchill got on with General Eisenhower who had demonstrated his competence as a commander in Operation Torch and the landings on Sicily and Italy. But under him, actually running the landings there would be four British officers – Eisenhower's deputy Air Marshal Sir Arthur Tedder; Admiral Sir Bertram Ramsay, commanding the operation at sea; Air Chief Marshal Sir Trafford Leigh-Mallory in the air; and on the ground General (later Field Marshal) Bernard Montgomery. This caused some resentment among American officers, who felt that they should have been represented at the high levels of command. However, one of the reasons Eisenhower had been picked as overall commander was the skill he had already shown in handling the rivalries between the British and the Americans.

When Montgomery was appointed on New Year's Day 1944, the first thing he did was to throw away the invasion plans American planners had been working on since 1942. He considered that the front in the American plan was too narrow and that the assault force was not big enough to do the job. He upped the number of divisions landing on the beaches from three to five and the number of airborne divisions from one to three. Montgomery presented his plan to the military commanders and senior politicians at St Paul's School in West Kensington on 15 May 1944. It was accepted. A key part of the plan was that, on D-Day itself, equal numbers of British and American troops would be landed. But, as losses mounted, the battle-ravaged British would be unable to sustain this commitment, while the US had an almost bottomless well of recruits. Eventually, the war in western Europe would become a predominantly American affair. To reflect this, Eisenhower himself would take over command of the land forces once the beachhead was well established.

D-Day was to be 5 June 1944. By that time, the Allies had complete air superiority over France and the bombing campaign had softened up the enemy. Much of it was directed against the railways to prevent men, weapons and ammunition being brought to the front. Bombing and sabotage by the French Resistance had knocked out 1,500 of the 2,000 locomotives available. Eighteen of the 24 bridges over the Seine between Paris and the sea had been destroyed, along with most of those over the Loire. Marshalling yards, crossings and other vital parts of the railway system had been attacked, and bombs and rockets had knocked out nearly all the radar stations along the northern coast of France.

As 5 June approached, the fine, sunny days that had lasted throughout May came to an end. The defenders along the Atlantic Wall, who had been kept on constant alert by false alarms for months, began to believe that the Allies had missed their chance. Rommel himself took the opportunity to go back to Germany to see his wife on her birthday. On the following day, 6 June, he was to have a meeting with Hitler.

The Allied first-wave troops had already embarked on 4 June when the weather worsened and a storm blew up. Eisenhower had no option but to postpone the invasion. However that night, the meteorologists thought that there might be a break in the weather the next day and Eisenhower gave the order for the invasion fleet to sail. Broad lanes across the channel had been swept by navy minesweepers and, as the invasion fleet headed out to sea, huge waves of RAF heavy bombers flew overhead to blast the coastal defences with 5,200 tonnes of bombs. As dawn broke on 6 June, the USAAF's medium bombers and fighters took over and continued the pounding of the emplacements behind the invasion beaches.

Under Montgomery's plan, the US had two landing beaches – Utah at the base of the Cotentin peninsula and Omaha further to the east along the Calvados coast. The three British beaches – Gold, Juno and Sword – lay to the east of that. The two fronts were each about 20 miles long. During the night, between midnight and 0300, one British and two American airborne divisions landed on what Hitler called Festung Europa – Fortress Europe – behind the

Atlantic Wall. The British 6th Airborne Division landed east of Caen to seize vital bridges across the River Orne, to prevent the Panzers that were stationed to the east attacking the landing force's left flank, while the American 82nd and 101st Airborne dropped at the base of the Cotentin peninsula to prevent troops stationed in Cherbourg counter-attacking. They were also to secure the causeways across the flooded areas behind the invasion beaches.

The paratroopers had been carried across the Channel on 1,100 planes from twenty different airfields. The British paratroopers were dropped too far east, but they caught the enemy by surprise, took the village of Ranville and secured the landing zones for the gliders carrying more men and anti-tank guns that would arrive two hours later. These dropped close to the bridges and seized all but one of their objectives – the bridge at Troarn which carried the main road from Caen to Le Havre and Rouen. A team under Major Rosveare grabbed some explosives, commandeered a jeep, drove hell-for-leather for the bridge and blew it up. Meanwhile 150 British paratroopers attacked the coastal battery at Merville whose guns covered Sword beach. After hand-to-hand fighting which cost half their number, the paras took it and destroyed its guns.

The American airborne landings fared less well. Heavy flak and clouds caused the transports to disperse. The pilots flew too high and too fast, scattering the paratroopers of the 101st Airborne over 375 square miles. Of 6,100 men dropped, only 1,000 made it to their rendezvous point. The 82nd had better luck and managed to capture St Mère Église on the road from Cherbourg. It was the first town in France to be liberated and, by dawn, the Stars and Stripes hung outside the town hall where the Nazi swastika had hung for four years. The American gliders also had a bad time. Only twenty-two of the fifty-two gliders landed in the drop zones and most were badly damaged on impact. This left the airborne troops short of transport, signals equipment and anti-tank guns, which made it impossible for them to capture the bridges across the River Merderet. The paratroops cut off west of the Merderet found themselves dropped into a region bristling with German strongpoints. They were so widely dispersed that all their efforts went into survival rather than securing their objectives. But although they did not take the bridges, they fully engaged the German 91st Division where it stood and it made no move against the beaches.

Throughout the night, German headquarters received sporadic reports of paratroopers landing. But the troops and the French Resistance set about cutting the telephone wires so it was impossible for anyone in command to get a clear picture of what was going on. At 0245, General von Rundstedt's headquarters received a report saying, 'Engine noise audible from the sea on east coast of Cotentin'. This was dismissed, and the Germans only became aware of the impending invasion when the landing craft were twelve miles off shore. Even then, it was thought to be a diversionary attack to draw the German defenders away from the Pas de Calais where the real invasion would come.

At first light, a combined Allied fleet of 200 warships began bombarding the Normandy coast. Then the landing craft started their run in. The seas were heavy and most of the men, who had been fed a hearty breakfast, were seasick. To add to their misery they were soon soaked to the skin from the spray as waves broke over the front of the landing craft. A piper played a highland reel in the front of one of the British landing craft. In another Major C.K. 'Banger' King, of the East Yorkshire Regiment, read stirring extracts from Shakespeare's *Henry V* over the Tannoy. In front of the landing craft that carried the troops were a line of amphibious tanks. Behind, craft carrying the artillery and multiple rocket launchers opened up. The German fortifications had been built to stand bombing and naval gunfire. Although the occupants were dazed from the bombardment, most of the emplacements were still intact and ready to mow down the infantry as they came rushing from their landing craft. But they did not expect artillery fire from the landing craft as they ran in, or to be confronted with amphibious DD (Duplex Drive) tanks, trundling up the beaches ahead of the troops.

There were more surprises. Crabs, modified Sherman tanks with huge revolving drums of flailing chains mounted on the front, landed to clear minefields; AVREs (Assault Vehicle Royal Engineers) carrying bridges or bundles of logs to breach walls or fill in ditches; perhaps most terrifying were the Crocodiles, Churchill tanks fitted with flame-throwers to clear out machine-gun nests. The whole idea of the Atlantic Wall was to destroy the invaders before they had a chance to get off the beaches. This would prove impossible.

Montgomery's plan was for the British to engage the German Panzers around Caen, hold them there and destroy them, while the Americans cleared the Cotentin peninsula. Once they had taken Cherbourg, the Allies could build up their strength and break out of the beachhead to the south. Key to this was for the British 1st Corps, which landed on Sword and Juno beaches, to join up with the 6th Airborne on the Orne. The British 3rd Division landing on Sword beach, near the mouth of the Orne, took less than an hour to secure the beach and push inland. They had travelled nearly two miles from the shore when they were stopped by the infantry and the 88mm self-propelled guns of the 21st Panzers. This took the British troops by surprise. They had been trained extensively for fighting on the beaches, where many of them had expected to die. Once they had survived that, they were not quite sure what to do and it took eight hours before they linked up with the 6th Airborne.

To the west of the British sector, the 50th Division – which had seen action in North Africa – and the 8th Armoured Brigade fought their way through the enemy defences within an hour. By 1200, the beachhead was three miles wide and two and a half miles deep. And by sunset, the British infantry and armour, supported by further naval barrages, had cleared the beaches around Arromanches, the site of one of the Mulberry harbours. With that, word was sent for the harbour's huge caissons to begin their journey across the Channel. And by the time it was dark, British patrols had reached the outskirts of the historic town of Bayeux and the 50th Division's beachhead was six miles wide and six miles deep.

The Canadians who landed on Juno beach, which lay between Sword and Gold, had a harder time as their landing zone was obstructed by a reef which delayed their landing by half-an-hour. The amphibious tanks and obstacle-clearing tanks that should have gone ashore ahead of the infantry were held back. But when the tanks finally came ashore, it still took the Canadians several hours to overcome the enemy strongpoints at the mouth of the Seulles. Then they found that they did not have the specialised armour they needed to clear the beach exits, and men and vehicles backed up on the sands.

To the east of Juno the lack of tanks meant the Canadians took heavy casualties in the 100-yard dash to the shelter of the sea wall. But then a ship almost beached herself to blast the German defences and the Canadians began to stream off the beach. By nightfall, they had taken the town of Bernières and had travelled seven miles inland – the furthest any of the Allied forces had reached on the first day. They were probing the main Bayeaux-Caens road within three miles of Caen and joined up with the British 50th Division, giving a joined Anglo-Canadian beachhead twelve miles long and almost seven miles deep.

On Utah Beach, to the west of the American section, thirty-two amphibious tanks went in under a huge bombardment by two battleships, two cruisers and twelve destroyers. Twenty-eight of the tanks made it the two miles to shore. When the first wave of infantry hit the beaches, they found that, as they covered the 500 yards to the foreshore, they were met by only occasional gunfire. This sector had been lightly defended because the area behind it was flooded and no attack had been expected there. The 4th Infantry Division had actually landed on the wrong beach. But within three hours they had cleared avenues through the beach obstacles and minefields, and their tanks rushed forward to seize the causeways over the flooded areas.

By contrast, the landings on Omaha Beach were little short of a disaster. The beach itself was far from ideal. The 300 yards of sandy foreshore was backed by a steep bank of shingle. Behind that was a sea wall or sand dunes. Beyond was a 150-foot plateau with defensive positions along the top. Four ravines cut the face of the plateau. These were the only beach exits and they were well defended. And at either end of the plateau there were 100-foot cliffs.

Although the beach was unsuitable for an amphibious assault it was chosen because the Allies had to take a beach between Gold and Utah if a single beachhead was to be established. To make matters worse, this was where the battle-hardened 352nd Infantry Division had been stationed. The Allied High Command knew this, but American troops, who were new to combat, were not told in case it sapped their morale.

Omaha was more exposed than Utah, and only four of the amphibious tanks made it the four miles to shore without being swamped. Poor visibility meant that the initial bombardment had failed to neutralise the enemy's defences, and the rockets from the multiple rocket launchers that followed the infantry in, landed harmlessly in the shallows.

When the landing craft hit the beaches and their ramps were dropped, the troops rushing out were met with a withering fire. Soon the sea was choked with blood and dead bodies. Those who survived did so by hiding behind beach obstacles that the engineers were supposed to blow up. The second wave of troops met a similar fate, apart from a small section who had managed to land on a part of the beach that was now wreathed in smoke. Nearly a whole infantry company, which had been blown to the east of its designated landing zone, managed to reach the sea wall and pick their way through the minefield behind. Strengthened by a formation of Rangers following behind, they made it up onto the plateau in time to prevent a counter-attack on the beach. Even further to the east, two battalions had got ashore under the cover of heavy smoke from undergrowth and a building set on fire by the naval bombardment. They made their way off the beach before German artillery got the range of those who followed them.

The main force found themselves pinned down behind the shingle bank, subjected to murderous machine-gun and artillery fire. Colonel G.A. Tayler rallied his regiment. 'Two kinds of people stay on this beach,' he told them, 'the dead and those who are going to die.' Some brave men then picked themselves up and attacked the German defences. Others scaled the cliffs to the left and moved off to join up with the British.

Even so, General Huebner, commanding officer of the 1st Infantry Division, realised something drastic had to be done. He called in another naval bombardment on the German fortifications, despite the risk of hitting his own men. The destroyers sailed so close to the shore that they were hit by rifle fire, but they did their job so effectively that the Germans came out with their hands up. But it was not until 1900 that the paths through the minefields had been cleared and obstacles blown up or bulldozed aside so that the armour could leave the beaches. They advanced on the fortified villages behind.

By dusk, the Omaha beachhead was only 1,200 yards deep. Beyond it the enemy was massing for a counter-attack. But instead of pushing the Americans back into the sea at Omaha, the Germans rushed all their armour towards what they considered a greater threat – the British and Canadians advancing on Caen. The mobile defence forces were sent against the British at Bayeux. One battalion of the 352nd Infantry Division were sent to deal with the American paratroops in Cotentin, another sent against the British, leaving only one battalion to check the Americans pouring off Omaha.

The following morning, the British from Gold turned eastwards to join up with the Canadians from Juno. Towards evening, they had cleared the remaining strongpoints between them, and the British beaches now formed one continuous beachhead. However, the move on Caen had stalled. The landscape of northern Normandy is known as *bocage* country. This is characterised by small fields separated by thick hedges on high banks and sunken roads. It is easy terrain to defend. Hundreds of German tanks and 88mm guns were dug in and camouflaged, and the Allied forces had to fight their way hedgerow by hedgerow through this country. However, the Allies' bombers, fighters and accurate naval gunnery support – which could lob shells sixteen miles inshore – made it difficult for the Germans to form up into the formations necessary to stage a concerted counter-attack. The best the defenders could do was slow the Allied advance, never halt it entirely or turn it back.

The 260 tanks of the Panzer Lehr Division, formed from various units of the German Army training and demonstration units, otherwise known as Lehr or teaching units, hence the name, who tank warfare expert Colonel-General 'Fast Heinz' Guderian boasted would 'throw the Anglo-Americans into the sea', were beaten back by air assaults. On D+1 (i.e. the day after D-Day) an SS Division was sent to the front. But it simply disintegrated under air attacks using bombs and rockets, and its men ended up hiding in the woods until dark. The Allied planes did not even have to wait until the enemy reached the battlefield before engaging them. They would attack the remaining trains bringing them to the front up to 30 miles away.

On D+1 the American airborne troops had begun to form themselves into a coherent fighting force. But the ten miles between Utah and Omaha beaches were still held by the enemy. However, with the help of RAF Typhoons and naval bombardment, Royal Marines from Gold beach had taken the small fishing port of Pont-en-Bessin halfway between Gold and Omaha's left flank and the following day forces from the British and American beaches linked up.

Montgomery kept up the pressure on Caen, often in bloody battles designed to keep the enemy off balance. They were costly in British casualties, but forced the Germans to use their tanks as dug-in artillery and took the pressure off the Americans. The 160 British troops who took the key village of Breville suffered 141 casualties. Once it was taken, though, the eastern end of the beachhead was secure. After fierce fighting, US troops took Carentan on 12 June and the Omaha and Utah beachheads were finally joined, giving the Allies one huge enclave along the Normandy coast sixty miles long and fifteen miles deep. The German front in the west began to crumble. An American thrust across the Cotentin peninsula to Barneville on the Atlantic coast cut off Cherbourg. Another push created a twenty-mile salient to the south.

By D+12, there were 50,000 men ashore. With twenty divisions now in Normandy, the Allies had managed to build up their forces faster than the Germans. The destruction of railways and bridges and constant air attacks – by then from planes flying from airstrips inside the beachhead – made it impossible for Rommel to bring battle-ready formations into the area. Divisions had to be broken up and travel at night, with the infantry often on foot or on bicycle. Tanks could not be massed for a large assault on the beachhead and were used piecemeal to plug the line. Two SS Panzer Divisions brought from the Eastern Front were devastated long before they reached the battlefield.

On 19 June, however, disaster almost overtook the Allies when the worst storm for nearly fifty years blew up in the Channel. Over three days and three nights, a dozen ships out to sea were sunk and 800 vessels were driven ashore. The Mulberry harbour at Arromanches was badly damaged but still usable. The one off Omaha beach was smashed to pieces. Suddenly the Allies were short of supplies and ammunition, and robbed of their air cover. It was the perfect opportunity for Rommel to counter-attack. But his forces were deployed for defence and were in no position to seize their last chance to push the Allies back into the sea.

Once the storm broke, the amphibious trucks used during the beach assaults were employed to ferry supplies ashore. By the end of the month the daily tonnage landing was back to pre-storm levels. Bits of the Mulberry harbour at Omaha were salvaged and used to patch up the one at Arromanches. Within two weeks 700 out of the 800 ships beached were repaired and refloated, and by 27 June, the port of Cherbourg was in American hands, although it had been so badly damaged and booby-trapped that it could not be used for several weeks.

The British had planned an attack on Caen on 19 June. This had been delayed and was finally launched on 26 June. With massive artillery support, the British managed to take the key highpoint Hill 112 to the south of Caen. The following day there was a massive armoured counter-attack which employed both the remnants of the SS divisions brought in from Russia and a Panzer division brought up from the south of France. These formations came under withering air attack from the RAF's rocket-firing Typhoons. As the German tanks advanced through the bocage country, they were vulnerable to the British Piat anti-tank weapon that could be fired at close range from behind the hedgerows. Both sides threw everything they had into the fray. A five-day battle raged over Hill 112 and the fighting became so intense that the little River Odon was dammed with human bodies. The result was a stalemate and the British did not completely overrun Hill 112 until 10 July.

It rained heavily throughout July. The fighting became – literally – bogged down and both sides feared that the battle for Normandy might turn into the kind of trench warfare and endless carnage seen in the First World War. Public opinion in Britain and America became restive. Meanwhile Hitler replaced his commander in the west, Field Marshal Gerd von Rundstedt with Field Marshal Gunther von Kluge, fresh from the Russian Front.

At the cost of 11,000 casualties, US troops had crossed the fields and marshes of western Normandy to take the smouldering ruins of St-Lô. This stood at the head of a good road that ran south to the Loire Valley. A plan code-named Operation *Cobra* was hatched to make a break-out here with a fast-moving tank column under General Patton. To pull this off, Montgomery would need to keep the German tanks pinned down to the east. The Canadians attacked on the airfield at Carpiquet, suffering grievous casualties. The British then launched a renewed onslaught on Caen, after the RAF had dropped 2,500 tonnes of bombs on it. After two days of fierce fighting, the British took the north-western part the city, above the River Orne. A renewed attack from Hill 112 cost the British 3,500 casualties.

Montgomery planned to keep up the pressure with Operation *Goodwood*, a massive attack against prepared positions to the east and south of Caen. On the eve of the battle, Rommel was machine-gunned in his staff car by an RAF fighter. He took no further part in the fighting and committed suicide while convalescing after being implicated in the July plot to kill Hitler.

On the first day of Goodwood, the British lost 1,500 men and 200 tanks, and failed to make a breakthrough, although Montgomery kept up the pressure for three days before the offensive was halted by a thunderstorm. Goodwood had one unexpected effect. It finally convinced Hitler that there was going to be no attack on the Pas de Calais – the Normandy landings were the real thing and he ordered the 250,000 men of his Fifteenth Army into the battle. Because of the devastation caused by Allied air attacks it took them a month to reach Normandy. By that time the Allies had 1,000,000 men ashore and the Fifteenth Army proved to be too little too late.

Montgomery took a great deal of criticism for the failure of Operation Goodwood. But, as Field Marshal Brooke pointed out, not only had it drawn in most of the German armour as planned, it had also destroyed it faster than it could be replaced. General Omar Bradley, now commanding the US forces in Normandy, also appreciated the strategy. It had allowed him to get his men in position for a break-out.

Patton had landed on Utah beach on 6 July without even getting his feet wet and, from a well-camouflaged bivouac on the Cotentin peninsula, he began to assemble his Third Army. With the Fifteenth Army on its way to the east of the front, Hitler felt it was safe to move seven of his divisions, including two Panzer divisions, to the west, bringing the number there up to sixty-five. This strengthened the German line against any US break-out, it also lured them into a death trap. On 25 July, 3,000 USAAF bombers dropped 4,000 tonnes of high-explosive, fragmentation and napalm bombs on a five-mile stretch of the German front to the west of St-Lô. The German commander General Bayerlein claimed that this raid turned the area into a Mondlandshaft – a moonscape. He estimated that seventy per cent of the German troops in that section were put out of action – either dead, wounded or demented. Patton's troops slowly moved forward through the bocage country – what the GIs called the 'Gethsemane of the hedgerows'. By 27 July, Coutances was taken; by 30 July, Avranches and the German retreat had turned into a rout. Within twenty-four hours,

Patton pushed three divisions through the five-mile gap that had opened at Avranches. His men were now out of the bocage country and onto the open roads of Brittany.

Montgomery was still making slow progress in the east and turned his troops to the south with the Canadians advancing on Falaise. Bradley sent Patton and his Third Army on a long sweep south, then east, to encircle the Germans. Hitler saw the danger too late. He had ordered Von Kluge to switch four armoured divisions from the British front to attack the Americans, but Von Kluge could not disengage them until 7 August. Hitler planned a counter-attack against the bottle-neck at Avranches, closing the gap there and cutting off Patton's supply lines. But Hitler was 800 miles away in his headquarters, the Wolf's Lair, in East Prussia. His commanders on the ground in Normandy were against the attack. They knew that the battle of Normandy was lost and that they should make an orderly retreat across the Seine.

Hitler threw in four divisions of the Fifteenth Army, fresh from the Pas de Calais. Allied bombers cut off the German retreat by bombing the remaining bridges along the Seine. Meanwhile, Patton was making quick time across the open roads of northwest France, taking Le Mans on 8 August. To the north, on their way to Avranches, five Panzer and two infantry divisions ran into a single American division at Mortain, which however managed to hold them until other Allied units came to its aid. Powerful US formations struck back through Vire, while the British pushed from the north against Condé and Patton turned north closing the trap. The Germans were now caught in small pocket between Mortain and Falaise, where the Allied air forces relentlessly bombed and strafed them. By 14 August, the only way out was through a eighteen-mile gap between the Canadians at Falaise and Patton's Third Army. Patton wanted to drive on to Falaise and close the gap but, by then, his speeding army had lost its coherence and Bradley ordered him to stop. By this time German units were being cut down by the French Resistance or surrendering wholesale to Allied forces. Von Kluge got lost in the confusion. Soon after he reappeared hewas relieved of his command and committed suicide. By 17 August the Falaise gap was down to eleven miles and the German forces were streaming eastwards through it. By 18 August, it was squeezed to six miles and air attacks on it were so relentless that any attempt to get through it resulted in almost certain death. It was sealed on 20 August.

Eisenhower said later of the battle:

The battlefield at Falaise was unquestionably one of the greatest killing grounds of any of the war areas. Roads, highways and fields were so choked with destroyed equipment and with dead men and animals that passage through the area was extremely difficult. Forty-eight hours after the closing of the gap, I was conducted through on foot, to encounter a scene that could be described only by Dante. It was quite literally possible to walk for hundreds of yards at a time, stepping on nothing but dead and decaying flesh.

Some 10,000 Germans were killed in six days in the Falaise Pocket and 50,000 prisoners were taken. Of the 20,000 to 50,000 who escaped, many more were killed before they reached the Seine. Thousands more who were cut off elsewhere gave themselves up. Two Panzer divisions and eight divisions of infantry were captured almost complete. In all, German casualties in Normandy amounted to 400,000 men, half of whom were captured. Allied casualties totalled 209,672 men, of whom 36,976 were killed. The Germans also lost 1,300 tanks, 1,500 guns and 20,000 vehicles. What remained of the German army in western Europe ran headlong for the German border. On 25 August 1944 Paris was liberated.

OPERATION MARKET GARDEN

On 1 September 1944, Montgomery formally relinquished command of the Allied forces in France to Eisenhower. And while US forces dashed across France and Belgium towards the German border, Montgomery and his 21st Army Group headed north-eastwards to clear the V1 and V2 sites which were raining down flying bombs and ballistic missiles on London, liberate the port of Antwerp and drive into northern Germany.

Normally chided for his caution, Montgomery now planned a bold move. He wanted to use airborne troops to capture five bridges on the road from Eindhoven to Arnhem. He would then drive his Second Army down this corridor across Holland through the German border defences and into the Ruhr, Germany's industrial heartland. The airborne part of the operation was code-named Market and the infantry and armoured part Garden. So the combined operation became known as Operation Market Garden.

The operation was to be mounted within a week. Although he gave the go-ahead Eisenhower had misgivings. So did Lieutenant-General Frederick Browning, deputy commander of the First Allied Airborne Army. In a planning meeting, he asked how long it would take for the Second Army to relieve the airborne troops holding the last bridge, the bridge at Arnhem. Montgomery said, 'Two days.' Browning studied the map and replied, 'Sir, I think we might be going a bridge too far.'

Five thousand aircraft were assembled for what would be the largest ever airborne operation. Three divisions – the British 1st Airborne and the US 82nd and 101st Airborne, plus the 1st Polish Parachute Brigade – would be dropped over three days, as there were not enough planes to drop them in one go. The 101st Airborne would land around Eindhoven at the southern end of the corridor. The 82nd would take the central section around Nijmegen. The 'Red Devils' of the 1st Airborne and the Poles, under Major-General

Robert Urquhart would take the final section at Arnhem. They would have the longest to hold out and, until the Second Army reached them, they would be on their own.

Aerial reconnaissance photographs and reports from the Dutch Resistance indicated that there were Panzers in the area of Arnhem, but the 1st Airborne were briefed to expect weak opposition from second-rate troops. The plan called for the 1st Airborne to take the defenders by surprise by being dropped near the bridge in close formation. But the pilots refused to fly slow, straight and level near the bridge, believing that it was defended by anti-aircraft batteries. Instead, the Red Devils would have to land on areas of open ground to the west, losing them the element of surprise.

The huge fleet of aeroplanes and gliders set off on the morning of 17 September. The landings in the early afternoon went well. However, the 1st Airborne soon found that the bunch of old men and boys they had been told they would be up against were actually two combat-hardened divisions of Panzers and a Panzergrenadier battalion armed with the new multi-barrelled, rocket-propelled mortars. But the 1st Airlanding Brigade fought off a German counter-attack and held the landing zone, while the 1st Parachute Brigade set out for the bridge. Their progress was hampered by Dutch civilians who treated them as liberators and wanted to ply them with drinks and food and the other spoils of victory. Later they discovered that their radio sets were not working.

The 1st and 3rd Battalions were stopped by heavy enemy fire on the main road, but the 2nd Battalion under Lieutenant-Colonel John Frost advanced quickly along a secondary road alongside the river. The Germans had blown up a railway bridge before they could get to it and a pontoon bridge upstream proved to be unusable. But the main road bridge, their objective, was still standing. As night fell, Frost and his men occupied houses overlooking the bridge's long northern approach ramp.

An attempt to take the bridge was repulsed by the Panzer-grenadiers. However, Frost's men prevented the commander of Second SS Panzer Corps, under Lieutenant-General Wilhelm Bittrich, sending one of his divisions across it to fight off the Allied attack at Nijemegen. Instead Bittrich tried to get his tanks across the river using a ferry upstream – a slow business – and sent his remaining troops to take the bridge. A fierce gun battle broke out between the SS troops and the paratroopers, who managed to destroy a column of twenty-two half-tracks and scout cars that tried to cross the bridge from the south. The Germans brought down artillery fire on Frost's position at the north end of the bridge. Soon the houses there were on fire and the cellars beneath were full of dead and wounded.

Unable to contact his men by radio, Major-General Urquhart left his divisional headquarters in the drop zone. He grabbed a jeep and went to try and find out what was going on. Eventually he caught up with his deputy, Brigadier-General Gerald Lathbury, commander of the 1st Parachute Brigade, who was advancing with the 3rd Battalion. It was then that fierce street fighting broke out. Lathbury was injured in the leg and was taken prisoner, while Urquhart had to hide in an attic overnight until he could make it back to British positions. He then discovered that divisional head-quarters had been moved to the Hartenstein Hotel in Oosterbeek, three miles west of Arnhem and headed there. On the way his jeep was fired upon. When he arrived, he learnt that, in his absence, he had been reported captured.

During the time he had been missing, the second wave of air-borne troops had been delayed by bad weather and the Germans had found a copy of the plan for Operation Market Garden in a crashed glider at Nijmegen. They organised a rough reception for the rest of the 1st Airborne when it arrived at 1600 on 18 September.

Urquhart's forces on the ground were scattered and only had rifles grenades and Sten guns to hold off Tiger and Panther tanks, and self-propelled assault guns. However, the 2nd Battalion was still holding on north of the bridge, though it was taking severe losses. If Market Garden had been going to plan, the Second Army should have been nearing the bridge by them. But there was no sign of them.

On 19 September, a renewed effort was made to join up with the 2nd Battalion, but this was halted a mile from the bridge by German reinforcements. The weather intervened again. Most of the 1st Polish Parachute Brigade was delayed. The glider force got through though, but it landed in the middle of the battle zone and was caught in the crossfire. With the drop zones now in German hands, Urquhart radioed for supplies to be dropped near his head-quarters at the Hartenstein Hotel. But the radio was still not working properly and the message did not get through. Of the 390 tonnes of food, medical supplies and ammunition dropped by the RAF, only thirty-one tonnes arrived in Allied hands.

By nightfall on 19 September, the Second Army had broken through and British tanks were only ten miles away, down the road they were now calling 'Hell's Highway'. But the 1st Airborne were taking terrible punishment and Urquhart took the reluctant decision to pull his scattered forces back into a box around the Hartenstein Hotel, leaving Frost's 2nd Battalion to fend for itself. Even in this defensive position his lines were only thinly defended and the crossroads at Oosterbeek came under such intensive fire that the 1st Airborne called it the Cauldron.

By the evening of the 20th, the Second Army had still not arrived. Colonel Frost was wounded. Ammunition was running low and he realised that their three-day stand was coming to a close. That night, they were overrun. At dawn on 21 September Bittrich's Panzers crossed the bridge and went to confront the Second Army. Later that day, the Polish paratroopers were dropped at Driel, south of the river, straight on top of the Germans. Those who escaped headed for a small ferry across the river. When they got there they found it was not working. Some 200 swam across the river to joint Urquhart, while the remainder dug in on the south bank.

Early on the morning of 22 September, a detachment of armoured cars from the Second Army reached Driel and made contact with the 1st Airborne across the river. Over the next two days the British infantry came up, but the situation for Urquhart's men on the north bank was deteriorating. Their stores were running low and attempts to resupply them had failed. The 4th Battalion of the Dorset Regiment tried to cross the river, but failed. Eventually at 0600 on 25 September Urquhart was ordered to withdraw. That night with muffled boots, they slipped down to the Rhine, where a few boats waited to ferry them across.

No one had expected so many men to escape and there was insufficient transport to carry them to the rear. So Urquhart's men, exhausted by eight days of fighting, had to march the 11 miles to the Second Army's main position at Nijmegen. They left behind 1,200 dead, 6,642 wounded, captured or missing. The German casualties were 3,300, of whom a third were dead. The people of Arnhem also suffered. For greeting the British as liberators, the Germans drove the entire population of Arnhem out of the town. They were only able to return the following spring. When they did, they found that their homes had been reduced to rubble.

THE BATTLE OF THE BULGE

Throughout the summer of 1944, the German army was on the retreat on all fronts. By then Germany was so weak that even Hitler realised that victory by force of arms was no longer within his grasp. But he thought that if one decisive battle went in his favour the situation might still be turned to Germany's advantage.

A victory on the Eastern Front was out of the question as the Red Army was too strong. However, the failure of Operation Market Garden showed that the Western Allies with their over-extended supply lines could still be halted and he realised that they would be particularly vulnerable if he hit them between the advancing British and American armies. A decisive victory there might force the Allies to the negotiating table – and they might even be persuaded to join their former enemy to take on Communist Russia together.

On 16 September, while listening to a situation report on the Western Front, Hitler suddenly announced, 'I shall go on the offen-sive... out of the Ardennes, with the objective, Antwerp'. An attack through the Ardennes had worked in 1940. As it fell between the British and US sectors, it was only lightly defended. A sweeping attack would sever the American's supply lines and cut off the British in Belgium and Holland. The operation was called Wacht am Rhein – Watch on the Rhine – and it would put at risk 20 divi-sions. If it failed, there would be no stopping the Allies.

Hitler and his closest aides planned the operation in secret. When Von Rundstedt, who had recently been reinstated as com-mander in the west, heard about it he was horrified. 'It was obvious to me that the available force was far too small for such an extreme-ly ambitious plan,' he said after the war. 'It was a nonsensical operation, and the most stupid part of it was setting Antwerp as its goal. If we had reached the Meuse we should have got down on our knees and thanked God, let alone try to reach Antwerp.' Indeed, Von Rundstedt pleaded for a 'little solution' – an offensive that stopped at the Meuse.

Von Rundstedt had sent 2,500 tanks into France on the Blitzkrieg in 1940. Now, against far superior forces, Hitler planned to send just 1,420, which would have to supply their own fuel by capturing American gasoline on the way. The Germans had enjoyed air superiority in 1940. That was now lost. They had had 2,000 fighter-bombers back then. In 1944, they had just 1,000. And the Germans no longer had the overwhelming number of men they could call on in 1940. It was the Americans who had the limitless numbers now. By the fourth day of the offensive, US reserves had doubled the number of men in the Ardennes to 180,000. But, running true to form, Hitler ignored what the professional soldiers told him and decided to go ahead. However, he was persuaded to change the name of the operation from *Wacht am Rhein* to *Herbstnebel* (Autumn Fog) and delay the attack from 25 November to 10 December, then to 16 December to muster enough troops for the offensive.

Spearheading the break-out would be the Fifth Panzer Army under General Hasso von Manteuffel and the newly formed Sixth SS Panzer Army under Colonel-General Joseph 'Sepp' Dietrich. They would be supported by the Seventh Army under General Erich Brandenberger. The Panzers would attack on a 90-mile front from Echtnernach in the south to Monschau in the north. The Fifth Panzer Army would be on the left, the Sixth on the right, while the Seventh Army would protect the armour's southern flank.

To blunt any counter-offensive, Hitler sent a hand-picked force of English-speaking troops behind the Allied lines carrying American weapons and wearing US uniforms. They would disrupt the Allied forces by misdirecting traffic and switching signposts. Their commander would be SS Colonel Otto Skorzeny, who had recently headed the daring raid to rescue Mussolini from his mountain prison, allowing Hitler to set the Italian dictator up in a new Fascist state in northern Italy.

Although Hitler was ill and exhausted, he switched his headquarters from the Wolf's Lair in East Prussia to the Eagle's Lair near Bad Neuheim in the Rhineland, where he would direct the battle personally. He had been there in Eagle's Lair in the 1940 when the German offensive had crushed the Allies in France. Those who accompanied him were increasingly of the opinion that he was rapidly losing touch with reality.

In November, while preparations were underway, the Allies had breached Germany's 'West Wall' frontier defences – the Siegfried Line – and had taken Aachen, the first German town of any size to fall to the Allies. However, the Allies were beginning to show signs of hubris. The front Hitler planned to hit was manned by just four divisions of the US 8th Corps, under Major-General Troy Middleton. They were spread thinly. The 4th and 28th Divisions had just been pulled out of the line to recuperate after heavy fighting, while the 9th Armoured and the 106th Division had never seen action before. Either side of the Ardennes front were the inexperienced and understrengthed First, Third and Ninth Armies of General Omar Bradley's 12th US Army Group. This hardly seemed to matter as Army Intelligence ruled out a German offensive in this area, despite the lesson of 1940. These men were about to be hit by three German armies, twenty-five divisions in all, eleven of them armoured.

Eisenhower was taken completely by surprise when, at 0535 on 16 December, 2,000 guns opened up in the Ardennes. The Germans attacked with a message from Von Rundstedt ringing in their ears. It read, 'Soldiers of the Westfront. Your great hour has arrived. Large attacking armies have started against the Anglo-Americans. I do not have to tell you anything more than that. You feel it yourselves. We gamble everything. You carry the sacred obligation to give everything to achieve things beyond human possibilities for our Fatherland and our Führer.'

The offensive took place during a period of bad weather when the Allied air forces were grounded and the Germans quickly developed a salient fifty miles deep in the American lines. Churchill quickly dismissed this as 'The Battle of the Bulge', a title he had first given to the 1940 Ardennes offensive. This time it stuck.

Skorzeny's troops in American uniforms went in first. They fooled no one and most of them ended up facing a firing squad. Seventh Army was held up not far from their starting point, but the Panzers did better. The Sixth SS Panzers struck through what was called the Losheim gap and made significant gains, which they could not exploit due to lack of fuel. The Fifth Panzer Army swept through the 28th and 106th Divisions, reaching Celles, six miles short of the River Meuse, where it was halted then the weather cleared and the Allied air forces took to the air again. Despite this initial success, the Fifth Panzers' supply route ran through the town of Bastogne, which was held by the 101st Airborne Division under Brigadier-General Anthony McAuliffe. He found himself completely surrounded in what was called 'the hole in the doughnut'. When he was asked to surrender, he replied famously, 'Nuts.' The 101st held out for six days, supplied by air.

By 19 December, the offensive was stalled, but Hitler refused Von Rundstedt's suggestion that part of Dietrich's Fifth Panzers should be moved north to support Von Manteuffel's Sixth SS Panzers who had done marginally better. Hitler wanted the SS to have all the glory. At a meeting at Verdun on the same day, Eisenhower told his generals, 'The present situation is to be regarded as one of opportunity for us and not disaster. There will be only cheerful faces at this conference table.' The outcome of the meeting was to shift Patton's Third Army 150 miles north to the left flank of the salient, while Montgomery, newly-promoted to Field Marshal, would attack the northern side with some of Bradley's troops temporarily assigned to his command.

Although on 21 December, the Fifth Panzers took the town of St Vith, Von Rundstedt felt the advance had run out of steam and, on 22 December, he asked Hitler's permission to withdraw. It was refused. But on Christmas Day, Sixth Panzer Army suffered a crushing defeat and the following day Bastogne was relieved, at the cost of 3,900 American dead and 12,000 Germans. The Americans lost 150 tanks in the action, the Germans 450.

Hitler had no choice but to withdraw now as German atrocities had inspired the US troops to fight with renewed determination. In the advance guard of the German assault was Lieutenant-General Jochen Peiper, commanding 140 tanks and a battalion of motorised infantry. At Honsfeld, his men shot nineteen GIs and robbed their dead bodies. At an airfield near Bullingen, Peiper forced captured Americans to refuel his tanks. Afterwards, he shot them. Eight more prisoners of war were killed at Lignueville. A hundred American prisoners were machine-gunned in Malmédy. Twenty Americans who miraculously escaped hid in a café. It was set on fire and they were machine-gunned when they ran out. Hitler thought that news of these massacres would demoralise the American troops. In fact, it gave them a first-class incentive to fight back. By early January 1945, the front line was almost back where it had been before the Battle of the Bulge. Hitler claimed that Herbstnebel had been worth it, but the autumn fog had been dispersed by the crisp air of winter. The Germans had lost 10,000 men, the Americans 81,000 and the British, who played only a minor part in the action, 1,400. The Americans had also lost 733 tanks, the Germans 600 and an enormous number of guns and other equipment had been lost. However, the complete destruction of German cities by relentless bombing meant the Germans could not replace their equipment. The Allies could. All Hitler had bought with the loss of his final strategic reserve was six weeks to prepare the defences on the Rhine.

THE CROSSING OF THE RHINE

By the time the Allied forces reached the frontier of Germany, the total defeat of Hitler's Third Reich was only a matter of time. But, for the British and American forces there was still one huge obstacle to overcome – the fast-flowing River Rhine which ran along much of Germany's western border.

In the early weeks of March 1945, the US First and Ninth Armies reached the Rhine and a unit of the First Army, finding the railway bridge at Remagen only lightly defended, swept across on 7 March. On 22 March Patton's Third Army established a bridgehead near Nierstein, ready for a drive across southern Germany. To the north, Montgomery's 21st Army Group had also reached the Rhine and halted while the western bank was cleared. On the other side of the river were five divisions of Hitler's elite paratroopers, with one Panzer division and one Panzergrenadier division as a mobile reserve. They were a formidable force and it was feared that they would be highly motivated as they were now fighting for their home territory. And after Arnhem, Montgomery had resumed his cautious demeanour. He was determined to cross the Rhine with the minimum loss of life for his men.

Montgomery planned an airborne assault called Operation Varsity, using the US 17th Airborne and the British 6th Airborne, and an amphibious assault called Operation Plunder, using the British Second Army and the US Ninth Army under his command. The airborne troops would seize the high ground on the other side of the river overlooking the crossing points to prevent the Germans deploying artillery there. To gain the element of surprise, he would reverse the normal order of things with the airborne assault going in after the amphibious landings, rather than the other way around. First, bombers from the US 8th and 9th Air Forces would cut off the Ruhr on the other side of the river to prevent the Germans bringing up reinforcements, while 1,000 fighter-bombers of the 2nd Tactical Air Force would provide close air support.

At dawn on 24 March, the British Second Army crossed the Rhine. By that time, the British paratroopers had already left their bases in southern England. Meanwhile, the US troops, resting in

Paris after the Battle of the Bulge, enplaned at seventeen bases around Rheims, Orléans, Evreux and Amiens. The two forces met up over Brussels. Between them they had 1,696 transport planes and 1,348 gliders carrying 21,700 men, 600 tonnes of ammunition and 800 guns and vehicles. And they were protected by a close escort of 889 fighters.

Airborne operations had been going on throughout the war, but there were still two schools of thought concerning tactics. The US forces liked to drop their airborne troops and release their gliders as low as possible to reduce the time they spent in the air, where they were particularly vulnerable. The British preferred to drop their airborne troops and release gliders high, to reduce the chances of the planes being hit by anti-aircraft fire. Both tactics worked in their fashion. The US suffered less casualties, but lost more planes. This was partly because they were using the Curtis C-46 Commando for the first time because it had two doors for the para-troopers to jump from, instead of the C-47 Dakota's one. But it also had a tendency to catch fire and was never used for paratroop drops again. However, flak suppression from the Allied artillery was so good that only forty-six transport planes and three per cent of the gliders were lost.

Both the British and American parachutists went in twenty minutes after the amphibious assault began. The British gliders followed three-quarters of an hour later, the American gliders forty-three minutes after that. The British 3rd Parachute Brigade landed on the left, along the north of the village of Bergen. They came under heavy fire from anti-aircraft guns which were being used as ground support, but succeeded in taking the village of Schappenburg. The 5th Parachute Brigade suffered casualties during the drop. They landed near the woods on the Hammiklen-Rees road and rapidly moved on to take their objectives. The 6th Airlanding Brigade also sustained casualties in the air. They landed in open fields to the south of Hammiklen. Their objective was the village itself.

Even though the American paratroopers were dropped lower, when they hit the ground they were more dispersed. Two battalions of the 507th landed in the drop zone between Diersfordterwald and the Rhine. However the third battalion and the regimental headquarters landed well to the north. They found themselves just short of Diersfordt. A fierce firefight erupted and the Germans put up stiff resistance for most of the day until, about 1500 they surrendered.

The 513th also landed north of their designated drop zone and found themselves alongside the right-hand battalion of the 6th Airlanding Brigade and 13th Devons. Together they secured the British objective, Hammiklen village, before the 513th moved on to take its own objectives.

During the airborne operation, the British lost 347 killed and 731 wounded; the Americans 159 killed and 522 wounded. Some 3,789 German prisoners were taken and the 84th Division practically annihilated. By dusk the airborne troops had joined up with the Second Army's amphibious forces. German resistance, though initially stiff, was soon crushed, though the Allies took heavy casualties. Montgomery has been criticised for using such a great force to achieve so little. However, with the Allies now moving onto Germany's own soil, it was perhaps not unwise to think that the Germans might put up the fight of their lives.

By this time, though, most Germans wanted to see the Western Allies sweep through Germany as quickly as possible, rather than let it fall into Russian hands. Having suffered terribly at German hands, the Soviets would be bent on revenge. And no one wanted to institute Hilter's scorched earth policy in front of the advancing Allies.

On 25 March the German Fifteenth Army containing the bridgehead at Remagen collapsed. The American First Army then broke through. The Third Army crossed the River Main at Aschaffenburg and Hanau. Then the First and Third Armies used the autobahn system, which Hitler had built to move his troops, to race across southern Germany.

On 15 April 1945, near where the Rhine crossing had been made at Bergen, horrified British troops found a concentration camp: Bergen-Belsen. Between the villages of Bergen and Belsen, it had been designed for 10,000, but it then held 41,000 people. Although this was not an extermination camp – there were no gas chambers there – some 37,000 prisoners died from starvation, overwork and disease, and their corpses were bulldozed into mass graves. Anne Frank, whose wartime diary would later become world famous, died of typhus at Bergen-Belsen in March 1945, while the Allied armies were massing a matter of miles away.

THE BATTLE OF BERLIN

Following the Battle of Stalingrad, Germany was on the run in Russia. However, the German Field Marshal von Manstein, who had nearly managed the relief of Paulus' trapped Sixth Army at Stalingrad, had managed to get his Army Group Don, named after the Russian River Don, back to the River Donetz. Then in February 1943, he retook Kharkov in the Ukraine, leaving the Soviet troops around the city of Kursk in a salient. This stretched 150 miles from north to south and protruded 100 miles into the German lines. In an attempt to regain the initiative on the Eastern Front, the Germans planned a surprise attack on the salient in a pincer movement from both north and south. They hoped to cut off, surround and destroy the Red Army in the bulge. For the attack, the Germans massed almost fifty divisions containing 900,000 troops, including seventeen motorised or armoured divisions with 2,700 tanks and self-propelled assault guns. However the Soviets had anticipated the German attack and had withdrawn their main forces. They had built eight concentric circles of defences and had massed forces that were numerically superior to the Germans in both men and tanks. When the Germans launched their attack on 5 July, they soon found themselves embroiled in deep anti-tank defences and minefields and only advanced into the salient thirty miles in the south and ten miles in the north, losing many of their tanks along the way. On 12 July, the Soviets counter-attacked. They successfully developed a broad front and recovered the nearby city of Orel on 5 August and Kharkov on 23 August. The Battle of Kursk was the largest tank battle in history and involved some 6,000 tanks, 2,000,000 troops, and 4,000 aircraft. It was the last German offensive on the Eastern Front and, from that point on, the German armies in the east were always on the retreat.

In early 1945, the race to Berlin was on. Although the Soviets had three army groups poised on the Oder-Neisse Line, the present-day Polish border, Montgomery's 21st Army Group was moving at such a pace that it was thought it might get to the German capital first. Montgomery proposed a single thrust in overwhelming strength from the Ruhr to take Berlin and finish the war. However, Eisenhower vetoed his plan. He had favoured Montgomery over his own generals throughout in the invasion, now he switched his resources to General Omar Bradley's 12th Army Group in southern Germany which, he thought, could make a quick dash to join up with the Red Army in the area around Dresden. This would cut Germany in two. Eisenhower feared that Hitler might abandon Berlin and prolong the war, fighting in the mountainous region to the south. On 28 March, he sent an outline of his plans to Stalin and asked about the Soviet plans. When Churchill found out, he protested vigorously. He wrote to the ailing Roosevelt, pointing out the political necessity of taking Berlin as 'the supreme symbol of defeat'. But Churchill had another agenda. He was a fervent anti-Communist and had been one of the architects of the 1919 Allied intervention into Russia, which attempted to strangle the

Bolshevik state at birth. He now feared that the Russians might roll on across western Europe and had even made plans to rearm the German army, once Hitler was dead, to fight Stalin.

'If the Russians take Berlin, will not their impression be that they have been the overwhelming contributor to the common victory be unduly imprinted on their minds, and may this not lead them into a mood which will raise grave and formidable difficulties in the future?' he wrote. It was of utmost necessity that Berlin be taken by an Anglo-American force.

However, leaving the politics aside, Eisenhower was right militarily, and his staff backed him. Stalin replied on 2 April, agreeing that the plan for their two armies to meet up near Dresden was strategically sound. As a result, he said, he would only send a second-rate force against Berlin which had 'lost its former strategic importance'. Nothing could have been further from the truth. Stalin was a politician not a general. He knew the political importance of taking Berlin and suspected that Eisenhower was playing a trick on him. Before he replied he spoke to his two senior field marshals, Ivan Koniev and Georgii Zhukov. They were great rivals and both begged for the chance to take Berlin. He gave them each forty-eight hours to come up with a plan.

Although Stalin told Eisenhower that he intended to attack Berlin in May, Koniev and Zhukov were clear that he wanted to do it before that, even though their armies were exhausted after weeks of heavy fighting. Koniev's 1st Ukranian Front – or Army Group – was on the eastern bank of the River Neisse, some seventy-five miles south-east of Berlin. He proposed starting his offensive with a two-and-a-half hour artillery bombardment with 7,500 guns. At dawn, he would lay a smoke-screen, and force a river crossing with two tank armies and five field armies, over 500,000 men in all. He would keep his tanks on his right flank. They would smash through the German defences, then swing north-westwards and make a dash on Berlin. Unfortunately his plan relied on two extra armies which, although promised, could not be relied on to arrive in time.

Zhukov's 1st Belorussian Front was on the Oder river, fifty miles east of Berlin, with a bridgehead on the western side of the river at Küstrin. He proposed pre-dawn bombardment with 10,000 guns. Then he would turn 140 anti-aircraft searchlights on the German defenders, blinding them while he attacked. Two tank armies and four field armies would stream out of the Küstrin bridgehead, with two more armies on each flank. With complete air superiority and 750,000 men as his disposal, Zhukov was confident of a quick victory.

Stalin gave Zhukov the green light as he was closer to Berlin and better prepared. But, still encouraging the rivalry between the two field marshals, he also let Koniev know that he was free to make a dash on Berlin if he thought he could beat Zhukov to it. The starting date set for the offensive was 16 April. The two field marshals had just thirteen days to prepare.

On 15 April, the Americans entered the race when Lieutenant-General William Simpson's Ninth Army crossed the Elbe. Between him and Berlin stood the remnants of the German 12th Army under General Walther Wenck. There would be little that it could do to prevent Simpson making a dash for the capital. But Eisenhower ordered Simpson to halt on the Elbe until the link-up with the Red Army had been made at Dresden. The following morning at 0400, three red flares lit up the skies over the Küstrin bridgehead. It was followed by the biggest artillery barrage ever mounted on the eastern front. Mortars, tanks, self-propelled guns, light and heavy artillery – along with 400 Katyushas – all pounded the German positions. Entire villages were blasted into rubble. Trees, steel girders and blocks of concrete were hurled into the air. Forests caught fire. Men were deafened by the guns and shook uncontrollably. They were blinded by the searchlights. Then, after thirty-five minutes of pounding, the Soviets attacked.

In his fortified bunker under the *Reichskanzlei* (the Reich Chancellery) Hitler still believed that he could win. He predicted the Russians would suffer their greatest defeat at the gates of Berlin. His maps told him so. They were still covered in little flags representing SS and Army units. Unfortunately, most of these little flags were just... little flags. The units they represented had long since ceased to exist or were so chronically under strength that they were next to useless. Anyone who pointed this out was dismissed. Even 'Fast Heinz' Guderian was relieved of his position as Chief of the General Staff on 28 March for suggesting that it was time to negotiate.

Hitler also sacked *Reichsführer-SS* Heinrich Himmler, the chicken farmer who had become Hitler's secret policeman and the architect of the Holocaust, from his position as Commander of Army Group Vistula. Although named Vistula, after the river that runs through Warsaw, this army group had not in fact seen the Vistula for some time. Himmler was replaced by a veteran military man, Colonel-General Gotthard Heinrici. At his disposal were the Third Panzer Army under General Hasso von Manteuffel, which occupied the northern part of the front. The centre was held by General Theodor Busse's Ninth Army, while the south was held by the depleted army group of Field Marshal Ferdinand Schörner. And there were 30 other divisions in the vicinity of Berlin he could call on.

Heinrici was an expert in defensive warfare. On the eve of the Soviet attack, he had pulled his front-line troops back so that Zhukov's massive bombardment fell on empty positions. The Ninth Army had dug in on the Seelow heights, blocking the main Küstrin-Berlin road. Zhukov's men attacking down the road suffered terrible casualties. They eventually overwhelmed the Seelow line with sheer weight of numbers, but then they came up against more German defences, reinforced by General Karl Weidling's 56th Panzer Division, and were halted. Stalin was furious. He ordered Koniev, who was making good progress to the south, to turn his forces on Berlin. And on 20 April, Marshal Konstantin Rokossovsky's 2nd Belorussian Front made a separate attack on von Manteuffel.

Busse's Ninth Army began to disintegrate and Zhukov got close enough to Berlin to start bombarding the city with long-range artillery. Koniev's forces were also approaching from the south and the German capital was caught in a pincer movement. To ensure that the Americans would not come and snatch their prize at the last moment, both Zhukov and Koniev sent forces on ahead to meet up with Simpson on the Elbe. They made contact at Torgau on 25 April to find Simpson sitting on the Elbe facing no one. Two days earlier, Wenck had been ordered back for the defence of Berlin. By 28 April, he had reached the suburb of Potsdam. There he met fierce Soviet resistance, but managed to extricate his force and tried to link up with remnants of the Ninth Army. He then headed westwards in the hope of surrendering to the Americans. Hitler cursed his treachery.

What propaganda minister Joseph Goebbels now called 'Fortress Berlin' was defended by 90,000 ill-equipped boys from the Hitler Youth and elderly men from the Volkssturm, the Home Guard. The two million Berliners still trying to go about their business in the ruined city joked, 'It will take the Russians exactly two hours and fifteen minutes to capture Berlin – two hours laughing their heads off and fifteen minutes to break down the barricades.'

Himmler, Goebbels and other top Nazis left the city. Hitler refused to go, pretending, for a while, that the situation could be reversed. He issued a barrage of orders to his non-existent armies. Then, as the Soviets drew the noose tighter and 15,000 Russian guns began to pound the city, Hitler dropped all pretence of running things and announced that he would commit suicide before the Russians arrived.

As Soviet troops entered the city, Hitler sacked his designated successor Göring, for trying take over while he was still alive, and Himmler, for trying to put out peace feelers to the British and Americans. Grand Admiral Karl Dönitz was named as his new successor. Then news came that Mussolini was dead. Captured while trying to escape into Austria in a German uniform, he was executed with his mistress, Claretta Petacci, on 28 April and their bodies were hung upside-down in the Piazza Loreto in Milan. On 29 April, Hitler married his mistress Eva Braun. The following day, he dictated his will and his final political testament. That afternoon, in their private quarters, Hitler and his wife of one day committed suicide. Their bodies were burnt in a shallow trench in the Chancellery Gardens.

Both Zhukov's and Koniev's troops were now in the city. But Koniev was ordered to halt so that Zhukov's men would have the honour of raising the Red Flag on the Reichstag. Zhukov's resulting popularity was seen as a threat by Stalin who banished him to obscurity in 1946.

There were still pockets of resistance and those remaining in Hitler's bunker tried to negotiate surrender terms. The Soviets would accept nothing but unconditional surrender – which General Weidling conceded on 2 May. The surrender of the German forces in north-western Europe was signed at Montgomery's headquarters on Lüneburg Heath on 4 May. Another surrender document, covering all the German forces, was signed with more ceremony at Eisenhower's headquarters at Reims. And at midnight on 8 May 1945, the war in Europe was officially over.

It is not known how many people perished in the Battle of Berlin. Estimates put the number of German dead as high as 200,000 and the Russian at 150,000. The Soviet troops then went on an orgy of drinking, looting and raping. It is thought that as many as 100,000 women were raped – often publicly – during that period in Berlin, an estimated two million in the whole of eastern Germany. The Russians often shot their victims afterwards. Other women committed suicide. In one district of Berlin alone, 215 female suicides were recorded in three weeks.

It had been agreed at the Yalta conference in the Crimea in February 1945 that Berlin would be divided between the four powers – Britain, France, the US and the USSR. By the time the Four Power Control Commission arrived to take control the orgy was over. Almost immediately, the Cold War started. The part of the city in the hands of the western powers became West Berlin, an enclave of democracy and free-market capitalism deep inside the region dominated by the Soviet Union which extended, by common consent, 100 miles to the west of the capital. This would become a bone of contention for the next fifty-five years, until the reunification of Germany in 1990.

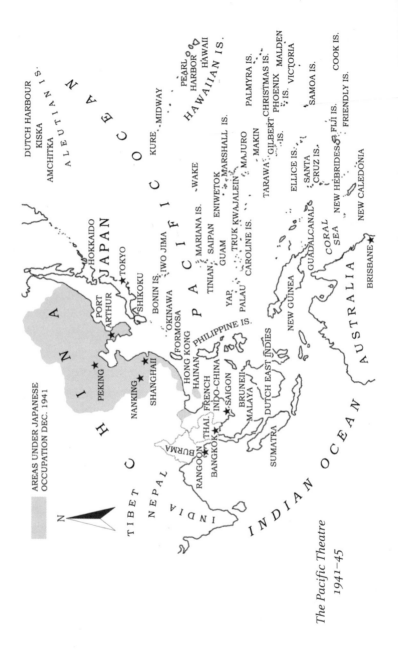

The Pacific Theatre
1941–45

6

VICTORY IN THE PACIFIC

DURING THE EXPANSION of their 'Co-Prosperity Sphere', the Japanese had occupied much of south-east Asia and numerous Pacific islands. While the British fought their way back across south-east Asia, the Americans turned their attention to the Pacific islands. The strategy was to hop island by island across the Pacific, until they were within striking distance of Japan itself. As they were pushed back closer and closer to their homeland, however, the Japanese put up an increasingly fanatical defence of their island conquests.

The defeat of the Japanese at the Battle of Midway called for an immediate American initiative. The plan was to start from the south, where their own men could be supplied easily from Australia and New Zealand. There would be two thrusts, one up through Port Moresby to clear northern New Guinea, the other would come though the Solomon Islands. Both would have as their objective the capture of Rabaul on the northern tip of New Britain, which was, by then, the principal Japanese naval base in the south-western Pacific.

The Japanese had landed on New Guinea at Salamaua, 200 miles due north from Port Moresby on the other side of the island. They were kept at bay by a successful guerrilla campaign in the mountains. The main invasion force heading for Port Moresby itself was turned back in the Battle of the Coral Sea. This allowed the Allies to reinforce the island with the Australian 6th and 7th Divisions who had returned from Europe. By June 1942, the Allies had

369,000 Australian and 38,000 US troops on the island, under over-all command of General Douglas MacArthur.

There were two areas considered crucial by both sides. One was Buna, which lay on the north side of the island at the head of the Kokoda trail, a track just wide enough for men to travel single file across the mountains to Port Moresby. The other was Milne Bay, which lay at the extreme eastern end of the island. Two Australian Brigades, under Brigadier Porter, were on their way down the Kokoda trails when, on the night of 21 July, 1,800 Japanese landed at Sanananda, just north of Buna. They met at Wairope on 23 July, where the Australians held them for four days, before falling back on Kokoda. The Japanese were soon reinforced in overwhelming number and forced the Australians back. But the Australians con-ducted a valiant rear-guard action, inflicting heavy casualties on the Japanese forces that now numbered 13,000. The Japanese had other problems. They were constantly harassed from the air. Their supply lines were over-extended and they could not handle the steamy jungle climate. But still they kept coming.

On 29 August, the Japanese received orders not to advance past Ioribaiwa, 30 miles from Port Moresby, which they reached on 17 September, while resources were concentrated on Guadalcanal. On 28 September, the Allies, under General Blamey, began a counter-offensive. By now, the Australian troops were experienced in jungle fighting. The Japanese put up no more than token resistance and, by 2 November, the Allies had retaken Kokoda. Throughout November, the Japanese continued retreating, but found them-selves in difficulties at Wairope, where the bridge had been destroyed. The Japanese commander General Horii was drowned while trying to ford the river and was replaced by General Adachi. The Australians took Gona, which was strongly fortified, after two attempts, then made straight for the Japanese base at Sanananda, while the US troops came under some criticism for their feeble attacks until their commander was replaced by Lieutenant-General Eichelberger. Buna fell on 2 January and Sanananda on 22 January 1943. By this point in the campaign the Japanese had lost 12,000 men, the Australians and the US 2,800 – though they experienced three times as many casualties from disease as from fighting.

Once Gona, Buna and Sanananda were in Allied hands, 5,400 Japanese fled westwards towards Salamaua, Lae and the Markham Valley. They hacked their way through the jungle and, on 30 January, attacked the airfield at Wau. This was held by the local Kanga force and the Japanese were repulsed with 1,200 casualties. Troops were sent from Rabaul to reinforce them but, on 3 March, 3,000 were drowned when their convoy was sunk in the Battle of the Bismark Sea.

The Japanese retreated towards Mubo and dug in. To break the deadlock, on the night of 20 June, 1,400 US troops made an amphibious landing at Nassau Bay and threatened Salamaua. General Adachi considered Salamaua so import to the defence of his position at Lae that he sent all but 2,000 of his 11,000 troops to defend it. This allowed the Australians to take Mubo on 17 July, then advance around the ridges behind Salamaua. Rather than be encircled, the Japanese withdrew and US troops entered Salamaua on 11 September. During this operation, the Japanese lost 2,722 killed and 7,578 wounded; the Australians 500 killed and 1,300 wounded; and the US 81 killed and 396 wounded.

The Allied forces then split in two. The Australian 7th Division pushed down the Markham Valley towards Madang on the coast, cutting off the Huon Peninsula. They reached Dumpu, some 50 miles from Madang in early October. Meanwhile the Australian 9th Division and the US forces hopped along the coast of the Huon Peninsula in a series of amphibious landings, though they were held up by fierce fighting along the Bumi River and a counter-attack outside Sattelberg, which they eventually took on 25 November.

General MacArthur then halted the advance to allow the Allies to build up supplies. This pause further weakened the Japanese who now had no air or naval support in the area. Six under-strength Japanese divisions had been left to fight 15 Allied divisions. On 2 January 1944, the US 32nd Infantry landed at Saidor, 100 miles ahead of the Australians advancing from Sattelberg. This cut off 12,000 Japanese on the Huon Peninsula. The Australian 7th Division forced their way over the mountains west of Saidor and took Bogadjim, Madang and Alexishafen on 24–26 August, forcing General Adachi's Eighteenth Army and his remaining 30,000 men back towards Wewak. The Allies left Adachi's men, along with 20,000 civilians, there without supplies while they made a series of further amphibious landings up the coast, taking their objectives with no significant opposition. Meanwhile Adachi tried to break out, but the US II Corps were ready for him. Some 8,800 Japanese died, while US troops suffered 450 killed and 2,500 wounded.

MacArthur decided that the tactic of leaving enclaves of Japanese troops in position without any supplies worked well and made a further series of amphibious assaults isolating enemy troop concentrations. However, someone would eventually have to take the enclaves on. The Australians advanced through the Toricelli mountains under terrible conditions, they took Wewak on 11 May at the cost of 442 killed and 1,141 wounded. Another 16,203 were hospitalised. The Japanese lost 9,000. But Adachi and his remaining 13,500 men only surrendered at the end of the war, which had long passed them by.

GUADALCANAL

At the same time as the offensive in New Guinea, the US made an advance in the Solomons, landing on a small, volcanic island that would give its name to one of the most famous engagements in Marine Corps history – Guadalcanal. The largest island of the

Solomon Islands – some 2,047 square miles in area – it was named by the Spaniard Álvaro de Mendaña de Neira when he visited it in 1568, but in 1942 it was a British protectorate. Its mountainous spine, the Kavo Range, rises to 8,028 feet at Mount Makarakomburu. Many short, rapid streams, including the Mataniko, Lunga, and Tenaru, tumble from the jungle-clad mountains to the coast, which is dotted with mangrove swamps.

On 3 May, Admiral Takagi had landed a small force unopposed at Tugali, immediately to the north of Guadalcanal across the Ironbottom Sound. On 1 July, a radio message from Martin Clemens, a young British district officer on Guadalcanal, reported that 1,000 Japanese troops had landed at Lunga, on the north of the island. By 5 July, they were clearing an area just inshore from their beachhead to build an airstrip. This made an attack on Guadalcanal a priority. It was to be under the strategic command of Vice-Admiral Robert Ghormley and the tactical commander would be Rear-Admiral Fletcher.

Operation *Watchtower* – or Operation 'Shoestring' as the invasion of Guadalcanal and Tugali became known among the men – was prepared hastily. Its commanders fell out and the troop morale was low. The under-strength 1st Marine Division commanded by Major-General Archer Vandergrift, a gritty Virginian of thirty-three years service, was assigned the task. With just a few weeks to go before the attack, half of Vandergrift's men were in Samoa or still at sea. They were green – few of them had been in uniform before the beginning of the year. However, time was of the essence. Once the airfield was up and running and the Japanese moved their Zeros and attack-bombers in, any amphibious invasion would be suicidal.

All Vandergrift knew about the island came from a handful of old photographs taken by missionaries, an ancient maritime chart and a short story by Jack London. However, he was getting good reports from Martin Clemens whose local scouts now said that there were between 2,000 and 10,000 Japanese troops on the island, with a smaller force on Tulagi and the twin islands to the north, Tanambugo and Gavutu.

As D-Day for Guadalcanal approached, some Australians were found who had lived on the Solomons. They were flown in to advise Vandergrift and helped him draw up sketch maps of the landing area. These would be out of range of the guns that now dominated the beaches at Lunga, east of the Ilu River. Unfortunately the Australians mis-identified the Tenaru River as the Ilu. Normally this stream was dry in August, but a sudden deluge had turned it into a raging torrent.

Things did not augur well. The unseasonable rains also soaked the men who were loading the transports. These were inadequate, only carrying enough ammunition for ten days' fighting and enough food and fuel for sixty days. The 19,000 men of the 1st Marines were to be put ashore by a huge invasion fleet of eighty-nine ships. Vandergrift had hoped that the Navy would give his Marines artillery and air support throughout the operation. But Admiral Fletcher was convinced that the invasion was going to be a failure. He did not want to risk his three precious aircraft carriers in the restricted waters of the Solomons and planned to pull out after two days.

Fortunately, the enemy were no better prepared. The Japanese Army commander Lieutenant-General Haruyoshi Hyakutake in Rabaul had not been told about the Imperial Navy's defeat at Midway. He believed the propaganda claims that numerous American ships had been sunk and their planes annihilated, so he dismissed the possibility of an American counter-attack. The Navy had not even told him about the airstrip they were building on Guadalcanal. So he concentrated all his forces on the invasion of New Guinea, imagining the seas around him were patrolled by the all-powerful Imperial fleet.

At 0613 hours on 7 August, the Japanese were still asleep on Tulagi and Guadalcanal when the bombardment began. Clemens had picked out key targets which were taken out by Dauntless dive-bombers and Avengers. On Tulagi, the Marines, supported by a battalion of Raiders and paratroopers, overran most of the island with hardly a shot being fired. Then they encountered fierce resistance. In the end, it took 6,000 Marines two days to defeat 1,500 Japanese soldiers. On 9 August Admiral Gunichi Mikawa, commander of the Japanese naval task force 600 miles to the north-west, received a despairing message. It read, 'The enemy force is overwhelming. We will defend our positions to the death, praying for everlasting victory.'

However, Gavutu and nearby Florida Island fell easily. But the Marines who stormed Tanambugo met withering fire. The island had to be bombarded by dive-bombers and destroyers before it fell the next day.

By comparison Guadalcanal was a walk-over – at first. At 0900, the Marines came swarming ashore on the palm-fringed beaches practically unopposed. The 2,200 Japanese on the island were largely construction workers who had fled when the first bomb fell. By nightfall, 17,000 Marines were ashore. The 10,000 men of main force had then moved on to Landing Beach Red in the middle of Guadalcanal's northern coast. Again they stormed 2,000 yards of sandy beach unopposed. The 5th Marine Regiment moved westwards towards the fishing village of Kukum, while the 1st Marine Regiment who followed them ashore advanced south-west towards the high ground that overlooked the airstrip. The heat and humidity were overpowering and they made slow progress through the jungle and over the switchback terrain. The rain came down in torrents and they had to wade chest deep through unexpectedly swollen rivers. But four miles inland they reached the grassy knoll above the airstrip. There they dug in for the night, alert for the enemy. But all they heard were the grunting of wild pigs, eerie bird calls, the scuttling of land craps and the whine of ubiquitous mosquitoes. It was all too easy.

Admiral Mikawa had also picked up a message from Guadalcanal. It said, 'American landing forces encountered, we are retreating into the jungle.' He passed this on to Admiral Nagumo, who ordered the fleet to make the recapture of Guadalcanal their immediate objective. And Mikawa was given permission to launch a night attack on the US fleet in the New Georgia Sound, the narrow body of water that runs the 300 miles north-west from Guadalcanal to Bougainville Island. Soon twenty-four Mitsubishi G4M 'Betty' torpedo bombers, escorted by twenty-seven Zeros were on their way. They were spotted by the fleet when they were still an hour's flight away and six Wildcats went up after them. They waited at 20,000 feet, shot several of the Betties down and harassed the rest enough to make their bombing ineffective. A number of Zeros were downed too and, of the fifty-one planes the Japanese sent, thirty were shot down.

After an uncomfortable night on the knoll, 1st Marines seized the airfield with hardly a shot being fired. They found it was much more than an airstrip. Some 17,000 Japanese naval pioneers had already built a road to the shore and dug deep bunkers that housed a radio station, warehousing facilities and power and oxygen plants. This was quickly named Henderson Field, after Major Loften Henderson, a Marine flying ace who had been killed at Midway.

The 5th Marine Division took Kukum unopposed and found that the Japanese defenders had fled in panic. They had abandoned their rifles, uniforms, mosquito nets and large amounts of mouldering rice. By 9 August, the Marines had set up a perimeter along the high ground and rivers surrounding Henderson Field and Kukum. With the airfield not yet operational, they were still being supplied across the beaches. Dozens of small craft shuttled back and forth bringing food, fuel, water, arms and ammunition quicker than it could be moved from the dumping grounds on the shore up to the airfield. These small craft were sitting ducks – or so the Japanese thought. Escorted by Zeros, another forty-five Betties attacked. But in the withering fire put up by the Navy, only one limped away, having caused little damage.

Despite these two easy victories, Fletcher felt that the risk to his three carriers was too great and withdrew them, along with their escort of sixteen destroyers, six cruisers and one battleship. But Admiral Mikawa was not discouraged by the failure of his fliers. He steamed southwards towards the New Georgia Sound, aiming to attack the transport fleet bringing in the Marines' supplies. Luck was on his side. US daylight reconnaissance planes did not spot him and, when he was sighted at last, the report took eight hours to reach Admiral Richmond Turner at his headquarters in Australia. He was furious when he discovered that Fletcher had withdrawn leaving the Marines undefended and ordered Rear-Admiral Sir Victor Crutchley, commanding the Australian naval squadron, to block the western approaches of the Sound, while another naval force under Rear-Admiral Scott would block the eastern approaches.

However, the Japanese spotted Crutchley's squadron of six heavy cruisers and four destroyers in the narrow straits between Guadalcanal and Savo Island and attacked. Within half-an-hour the American cruisers *Astoria* and *Quincy*, along with the Australian cruiser HMAS *Canberra*, were blazing hulks, bound for the bottom of Ironbottom Sound. The USS *Vincennes* hit the Japanese cruiser *Kinugasa*, but followed the others to the bottom. Another cruiser was badly damaged, 1,270 men were killed, drowned or devoured by sharks, and over 700 wounded were rescued. In memory of this action, the next US Navy heavy cruiser to be commissioned was named *Canberra*, the only American warship ever to be named after a foreign city.

Turner had to withdraw the undefended transports and supply vessels to New Caledonia. Next morning, when the Marines from Henderson Field arrived at the beach all they could see was blue sea, the supply ships and warships gone. They were now on their own.

They gathered up what supplies remained on the beach, then set about completing the airstrip in the hope that they might get some fighter support. To hold the airfield, which would become their lifeline, they had to maintain a perimeter that was 3,500 yards deep at its widest and 7,500 yards long. It ran inland from the beach between Kukum and the village of Tenaru to a tortuous ridge of hills along the southern flank. The Matanikau river and Kukum hills formed the western flank, the Tenaru River the eastern. Defences were dug and positions manned, while Vandergrift massed his artillery and tanks in the middle of the enclave so that he could bring down concentrated fire on any point around it. The airfield was defended by 90mm ack-ack guns dug in to the north-west of the airstrip and 75mm guns on half-tracks which were dug into the north. Positions were also prepared for the half-tracks on the beaches, so they could defend against any sea-borne landing. This was where Vandergrift expected the Japanese to attack, so extensive trenchworks were dug along the top of the beaches with other further defensive lines inland.

The first air attack came on 9 August. Anti-personnel bombs that burst into a thousand flying steel slivers were dropped, along with 500-pound bombs. Next came a naval bombardment from Admiral Mikawa's cruisers and destroyers sailing up and down the coast in what the Marines came to call the 'Tokyo Express'. Three days later came the gruesome curtain-raiser to the land battle, when a Japanese force landed at night near Matanikau. On 12 August, they ambushed a 26-man patrol, cutting the Marines down with hidden machine-guns. The three survivors who made it back told their fellow Marines that the wounded had been hacked to death with sabres. From then on, the Marines decided that they would be every bit as brutal.

On 13 August General Hyakutake received orders from Imperial General Headquarters in Tokyo to retake Guadalcanal without delay. He sent Colonel Kiyono Ichiki with 2,000 crack troops who had been trained for the invasion of Midway. On 16 August, Colonel Ichiki and the 915 men in his preliminary force set sail on six destroyers. The rest would follow later in slower craft. The main advance force landed at Taivu Point, 22 miles east of the Tenaru River, with a diversionary force going ashore to the west. Vandergrift had every reason to know about the landings. At night, in the South Seas, the wash of boats becomes luminous. This had been spotted by a sharp-eyed sentry. Clemens and ten of his scouts had put themselves at Vandergrift's service and told him of the arrival of the Japanese. US Naval Intelligence confirmed the reports. On top of that, a message bound for the original Japanese force hiding to the west of Kukum fell within the perimeter. It read, 'Help is on the way. Banzai.'

The Imperial High Command believed that the battle for Guadalcanal would force the US to return the remains of its Pacific fleet to the area. Eager for revenge for Midway, Yamamoto mustered three aircraft carriers, three battleships, five cruisers, eight destroyers and a sea-plane carrier and sent them to the Solomons. Admiral Mikawa already had four cruisers and five destroyers there, supported by 100 warplanes flying from Rabaul.

Yamamoto was right in his assessment of the situation. When the Allies saw where his fleet was heading, Ghormley ordered Fletcher to guard the approaches to the Solomons and sent the carrier *Hornet* and its escort of destroyers and cruisers as reinforcements.

Unsure of the enemy's deployment, Vandergrift sent three companies of Marines to attack the Japanese defences along the

Matanikau. At the same time he sent a patrol in force to the east. The Matanikau attack was successful and the Marines mounted an amphibious assault further to the west at Kukumba. This came under fire from the Tokyo Express and a Japanese submarine. But the Marines got ashore and managed to drive the Japanese defenders into the jungle.

A patrol from Colonel Ichiki's force to the east was surprised by the Marine patrol and a map was taken from them showing that Ichiki knew the weakest point along the Tenaru defence line. Vandergrift strengthened it immediately. Shortly after 0010 on 21 August, 500 of Ichiki's men rushed the Americans guarding the sand spit at the mouth of the Tenaru River. Mortars rained down on the defenders. The attackers yelled 'Banzai!' and sprayed the Marines' positions with automatic and machine-gun fire. But the Marines kept their cool and held their fire – then opened up with everything they had. It was a blood-bath. At 0500 Ichiki sent a second wave of 400 men. This time they were cut down before they even reached the American wire. Ichiki's elite force was wiped out without even making so much as a dent in the American line. In shame at his utter failure, Ichiki burnt the regimental colours and shot himself. But some of his men fought on. Wounded Japanese soldiers tried to kill the American medics who were going to help them. Vandergrift sent in light tanks to make sure that there was no further resistance.

But Yamamoto was not to be thwarted. Operation Ka to recapture the airfield on Guadalcanal would continue. The remaining 1,500 men of Ichiki's main force were still on their way. Yamamoto reinforced them with another 1,000 men sent on fast transports. Meanwhile, he was determined to get the better of Fletcher. On 22 August, he sent twelve submarines to set up a screen south-east of Guadalcanal, while his main force was concentrated 200 miles north of the southern-most of the Solomons. The light carrier *Ryujo* was then sent out as bait. Yamamoto's plan was to destroy the American carriers while their planes were attacking the *Ryujo*. Then his massive battleships could sail though Ironbottom Sound and annihilate the Marines, while his troops retook the airfield.

Fletcher took the bait and torpedo planes and dive-bombers from the *Enterprise* and the *Saratoga* obliterated the *Ryujo* completely. Yamamoto had counted on Fletcher keeping his three carriers together for the attack, but he had already sent the *Wasp* to refuel. He was also ready for Yamamoto's counter-attack. The *Enterprise* had kept back fifty-three Wildcats which were circling in the clouds as the carrier waited for its attack planes to return from the *Ryujo*.

Then thirty Val dive-bombers came screaming from the sky. The battleship *North Carolina* fired a canopy over the *Enterprise*, but still three dive-bombers found their mark. The *Enterprise* sped on at 27 knots, ablaze. An hour later she was able to swing into the wind to pick up the returning planes, but after that she was out of action for two months. However, in the Battle of the Eastern Solomons, the Japanese lost daytime control of the sea, along with one more carrier and numerous planes, although some of the surviving Japanese pilots claimed that two US aircraft carriers had been sunk. In Rabaul, Admiral Mikawa gave the okay for the invasion convoy to continue to Guadalcanal.

In preparation for the invasion, Admiral Tanaka, commander of the invasion fleet, sent five destroyers into New Georgia Sound to bombard Henderson Field. This left the convoy undefended. On the night of 24 August, with the transport just over 100 miles from Guadalcanal, a formation of Dauntlesses caught up with them. The Japanese were so confident that the US carrier force had been dealt a serious blow in the Battle of the Eastern Solomons that they did not even have their guns loaded. The American dive-bombers hit Tanaka's flagship, the cruiser *Jintsu*, and a large troopship laden with men. They then called up Flying Fortresses which finished off the burning transport and a destroyer that was trying to rescue the men. The other ships turned northwards and fled out of range.

Yamamoto then decided to change tactics. Instead of landing a large invasion force, he would build up slowly, landing men on the island by stealth at night. Next ashore was to be the crack Kawaguchi Brigade. But their advance units were so eager to get into the fray that they left Borneo on destroyers at night, guaranteeing that they would be in New Georgia Sound in broad daylight. Marine dive-bomber pilots spotted them and soon two of the four destroyers had been torn apart with explosions and a third was on fire.

General Kawaguchi and his main force were on shore in the Shortland Islands south of Bougainville with Yamamoto. A row broke out. Kawaguchi refused to have his men transported by destroyers, insisting that they be landed by barge. A compromise was reached. Eight destroyers would carry the bulk of the force. The rest would follow up in the limited number of barges available. Some 3,500 men were landed from destroyers at Taivu Point on Guadalcanal on the night of 31 August. Several nights later, the remaining 1,000 men turned up in their barges, but a heavy swell prevented them from landing. At first light, they were caught out to sea by the Marine aircraft now flying from Henderson Field and decimated.

The Imperial General Headquarters was now getting impatient with the loss of life the recapture of Guadalcanal was costing. They sacked Admiral Tanaka, though he had frequently warned against the use of barges, and made the taking of Henderson Field their top priority. The already over-stretched General Hyakutake was ordered to go on the defensive in New Guinea and concentrate his forces against Guadalcanal. This halted the Japanese forces within thirty miles of Port Moresby and allowed the Allies to regroup for their counter-offensive which eventually pushed the Japanese back across the island. The entire resources of the Southeast Area Air

Force would also be put at Hyakutake's disposal and he would be supported by the powerful 8th Fleet.

Henderson Field was being bombed daily and the Japanese were now deploying fifty-eight more planes against it. However, Henderson now had its Cactus Air Force – as they called themselves – who quickly shattered the myth of the invincibility of the Zero with their new Wildcats. With its superior firepower, the formation flying of the US pilots outweighed the greater speed and manoeuvrability of the Zeros. Spotters along the coast gave Henderson an early warning of the approach of enemy aircraft. This meant that the stubby, radial-engined Wildcats could get airborne and attack the incoming bandits out of the sun. Enemy planes were being shot down at a rate of between six and eight for every Wildcat lost. However, they could do nothing to counter the nightly Tokyo Express and the US Navy still did not dare to enter the New Georgia Sound.

The situation at Henderson Field grew dire. The Japanese forces around them were building up. The Tokyo Express meant that the Marines got little sleep at night and were subjected to surprise attacks during the day. They were also suffering from dysentry, jungle rot, malaria and the effects of eating little but stodgy rice. But things picked up when the First World War fighter ace Brigadier-General Roy Geiger flew in to take command of the Cactus Air Force and a battalion of Navy Seabees, expert in airfield construction, arrived to make improvements to Henderson Field.

Vandergrift was short of reinforcements and called in the Raiders and paratroopers from Tulagi. They were ferried across the Ironbottom Sound at night by the light destroyers Gregory and Little. But after they had delivered their precious cargo, the ships were mistakenly illuminated by an American flare and shot to pieces by the Japanese Navy.

With the airfield now extended, Skytrain air transports brought in machine-guns and took out the wounded. This became a regular service and did much to boost the Marines' morale. Then two transports got through with reinforcements, bringing the garrison up to 23,000.

On 12 September, the Japanese began a massive air and sea bombardment to cover the advance of Kawaguchi's 6,200 men in a three-pronged attack. However, he had overestimated how quickly his men could move through the slimy swamps and tangled jungle that characterised the terrain. Soon they were strung out and disorganised.

Forewarned, Vandergrift reinforced the steep ridges the Japanese were aiming for and brought his headquarters up. But the bombardment left Henderson Field with only 11 Wildcats airworthy. Despite protests, Admiral Nimitz ordered Fletcher to sent 24 of his fighters from the *Saratoga* to reinforce Henderson. This was done reluctantly as Ghormley now considered the position of the Marines on Guadalcanal untenable. As there was no way that the US Navy could risk taking on the Japanese Imperial Navy in the confined waters of the Solomons, he ordered the fleet to stay away.

On the night of 12 September, the American defenders on the ridge above the Tenaru River saw a rocket. Next they heard the crackling of automatic fire and the cry of 'Banzai' as the Japanese came charging up the hill. In some places they forced the Marines back. In others they broke through. But Kawaguchi had misjudged the jungle. He had sent his first wave in, while the second were still clawing their way through the undergrowth. Vandergrift then concentrated artillery fire on the places the Japanese had broken through, causing any who had survived the bombardment to flee back into the forest. A counter-attack by the Marines at dawn retook what they were now calling Bloody Ridge. As it seemed certain that the Japanese would attack there again, they rolled out barbed wire and cleared the slopes so that, next time, the Japanese would have to charge across a hundred yards of open ground raked by machine-gun fire.

Back at Henderson Field, three air raids had depleted the complement of Wildcats again, but sixty more planes, including six Avenger torpedo bombers, arrived from the *Wasp* and the *Hornet*. At the same time, 140 new planes arrived at the Japanese bases on Bougainville and at Rabaul.

Henderson was given a day's rest, while General Hyakutake waited for the news that Kawaguchi had taken the ridge. His planes would, instead, be sent to bomb Tasimboko, to Kawaguchi's rear, where there had been an erroneous report of an American landing. Mistaking them for Americans, the Japanese planes made a devastating raid on Kawaguchi's rear echelon troops.

In the jungle below Bloody Ridge, Kawaguchi tried to muster his remaining 2,500 troops into an organised assault. That night, while Henderson Field was under bombardment from seven destroyers, he sent 2,000 men in six waves up the slope against just 400 Raiders under 'Red Mike' Edson. Some made it across the newly-prepared killing grounds and threw themselves into hand-to-hand fighting. The American artillery decimated the oncoming Japanese. Others were knifed to death as they jumped into American foxholes. The Japanese also called their naval gunfire from the Tokyo Express, though soldiers from both sides were in the close combat. The American line bent, but held. The surviving Japanese were put to flight by P-400s swooping in low with cannon firing, and chased away by five Marine tanks. The Raiders had suffered 224 casualties, the paratroopers 212, and the Marines who had been sent in as reinforcements 263. The Japanese dead were uncountable and Kawaguchi's men carried away 400 wounded on litters through the jungle towards Matanikau. Meanwhile, six more transports got through carrying 4,000 more Marines. They had been escorted by a substantial force including the *North Carolina*, the *Hornet* and the *Wasp*. These big ships were quickly withdrawn under cover of darkness on the night of 14 September. The following day, the *Wasp* was fatally hit by torpedoes and a battleship and destroyer were damaged, but Yamamoto could not follow up and finish off the US fleet because his ships had been recalled for refuelling, only for the carriers to be ordered back to home waters. Instead, he continued his tactic of building up the ground forces on the island, sending in the battle-hardened Nagoya Division and the crack Sendai Division.

On 18 September, in a lightly defended convoy, Admiral Kelly Turner landed more Marines inside the perimeter at Guadalcanal. He also brought 155mm 'Long Toms' and 5-inch naval guns. Also on their way were USAAF Lightnings, diverted from the Anglo-American landings in North Africa, which had the range to attack the Tokyo Express when the ships stayed away from the island during the day.

Although the conditions at Henderson Field were by no means luxurious, the Japanese out in the jungle were in a pitiful state – disease-ridden and starving, with no prospect of evacuation. Vandergrift decided to increase their woes. On 27 September, he sent a three-pronged attack against their strongpoint at Matanikau. The Marines would rush across the sand spit at the mouth of the river, while the Raiders were to cross the river a mile inland, wheel around to the Japanese rear and meet up with another Marine battalion that was to land behind them. But the Marines charging across the spit were driven back, the Raiders were pinned down and the landing force found that they had walked into a trap. Vandergrift cancelled the offensive.

The monsoon was on its way and Admiral Nimitz landed amid heavy rain to reassure the defenders that he would support them with the 'maximum of our resources'. The embattled defenders were in need of reassurance. The ground troops arrayed against them seemed to increase every day. The Marines were, however, winning the war in the air. The next two air raids on Henderson Field cost the Japanese six fighters and twenty-nine bombers, without destroying a single American plane. By the end of September, the Cactus Air Force had lost thirty-two planes; the Japanese more than 200.

Determined to make sure that the Japanese forces did not fail again, Hyakutake left Rabaul for Guadalcanal on 9 October to direct operations personally. He estimated Vandergrift's strength at just 10,000 – it was over 19,000 – and believed that his Sendai Division alone could vanquish them. Nevertheless, he took the precaution of bringing the 38th Division in from Borneo and established his Seventeenth Army headquarters on Guadalcanal. The plan was to attack in force from Matanikau on 17 October. The Sendai commander Lieutenant-General Masoa Maruyama issued an order of the day setting the tone for the engagement. It said, 'The occupying of Guadalcanal island is under the observation of the whole world. Do not expect to return, not even one man, if the occupation is not successful.'

At the same time, Vandergrift decided to launch another attack, this time in more force, against Matanikau. On 7 October they met head-on in the jungle. Furious fighting ensued. By nightfall both sides were pinned down as the monsoon started. The following day, the Marines caught a battalion of Sendai resting in a ravine and called artillery fire down on them, killing them all. Around 1,000 Japanese died at the cost of sixty-five Americans, and the unbeatable Sendai were then forced to retreat.

As the Marines had held their position on Guadalcanal for two months now, their prospects were now viewed with more optimism. Even the Army chipped in. The 164th Infantry Regiment sent 3,000 men on two transports from New Caledonia and the USAAF sent twenty Wildcats. And Ghormley sent all the warships available to challenge the Japanese's dominance in the New Georgia Sound. The landing on Guadalcanal had started out as a small-scale engagement. Now it was a major battle.

The Japanese were reinforcing too. Hyakutake brought in 1,000 more men from the Sendai Division on six destroyers, and another battalion on sea-plane carriers. The convoy was guarded by a huge force including three cruisers, two destroyers and numerous aircraft. Artillery, stock piles of medical supplies and ammunition and sixteen tanks were landed. The ships, under Admiral Aritomo Goto, were then to bombard Henderson Field, putting it out of action. That night, 11 October, they were to run straight into Rear-Admiral Norman Scott's convoy coming in from New Caledonia, which had four cruisers and five destroyers protecting the troopships. Goto felt safe, believing that the Americans would not attack after nightfall. But Scott's convoy had radar so he could see where the Japanese ships were and his crews had been extensively trained in night fighting.

Scott's fleet almost gave their position away when a spotter plane caught fire on take-off, but Japanese look-outs mistook the conflagration for a signal fire on the landing beaches. At 5,000 yards, the American ships opened fire. The first salvoes hit the cruiser *Aoba*, Goto's flagship, setting it on fire and fatally wounding the Admiral. To take stock in the midst of the confusion, Scott ordered a ceasefire. Not all the gun crews heard the order and before the guns fell silent the cruiser *Surutake* was also on fire. Searchlights also revealed that the destroyer *Fuvuki* had been blown to pieces. On the US side, the destroyer *Duncan* had been caught in the crossfire and sank, and the cruiser *Boise* was badly damaged. The Battle of the Cape of Esperance, as the engagement became known, ended Japanese domination of the waters around Guadalcanal for the time being. This point was rubbed home when the Japanese destroyers that landed the Sendai reinforcements were attacked by dive-bombers from Henderson Field and annihilated.

Progress was being made by the US forces, but painfully slowly. As the 3,000 American infantry men Scott had brought set foot on Guadalcanal there was a massive Japanese air raid. Japanese ground troops had attacked and killed the coastal spotters, so Henderson Field had no warning. The Wildcats could not climb fast enough to intercept the attackers. Planes on the ground were badly damaged and fuel stores set ablaze. The Japanese had now brought in artillery that could out-range the American guns and an artillery barrage hit the runways, putting the airfield out of action for the first time.

Another 10,000 Japanese troops were to be landed on the night of 14 October, ready for an all-out offensive on the 20 October. They were supported by Yamamoto's massive fleet which comprised five aircraft carriers, five battleships, fourteen cruisers and forty-four destroyers. The battleships bombarded Henderson Field for an hour-and-a-half, leaving the men there speechless and barely sane. Forty-one had been killed, many of them pilots. All thirty-four Dauntlesses had been badly damaged, along with nearly all the Avengers and sixteen out of the forty Wildcats. And both runways were pitted with huge craters.

The Seabees got to work on the runways and, using fuel siphoned from two wrecked Flying Fortresses and a slash captured from the Japanese, the remaining twenty-four Wildcats got airborne to fend off further air raids. Ten Zeros and nine bombers were shot down at the cost of one Army pilot and two Marines. Then, working around the clock, the mechanics managed to patch up the P-400s, Aerocobras, Dauntlesses and more Wildcats which went out to strafe and bomb the incoming troopships. Fuel was flown in and, towards the end of the day, a formation of Flying Fortresses from the New Hebrides joined in the attack. Four motor torpedo boats began harassing the convoy by night, while the Cactus Air Force threw everything they had at them by day. Two of the transports were wrecked. Another three turned back. In all Hyakutake only got 4,500 of the reinforcements for his big offensive.

Yamamoto's fleet continued pounding Henderson. On the night of 15 October, hundreds of 8-inch shells finished off the fuel stocks and smashed the planes until there were only twenty-seven left. The converted destroyer *McFarland* arrived with 40,000 gallons of aviation fluid. It was unloading as fourteen Japanese dive-bombers came screaming from the sky. At that moment a squadron of Wildcats sent in from the New Hebrides, at the limit of the range, arrived. With his fuel tanks almost empty, the squadron's leader, Lieutenant-Colonel Harold Bauer, shot down four Vals in one swoop and the McFarland finished unloading.

Hyakutake now prepared his attack with 22,000 men. General Maruyama was to take 7,000 men on the same route as Kawaguchi's ill-fated assault. But this time, a road would be hacked through the jungle. He would then break through the perimeter and take the airfield. Meanwhile, the remaining 15,000 men would stage diversionary attacks to prevent the Americans reinforcing Bloody Ridge. And the defenders would be harassed constantly by land-based planes flying from the airfields at Rabaul, on the nearby island of Buka, and from the Buin airfield on Bougainville. They would be joined by planes from Yamamoto's carriers and the fleet would be on hand if any further bombardment were needed. The Japanese strength was so overwhelming, Hyakutake believed that the whole thing would be over in two days.

However, the jungle came to the defenders' rescue again. On 22 October, after five days marching, General Maruyama's Sendai had only covered twenty-nine of the thirty-five miles to their starting point. Nevertheless Maruyama reported that he would be ready to start the battle on 23 October. That day, the Japanese sent in a formation of bombers. The Wildcats took off to greet them and take on their escorts. In the attack twenty Zeros were downed for the loss of not one single Wildcat. None of the bombers got through.

On the ground, things were going even more badly for the Japanese. Maruyama was in position, but Kawaguchi, who was supposed to attack on his right, was not yet in place. Kawaguchi was relieved of his command and the attack was rescheduled for the 24 October. However, news of the delay did not get through to Major-General Sumoyoshi. At dusk he attacked across the mouth of the Matanikau River. His men and his tanks were blown to pieces by the American artillery.

Vandergrift was away at the time, seeing the new commander in the South Pacific Admiral Halsey. Intelligence reported that an all-out attack was expected on the night of 24 October. Halsey sent in the *Enterprise* and the *Hornet* to take on Yamamoto's fleet while the battle raged on land. In Vandergrift's absence, Geiger was in command. Sumoyoshi's premature assault on the Matanikau River convinced Geiger that the attack would come from the west and he switched a battalion from the southern defence line to reinforce his right flank.

Maruyama's attack was due to begin at 1700. But at that moment the monsoon came. The jungle tracks turned into seas of mud. His units lost touch with each other and communications broke down. He postponed the attack for two hours. At 1900, the rain had stopped, but Kawaguchi's successor, Colonel Shoji, had still not managed to get his men up to the start line to the right. Nevertheless, Maruyama sent his left wing in. The jungle was so dense that it was impossible to advance with any degree of stealth. An American outpost warned their comrades on the ridge that the attack was coming. The Marines held their fire until the Japanese reached the wire. The first wave was cut down to a man. The second wave tried to scramble over the corpses of their fallen comrades, but even the Sendai could not take this kind of slaughter and a few survivors fled back into the forest. At one point, however, the Japanese did make it through. Led by Colonel Furumiya with his sword held high, they rushed the American machine-guns, killing a number of Marines. The line simply closed behind them and, when they were all dead, the positions were remanned.

At 2130, the Sendai tried again. This time Shoji had his men in place on the right wing and they were determined to cleanse the dishonour of being late for the battle with their ferocity. At a number of places they managed to penetrate the Marines' line. Thinking that his men had got through, Maruyama radioed that he had taken the airfield and Hyakutake sent a message to Admiral Mikawa asking him to land the remaining men he had on three destroyers at Koli Point to the east of Tenaru to finish off the Americans once and for all.

All this was very premature. The Marines' line had been penetrated, but not broken. Soldiers were sent up to fill the gaps and the Japanese troops who had got through were hunted down and killed. At 2330, a fourth wave of Sendai warriors were sent in. Instead of finding the line broken, they were met with intense fire. When the slaughter abated, a few survivors slunk away into the dark depths of the jungle. At dawn, the Americans saw the terrible carnage around their positions. At one place, an anti-tank gun had hit an entire Japanese column point-blank, blasting them to pieces. Shamefacedly, Maruyama radioed Hyakutake, 'Am having trouble capturing the airfield.'

But it was too late to stop the landings. As the destroyers carrying the troops approached Koli Point, they met five-inch shells from the Marines' guns and were forced to turn away. Once the morning sun had dried out the airfield, a wing of Dauntlesses took off to attack the convoy. They set one Japanese cruiser on fire, sent four destroyers fleeing for the open seas and forced another on to shore. Twenty-six Japanese planes were shot down over Henderson

Field and Admiral Nagumo, fearing another Midway, turned tail, taking with him the carrier Junyo whose planes were to have landed at Henderson, once it was safely in Japanese hands.

That night Maruyama tried to redeem his honour with one more assault. This time he got all his men in place and in communication. Then they came screaming out of the jungle. Hundreds were slaughtered, but as the battle developed the attack swung towards Hill 67 and the sea. The Sendai charged headlong at the machine-gun nests. Those who got through hacked at the Marines with knives and swords. Such was the ferocity of the attack that some of the machine-gun positions were overrun. But the Marines counter-attacked, forcing the Sendai back, leaving some 2,500 of their dead on the ground. Maruyama ordered a full retreat. The land battle had been won. There now followed a battle at sea.

While the Sendai were being decimated in the jungle and America was winning its first land battle of the war, the *Enterprise* and the *Hornet* were steaming with their escort ships towards Guadalcanal from the Santa Cruz Islands in the south-east, under the command of Admiral Thomas Kincaid. The huge Japanese fleet, with its four carriers, turned south looking for them. On 26 October, a reconnaissance plane from the *Shokaku* found the US ships 200 miles to the east. Admiral Nagumo sent bombers from all three of his carriers, while the Junyo, a 100 miles to his rear, launched a separate attack. At about the same time, an American spotter plane found Nagumo's fleet.

Shortly before 0700, a patrol of Dauntlesses came hurtling down through the canopy of Zeros onto Nagumo's carriers. They quickly made smoke and zigzagged, but two bombs hit the *Zuiho*, putting her out of action.

The Japanese pilots could not find the *Enterprise*, which was hidden under cloud. But the *Hornet* was caught out in the open by fifteen dive-bombers and twelve torpedo planes. A Japanese pilot smashed his plane through the flight deck in a kamikaze attack, starting a huge fire. Two torpedoes then struck home, followed by three bombs. Although the whole ship threatened to blow up, the fires were soon brought under control.

Meanwhile, the *Hornet's* dive-bombers had located the *Shokaku*. Diving through heavy flak, they put 1,000-pound bombs through her deck, setting the whole ship on fire. Unfortunately, the Avenger torpedo bombers did not find her to finish her off. Instead they disabled the cruiser *Chikuma*. The *Shokaku* also headed out of the battle, but in nine months she was at sea again.

While she was turning to avoid torpedoes from a Japanese submarine, the *Enterprise* was hit on the flight deck by two bombs. She evaded more torpedoes dropped by Kates and survived in good enough shape to take on her returning aircraft. The battleship *South Dakota* downed 26 of the Japanese dive-bombers that attacked her, taking scarcely a scratch herself. The *Hornet*, which was being towed by the cruiser *Northampton*, was hit again by Japanese bombers and Admiral Kincaid ordered that she be scuttled. American destroyers tried to torpedo her but, of the eight Mark 15 torpedoes launched by the USS *Mustin*, only three ran straight. And they failed to do the job. So, while American float planes illuminated the target with flares, the destroyer hit her with 430 five-inch shells. Still she would not go down and had to be abandoned. Eventually the Japanese sunk her with four 'Long Lance' torpedoes.

As Kincaid sped away from the advancing Japanese fleet, the Japanese announced that they had won the Battle of the Santa Cruz Islands. But Nagumo was replaced. He had won victory at too high a price. The *Shokaku* and the *Zuiho* had been put out of action and more than 100 planes, along with their highly trained crews, had been lost. On top of that, the *Hiyo* had damaged its engines during the engagement. But at least the defenders on Guadalcanal did not have to worry about being attacked by carrier-borne planes for some time.

Since late October, things had been stalemated on the island. But soon both sides began to reinforce again. It had come to the attention of President Roosevelt how vital the battle for Guadalcanal was becoming. Cactus Air Force was now down to 29 planes and he ordered all available aircraft, ships and weapons to be rushed there. Meanwhile, Japanese Imperial Headquarters planned yet another all-out offensive from Matanikau, accompanied, once again, with a massive naval bombardment.

On 1 November, Vandergrift did his best to upset these plans by sending 5,000 Marines to stop the Japanese consolidating their position to the west of Matanikau and to silence their long-range artillery there. Fierce fighting ensued, but the Japanese were eventually pushed back. Then two battalions of 155mm 'Long Tom' guns were delivered to the defenders giving the US artillery the ascendancy again.

On 3 November, Nagumo's successor, Admiral Tameichi Hari, transported more troops to reinforce the Sendai survivors who were quietly starving at Koli Point and renewed the Tokyo Express with three cruisers and eight destroyers. By 10 November, the Japanese had built up their forces on the island to 30,000, against Vandergrift's 20,000 Marines and 3,000 soldiers. Another 6,000 were on their way. But before they were to attack again, the Japanese wanted overwhelming superiority. On the night of 12 November, they planned to land 28,000 more troops and add two aircraft carriers, four battleships, eleven cruisers and forty-nine destroyers to the Tokyo Express. These were spotted by Australian coastal watchers on occupied Bougainville and Halsey decided that he would have another crack at the Imperial fleet. In Noumea harbour on New Caledonia, hundreds of engineers were working day and night on the Enterprise. The Imperial Fleet was expected to arrive at Guadalcanal on 12 November. On 11 October, the *Enterprise* sailed from Noumea with repair teams still working on board. She was escorted by the battleship *Washington* and the damaged *South Dakota*, two cruisers and eight destroyers.

Under cover of a rainstorm, the Japanese fleet slipped into New Georgia Sound. American reinforcements were landing when eight Zeros and twenty-four Betties flying from the fleet attacked. But the guns of the American naval escort downed three Zeros and twenty-three Betties in just a couple of minutes.

In the forthcoming battle, the planes on Henderson Field were a vital asset, so Admiral Turner sent two heavy cruisers, the *Portland* and the *San Francisco*, three light cruisers, the *Atlanta*, the *Helena* and the *Junea*, and eight destroyers to attack the Japanese fleet in an attempt to stop it bombarding Henderson Field. Admiral Hari had not anticipated this. When his fleet arrived off Savo Island, its decks were stacked with high-explosive shells to bombard Henderson. When the look-outs spotted the American ships, there was consternation. One shell hitting the ammunition would blow the ship out of the war. Quickly the high-explosive shells were taken below, the gunners reloading with armour-piercing shells to take on the American ships.

The American ships, under Rear-Admiral Callaghan, advanced in a single line because his ships had not trained together as a squadron. Even this simple manoeuvre required more co-operation between the ships than they could manage and the situation was not helped by the fact that Callaghan's flagship *San Francisco* did not have radar. At 0140, in the darkness, the destroyer *Cushing* almost ran into the two Japanese destroyers, *Murasame* and *Yudachi*. Only five minutes later did Callaghan give the order to open fire. Almost immediately, the Cushing was blown to bits by the battleship *Hiei*. A point-blank blast from the *Laffey* set the *Hiei* on fire, but the counter-blast blew the *Laffey* out of the water. The

Portland and the *San Francisco* hit the *Hiei* and damaged two Japanese destroyers, the *Yudachi* and the *Akatsuki*. But when Callaghan found that the *San Francisco*'s guns had also crippled the *Atlanta* he gave the order to cease fire. This allowed the 14-inch guns of the battleship *Kirishima* to fire a massive broadside into the *San Francisco*, killing Callaghan and his staff. The crippled *Atlanta* was also caught in the Japanese searchlights and blasted, killing Admiral Scott. In the maelstrom, the Americans lost five destroyers and two light cruisers, and the *San Francisco* was badly damaged. Only one Japanese ship, the *Akatsuki*, sank, though the *Yudachi* had to be abandoned. Nevertheless, the Japanese abandoned their plans to bombard Henderson and withdrew, leaving the damaged *Hiei*. The next day, it was bombed and sunk.

But Henderson was not to be spared for long. The next night, Admiral Mikawa's flagship, the *Chokai*, three heavy cruisers, the *Kinugasa*, the *Maya* and the *Suzuya*, and six destroyers arrived off Savo Island at midnight. The *Enterprise* was still too far away to be of any help. Kincaid sent the greater part of his escort – the battleships *South Dakota* and *Washington* and four destroyers – but they would not arrive before dawn. Mikawa's ships bombarded Henderson at will on the night of the 13 November, destroying eighteen planes. But next morning the Cactus Air Force would have its revenge. Its planes torpedoed the *Kinugasa* and the destroyer *Izuso*. Then planes from the *Enterprise* turned up to finish off the *Kinugasa*. Soon after noon, eleven Japanese troop transports were spotted by US planes some 150 miles from Guadalcanal. By nightfall, there were only four left.

On the night of 14 November, the Japanese attempted to bombard Henderson Field again. A squadron under Vice-Admiral Kondo – the heavy cruisers *Atago*, *Kirishima* and *Takao*, the light cruiser *Nagara* and three destroyers – sailed into Ironbottom Sound. The US submarine *Trout* spotted them as they passed Savo

Island and warned Rear-Admiral Willis Lee. The *Washington* and the *South Dakota*, supported by four destroyers, went to attack them. But the Japanese had split their force into four groups. The cruiser *Sendai* was sent to shadow the American ships. When Lee realised this, he opened fire. While the *Sendai* returned fire from the rear, the *Ayanami* and the *Uranami* attacked them for'ard. In the gun battle that followed, the American destroyers *Preston* and *Walke* were sunk.

The destroyer *Gwin* was also out of action and a shot from the *Kirishima* knocked out the *South Dakota*'s electrics so it could not move its guns. At this point, only the *Ayanami* was damaged, so Kondo and his squadron closed in. They fired three torpedoes at the *South Dakota*. All three missed. The *Washington* retaliated. Soon the *Kirishima* was crippled and sank. Kondo broke off at 0030, his destroyers also having been badly mauled. However, the Japanese did manage to drive their transports aground at Tassafaronga and the reinforcements disembarked under fire. Only 2,000 got ashore, along with 250 cases of ammunition and 1,500 bags of rice. On 30 November, eight Japanese destroyers attempted to land more troops and were beaten off in the Battle of Tassafaronga, losing one destroyer sunk and one crippled – the cost to the Allies was one cruiser sunk and three damaged.

Even though the Japanese forces on Guadalcanal outnumbered their American counterparts, the Japanese had lost the battle for the sea: the forces on Guadalcanal could not be resupplied. During the naval battle, they had lost two battleships, one cruiser and three destroyers to the Americans' two cruisers and five destroyers. It would become increasingly difficult to resupply their men while the Americans still held Henderson Field. The Japanese mounted a fifth and final offensive on Guadalcanal, but it never really got off the ground. And the Japanese troops on the island were soon reduced to eating grass and roots.

On 4 January 1943, after bitter disputes between the Army and the Navy, Imperial General Headquarters decided to evacuate their forces from Guadalcanal. Between 1 and 7 February, the Japanese withdrew the 13,000 survivors so stealthily that the Marines, now 50,000 strong but still fearful of a new attack, did not even know about it. Nevertheless Guadalcanal was the first land victory in the South Seas and the beginning of the end for the Japanese Empire. During the six-month campaign on the island, the Japanese lost 50,000 men, 25,000 of those on land and 9,000 to disease. But the greater loss, militarily, was 600 planes and their crews – all for what the Imperial High Command called, at the time of the first American landing, an 'insignificant island in the South Seas'.

Guadalcanal had cost the Marines 1,592 lives. And for America the island was not so insignificant. It kept open the route to Australia which was fast becoming a forward base in the war against Japan. The battle for Guadalcanal had also been well covered in the press and newsreels, and victory there gave the Allies' morale a much-needed boost.

RABAUL

On 21 February 1943, the US infantry landed on the Russell Islands to support advances on Rabaul. In the summer of 1942 British forces had begun an invasion of Vichy French-held Madagascar. Hostilities ceased on 5 November and the Free French took over on 8 January 1943. In the North Pacific, the United States had decided to expel the Japanese from the Aleutians. Landing forces on Adak in August 1942, they began air attacks against Kiska and Attu in September while a naval blockade prevented the Japanese from reinforcing their garrisons. Bypassing Kiska, US forces invaded Attu on 11 May 1943 and killed most of the island's 2,300 defenders in the following three weeks and the Japanese evacuated Kiska. With bases in the Aleutians, the US could bomb the Kuril Islands at the north of the Japanese archipelago.

In mid-1943, the Allies drew up new plans for the invasion of Japan proper. It was decided that the main offensive should come from the south and the south-east, through the Philippines and through Micronesia, rather than from the Aleutians or from the Asian mainland, where the Chinese with Allied backing were still fighting the Japanese while the British were taking on the Japanese in Burma.

The key to the invasion plan was the Philippines, which the Japanese had taken in 1941. Retaking them would disrupt Japanese communications with the East Indian islands and Malaya. And the conquest of Micronesia, through the Gilbert Islands, the Marshalls, the Carolines and the Marianas, offered the prospect of drawing the Japanese into a naval showdown and winning land bases for massive air raids on the Japanese mainland in the run-up to any invasion.

To reach the Philippines, it would be necessary to encircle Rabaul – the strategy was to isolate it rather than attack it directly. The encirclement of Rabaul began with the capture of the Treasury Islands in the Solomons by New Zealand troops in October and November 1943. And on 1 November, US troops landed at Empress Augusta Bay on the west of Bougainville. US reinforcements subsequently held off Japanese counter-attacks in December 1943, when they sank two American destroyers, and in March 1944, when they killed some 6,000 men. But by then what remained of the Japanese garrison on Bougainville no longer had the strength to fight, although it did not surrender until the end of the war.

On 15 December 1943, American troops landed at Arawe on the south-west coast of New Britain. This drew the Japanese away from Cape Gloucester on the north-west coast, where there was a major landing on 26 December. By 16 January 1944, the airfield at Cape Gloucester had been secured. Talasea, on the road to Rabaul, was captured in March 1944. With western New Britain now in

American hands, the Allies controlled the vital straits between New Britain and New Guinea.

On 15 February, New Zealand troops took the Green Islands south-east of New Guinea. American forces invaded Los Negros in the Admiralty Islands on 29 February and captured Manus on 9 March. With the fall of the Emirau Islands on 20 March, the Allies' stranglehold on Rabaul was virtually complete and the 100,000 Japanese troops there could be ignored for all practical purposes. Then when the Allies subdued the Japanese in western New Guinea in 1944 and built airbases there, they were all set to push on towards the Philippines.

TARAWA

Although there was no plan to make a major offensive westward across the Pacific until mid-1944, the US Joint Chiefs of Staff decided to launch a limited offensive in the central Pacific in 1943, hoping to draw the Japanese away from other areas and to speed the pace of the war. In November 1943, Admiral Nimitz's central Pacific forces invaded the Gilbert Islands. Makin fell easily, but the amphibious landings on the Tarawa atoll became another blood-bath.

Tarawa is an atoll to the north of the centre of the Gilbert Islands, comprising fifteen islets, with a total land area of twelve square miles. They are laid out in the shape of a right-angled triangle – the hypotenuse being the north-eastern side. This is made up of a string of islands. The southern side is the same, but the western leg is largely a reef which shelters the central lagoon. The only entrance to the lagoon is through a break in the reef on the western side, just north of Betio Island in the south-western corner. Before the war, Betio had been the British administrative headquarters and, on the north side, in the lagoon, there was a pier where a small boat could land at high tide. The island was just two miles long and only a few hundred yards wide. But it was flat, rising no more than ten feet above sea level, and the Japanese had built an airstrip there for medium bombers. It was the main air facility in the region. Consequently, the island was well fortified.

Despite having been British territory before the war, detailed information about the island was scant. The only charts of the area were over a hundred years old and carried no information about currents and tides. However, aerial reconnaissance had located an estimated 90 per cent of the Japanese defensive positions. It was also estimated that the Japanese had 200 artillery pieces on Betio, ranging from 8-inch guns to 20mm cannon. As the island was so small, almost all the beaches were within range of almost all the guns. Although the island had palm trees and a little undergrowth, there were absolutely no natural features to provide cover. Any invasion was going to be bloody.

With little information to go on, the 2nd Marine Division, who were to make the assault, decided to use amphibious tractors – Amtracs – to get its men ashore, although these had only been used to land supplies on beaches before. The Marines acquired seventy-five of them and began fixing machine-guns to them and welding armour plating in position, while Marine drivers were taught how to manoeuvre them over coral. Fifty more Amtracs, of a newer type designed for beach assaults, were shipped out from San Diego the day before the invasion. But even that was not enough. The divisional commander Major-General Julian C. Smith's plan called for 100 tractors to carry the first three waves of the assault, with twenty-five tractors being held in reserve. That meant that the fourth and fifth waves would have to be brought in on landing craft. These would need at least four feet of water over the reef which ran between 800 and 1,200 yards out to sea all around the island. No one knew much about the local tides but, for strategic and logistical reasons, the assault would have be made during a neap tide. If they waited seven days for a spring tide, the high tides came at night, which was no good for a beach assault. Delaying for over a month until spring high tides came during the day would have been too late. So D-Day was set for 20 November 1943 and H-Hour was 0830.

The Japanese were expecting an invasion. At the top of the beach all around the island they had built a wall of palm logs three to five feet high, reinforced with wire. Behind it they had dug machine-gun emplacements and rifle pits. Behind those there were more well-fortified machine-gun posts made of logs, coral and reinforced concrete, and covered with sand. They were hard to see and even more difficult to silence. Further back there were another twenty-five pillboxes and concrete emplacements housing 75mm field guns and 37mm anti-tank guns trained on the shore. At each corner of the island and dotted in between the other emplacements, there were fourteen coastal defence guns ranging in calibre from 80mm to 203mm. Their magazines and crews were protected by bombproof shelters. The guns were trained on the sea approaches and the beaches themselves, and concrete beach obstacles had been laid to concentrate any invasion force into their field of fire. The Japanese also had seven Type 95 light tanks, each armed with two machine-guns and a 37mm, acting as a mobile reserve.

The defenders were commanded by Rear-Admiral Keiji Shibasaki. Under his command, there were 1,497 sailors from the 7th Special Naval Landing Force and 1,122 sailors from the 3rd Special Base Force. Also ashore were 2,170 Korean construction workers.

Careful study of aerial photographs showed that the south and west of the island were most heavily defended. The Japanese plainly expected the attack to come from the open sea. But the beaches there lay in a series of concave bays where it would be easy for the defenders to concentrate their fire. The northern beaches, however, were convex, so it was decided to attack the island from the lagoon side. A scouting platoon would be sent in to clear the jetty there, which could be used for resupply and the evacuation of the wounded. Three reinforced battalions would then land on the beaches Red 1 and Red 2 to the right of the pier, and Red 3 to the left. A separate landing would take place on Green Beach at the western end of the island. The 2nd Marine Regiment, under Colonel David M. Shoup, was to lead the assault on Betio, reinforced with a battalion of the 8th Marines.

The 2nd Marines had some experience of jungle fighting on Guadalcanal, but their intensive training with the tractors gave them the impression that they were going to be involved in a landing rather than an assault. They thought it was going to be a walk-over.

On 18 November, the 2nd Marines were joined by the 27th Army Division, under Major-General Ralph C. Smith. Along with the 2nd Marines divisional commander Major-General Julian C. Smith, there was yet another Major-General Smith involved in the operation, the Marine Corps commander Major-General Holland M. Smith – known to his men as H.M. 'Howling Mad' Smith – who had supervised the 27th Division's amphibious training on Hawaii.

On the night of 19 November, the assault force closed on Tarawa. Long before they reached the beaches things began to go wrong. Unbeknownst to the planners, the area where the Marines were supposed to transfer from their ships into the Amtracs and landing craft was subject to strong currents. The ships began to drift and in the darkness what was supposed to be an orderly transfer turned into chaos.

Air raids over the previous few nights were supposed to have knocked out the shore batteries. At first light, it was discovered that they hadn't. However, the Japanese aim was bad – perhaps because the fire control system had been damaged. No ships were hit, but shells landing all around them in the water did little for the men's morale. The Navy then opened up in an attempt to silence the Japanese guns, but the vibration knocked out the communications equipment on board the command ship USS *Maryland*. This meant the invasion force had no communication with the carrier-borne air attack that was to come in and soften up the beach defences. This had been scheduled for 0545, so the Navy stopped their bombardment at that time to avoid hitting their own planes. When no planes appeared, they started it again. When the bombers eventually turned up at 0615, the naval bombardment had kicked up so much dust that they could not see their targets.

At the same time, two minesweepers moved into the lagoon, followed by two destroyers who laid smoke-screens and bombarded the beaches from close range. After an hour the gunfire was supposed to slacken as it was assumed the Marines would be nearing the beaches, but a strong off-shore wind had slowed their progress and they were still nowhere near their start line. This line was supposed to be marked by the minesweepers, but one of them had drifted out of position, adding to the confusion. Rear-Admiral Harry Hill worked out that it would take the Amtracs forty minutes to travel from the start line to the beaches, so he stopped his bombardment at 0855 to avoid hitting his own men as they landed. However, the Amtracs were a lot slower in the water than he had calculated. So, when the bombardment stopped, they were still a long way from the beaches.

The carrier-borne planes were then supposed to strafe the beaches but, due to the breakdown in communication, few turned up and those that did left a full ten minutes before the first Marine arrived. Meanwhile, the carrier pilots were telling their debriefers that the island's defences had been completely destroyed. Along with their bombing and strafing, 3,000 tons of shells had hit Betio and the Marines, it was said, would walk ashore.

Shortly before 0910, Lieutenant William D. Hawkins and his

scout patrol arrived on the pier and cleared it of Japanese snipers. A few minutes later, the three assault battalions reached the beaches and landed with little opposition. They ran up the beaches to the log wall, where they stopped. By this time, the Japanese began to recover their senses after the bombardment. A few men got over the log wall, but the majority were pinned down behind it.

The men coming in behind them were in even more trouble. There was only three feet of water over the reef, so the landing craft had to drop them at the edge and let them wade ashore, presenting irresistible targets to the Japanese gunners. Amphibious assaults from landing craft were at this time still relatively new. By the time the Allies stormed the Normandy beaches they had learnt to put the officers and NCOs at the back. At Tarawa, they were at the front and they got shot down, leaving those men that did get ashore leaderless. Only one of the battalion commanders from the landing craft reached the beach alive. The men from the landing craft were in danger, not just from enemy fire, but from the reef itself, which had deep holes in it. Fully-laden Marines disappeared into them and drowned.

At noon, the next wave arrived with the tanks. These drove in across the reef. On Red 3, one platoon of four medium tanks helped the 2nd Battalion of the 8th Marines under Major Henry P. Crowe consolidate their position, but they made little progress inland. By the end of the day, three of the tanks had been destroyed – two of them hit by American bombs. A battalion from the reserves, under Major Robert H. Ruud, was sent in to help Crowe. Again they took heavy casualties crossing the reef, especially among the officers and NCOs, though Ruud himself made it ashore; by the time they reached the beach, their number was less than that of the battalion they had come to support. There was no prospect of making an attack on the Japanese and, by nightfall, the Americans controlled a stretch of beach only 300 yards long and had penetrated no further than 250 yards inland.

On Red 2, the situation was worse. Intense fire during their landing had dispersed the landing force and their commander had been landed so far to the right that the men effectively had no leader. But a liaison and observing officer from Corps Headquarters, Lieutenant-Colonel Walter I. Jordan, was with them. He took charge but, as he pointed out later, Marines are not inclined to take orders from people they do not know. Nevertheless, under his command, the Marines moved inland some seventy-five yards before being pinned down by sniper and machine-gun fire.

Seeing that the centre of the beach was in trouble, Colonel Shoup committed his 3rd Battalion. Enough of the Amtracs had made it back through the intensive shelling to the start line to carry two of its three companies back to the beaches. The other company would have to wait until the Amtracs dropped off those men and made the hazardous return journey.

The first two companies approached the beaches at about 1130. On their way they passed the mouth of a small valley which was bristling with Japanese guns. They took 200 casualties before the tractors even hit shore. Some landed on the wrong beach and those who had arrived on the right one had lost most of their equipment.

Shoup followed them ashore, followed by four 75mm howitzers. He set up a command post and established contact with Crowe to his left. But no communication was possible with Red 1, as the Japanese were dug in between them. He had no communication with his divisional commander J.C. Smith either as most of the radio sets had got wet during the landings and were not working.

Neither Smith nor Shoup had any idea what was happening on Green Beach. The 3rd Battalion under Major Michael P. Ryan landing there found they were facing a considerable Japanese force. But with stragglers who had drifted there from other beaches he managed to consolidate a position on the north-west tip of the island. At midday, two tanks drove in across the reef to support them. Engineers then blew a hole in the log wall and, following the tanks, Ryan's men advanced 500 yards before the tanks were knocked out. But they were unable to hold this forward position as they had bypassed several Japanese positions, lacking the heavy weapons to take them out. So at nightfall, he fell back to a defensive perimeter.

That evening, one of Ryan's radios dried out sufficiently to work. He reported to J.C. Smith that, without heavy weapons, he could not advance. Smith got the impression that the situation was far worse than it was and, although reinforcements could have been landed safely, he sent none. Instead he called up the Corps reserve and prepared to send the 1st Battalion of the 8th Marines to make a fresh landing east of Crowe, fearing that the Japanese had a force there set to counter-attack. Due to a mix up, this landing never took place – which was fortunate as it would surely have resulted in a massacre. Before Smith had issued his orders, a Marine spotter plane saw Shoup's howitzers going ashore on Red 2 and assumed it was the 1st Battalion. Smith was told that the 1st Battalion had already been committed and binned his plan. As it was, the men of the 1st Battalion suffered an uncomfortable night in the landing craft. The following morning, they were sent to Red 2. A message from Shoup saying that there was a deep-water channel running all the way up to the jetty did not get through and the 1st Battalion sustained heavy casualties as they waded ashore across the reef. The survivors were sent to defend Shoup's right. He then pushed forward and, by the end of the day, Marines from Red 2 had made it across the island to the opposite shore, cutting the Japanese in two.

Although Ryan had been denied troop reinforcements, he received two more medium tanks and some flame-throwers during the night. Air strikes were called in on the Japanese artillery and at 1000 hours he moved out against little opposition. Soon he had cleared the western beach and arrived at the southern coast opposite the pier.

That evening, two battalions of the 6th Regimental Combat Team under Colonel Maurice Holmes were to land on Green Beach. In the morning they were to advance on the airstrip, while the rest of the Marines were to attempt to break out of their beachheads. The Japanese had been seen moving off Betio onto the next island in the southern chain, Bairiki. As J.C. Smith's orders were to clear the entire atoll, he sent a battalion of 75mm howitzers and a battalion of the 6th Marines to Bairiki to prevent the enemy making a stand there. On Bairiki they met two machine-gun posts manned by fifteen Japanese. But Bairiki was also used as a fuel dump. A preliminary air strike strafed the island and hit the dump with .50 incendiary bullets. The resulting explosion burnt out the machine-gun posts and the Marines landed unopposed. Once the howitzers were in position, they could cut off the retreat of the Japanese, leaving the infantry free to return to the battle on Betio.

Late that afternoon, the 1st Battalion of the 6th Marines under Major William K. Jones landed on Green Beach. They were the first unit to reach the island in an organised condition. During the night they moved forward to reinforce Ryan's position. The following morning they pushed along the southern coast until they met up with the Marines who had crossed the island from Red 2 the day before. With the aid of flame-throwers, naval gunfire, the one remaining medium tank and seven light tanks, they pushed forward a mile and a half by midday. The rate of progress slowed that afternoon, partly because the light tanks were found to be ineffective. Their 37mm guns made little impression on even the defensive positions made out of coral and logs and they did not have enough weight to crush them. However, the M4 medium tank worked wonderfully and, by the end of the day, they had joined up with Crowe, Ruud and the 8th Marines at the end of the Japanese airbase's runway. With the exception of small pockets, the Japanese forces were now corralled in the eastern end of the island. There they were pounded by naval gunfire and the howitzers on Bairiki.

On the morning of 23 November, Shoup began clearing the remaining Japanese resistance in the valley that ran inland from Red 2. By midday he had driven through to the southern tip. Meanwhile, the 3rd Battalion of the 6th Marines passed through the American lines and advanced on the Japanese positions. At 1312, J.C. Smith announced that Beito was clear. The rest of the atoll was cleared by 28 November. The defenders lost 4,690 killed, and 146 were taken prisoner. Only seventeen of them were Japanese. The rest were the remnants of the benighted Korean construction workers.

Tarawa had cost the Marines over 1,000 killed and 2,100 wounded. The casualty list would have been longer if the Japanese commander had not depended on stopping the invasion on the beaches and prepared a more effective defence inland – admittedly, as Admiral Shibasaki was killed by a shell in the preliminary bombardment, he was in no position to organise this as the battle developed. But as it was, the Battle of Tarawa shocked the American public because of the huge number of casualties sustained in so short a time. However, it had taught the military some important lessons. Programmes were developed to improve the accuracy of naval gunfire and aerial bombing and strafing, and changes were made to the organisation of amphibious assaults that would pay dividends on other islands and on the beaches of Normandy.

THE MARIANAS

Having lost the Gilbert Islands, the Japanese defended the Marshalls in an effort to tie up Allied forces and put a strain on their extended lines of supply. Nimitz made his first attack on the Kwajalein Atoll, which he subjected to so heavy a preliminary bombardment that the Allied infantry had no problems landing on 30 January 1944. Enewetak fell on 17 February.

To support their landings on the rest of the Marshall Islands, the US fleet began day and night attacks on the Japanese base at Truk in the Carolines on 17 February, destroying 200,000 tonnes of merchant shipping and around 300 aircraft. That put the base out of action and the Allies could safely bypass it. The Allies then mustered over 125,000 troops and 500 ships to attack the Mariana Islands, which lay 3,500 miles from Pearl Harbor and 1,000 miles from the western-most limit of their advance, Enewetak.

Knowing the attack was coming, the Japanese planned to counter-attack using their remaining 1,055 land-based aircraft in the Marianas, the Carolines, and western New Guinea, along with the 450 aircraft on their nine aircraft carriers. But in the spring of 1944 the Allies were winning the war in the skies. Yamamoto had died when his plane had been shot down over Bougainville in April 1943 and his successor, Admiral Koga Mineichi, who had come up with the plan, was killed along with his staff in a plane crash.

On 15 June, two divisions of US Marines went ashore on Saipan Island in the Marianas. But the 30,000 Japanese defending it put up a fierce fight. The Japanese fortified themselves in underground caves and bunkers that protected them from American artillery and naval bombardment. The same defensive tactics were used on other small islands. The only way to deal with the defenders was to clear out the bunkers and caves one at a time. This was time consuming and caused such a high rate of casualties that an entire Army division had to be brought in as reinforcements. Gradually, the Japanese defenders were pushed into smaller and smaller pockets. The Japanese position was hopeless. To encourage their men to fight to the last Admiral Nagumo, now the Commander-in-Chief on Saipan, and Lieutenant Gaito, head of the garrison, committed suicide. Organised resistance ended on 7 July with a suicidal counter-attack, the biggest of its kind in the war. Some 8,000 civilians also committed suicide en masse by jumping off the cliffs at Marpi Point. Only 1,000 out of the garrison of 32,000 survived. In all, 22,000 civilians also perished. American casualties were also high – 3,426 were killed and 10,595 wounded.

The loss of Saipan was such a setback for the Japanese that prime minister Hideki Tojo and his entire Cabinet resigned. Even some in the Imperial High Command realised that the loss of the Marianas meant the war was lost, but dared not say so. Even so, Tojo was succeeded by General Koiso Kuniaki, who pledged to carry on the nation's historic fight with a renewed vigour. The loss of Saipan meant that the US could build bases there for its new B-29 Superfortresses, which had been developed for the sole purpose of bombing Japan. Now the Japanese would have to suffer air raids like their German allies. The first flight of 100 B-29s took off from Saipan on 12 November 1944. It bombed Tokyo, the first air raid on the city since 1942.

While the Japanese were still resisting on Saipan, Admiral Jisaburo Ozawa put Admiral Mineichi's plan into action. The Japanese Combined Fleet was steaming from its anchorages in the East Indies and the Philippines to take on the American 5th Fleet, under Admiral Raymond Spruance. Ozawa had nine aircraft carriers against Spruance's fifteen, but he could count on help from land-based planes from Guam, Rota and Yap. They met west of the Marianas in the greatest carrier battle of the war known as the Battle of the Philippine Sea. It is also known as the 'Great Marianas Turkey Shoot'. Battle was joined on 19 June, but Ozawa had already lost. He did not know that raids on the Japanese airfields had put his land-based aircraft out of action. At 0830 Ozawa sent 430 planes in four waves against Spruance's ships. As the second wave left, the carrier *Taiho*, Ozawa's flagship, was hit by a torpedo from a submarine. US planes intercepted the Japanese aircraft and only twenty planes from the second wave got through to inflict minor damage on the *Wasp* and *Bunker Hill*. At 1220, the *Shokaku* was recovering the thirty of its planes that had made it back when it was hit by a torpedo from the US submarine *Cavalla*. The *Shokaku* blazed for three hours before it sank. Shortly after, at 1532, the *Taiho* exploded. Even then Ozawa did not realise what a disaster the battle had been, believing that his missing planes had landed on Guam. In fact, over 300 planes had been shot down. Hoping that they might return Ozawa held on until late in the afternoon of 20 June. US aircraft counter-attacked, sinking the *Hiyo*, damaging the *Zuikaku*, putting a hole in the flight deck of the *Chiyoda* and destroying nearly 100 more planes. As the Japanese fleet retreated northward towards Okinawa, the American pilots tried to make it back to their ships in the growing dark. That night only 43 of the 216 aircraft launched in the air strike found their carriers. Many ditched in the sea and most of the crews were picked up. The US lost only 16 pilots and 33 aircrew.

Despite the American aircraft losses the Battle of the Philippine Sea was ultimately of more strategic importance than the fall of Saipan. After it, Nimitz's forces could occupy other major islands in the Marianas. Of particular satisfaction was the retaking of Guam, which had been an American possession since the Spanish-American war in 1901. Garrisoned by 365 Marines, it was the first US possession to fall into Japanese hands when it was invaded on 9 December 1941.

The island of Guam was about ten miles long and thirty miles wide. There were mountains to the south and the centre was a flat limestone plateau. It had a fine anchorage in Apta Harbour and the Japanese had built an airbase on Orote peninsula, next to the old Marine Corps barracks. The invasion was delayed because the Marines were held up by the prolonged fighting on Saipan, so the Army's 77th Infantry Division was brought in from Hawaii to reinforce the assault force. After eleven days of bombing and shelling, the 3rd Marine Division were put ashore at 0829 on 21 July at Asan. By mid-afternoon they held a beachhead just 2,000 yards wide and 1,200 yards deep with the Japanese pouring fire down on them from the surrounding hills. Mortars were fired from the caves on the front of the hills and artillery from the reverse, causing huge casualties among the Marines. But accurate naval gunfire helped them fight their way up the slope and on 24 July they held the ridge. The following night seven battalions of Japanese soldiers with bayonets fixed charged, shouting, 'Banzai' and 'Wake up Yankee and die.' In heavy fighting some of the enemy got so far through the American line that the wounded in the field hospital had to pick up rifles and defend themselves from their beds. But the ferocious Japanese counter-attack failed to push the Marines back into the sea. It petered out leaving massive Japanese casualties.

A second landing on 21 July by the 1st Provisional Marine Brigade (Shepherd) to the south on Agat beach came under heavy Japanese artillery fire the moment they hit the beaches. Some 350 Marines died and 24 Amtracs were destroyed. But once ashore the Marines made rapid progress, soon penetrating to a depth of 2,000 yards. On the first day, they also managed to land 3,000 tonnes of supplies and a platoon of Sherman tanks which helped them hold off Japanese counter-attacks on the following few nights. When reinforcement arrived from the 77th Infantry, the Marines fought their way out of the beachhead and joined up with the Marines at Asan to the north. Together they fought north until they had cut off the Orote peninsula. This was defended by an infantry battalion, whose commander told his men to drink whatever alcohol they could lay their hands on. Intoxicated on beer, saki and synthetic whiskey, the Japanese staged a night attack. They charged, giggling hysterically, reeling about and firing their weapons indiscriminately. But just because they were drunk did not mean they were not dangerous. They were shelled and machine-gunned. In the morning, the Marines counted more than 400 Japanese corpses.

The 1st Provisional Marine Brigade then fought its way yard by yard up the Orote peninsula against fierce resistance. But fire support from naval artillery helped force the enemy back. Resistance cracked on 27 July. By 29 July, the peninsula had been cleared and the airfield was in action again – this time for American planes – on 31 July. But there were still Japanese units who put up a tremendous fight on the island. Gradually the 1st Marines and 77th Infantry drove them up into the northern tip of Guam. Resistance ceased on 10 August. Of the 54,891 US troops landed, 1,440 were killed, 145 were missing and 5,648 were wounded. Of the Japanese garrison 10,693 were killed and ninety-eight taken prisoners. The rest disappeared into the jungle to fight on. A lieutenant-colonel and his 113 men surrendered on 4 September 1945, but the last known survivor, Colonel Yokoi Shoichi, emerged in January 1972.

The last important island in the Marianas, Tinian, fell on 24 July, when two Marine Divisions from Saipan landed on the beach taking the Japanese commander, Admiral Kakuda, and his 9,000-man garrison by surprise. By the evening, the Marines had established a large beachhead and 1,200 Japanese died when they tried to force them back into the sea. The 4th Marines cleared the southern part of the island, while the 2nd took the north. Within a week the island was in American hands. The Marines had lost 327 killed and 1,771 wounded. The Japanese had lost their garrison almost to a man. In all, the Marianas cost the Japanese 46,000 killed or captured, the Americans 4,750 killed.

THE PHILIPPINES AND BORNEO

On 28 July 1944, President Roosevelt had approved General MacArthur's plan to take the Philippines Archipelago. This was of special interest to MacArthur as he had been commander of the

US forces on the Philippines when the Japanese attacked in 1941. With 180,000 men under arms he thought he could hold the islands, but by 27 December he was forced to abandon the capital Manila and withdraw to the peninsula of Bataan. They fought a delaying action there, but found themselves short of supplies. MacArthur left on 11 March 1942 with the words, 'I will return'. The men in Bataan fought on until 8 April. Six days later they were subjected to a march into captivity, the infamous Bataan Death March. Some 16,000 died. A small US force fought on, on the island of Corregidor until 6 May.

In preparation for the invasion, MacArthur's forces from New Guinea seized Morotai, the most north-easterly island of the Moluccas in mid-September 1944. This was on the direct route to Mindanao, the southernmost landmass of the Philippines. Meanwhile, Nimitz's fleet from the east landed troops in the Palau Islands.

US intelligence had discovered that the Japanese forces were unexpectedly small both on Mindanao and on Leyte, a smaller island north of the Surigao Strait. It was decided that they should bypass Mindanao and begin the invasion of the Philippines on Leyte. On 17 and 18 October 1944, US forces seized offshore isles in Leyte Gulf. And on October 20 they landed four divisions on the east coast of Leyte itself. The threat to Leyte was the cue for the Japanese to put into action their latest plan *Sho-Go* – 'Operation Victory'.

Under Sho-Go, the next Allied invasion would be met with concerted air attacks. The problem was that the Japanese Army and Navy air forces only had 212 planes in the immediate area. However, Admiral Ozawa would send four carriers with 106 planes south from Japanese waters. It was also hoped that this carrier force would lure the US aircraft carriers into a new engagement. By this point in the war, the Japanese were training 'kamikaze' pilots who would fly planes loaded with fuel and explosives into the Allied shipping. They hoped to knock out the US carrier fleet in a desperate effort to protect their homeland.

At the same time, a Japanese naval force from Singapore would split itself into two groups and converge on Leyte Gulf from the north and from the south-west. The weaker of the two groups, with two battleships, one heavy cruiser and four destroyers under Vice-Admiral Nishimura Teiji, would pass through the Surigao Strait. The stronger group, consisting of five battleships, twelve cruisers and fifteen destroyers under Vice Admiral Kurita Takeo, would enter the Pacific through the San Bernardino Strait between the Philippine islands of Samar and Luzon. On the way, two of Takeo's heavy cruisers were torpedoed by US submarines on 23 October and one of the mightiest of Japan's battleships, the *Musashi*, was sunk in an air attack the next day. However, three groups of American escort carriers Takeo met on the way also suffered heavy damage.

As the commander of the US 3rd Fleet, Admiral Halsey, had diverted his main strength towards Ozawa's fleet farther to the north, Takeo made his way unopposed through the San Bernardino Strait on 25 October. But Teiji's fleet had been spotted going through the Surigao Strait and, when it arrived in Leyte Gulf in the early hours of 25 October, it had been practically annihilated by the US 7th Fleet under Admiral Kincaid. Finding himself all alone in Leyte Gulf, Takeo turned back. Meanwhile Halsey had destroyed all of four Ozawa's carriers, together with a light cruiser and two destroyers. 'Operation Victory' had been a terrible defeat. Japanese losses amounted to one large aircraft carrier, three light carriers, three battleships, six heavy cruisers, four light cruisers and 11 destroyers. The US had lost only one light carrier, two escort carriers and three destroyers. However, this was the first time the American fleet faced the kamikaze in force and their deliberately suicidal attacks meant that the war was going to be hard won.

After the Battle of Leyte Gulf, the Japanese Navy was no longer a threat and the way was clear for the invasion of the Philippines. But that did not mean the Japanese were going to give them up easily. Even after their naval defeat in the Leyte Gulf, they landed reinforcements on the west coast of Leyte. Japanese resistance was so stubborn that the Americans had to be reinforced before the main city of Ormoc fell on 10 December 1944. Only on Christmas day could the US claim control of the whole of Leyte – even then, there was still some mopping up to be done. The defence of Leyte cost the Japanese some 75,000 killed or taken prisoner.

From Leyte the Americans took Mindoro, the largest of the islands immediately south of Luzon, on 15 December. Again the kamikaze made the victory costly. Suicidal attack continued after the US forces surprised the Japanese by landing at Lingayen Gulf on the west coast of Luzon itself, the most important island of the Philippines, on 9 January 1945. There was no hope of reinforcement and, in the long run, there was no prospect of victory, so the Japanese commander, Lieutenant-General Yamashita Tomoyuki, tried to tie down the American forces as long as possible in the mountains. Manila itself was strongly defended. One American corps approached it from Lingayen over the Central Plains. Another was landed at Subic Bay, at the northern end of the Bataan Peninsula, on 29 January. The two corps met up at Dinalupihan a week later. More troops landed at Nasugbu, south of Manila Bay, on 31 January, surrounding Manila. It fell on 3 March but Japanese resistance continued in the mountains until mid-June 1945. Meanwhile, an American division landed on Mindanao at Zamboanga, on the south-west peninsula, on 10 March and a corps began the occupation of the core of the island on 17 April.

While US forces consolidated their positions in the Philippines, the Australians started the reconquest of Borneo by bombarding Tarakan Island, off the north-east coast, on 12 April. On 30 April, they landed on nearby Sadau Island in the Baragan Straits, from where they could shell the beach fortifications. They landed on Tarakan on 1 May. After four days of fighting the town of Tarakan fell at a cost of 225 Australians killed and 669 wounded, 1,540 Japanese were dead. On 10 June, 2,900 Australians went ashore in Brunei on the north-west coast, where they met little opposition. And Balikpapan, on the east coast far to the south of Tarakan, was attacked on 1 July and the Japanese defences collapsed, depriving Japan of oil supplies for southern Borneo. The British then began preparing an advance base for the retaking of Singapore there. But by the time the air base in Borneo was built, Japan had surrendered.

IWO JIMA AND OKINAWA

While the campaigns on the Philippines and on Borneo were still under way, plans were being laid for invasion of Japan. This would begin, the planners decided, with landings on Kyushu, the most southerly of the major Japanese islands. In preparation, B-29 Superfortresses under General Curtis E. LeMay stationed on the Mariana Islands began a campaign of bombing in the closing months of 1944. But it was a round trip of 3,000 miles from Saipan to mainland Japan, a long flight even for the Superfortresses. However if US forces took the little volcanic island of Iwo Jima in the Bonin Islands, which lay some 760 miles south-east of Japan, they would halve the distance to Tokyo and, with fighters stationed there, the USAAF would be able to defend its bombers over their targets. Iwo Jima was a doubly important target because Japan considered the island its 'unsinkable aircraft carrier'. It was a radar and fighter base whose aircraft intercepted the Superfortresses on their bombing missions over Japan.

Irregularly shaped, Iwo Jima is about five miles long and anything from 800 yards to two and a half miles wide. The Japanese were determined to hold on to it. They garrisoned the island with

21,000 troops under Lieutenant-General Kuribayashi Tadamichi and it had the strongest defences of all the Japanese possessions in the Pacific. It had been under constant bombardment since the fall of the Marianas, but the prolonged fighting in the Philippines had delayed the attack, giving the Japanese a few months to build up the island's already formidable fortifications. As on other Pacific islands, they had created underground defences, making the best possible use of natural caves and the rocky terrain.

For days before the landings, Iwo Jima was subjected to massive bombardment by naval guns, rockets, and air strikes using bombs carrying the recently developed napalm. But the Japanese were so well dug in that no amount of shelling or bombing could knock them out.

On 19 February, the 5th Amphibious Corps under General Harry Schmidt went ashore on the south of the island, confidently predicting that he would take the island in four days. Of the 30,000 men landing on the beaches on the first day, 2,400 were hit by the Japanese. The Marines soon had a 4,000-yard long beachhead, but they were slowed down inland by the island's ashy volcanic soil. 5th Marines then divided their forces. Half struck inland and took the first of the two Japanese airfields – a third was under construction. The other half turned south to take Mount Suribachi, an extinct volcano soon nicknamed Meatgrinder Hill for the casualties taken there. The Marines eventually took Mount Suribachi on 23 February. The raising of the American flag on its summit was photographed by Joe Rosenthal of the Associated Press. It became one of the best-known images of the Pacific war and statues, paintings and American postage stamp designs have been based on it. However, the photograph actually depicts a second flag being raised over Mount Suribachi. The first flag was raised some hours earlier, but it was too small to be seen by the other troops on the island.

While 5th Marine Division moved up the west coast, 4th Marines fought their way up the east, but the fighting was so fierce that 3rd Marines, a floating reserve, had to be landed. They moved up the centre and by 9 March they had reached the north-east coast. On 26 March the Japanese staged their last suicidal attack with 350 men near Kitano Point on the northern tip of the island. After that, resistance collapsed. Some 20,000 Japanese were killed, the remaining 1,000 captured. The Marine and Army losses were 6,812 killed and 19,189 wounded. The Battle of Iwo Jima was a costly, but decisive victory. Now the all-out assault on the Japanese mainland could begin and, in the next five months, over 2,000 Superfortresses flew bombing missions from the airfields of Iwo Jima.

While the fighting on Iwo Jima had been going on, the war in the air took a new turn. The USAAF abandoned high-altitude strikes during daylight as they seemed to be making little impact on Japan's industrial output. Instead they began low-level strikes at night, using napalm. These were a startling success. As Japan was in an earthquake zone, buildings were traditionally made out of light-weight wood and paper. They burnt easily. In the first fire-bomb raid on the night of 9 March 1945, about twenty-five per cent of Tokyo's buildings were destroyed, killing over 80,000 people and leaving 1,000,000 homeless. Strategic planners then came to believe that Japan could be defeated without an invasion by ground troops and the massive casualties that would entail. Similar fire-bombing raids were launched against other major cities – Nagoya, Osaka, Kobe, Yokohama and Toyama. However, the invasion plans were not discarded immediately and there would be one more island hop before the end of the war. It would be the largest amphibious operation of the Pacific war. Its objective was Okinawa, an island some seventy miles long and seven miles wide just 350 miles south of Kyushu. Okinawa was considered the last stepping-stone before the invasion of Japan itself.

American reconnaissance planes put the strength of Okinawa's garrison at 65,000. In fact, the Thirty-Second Army under General Mitsuru Ushijima was almost 120,000 strong. Some 10,000 aircraft defended the island and the Imperial Navy sent a task force headed by the *Yamato*, the biggest battleship ever built.

For the invasion of Okinawa, code-named Operation *Iceberg*, the commander of the US ground forces Lieutenant-General Simon Bolivar Buckner assembled the largest array of battle-hardened troops yet deployed in the Pacific. There were three Marine Divisions and four Army Divisions: over 155,000 men in all. But by the time the fighting was finished, over 300,000 Americans had been committed to battle. Admiral Spruance assembled over 1,300 vessels of all sizes for the landing, including a large British carrier force under Vice-Admiral Sir Bernard Rawlings.

Air raids on Okinawa began as early as October 1944 and culminated in March 1945 in an attack that destroyed hundreds of Japanese planes. The invasion was scheduled for 1 April and the preliminary naval bombardment began on 18 March. US forces then began taking some of the outlying islands, including the Kerama Islands which would be used as a forward base. On the Keramas, 77th Infantry captured 200 suicide boats, packed with explosives which would have posed a major threat to the 5th Fleet, who were already being harassed by kamikazes. In all, twenty-seven suicide pilots penetrated the wall of fire the escorts put up to reach their target. Four carriers were damaged in the run up to the landings. The USS *Franklin* and the *Wasp* were knocked out and kamikaze also hit a battleship, a cruiser, four destroyers and six other ships.

On 1 April, the island was bombarded with 44,825 rounds of five-inch and larger shells, 32,000 rockets and 22,500 mortar rounds. The troops clambered into their landing craft at 0400 for the four-and-a-half hour run into Hagushi beach on the west coast of the island, which had just been cleared of mines. They hit the beaches at 0830 and found, to their surprise, no opposition. By nightfall, 60,000 men were ashore, holding a beachhead eight miles wide and three miles deep.

The next day US troops drove across the island to the east coast, occupied the entire central zone of the island and captured two airfields. Buckner then sent three Marine divisions south, while 6th Marines went north where they met some resistance on the Motubu Peninsula. By 21 April, they had cleared the north of the island, killing 2,500 Japanese defenders at a cost of 218 Americans killed and 902 wounded.

On 4 April, the 24th Corps under Major-General John Hodge reached the Japanese southern defences at Shuri, where Ushijima was determined to fight a war of attrition that he could not win. Meanwhile on 6 April the 77th Infantry Division took the small island of Ise Shima off the north coast of Okinawa. It was held by 2,000 Japanese who put up a fierce fight for five days.

That same day the kamikaze resumed with new vigour. Some 700 suicide planes attacked the 5th Fleet damaging or sinking thirteen destroyers. The *Yamato* along with its escort of the cruiser *Yahagi* and eight destroyers were also sent on a suicide mission. With their tanks filled with nearly all Japan's remaining stocks of oil, they did not have enough fuel to sail back to port. So the flotilla had been ordered to beach itself on Okinawa and use their guns to defend the troops there. But the mighty *Yamato* was spotted by a submarine just off the southernmost tip of Kyushu. She had no air cover and was a sitting duck when carrier planes caught up with her the next day. In two hours, she was hit by seven bombs and twelve torpedoes, blew up and sank. Then, in what proved to be the last naval action of the war, the *Yahagi* and four destroyers were also sunk.

Meanwhile, despite reinforcements, 24th Corps could not make much of a dent in Ushijima's defences and were suffering high casualties. Even though his men were suffering ten times the casualty rate of the US force, on 12 April, Ushijima went on the offensive. For two days, he sent wave after wave of men in suicidal attacks on the American positions. All of them were repulsed. Then 32nd Army went back on the defensive again.

That same day a new Japanese suicide weapon – christened the *baka* by the Allies from the Japanese word for fool – claimed its first victim, the US destroyer *Abele*. The baka was a rocket-powered glider that was towed into range by a bomber. When released its solitary pilot flew at the target. There was no parachute and no way to get out. Dropped usually from an altitude of more than 25,000 feet and over 50 miles out, the baka would glide to about three miles from the target before the pilot ignited its three rocket engines, accelerating the craft to more than 600 miles an hour in its final dive. The explosive charge in the nose weighed more than a tonne. Plane, pilot and – in thirty-four cases – ship were destroyed in one massive explosion.

Frustrated with the slow progress on land, Buckner ordered a more intensive bombardment. But the Japanese fortifications were well prepared and costly to overrun and the Marines could make no breakthrough. On 2 May Ushijima went on the offensive again, but was driven back, losing 5,000 men. On 11 May, Buckner ordered a new offensive to push back the Japanese flanks. Fearing that he was about to be encircled, Ushijima pulled back on 21 May to make a final stand on the southern tip of the island. A rearguard continued a ferocious fight against the 24th Corps, while the rest of Ushijima's men made an orderly retreat to a new line. On 31 May, the city of Shuri finally fell, after its defences and been reduced to rubble by bombardment.

The US Tenth Army made a last push, aided by 6th Marines who made an amphibious landing on Oroku Peninsula on the south-west corner of the island to take out a strongpoint and an airfield there. Buckner's main force moved forward painfully slowly using flamethrowers and high explosives to clear enemy positions. The Japanese fought on fanatically, but the front gradually began to crumble.

On 18 June, General Buckner was wounded and, later, died. He was replaced by General Geiger for the final stages of the battle. Three days later Ushijima was also dead, by his own hand. Scorning an American offer of surrender to prevent any further unnecessary loss of life, on 21 June he and his Chief of Staff knelt outside their headquarters and committed hara-kiri. His final order was that his men should revert to guerrilla warfare. They continued fighting until the end of the month when some 7,400 gave themselves up, the first time the Japanese had surrendered in large numbers. At least 110,000 Japanese soldiers were dead and there had been a large number of civilian casualties. For the Allies it was the costliest operation in the Pacific, with some half-a-million men involved in the fighting. US ground forces had lost 7,203 killed and 31,807 wounded. The navy had lost some 5,000 killed and a similar number wounded.

Japan had lost its entire navy and, during the Battle of Okinawa, 7,800 Japanese aircraft had been destroyed for the loss of 763 Allied planes. The Japanese mainland now lay wide open. It had no defence against the continual bombing raids the USAAF flew against it, and the British and American fleets that surrounded the islands could shell it at will.

General Joseph 'Vinegar Joe' Stilwell was brought in to command the Tenth Army and plans were laid to bring over the First Army, who had recently been victorious in Europe. They were to form a new army group under General Douglas MacArthur, ready for the invasion of Kyushu which was scheduled to begin on 1 November. But they were upstaged by history.

President Roosevelt had died on 12 April and President Harry S.

Truman was now in the White House. Military assessments of the situation given to Truman estimated that it would take well into 1946 to defeat Japan, at a cost of perhaps a million casualties. But on 16 July 1945, the atomic bomb was tested successfully in a desert area at Alamogordo, New Mexico. It had an explosive power equivalent to that of more than 15,000 tonnes of TNT, vastly more devastating than any previous weapon. Truman realised that it might be used to bomb Japan into surrender rather than waste more American lives in the invasion of the Japanese homeland.

When the victorious Allies met in the Berlin suburb of Potsdam in July 1945, they put out peace feelers to Japan, but received no reply. So on 6 August 1945, an atomic bomb was loaded onto a specially equipped B-29 Superfortress *Enola Gay* on Tinian Island in the Marianas. At 0815 local time *Enola Gay* dropped the bomb on Hiroshima, at the southern end of Honshu Island. The combined heat and blast obliterated everything in the immediate vicinity. Fires burned across four square miles of the city. Between 70,000 and 80,000 people were dead or dying and over 70,000 others were injured – though as many, if not more, were killed by conventional bombing and shelling that day. When this did not achieve the Japanese surrender, a second bomb was dropped on Nagasaki on 9 August. This killed between 35,000 and 40,000 people.

On 8 August, the USSR declared war on Japan, threatening the huge Japnaese army now cut off on the mainland of Asia. On 10 August, the Japanese government agreed to surrender on the terms offered at Potsdam on the understanding that they could retain the Emperor. The Allies agreed. On 14 August, Emperor Hirohito spoke on the radio for the first time and urged the Japanese people to accept the unacceptable. On 2 September, General MacArthur formally accepted the Japanese surrender on the deck of Nimitz's flagship, the USS *Missouri*, in Tokyo Bay. The Second World War was over.

BIBLIOGRAPHY

Beevor, Anthony, *Berlin: the Downfall 1945* Viking, London, 2002.

Beevor, Anthony, *Stalingrad*, Viking, London, 1998.

Carver, Michael, *Dilemmas of the Desert War – A New Look at the Libyan Campaign 1940–42*, Batsford/Imperial War Museum, 1986.

Cawthorne, Nigel, *Fighting Them on the Beaches*, Arcturus, London, 2002.

Churchill, Winston S., *The Second World War*, Penguin, London, 1985.

Deighton, Len and Hastings, Max, *Battle of Britain*, Wordsworth, Ware, 1999.

Evans, Martin Marix, *The Fall of France*, Osprey, Oxford, 2000.

Forty, George, *Road to Berlin – The Allied Drive from Normandy*, Cassell, London, 1999.

Gawne, Jonathan, *The War in the Pacific – From Pearl Harbor to Okinawa*, Greenhill Books, London, 1996.

Hamilton, Nigel, *Montgomery of Alamein, 1887–1942*, Allen Lane, London, 2001.

Hastings, Max, *Overlord*, Michael Joseph, London, 1984.

Healy, Mark, *The Battle of Midway*, Osprey, Oxford, 2000.

Kershaw, Robert J., *The Battle of Kursk*, Ian Allen, Shepperton, 1999.

Kershaw, Robert J., *War Without Garlands – Operation Barbarossa 1941–42*, Ian Allen, Shepperton, 2000.

Kiriakopoulous, G.C., *Ten Days to Destiny – The Battle for Crete 1941*, Franklin Watts, New York, 1985.

Latimer, John, *Tobruk 1941*, Osprey, Oxford, 2001.

Mueller, Joseph N., *Guadalcanal 1942 – The Marines Strike Back*, Osprey, London, 1992.

Perrett, Bryan, *Allied Tanks in North Africa*, Arms and Armour, London, 1986.

Prange, Gordon W., *At Dawn We Slept – The Untold Story of Pearl Harbor*, Penguin, London, 2001.

Ryan, Cornelius, *A Bridge Too Far*, Wordsworth, Ware, 1999.

Whiting, Charles, *The Battle of the Bulge*, Sutton, Stroud, 1999.

Wright, Derrick, *The Battle for Iwo Jima 1945*, Sutton, Stroud, 1999.

INDEX OF ARMIES, BATTLES & COMMANDERS

that the girl had even existed so there was no way that he could have stepped into the breach. It was Haggerty who had done that. He was the one who had married Mary Jane's mother, Abigail, and then gone on to have Malcolm and make the picture of the perfect family complete. He did a quick mental calculation. They must have met, got together, married and had Malcolm very quickly.

Anderson made a note to find out how they met, exactly, out of idle curiosity as Haggerty spoke of Oscar as if he was a close friend.

Anderson couldn't imagine losing Brenda and Peter, and being able to have a conversation that only barely mentioned them. As if they were completely something of his past, talking about the horror of the scene without giving a thought as to what his loved ones had gone through.

He had never once asked, 'Did they suffer?'

Alastair Patrick closed his eyes and waited, he didn't know these men. But he sensed that they shared one thing.

A history.

After a couple of weaves left and right, the Landie came to a halt, skidding jerkily to a standstill as if the driver had suddenly realized that they had arrived at their destination. The driver and the others got out; the cold wet air snaked into the vehicle. He saw another identical vehicle, the door opened as another man, dressed exactly as the others, dark blue and black got out. That made four, the perfect sabre. There was no light except for the beams of six spotlights that shone uphill into the infinity of the night, picking up nothing but the rain slicing like tracer fire in the beam. That and a few barren stone stacks, standing like wraiths, waiting.

Then one gorilla walked briskly back to the vehicle and opened Patrick's door. He took the hint and got out.

The Gorilla and the Glaswegian climbed back in the Land Rover and drove off without a word, leaving Patrick standing in the pouring rain that bit at his neck and face, he felt its sting and recoiled, the cold air snatched at his hood, pulling it from his head, then he felt the wind tug at his hat. Watching the three other men walking around. One then walked away and climbed into the other Landie. The other came towards Patrick, and he felt himself stiffen, rising on the balls of his feet, bracing himself, his fists clenching. Ready. Patrick scanned the face behind the black mask, looking for targets. Another old habit.

'Captain Patrick?' The voice came from somewhere behind the wool. 'Claymore. I am your commander, and as of now you are under my orders. Now, time to get about the night's business.'

Patrick recognized his reactivation command, and again that one word pushed unwelcome memories into his head, the smell of cordite, the sound of tracer fire. Faces flashed across his vision, bodies sprawled in bloodied heaps over the machine gun.

He pushed the fear away. 'Your business is none of mine, not now.' Patrick said to reassure himself.

'Shut it, Tonka, your file's about a foot thick. Don't ask, just obey.'

'It's a long time since somebody called me Tonka. I presume I don't know you.'

'No, but I know you by reputation.'

'Then we are not mates, so Captain Patrick to you.'

'Captain Patrick then. You are a police officer, you need to do your job, so we can do ours.'

For a short moment they stood a metre apart. Two men regarding each other, separated by a generation or more. One unit bonded them and that would be with them both until the day they died. No matter how hard Patrick tried to leave, he would still be one of them. Their blood was his blood, their fight his fight, even to the end.

There was a grunt, a nod. He walked away.

Patrick called after him. 'What are my orders?'

The boss turned and pointed. 'Up that gully. Fifty metres.'

The spotlights crashed off plunging him into total dark, his eyes dazzled by kaleidoscope images on his retina. He closed his eyes and waited, heard one vehicle depart and opened one eye. If it wasn't for the near invisible outlines of the vehicle that remained, he'd have thought that he was alone up here on the Bealach. Alone with the silent sentinels of the cairns and the ghosts howling in the wind. He saw the headlights of the departing Land Rover, the beam from the headlights consumed by the darkness, the noise of the engine eaten by the wind.

They were gone. He was alive but with no idea what he was doing here.

Qui audet adipiscitur.

Fifty metres. What the hell did that mean? Had they accidently killed somebody?

He was truly, completely alone. And the Land Rover was sitting, waiting, engine running. Left for him. He couldn't see anybody inside.

'But I can see that we still use Her Majesty's money to play silly buggers, always money for shite,' said Patrick into the wind, as he was bloody sure there was nobody there to hear it. Well, nearly sure. He faced uphill and now he had his night vision back and began to quarter the hillside in visual sweeps. He smiled. It had been a long, long time since he lived in a world where nobody knew your name because if you saw them as a person, then you might hesitate, and that could be fatal. He remembered the killing house, blacked out, and being told one man with a knife who kept his nerve could kill lots of people in the dark. Why? Because without hesitation he could murder every single one he met, while his enemies whispered, *'Is that you Frank?'* You were given a nickname the minute you walked in the door, the second you signed up and became one of them, one of the ten percent. The nickname meant you ceased being a person in your own right, you became one of them, one of the team. And he had been one of that team, he had been on a hillside like this many a time, cold and wet, pumped with adrenaline listening to the noise of gunfire and following the pattern of tracer fire back to its source. Four men going where an army couldn't. Small strong men, the four of them moving like an insidious, venomous little beast, working towards the heart of its prey.

And they had. Patrick closed his eyes for a moment and he was back on a hillside, clouds of smoke, the smell of cordite and burned flesh filling his nostrils, pushing on and up, climbing, running over rough ground and pushing through,

going in where angels failed to fly for fear of being shot down.
Slotting everyone in front of them.

He breathed deep in the air that was fresh and cooling to
his lungs, air untainted by the death of those like him, born
in a different belief system, in another country.

Like the past.

Valerie was hanging, swinging back and forth like a pendulum
inside a clock, the tightness around her neck getting worse.
She was back in the cupboard at the Blue Neptune, somebody
was strangling her. She passed out, a tangle of colours appeared
before her eyes, red bursting into yellow that faded to black
as she lost consciousness. She waited to die.

But didn't.

She was being strangled. She reached up to her throat,
clawing at the noose, her fingertips tugging at the soft fabric
that was winding round and pulling ever tighter.

Then it all went dark.

She opened her eyes. It was actually dark.

Valerie was back in the cupboard, panicking. She lifted her
other hand and slipped, hitting her head on the tiled floor. She
could see in her mind's eye the noose tightening, constricting
her throat until she couldn't breathe. She choked, rolling on
the floor, her eyes closing. Then she realized she was lying
down and not choking.

She was lying in the dark.

She walked her fingertips up to her neck, wondering
what she would find. Unable to get her arms free, she tried
to calm herself. She shuffled out the door of the bedroom,
aware of something sticky under her. But she kept going, she
had to get out of here. Shouldering the door open, she twisted
her body and waited for her vision to clear so she knew what
was on the other side of the door. She recognized this room,
but had no idea where from.

She could make out movement on the opposite wall,
somebody lying low and trying to stay hidden, somebody like
her, tied up and kept captured.

She closed her eyes and rested her head against the wall,
waiting for a noise or some clue. Her thoughts were all over

the place. This was her worst nightmare all over again, he had found her and put her back in the cupboard. She needed to get out and help the other woman. Looking up she saw the woman was looking back at her. She edged her way forward as she came forward to meet her halfway.

She was looking at herself.

She was there, in the mirror of the hotel room. She stared into her own eyes for a long time wondering if she actually recognized that woman who looked back at her. She looked so much older and more tired than Valerie.

She was old. On the floor after another blackout. Time had slipped somewhere, a few minutes or hours lost, a little bit of herself had escaped. She had no idea.

Then she heard footsteps on the corridor outside. Valerie's eyes fixed on the door, willing it to open. It seemed a long time before there was a very quiet double knock.

She thought she saw a light, thinking that she might be dying now. All that bloody effort and now dying when she wasn't ready. But God smelled familiar and said something, a voice she recognized as if he was far away down a tunnel, shouting at her. She presumed that, as she knew the voice, God has been talking to her before her final breath.

She reached her hand out, ready to meet her maker.

Her mouth was dry. It hurt to move her tongue. She thought she was forming the words correctly, she hoped she could be understood, but from God's uncomprehending face, which blurred and danced in front of her, she was making no sense at all.

She tried again. 'You need to help me.'

The Bealach was a terrible place to be in winter. It was like the surface of the moon but slightly less hospitable. Bealach Na Ba the locals called it, which meant the pass of the cattle or, as it was sometimes translated, the stink of burned-out clutch. Until recently, within Patrick's memory, it had been the only road that connected Applecross with the rest of the country. Up here, two thousand feet above sea level on an exposed summit, the wind was so strong, it whipped at his jacket, almost pushing him over. Reminded him of the screeching winds on South Georgia, the Fortuna Glacier, where they had to creep about like German snipers.

He took cover behind the shelter of the Land Rover, crouching against the body on the lee side where the wind and rain came under the Landie trying to get a bite at him. Once he got his bearings, he gave in to the aching in his knees, stood up and climbed into the shelter of the vehicle, fumbling to check the keys. He set the demister at full, thinking.

He moved the vehicle, pulling it forward and repositioning it so the lights shone right down the gully, but back enough from the edge to allow him to getaway easily without reversing.

This was not a place for him, this was home for deer and sheep, this was where city folk and hill walkers died of exposure. Well, in the past that was true, but now the National Park had built access roads everywhere, the hills belonged to everybody. Now there was an invasion of mountain bikers, motorhomers, stupid people who had seen the North Coast 500 drive on the TV and thought they liked the look of it. Puffer fish looked nice too, but they were still fatal to the ignorant.

So, there was something out on that hillside that was his business, or at least what Intel thought was his business. He'd no sure idea what his monosyllabic friends had been getting at but there was only one way to find out. Coming up with the story of how he came to be here might be more of a challenge, he thought. He could always tell the truth, no bugger would ever believe that, but that truth would already be being manipulated now, by faceless men in good suits, with no blood on their hands.

He picked up the torch, turned it on, flashing it a few times to make sure the beam was strong and that it was waterproof, rolled into the rear and out the back door behind the glare of his lights. He did a quick grid search in the darkness, making sure he was alone.

Then he walked quickly across the parking area till he was in the shadow again outside the arc of the lights and began to walk uphill, rolling silently on the outside of his boots, stopping at each perspective change and checking the ground. From the dark he could see every rock bathed in stark light.

Forty metres or so up he saw it. Pale and white, out of place, waving at him in greeting. He crouched and scanned the dark above the lights. He pulled his mobile but there was a better signal on the moon than up here. He had to hurry. Throwing caution to the wind he rushed towards the movement in the heather.

It was a hand, hanging from the sleeve of a jumper caught in a whipping gorse bush, the fingers caught in the wind, waving.

Two hours after he found the body, Patrick was alone again at the top of the pass, waiting for the circus to come to town. He had rather enjoyed the drive to the north, going down the Bealach, until his phone told him he had a signal. Then he had contacted his DC, Morna Taverner, getting her out her bed at four a.m., and gave her a list of instructions, checking the local hotels for guests who hadn't returned tonight, then check the list of young men reported missing, in Scotland for starters. Then any abandoned or burnt-out vehicles within a twenty-mile radius. It might be a long list, but she was a good police officer, despite that idiot she had married and a constant lack of a reliable babysitter. As an afterthought. He called the number of Lachlan McRae, who lived next door to Morna in Constance House, one street from the seafront at Port MacDuff and got him out his bed as well.

Then he turned around and drove back up, slower than the Gorilla had driven but still bringing back an old thrill.

The body on the hill had no ID on him, Patrick was not convinced of the most obvious answer; that the young man had been a rough tourist, not an extreme runner with the jumper he was wearing. Maybe more of an extreme walker, the big knitted jumper and border collie brigade, not the Rohan Craghopper super fit lot. They were both tough, both more than a little mad according to the mountain rescue. The real answer would be more tragic, brought about by human hand.

The Bealach was isolated and high but it wasn't steep. The road up twisted and turned, gaining height over nine kilometres, meandering its way up and over the pass. Who was he? Who took his ID and why he was dressed the way he was? And

how did he end up here on a night like this when the road
had been closed for a couple of weeks now. The uncomfortable answer to that was he was either somebody who knew
the place, or he had been placed here by somebody who
knew the place and whoever did that, well, that vehicle would
be covered in blood and that vehicle would have been spotted
somewhere along the way. At this time of year, strangers stuck
out. Patrick had a slight rethink there. The North Coast 500
was far too popular. Tourists were driving it all hours of day
and night, the holiday season now lasted twelve months.
Everybody thought they knew the road because they had read
about it in a magazine in a Sunday supplement, everybody
and their uncle. Folk with 4x4s sat in pubs in the West End
of Glasgow and talked about it, boasting about how they had
driven it in a gale in October, a snowdrift in January, backwards
at midnight while whistling the theme tune from *The Great
Escape*. That was all very well until one vehicle missed a turn
and plunged down into the glen, killing everybody on board.
Then it would be his fault.

Four hours after he found the body, Patrick was watching
the circus. There was no daylight up here in the middle of the
bleak wilderness, it was all spotlights and headlights, shadows
dancing over bleak rocks and cairns.

The scenes of crime team had pegged out the stony ground,
fine puddles lying on top of the moss and grass. The vehicles
were on the hard standing at the viewing point, there had been
a decision, made by Patrick, to leave the civilian vehicles at
the bottom of the hill. The road was closed anyway and probably would remain so until early in the new year. The forestry
commission ATVs were doing the running up and down,
safe and sturdy.

Despite the weather things were going well; the lights were
on, the plates were up. The body lay there, now bathed by
light, a young man with dark hair that took a deep ebony sheen
in the neon glow, a slight burnished copper tint when caught
by the harsh glare of the spotlights.

Alastair Patrick had taken one look at the man and knew
he had been beaten to death. It looked like somebody had
danced on his head, never mind the obvious wound across the

front of the man's throat which to Patrick's expert eye was both amateurish and non-fatal. There may have been torture, but looking too closely would involve adjusting clothing, and maybe losing trace evidence, so he left it. A quick look through the pockets of the baggy jeans revealed nothing.

This was no accident.

Somebody had pulled him from a vehicle and rolled him into the gully.

No rush. The victim wasn't going anywhere.

They could wait until they had him on the slab over at the mortuary, wherever he ended up. There was talk of taking him all the way down to Glasgow, and that could take another six hours or so. Maybe he could insist on Inverness.

Patrick looked round to see the photographer in the spotlight, clicking away, the crime scene officer was helping with the video. Two CSIs were on their knees searching the ground, getting soaked and finding nothing but doing the job anyway. He had instructed that the body be taken off the hill ASAP, they would find anything they needed to find once the sun was up. He looked at his watch and that would be another three hours away.

One of the CSIs shone her or his torch in the face of the young man, eyes closed, a pink, fresh face, as if he had decided to shave when he looked in the mirror on the day he died. His face was bloodied red, the rain running over it, giving him the look of both life and perspiration. He looked at peace in this desolate place.

After dying a brutal death.

The police surgeon turned up eventually, ignoring Patrick, picking his way over the ground, dressed in a huge downy anorak, and a woollen hat pulled far over his ears. He snubbed the group as he went about his business, then he stopped. Suddenly.

The two CSIs and the photographer ceased to move, stilled exactly where they were, turned to stone.

'Who is in charge here? Is that you, Patrick?'

'Yes,' he shouted over the screaming of the wind.

'Well, you'd better get a chopper here right now. He's not dead.'

Alastair Patrick's mind swiftly moved up a few gears. Oh, so he was not dead, so why was he here? Why had they thought he was dead? Had they checked? Had he checked? Of course he had, he had placed his bare fingers over the jugular and found nothing.

Alastair Patrick walked back to the Land Rover with greater purpose than he had left it, he was ready to drive back down the pass to get a phone signal as a stretcher, aluminium blankets, an oxygen tank and mask ready, was making its way back over to the body.

The paperwork just got problematic.

He was thinking of the long drive to Inverness as Patrick watched the body being placed on a stretcher, and placed into the back of the Land Rover, resting it on the top of the seat. There was no way a normal ambulance was going to get up here. They'd take him down to the coast and the Paraffin Budgie could meet them there.

That would be safer, in this night sky, this weather, this visibility.

He called the Multi Agency Briefing.

It was someone else's decision.

FOUR

Gareth Ahern had been volunteer ranger for as long as he could recall. He was better at it than most of the young professionals that came onto the lochside after graduation from university, all very good at the DNA of ferns and the breeding habits of otters, but not so bloody good at getting up at the crack of dawn and reading the signs of what had been going on in the wee dark hours of the night. And more recently they had had the hooligans from the city come up, making it out to the islands and killing the wildlife, most noticeably the wallabies. Last week one of the wallabies had been skinned on the beach and left in full view for the tourists on the loch cruise to see the next morning. Ahern had thought he would never see the day when there had to be security on twenty-seven square miles of water.

One of the students, a nice young bloke called Cowan who drove a VW camper, had explained it to Ahern; it was some kind of game they had, an initiation ceremony to become a fully paid up member of the gang by showing how tough you were. The aim of it seemed to be to get out to the islands of the loch unseen, then trap and kill whatever they could find. Birds, ducks, rabbits and, most recently, the wallabies. There had been signs of torture of the animals, the Wildlife Protection Unit were taking an interest now that it looked likely the attacks would affect tourism. They had asked Ahern and Cowan and others to keep watch and collect any evidence that they could.

That would be for a prosecution, Ahern knew that and knew that some defence counsel would argue some shite about the wee bastards being brought up on a council estate and deprived of the newest iPhone or designer jeans, or a job or a sense of self-respect. Aye well, self-respect came from yourself in Ahern's opinion, nobody else. You believed in yourself and others followed suit. Nobody could take your self-respect away, you had to give it away.

It made Ahern's blood boil, he had let it be known that he would do time for the wee shites. He'd take his bloody shotgun out and blow the shit they had for brains to where the sun didn't shine. The violence towards the animals angered him, the senselessness of it enraged him. But the lack of respect? That really got to him. It was everywhere in society these days.

As he walked on, in teaming rain that was caught by the gusty wind, hitting him in the face then snatching at the skin at the back of his head, he amused himself by considering how he would do it if he ever caught the perpetrators. He would take his time about it too, taking them one at a time, so they each knew what was coming. He was even thinking of some way he could get the boat away if they were on the island, so they would be stranded. And he would leave them there. He could sit on the shore and watch them as they waved for help, he'd wave back. They all had bloody mobile phones nowadays so they'd call the cruise services and get picked up and then blame the national park management or the social services when all the really needed was a loaded shotgun up their arse. And a twitchy finger on the trigger.

Ahern trudged up the hill walking south to the visit centre at Inveruglass, which had been ruined by that stupid viewing tower that folk kept setting on fire. They should ban the whole bloody lot of them; he walked on, gaining height until he saw his first full view of the loch. It was leaving eight thirty, the first hesitant flicker of dawn haloed the Ben. Every day it made his heart ache as it had done for the last fifty years, sixty years if he was honest. Bar deaths, marriages, two weeks annual holiday, he had been here every day, and even on his holidays he went north to look at Loch Maree instead.

Then he smelt it. Something bloody in the air, in the rain. And the blood was relatively fresh. His fury boiled over, he started cursing, battering the longer brown ferns with his walking stick, looking to spot the body of another animal in his torch beam. A deer from the look of it. He was furious, more death, more waste of life lost by the mindless acts of those less worthy.

He sniffed the air, thinking how unusually strong the smell

was. He stepped through the wet grass, slowly and carefully, keeping his eyes low but following the scent of the blood, and there it was. Well, there it wasn't.

A flattened area of grass, blades bent and broken, over a large area and the smell of blood hanging in the mist. Lots of blood, whatever had died here must have been a big animal. He walked around a little, the beam catching footprints in the mud. Trying to keep clear of them so he didn't mess it up for the wildlife unit and any further prosecution. He rubbed at his beard, this might be some of the evidence they were waiting for. Something had died here, but he wanted to be sure, so he looked around for the signs of an illegal snare or a trap. Finding nothing, he sighed and swallowed his anger before walking down to the café where Belinda had a mobile phone. The café wouldn't be open yet, but Belinda would be in and she'd report it for him.

Hannah was worried. The woman had come back from X-ray, there was a fracture in her occiput that had been the result of a blunt force trauma. But what worried her more was the smell of drink that had vanished when she took the clothes off her. The smell had followed the clothes to the bag. The woman's breath was clean, minty if anything, her hair smelled of shampoo – who shampooed over a huge head wound? Well, the answer to that was any Glaswegian drunk who got into a fight.

The day shift were talking about doing a rape kit. There was no chance of getting informed consent, but she could try and talk her round. Maybe get the patient to understand, talk her through it and see if she could be made to understand. But if it was true that the woman had suffered a very stressful event, been subject to physical violence, then showered, then that added up to some kind of sexual assault. Maybe from her permanent abuser. If there was any evidence it would probably have gone down the plughole.

Hannah believed there was a positive side to everything. The patient's psychotic break was doing its job, protecting the victim, keeping out the traumatic memories until psyche was strong enough to recall them. If she was a victim of a sexual attack, she was very calm, too calm. Hannah had seen that many times too, that ability to hand themselves over to a caring person but this one was more wary, far more calculating than distressed.

They were waiting for a psychiatric bed then there would be further assessments, so God alone knew how long that would be. At least she had been moved to a room rather than a cubicle with a curtain round her, dressed in a hospital gown, her head wound covered by a light dressing. Anything was better than lying on a trolley in an examination room, with everybody and their mother popping through to borrow this and that and never returning it.

She seemed to be able to hear, to understand, but did not speak or respond in any way, except . . . well, she did. Hannah couldn't pinpoint the common factor. The hospital didn't faze her at all. Was she a nurse somewhere, a cleaner, maybe a doctor? A light bulb went on in Hannah's head. Was that why the wound was cleaned? Something she maybe did by instinct, with a first aid kit or something.

Hannah found it all very confusing, but she had been told to stay here, keep monitoring her vitals, to get some form of communication going and get consent or even an ID. All hell was let loose around her as a couple came in high on all sorts of substances. She heard raised voices, swearing, then something being pushed and then a smash of something glass being broken, followed by the thump thump of security boots hurrying to the scene. Hannah felt she had had the Sunday night shift easy.

The blonde woman was lying easier now, head back, her hair swept up off her face. They had got the age wrong, Hannah thought, this woman was younger than her sixties, fifties maybe. Hannah had gone through her clothes and found nothing. Her clothes were clean apart from the bloodstains and she had good teeth, her nails were clean and cut evenly, no ingrained dirt. Two things that are rarely found on any poor bugger who is living on the street. She could have been foreign, so Hannah tried a few languages she knew hello in. The woman was fair-skinned so that cut out the Middle or the Far East, but she could be Eastern European or Scandinavian or any of those new countries that Hannah didn't really know the whereabouts of.

She nipped out to the main desk and picked up the laminated sheet with *Hello, you are in a hospital*, written on it in many languages. She showed it to the woman who looked at it, reached out a hand to take it. Hannah held her breath thinking that the woman was processing the writing and was going to point at one, or point at one and then say something.

She handed the laminated sheet back.

Hannah tried to explain that they were keeping her in for observation, to make sure she didn't have a brain bleed. 'Did somebody hit you over the head?' Hannah asked, lifting her own hand up as if she was going to hit herself. 'Did somebody punch you in the eye?' she mimed this also. The grey eyes looked right through her; they turned at the crackle of a police radio outside the room.

It looked like, to Hannah's mind, and Hannah loved mystery writing, that the woman had been assaulted. She had been caught by the shoulder, bruised and sore, hit over the head, the slashes on her back and lower arms were, well, one directional? Then she had been stabbed, but she had pulled away at the last minute. Was that possible, a sign that she had been running, a knife went out and the victim twisted as he caught her, she had put her arms up to protect herself, somebody had battered her on the head then got her on the ground and kicked her. That was what it looked like, she had worked in A & E for five years now. She had seen it all. Except why do that when they had a knife on her?

And, the woman was behaving as if she was safe in here.

Which, Hannah concluded, meant she might not feel safe outside or at home? If she had been battered by her hubby or partner then they wouldn't have listed her as missing. They would need to wait until a friend or a family member did that?

Or was this a sanctuary? Hannah turned back to look at her as the grey eyes followed her every move, not dull or dazed but alert. Hannah smiled; the woman's mouth twitched as if she had been going to smile then remembered the game she was playing.

Hannah told her they would get her a cup of something

once the doctors had cleared that, in case she needed an operation. No response. The doctor would be here in a minute – no response. In the NHS a minute can be a long time – no response.

She placed the switch for the buzzer in her hand, the patient took it. She put on a heart monitor as her pulse was fast but weak, and an oxygen tube on her top lip. All her vital signs were indicative of blood loss but there wasn't that much blood on her . . . It must be somewhere.

She left the cubicle to update the police. Her shift was over. Usually she was glad to be going home but not this time, she would like to stay to see how this panned out.

After talking to the duty doctor, Hannah tried an age-old trick, came in with a cup of tea and asked the woman if she would like it. The woman didn't respond in any language, except to hold out her hand for the tea, and proceed to drink it.

Well, that told her nothing, except the woman drank black tea and that there was nothing wrong with her vision.

Morna Taverner stood by the window staring into the rain-drenched street and tried not to make it too obvious that she was waiting. She loved her husband dearly, she loved her son and she loved her mother. She wished that some of them, any of them, or all of them, could be exactly where they were supposed to be. The child was in the bath – she could hear Finn doing his impersonation of the Death Star, so there would be more water on the bathroom floor than in the bath. Neil wasn't home from work yet, and he was supposed to be. He wasn't answering his mobile so he would be driving or out at a remote B and B to drop off luggage for those who thought it was fun to walk twenty miles a day in the freezing cold, pissing rain then go and sleep in a plastic bag in a field or in a stranger's lumpy bed. Morna thought they were bloody mad, but their madness did pay for her to go to Lanzarote once a year and it financed Neil's dream of building their forever home.

She leaned on the windowsill, peering through the glass. Should she phone her mum again? Mum had said she was just leaving the farm so she would be on her way and not able to answer if she was driving, not on these narrow country roads with their deceitful turns and hidden bends, much worse in this bloody weather and the bloody tourists doing three miles an hour on the single track road enjoying what they could see of the scenery.

Morna was needed at work and she was keen to go. She had to drive to Raigmore Hospital, two hours if she got a clear run. Somebody, or some body she corrected herself, had been attacked and left on the top of the Bealach Na Ba.

Morna fingered her mobile in her pocket. Patrick, her DCI, had phoned her twice now. She really wanted this job and if she wasn't able to respond quickly then he would call another DC. He had a mental list that he would work through and Morna was close to the top, born and living in Port MacDuff with a good local knowledge. She wanted the job and didn't want to pass it up. Something terrible had happened up on the Bealach, she was sure of it, and if DCI Patrick had contacted her . . . well, she was keen to get on and show her competencies. She wasn't going to get anywhere if she had to say to her boss again, *yes I'd like to come in and help out, I know I am late for work but there is nobody here to look after the wee guy and take him to school so on you go and I'll catch up with you when I can.*

She could imagine how well that would go down.

Why did he phone her? Was it because of something that she was already working on? Like that cut the list of possibilities down to anything. Or maybe . . . she cheered up as she saw some lights on the road, a car coming . . . then her heart sank as it went past the bottom of the road. Not her mother then. Shite, she was going to be really late.

And she didn't want to be, not after all that time off after the accident.

She looked out the window, hearing Finn splashing in the bath, all was dark outside.

Was it her pet project? Had he seen a link with that and that was why he had phoned? Patrick had warned her about becoming obsessed with the rape she was trying to link with other similar crimes. The disappearance of Jennifer Argyll in

1987 was not an isolated event. Jennifer had been the start of something, she was sure of it. Well, *she* was sure of it. And DCI Patrick had heard her out, he had looked at the file saying nothing as she spoke, voicing her thoughts and suspicions. He let her run out of steam, and then said, quietly, in that very direct way he had, that a database was only that. Ask it a stupid question and it will give you a stupid answer. Well, she could recall his exact words. All he had really said was 'Shit in equalled shit out'.

Morna had taken that to mean she was asking the wrong questions of the database, rather than 'stop wasting police time'. A few minutes here and there, she was back on it. Patrick knew she was still trawling the system, she wasn't hiding it from him, or drawing his attention to it, but she logged the minutes, and when he saw them he gave her a wry smile. He was a man of few words. That rare smile translated as 'God loves a trier'.

She turned back into the room and gave the logs on the fire another wee poke, closing the door tightly and closing the vents. She had stuck a towel over the radiator when she got the first call, but that had cooled off now. Last night Finn had been painting a wizard's outfit for a party later in the week, and had left the mask on the radiator to dry. It had a wide smile and huge ears, giving it a passing resemblance to Prince Charles at the dentist. Morna remembered she had forgotten to buy a present for whoever's birthday it was. She'd ask another mum. She looked out the window one last time, saw no car, then walked into the kitchen to write a reminder for the party on the blackboard that held her shopping list. She squirted some hand cream onto her chapped, bleeding hands and waved her fingers about drying them in the cold air.

Then Finn was shouting that he wanted out the bath so she grabbed the Darth Vader towel from the radiator and rushed down the hall. Finn was doing his impersonation of the Death Star while lying face down in the near empty bath, a snorkel covering his face.

'Up,' she said, 'out.'

He climbed out the bath, this pale-skinned creature with endless bendy limbs, red-headed and freckled. The Death Star kept pinging, the snorkel was steaming up, and Finn was waving a grey plastic X-wing above his head, keeping it to its deadly mission. He swapped it from hand to hand as he slipped his arms in his vest, then his school shirt, then his jumper. She picked him up, carrying him into the living room where his socks and wellies were warming in front of the dying fire.

She checked the clock.

'I have to go out now.'

'No mummy,' he sighed, wriggling and kicking as she tried to get socks on his feet, then the wellies on his legs.

'You will have to go next door until Granny gets here, then go to school.'

'Haribos?'

'No. That's a Thursday. You get Haribos on a Thursday.'

'What day is it today?' The X-wing executed an impressive turn.

'The day after Sunday.'

'Wednesday?'

'Nope, try again.'

'Can I get Haribos?'

'Nope.' She stood him back up, his head like an orange porcupine. She tightened the belt of his house coat then marched him, and the X-wing, out to the hall where she put an old waxed jacket over his shoulders. It was long enough to touch the floorboards. Then she plonked a flat cap on his head.

Brora looked up, but the collie judged it was too wet to be bothered about going for a walk so she promptly went back to sleep.

Morna opened the front door and shoved the boy out into the rain, frogmarching him down their short front path, through the gate then up the path of the neighbour's house. The three stories of the terraced looked gloomy and menacing in the glare of the streetlamps. The small windows looked mean; the dark closed curtains looked hostile.

Not the sort of place to run to if you were young, vulnerable and in trouble. A place where you could walk out the village and disappear. Like Jennifer Argyll.

The neighbour's front door opened immediately, Lachlan had heard her own door close no doubt and had a fair idea what was coming. He was dressed but looked as if he hadn't showered or combed his hair, the white streak in his hair was curled into a corkscrew. 'When you have to go, you have to go, Morna. Alastair has already phoned me.'

'Really?' she was annoyed that the shortcomings of her family had been so predictable to her boss.

'You want me to look after the lad.'

'Just for a couple of minutes. Mum will be here soon. Or if not, can you take him to school.'

'No problem, just watch yourself in that weather.' Lachlan placed his huge hand on Finn's head and guided both boy and X-wing into the house. 'He'll be OK here.' He looked up into the ebony sky then at her, his brown eyes creased slightly, an old cop looking at the young generation.

Morna turned to walk back down the path, pulling up her hood. 'Did Alastair say anything? Is it about Jennifer?'

'No. But I doubt it, why would it be? Take care,' and the door closed over, one final ping of the Death Star sonar.

Alone, in the street, pissing down, abandoning her son for the company of a dead body found at the top of the pass on a dark and stormy morning, thinking about a woman she had never met.

DC Wyngate drove into the car park at Inveruglass in response to a call from the Wildlife Protection Unit. Not his territory but they needed a hand and somehow the buck had stopped with him. It felt like demotion.

It had taken him an hour to drive the forty miles; much quicker once he had got out the city boundary and the rush hour traffic and he had made good time. The car park was largely empty, except a cop car, small van for the café and a Mini Clubman. It was too early in the day and too late in the year for the coaches full of old folk, on their three days' tour of the Highlands, staying in second-rate hotels but still cheaper than heating the houses at home. Nobody would go up to the viewing site. Not only was it too misty to see anything but the back of the head of the person standing in front of you, there was the small matter of the blue and white tape cordoning the area off.

He parked his car alongside the other, opened the door and looked at the sky, then opened the boot and put on his heavy duty jacket and his wellington boots.

Ahern introduced himself. He was still shaking slightly, not with nerves or shock but with finely controlled anger. Wyngate thought he looked the type, waterproof Rohans tucked into his serious Hunter wellies. The walking stick had been carved from a tree branch, the handle of it made from a horn or an antler of some kind. He was older than Wyngate had presumed; he had the air of a civil engineer or an architect out for a long country walk about him rather than a wildlife ranger. He was not far wrong as Ahern introduced himself as a volunteer ranger, now he was retired. Wyngate nodded as Ahern said he had been an architectural surveyor in his previous life, used to working with mines and underground waterways.

They walked across the car park, Ahern talking about the amount of blood, the rainfall, how much of it would have already been washed away so God knew how much the poor creature had lost at the time of the . . . He had difficulty finding the most appropriate word and ended up settling for 'event'. Wyngate struggled to walk and take notes but fortunately Ahern was clear, concise, accurate as to what he had witnessed and explained why he was there so early in the morning. As they started to walk up the hill on the path that passed the viewing point, Ahern became distressed, as he spoke of the amount of blood. He wiped his lips with the back of his hand. To his eyes it looked as though something had been chased, hunted down, he nodded to the north through the undergrowth saying there was another smaller path there that went in a long circuitous route back to the car park.

Ahern looked up at the sky, mimicking Wyngate's actions as he had left the car. 'Even with the rain washing some away. There's too much blood,' he repeated, as if the rain itself had stolen the blood, and would the guilty party like to give it back.

Wyngate looked at the ground, trusting Ahern's story rather than his own eyes. Ahern knew the area well and had got into the habit of staying away from the official car parks and laybys on the west side of the loch. He had come across a few rough sleepers and wild campers, illegal campsites littered with empty booze bottles and occasionally the odd syringe and bit of burned tinfoil. That morning he had been walking around the loch on the north-west side making his way down to the viewpoint from the north, when he had smelled the blood in the air.

'Smelled it?' asked Wyngate, panting a little with the effort of keeping up with the man old enough to be his father.

'Oh, yes, fresh and plenty. Somebody will have a deer in their freezer tonight and I hope it poisons them.'

'Any trouble up here with weird goings-on? Satanic stuff? Anything like that?'

'Nope. Just the devil that is the drugs, and that's enough.'

The two of them walked, Ahern leading the way, no sense of urgency, an easy stride of his long legs making easy of the steep hill. Wyngate was thinking about the wallaby killings, animal sacrifices? Killing animals to conjure up the spirit of Old Nick did at least make some kind of sense.

'There's no skin, no intestines, no internal tissue, just the blood? No sign that something was gralloched here?' Wyngate asked. 'Could it be human? I mean, can a human lose that amount of blood and live? I'm thinking about the drug wars that are raging in the city.'

'You are a city cop, I'm a country ranger. Both red deer and humans have eight pints of blood. One of those things you get to know doing this job.'

Wyngate realized that the prospect of a human victim had crossed Ahern's mind as well. 'The last three bodies up here were drug related, admittedly little more than kids out getting their kicks from illegal or legal highs, but they were all cold once they got to the pathologist's table.' Wyngate was already thinking that he was getting that blood tested, even if they found an antler and a copy of Bambi. He was sure the CSI team carried now an onsite blood test for that so they didn't spend too much money investigating the site of a dog fight. A two-test system, one to make sure it was blood, the second to make sure it was human. He knew it was an immunochromatic procedure and once they had that, they could then decide whether or not they needed to look for more samples for future DNA testing, but it was all time sensitive in this weather.

Ahern stopped, suddenly, putting his arm out to his side preventing them from going any further. He looked down at the grass, flattened and fractured, a main area, three-feet wide that narrowed to a tail over a space of about ten feet. There were bloodstains still easily visible, not complete, the veins of it had been washed away leaving droplets in the leaves and spikes in the channels of the grass leaves. There were traces of it, here and there all over.

By force of habit, Wyngate started looking around, half-listening to what Ahern was saying. His eyes scanning the ground for anything odd. He thought he saw a black bird, near the trunk of a sapling that was bending in the wind. It was small, jaggy and a black that was too dense to be natural.

He walked over and knelt down beside it. It hadn't been lying there for very long, the fractured plastic of the Samsung was clean. It was partially embedded into the ground.

Animals do many great things but they are not generally known for smashing brand new mobile phones. Wyngate make a quick calculation. Whoever it was had been wounded and was probably deceased. They now needed manpower to fan out and grid search the place of the attack. He turned to look out, the Ben was covered in swirling mist; the water was keeping its secrets.

This was now extremely time sensitive.

He excused himself from Ahern and started making his phone calls. Crime scene first and then hospitals.

FIVE

There was no doubt about it. Valerie Abernethy was feeling better. Her function was improved and her brain was clearer but she had always been a high-functioning alcoholic, and she was very bright. There was a lot she could do with very little thought or effort, it all came so easy to her. She had never really learned to challenge herself. Now she was learning the hard way just how difficult it could be for her to get up in the morning. For the first time she had accepted medication for depression and her mood swings. She had admitted that to the young doctor who had appeared at the door of the surgery where Archie had dumped her. He was a hard-faced man who spoke in terms that made it perfectly clear she had two choices, do as she was told or die.

It was up to her.

He was not going to waste his time and effort if she was not going to do anything about it right here and right now.

She had looked back at him and, in a quiet voice that did not sound like her at all, said that she had lost her entire family.

'So,' he said, with a beguiling tilt of the head. She knew this meant she had walked into a trap and he was about to close it. 'You were totally sober before that? I think not.'

The doctor had repeated, 'So I'm not going to do anything about it if you are not going to do anything yourself. You need to apply yourself to getting better.' He had leaned back in the seat, talking over what she had been through in the last few years, ticking the points off on his fingers, by the time he had finished Valerie had felt that she would have felt terrible for that person, and that person was herself. She was one step removed from it all. And then the doc had said, 'I don't think that this is a good time for you to be making big decisions. You need to keep your life on the straight and narrow, you need to let your blood chemistry stabilize. You need to regain the capacity for clear thought so you can get through the day. That will be your first challenge, once you get through that then we can look at the other options. And please, don't ever do anything on impulse. Recovering alcoholics can have severe issues with impulse control. If you get an idea, even if you think it's the greatest idea in the world, write it down and think about it again the following day. It will be that lack of filter that has got you into much of the mess you are in.'

She thought about the gun she had tucked away in the back of her bag that was leaning against her leg. She opened her mouth, getting ready to say that she still had the means to kill herself, and that was still her intention, but when she spoke all that came out her mouth was, 'I have nothing to do. I don't even have a cat to look after.'

'You have plenty to do, you just don't want to do any of it. You need to work on yourself.' Those were his final words as he pressed print and the prescription slips started to churn out. She tuned out, hearing him vaguely add something, spoken to the wall, or to himself, about being a bright young woman, with a good brain and that the brain will find something to worry about unless she gave it something constructive to do, something challenging but insignificant so she could get her teeth into it but not fret if she failed at it. Then she would be OK.

'And you are going to stay with your uncle?'

'So he tells me.'

'Best thing you can do'.

And here she was . . .

At Uncle Archie's house.

Valerie looked round the room, not recognizing it but she recognized the style – it was very Pippa. Very Marks and Spencer's. But she had no real idea when she had last been in this house, or if she had ever been in this neat little bungalow with the lawn cut in precise stripes at all. She could remember the detached house out in Milngavie where Archie and Pippa had lived before they downsized. When she was a child, Archie and her dad worked together in the fiscal service, and Pippa and her mum were housewives. Valerie and Abigail had played in that house often as children. Uncle Archie and Auntie Pippa were great fun in the way that parents can never be, giving too much freedom and too many sweeties.

They had been second parents to both girls.

It was only now, as an adult herself, that she wondered if Archie and Pippa had wanted children too, in the same way that she herself had yearned for them, once she knew that she couldn't have them. Archie and Pippa seemed to have everything else.

Having a family had never really worked out for them and they had sold up and moved to this lovely, but charmless bungalow. Small, neat, easily looked after.

Archie knew Abigail almost as much as he knew her, his god-daughter. He had been Uncle Archie to them both.

She thought back to what the GP had said earlier at her emergency appointment. 'We will get these prescriptions picked up, stay well, get plenty of rest, and after a week we will see where we are. We need to survive seven days. If we can do that, if you do that, then we can all move it forward. Here's the phone and contact details of the AA and support that is available. If you get stuck. pick up the phone and speak to them. I know you don't want to hear it right now but you are a very lucky woman, you have somebody who's willing to take you in and look after you.'

She did.

Archie Walker, bless him.

Knowing her was like cuddling a serpent.

Wyngate had felt quite the king pin, in charge of the locus on the bloodstained site at the loch. There were CSIs crawling everywhere. Cops he had not been on the same shift rotation with for ages had appeared to help out, or as he was starting to see it, they were here to get in his way and he started to wish that somebody else would come along and claim responsibility for the crime scene. It was becoming a poisoned chalice.

He had been told a SIO from Balloch had been appointed, but as they had no real idea what they were investigating, he had gone back to base and had so far refused to return to a site of a 'bad nosebleed and a stolen mobile phone'.

Then a smartly dressed young man had limped out of a very clean Audi and asked the nearest uniform who was in charge. A minute later DS Viktor Mulholland had introduced himself to Wyngate, very sarcastically. He had been seconded back down from West End Central so the bosses said, but it was obvious the people upstairs had been given the ideal opportunity to get them out the way, in a two for one deal.

'Do you have a clue what's going on?' asked Mulholland.

'You are the superior officer,' said Wyngate looking around. 'And that's the site up there.' He pointed up to An Ceann Mor.

'No way am I going up there. No chance, I have a bad leg.'

'Exactly,' said Wyngate, then explained that he thought the CID should already be here and that, if in charge of anything, it should be traffic. Coaches kept pulling into the car park and had to be helped to U-turn and get back out again, although the police activity was proving a bigger tourist attraction than the loch with its beauty hidden behind a bank of rain.

In the end, Wyngate and Mulholland had a quick resume of the situation, they both had been dropped in the shit by their superiors so they may as well make the best of it.

'The blood, is it human?'

'It is. They are looking for a body. So far, the nearest five A & E's have come up with no admissions that match this scenario. A search team is coming and I think we need traffic out to get the road signposted right at the start of the loch turn off.'

Mulholland nodded and looked up at the viewing point, seeing the CSIs walking around in their protective suits, looking rather unworldly high up in the mist. 'We'll hold the reins until the results come in, it will go up the tree quick enough. Where is McCaffrey? Has he gone up in the world or something?'

'Who?' Wyngate looked at his notebook, he had kept an inventory of names. 'No McCaffrey here.'

'Oh, he's here. I'm bloody sure that's his car in the car park, can't be that many Mini Clubmen around with three baby seats. He'll have sneaked in when your back was turned, he's an ambitious wee sod that one. I'll see what's happening over in the car park and let you know.'

He wandered off, leaving Wyngate to ponder his next move.

The search dog had been called out, they still had the chance of finding somebody alive. The divers were more expensive and that could wait until there was a higher presumption of death at the scene. It would be the easiest thing in the world to roll a human body down the steep hill into the loch, where it would fall down a sheer rock face into very deep cold water. The blood was human, no doubt about that. They had taken samples at four-inch intervals from the wide patch of grass that appeared to be the site of the first, and main, attack. Ahern was proving very useful as a wildlife tracker and backed up by a constable, the two of them were inching their way along a path that did not exist to the naked eye, both now wearing shoe covers in case they were right and they were walking in the footsteps of the victim. And maybe, whoever had been pursuing them. Or a killer fleeing the scene.

Wyngate felt he could leave Mulholland in charge at the car park so he too was following Ahern, knowing that the guys were on to something. Then the search dog arrived and immediately followed the path of the three men, nose in the air, rain glistening in baubles on his ebony saddleback, as he trotted along as if this wasn't difficult at all.

'A second site? What do we think?'

'Well, something happened at the peak there, then somebody ran or was chased down here.'

'Trying to get to the car park?'

'Why not go out the way they came in?'

'Because it wasn't safe to go back that way obviously. The path is really only wide enough for two side by side, not a huge amount of room to get past somebody who is trying to stop you from leaving. Or had stabbed you and was standing there with a knife? I'd run in the opposite direction.'

'Or if there was more than one of them chasing you?'

The dog was moving on, slower now, stopping every now and again to check, casting a glance at his handler to see if that was OK. Then he stopped. And did an about turn, curving his spine into the length of his own body, getting ready to come back the way he had come.

'Why is he doing that?' asked Ahern.

'The scent runs out, he'd follow it if it was there to be followed. Whoever was here retraced their steps and went back the way they came. Or was airlifted out by an alien.'

'Or,' said Wyngate, 'they caught the poor bugger here, dragged him across this grass and tossed him in the loch.'

'Then the dog would take us to the water's edge, but he hasn't. So it didn't happen like that.'

Wyngate looked at the dog, who looked back at him with eyes that seemed to be asking for a bacon sandwich. He didn't know how much to trust it. 'Yeah, thanks for that.' Wyngate's airwave crackled. He answered it, ready to point out that he wasn't a rank that got paid enough to do this job, some of those fat bastards back at Central could come out again now that this had gone up the priority list.

At the car park, Mulholland had been asking around about McCaffrey, keen to speak to the young officer who had got close to Costello during the Braithwaite case. His eyes kept gravitating towards the Clubman. The windows were condensed over. He checked the other cars that had been parked there for a couple of hours now. Light fog over the windows, McCaffrey's looked thick and dense, as if the car had been there all night.

Nobody had seen him.

He radioed in, locating the station where McCaffrey was based. And then gave them a quick call. He turned away instinctively as two other cops came close, aware of the silence in the still air and the ease with which he could be overheard.

'You still up at the lochside?' asked the desk sergeant.

'Yes.'

'Well, Isla McCaffrey has been on trying to locate her husband. He didn't appear for the start of his shift this morning and he didn't come home last night or the night before. That will be Isla McCaffrey as in . . .'

'The wife of the bloke who drives the Clubman? It's still here. I think it has been here for some time.' Mulholland read out the plate number.

'That's a match.'

'Yeah, can't be many with three kiddie seats inside.' Mulholland looked round to the deep water of the loch. He'd put an alert out for McCaffrey, talked to his senior officer, but had the sinking feeling he'd be calling out the underwater search team before darkness fell.

*   *   *

When Hannah got back to her cottage flat in Govan she thought about doing the hoovering, but she was too tired, almost too tired to sleep. She was always like this after doing a string of night shifts at A & E, she became a little excitable and found it difficult to sit down and relax. The flat was cold so she sat on the edge of the settee having a couple of quick cigarettes. It was still raining outside. She watched a neighbour walk her two wee girls past the flat, the neighbour looked in, saw her and waved. Hannah waved back and then settled back into the sofa, thinking about putting a log on the fire. Then have a shower, put on her jammys, light the fire and settle down with a cuppa and toast, thickly buttered with a teaspoon of Marmite on each slice. That would normally send her to sleep, and if that didn't do it, sticking some daytime TV with its simpering banality definitely would.

She went over to the fire; it was her proudest possession, this old flat with its original fireplace and a wood-burning stove reinstated. Kneeling down she dusted the ash away and brushed it into the ash box. She pulled out some old newspaper that her neighbours upstairs kept for her, and she started the dirty process of rolling them up five sheets at a time and tying a knot in them. There was something very pleasurable in getting her fingers so dirty, before having a shower and making sure she got them clean again.

She placed a small firelighter in the grate and tossed in a few knots of newspaper and added a few more logs. Leaning back on the carpet, she thought about having a cup of tea before the shower. She squared off the pile of newspapers and put her hand down on the carpet to lever herself up onto her aching feet, then looked down at the front of the newspaper that was facing up at her, and the two faces on it, a one-word headline: MISTAKES. She looked again, picking up the paper and holding it close, reading it with tired eyes, scanning the picture, then looking at the date. The fourth of October.

She looked closer at the face, and the name. She was sure it was her. Domestic abuse took place at home, not at work, and there was the name of a colleague, a safe person. She rubbed her hands down the front of her trousers, leaving jet streams of black ash on her thighs. So this woman might be this police officer. Might be. For all Hannah knew, her husband, the abuser, might also be a police officer. But she was involved with people like pathologists. Hannah read the caption under the photograph of the grey-haired man to confirm. These people knew all about the issues of patient confidentiality and the difficulties of identification. She was dealing with people who knew the score. It was worth a shot, she reached for her iPad.

And here she was, walking around Uncle Archie and Aunt Pippa's house. He had gone to work, after making it quite clear that he was not going to hold her hand, snoop or check up on her. She had asked him, as she always did, if the investigation into Abigail's death was making any headway. The answer was always no, but he did say they were now looking at wider CCTV, the timeline and the logistics again. And that had panicked her. Alone in the kitchen, she tried to think.

She sat for a long time, staring at the tabletop, letting the coffee go cold.

She heard the phone ringing through in the hall. It would be for Archie, she let it go.

It stopped then started again. Probably a sales call, so she walked over and put her hand out. It fell quiet as soon as she lifted it from its cradle. It wasn't her house, it wasn't her phone.

The problem was, she didn't know if she could actually do it. Not again. The water she poured from the kettle kept missing the cup, spreading over the worktop. She mopped it up; wishing the tremor in her hands would stop betraying her. The need for alcohol was intense; vodka, strong black coffee and a pro plus. She was supposed to be on decaff, vitamin C, Acamprosate and Fluoxetine, never on an empty stomach. Her larynx and the muscles of her throat had been damaged when she was attacked, so she had learned to eat and drink in a certain order. She had taken the pills out the dosset box and flushed them down the toilet. She was going to have an Americano and a couple of rich tea biscuits, a habit she had learned from Abigail when she had suffered from terrible morning sickness. The pain of that thought, the easy way the memory had popped up in her mind so unexpectedly, it punched her in the stomach

with more pain than any attack she had suffered in the Blue
Neptune. When Abigail had got pregnant with Malcolm, it
was as if her sister was rubbing her face in her own infertility.
The way Abigail looked at her sometimes, as if she had it all,
and Valerie deserved to have, and to be, 'lesser'. She closed
the lid of the kettle, thinking how funny it was, the way life
turned out. It was a true saying, it's not where you start, it's
where you finish.

A fleeting memory flashed through her mind, stubble on
her cheek and the impression of a scent that she couldn't
identify. Maybe a perfume of Abigail's. She gripped the side
of the worktop in Archie's pristine kitchen and tried to
remember. There had been a man, a kiss, a cheek against hers.

Sitting amongst the Robert Annan prints on the wall, at the
melamine table with its cream and light-brown striped bench
seat, she sipped her caffeinated coffee, and looked out the
window to a bare tree, an empty bird feeder swinging back
and forth in the wind. Her Agatha Christie biography, still
stuck at page fifty-six. She let the tears run. She was fed up
trying to be strong. Life beyond vodka had only been a few
hours old, and she had no idea what was causing the pain that
gnawed and chewed at her soul. The loss of her family? The
loss of herself? Mourning that her affair with the bottle might
be over? She was better than that, better off than that, she had
a brain and she had Archie behind her. He would treat her like
a daughter.

Her future.

The lack of future?

If she ever was arrested, locked up, she really didn't care.
She'd have a roof over her head at least. That wasn't the issue,
at least it was something. The future that is unknown was far
too awful to contemplate. She sipped at her coffee, letting the
tears roll until they made little star-shaped drops on the
tabletop. It was a future that was purposeless. It was a yawning
great void that stretched in front of her and she could see
nothing in it, nothing that was of any value to her.

Maybe she could get another cat. Yeah, she could just see
Archie's face when she presented him with a litter tray. She
looked out the window, there was a robin hopping around in

the garden. That wasn't something she saw when she had Alfred.

She brushed away a tear . . .

Who killed Cock Robin? It was the sparrow, with his bow and arrow.

It shouldn't be too bloody difficult to figure out who killed her sister.

Surely.

That was one question that wasn't going to go away. And, the thought struck her as another teardrop fell, that might be the one question that she was uniquely placed to answer. Yet she could not.

Where had she been at four o'clock that morning?

The phone rang, she jumped. Maybe she would be better answering it and give Archie a message or swear at the person if it was a bloody sales call. Or she could let them speak and then say, 'Now let me tell you all about the Baby Jesus'. That usually made them hang up. She walked, rather quickly and with no loss of balance she noticed, into the living room and lifted the handset. The voice on the other end said, 'Valerie? Can you give a message to Archie? His mobile is turned off.'

'Yes,' she replied, looking round for a pen, but knowing she used to have a very good memory. 'Yes, of course I can take a message.'

She was so touched that somebody used her name, and trusted her with a job that she started to cry.

The helicopter journey had been quick and uneventful, the blades cutting their way through the dark clouds to land on the pad at Raigmore, where an emergency medical team had been waiting with full clinical support, right from the minute the young man's stretcher had been clunked off its cradle on the chopper. Ten minutes later the patient was in a cubicle, on oxygen and plasma, platelets and four monitors, stabilizing him to give them time to work out what the bloody problem was. Apart from the big wide cut across his throat.

And, in amongst them all, moving between them quietly, was Morna Taverner, a female constable, dressed in civvies covered in a sterile gown, carrying a pile of brown paper bags which she held open as the young man's clothes were stripped and cut from him, and then delicately dropped into a bag, to be sealed, signed and removed from the premises.

Morna Taverner had been following their conversation from the moment the trolley hit the tarmac. He looked to her like every other hiker or walker that liked to take on the challenge of the hills during the winter. An extreme hillwalker. He was an outdoorsy type anyway, as his boots were dropped into the evidence bag, she saw the dried pine needles fall from the indentations in the soles. The weather on the Bealach was too severe for trees, so he had been walking elsewhere and transferred to the peak. Except if he was an experienced hillwalker, he would have been dressed more appropriately. And he would not have been out there on his own. Not in November. Not without having left notice with somebody to raise the alarm if he failed to return when expected. He wouldn't be the first to take off his jacket at the first sign of hypothermia. But there had been signs that he had been dragged to where he had been found. And the telltale cut on his throat.

He had no signs indicative of being hit by a car, no first impact abrasions on the shins, nor the impact of the bonnet and the roll off the vehicle to the road. A senior casualty officer popped his head in and looked at the chart, his vitals, and finally looked at his face.

'So throat cut and then what? He's been beaten? A crowbar? Then thrown off an elevated site?' The doctor looked a little confused.

'Agreed, he was found like this at the top of the pass, then maybe dragged to the gully. The cut throat suggests foul play. Obviously.'

'Are you the policewoman?'

'Police officers we are supposed to be called now,' Morna smiled. 'How is he doing?'

'Fair enough. We are going to wheel him down for an X-ray as soon as we get some bloods in him, get his temperature up. See if he's got any blood on the brain, we will take it from there. If he's ready, the scan will be within the next two hours but neurologically, there doesn't seem to be any panic. But right now, he's going to the high dependency unit.'

And the wheels on the trolley were clicked down, the stretcher stabilized and he was away, his dirty feet sticking out the end of the trolley, a passing nurse picking up the blanket and smoothing it down, smiling at his immobile black and swollen face. 'Any ideas who he is yet?' the nurse asked.

'Nope. Nobody has reported him missing as yet and he has no ID on him.'

'There are some bloody mad bampots out there.' She looked out the window, as if she meant Inverness itself.

Anderson was studying a printout of unsolved rapes over the last ten years, searching through it, looking for connections. The pad beside him was full of scribbles and doodles, mostly excluding those incidents from the connections he was trying to make.

He answered his phone automatically, surprised at the very quiet voice on the other end, very young, almost a girl. She pronounced his name Coleen Anderrrson, soft consonants, a Highlander, he thought. 'Yes, indeed, how can I help you?' He assumed the attitude he did when he talked to one of his daughter's friends. This sounded like a student wanting help with a dissertation. Probably passed on by Mitchum who obviously thought he didn't have enough to do and that he was only sitting at his desk, looking at a sequence of rapes for his own amusement.

'DCI Anderson, this is DC Morna Taverner. I'm up at Wester Ross, CID', she added, as if she had forgotten and had realized that he might like to know. 'I have been doing a cold case computer trawl . . .'

'Yes,' he said, and leaned back in his chair, knowing exactly where the conversation was going.

'And I came across your name more than once, about the A835 rape?'

'Not familiar with that.'

'No reason why you should be. It's the Sally Logan and Gillian Witherspoon cases you have been looking at. Our footprints over the archive keep crossing, so I thought you might be interested in Nicola Barnes, she was a twenty-three-year-old, out on her own, taken off the road – the A835 as it comes into Ullapool. It was the eleventh of July 2004.'

He heard her take a deep breath.

'And there was an incident in 1987? A seventeen-year-old girl disappeared at—'

'That's a long time ago,' Anderson said quietly. 'Do you have anything else?' Anything? He was encouraging, betting that this was usually as far as she got in her pitch. There would be nothing in this. She was young, trying to make connections, seeing them where none existed. She would be on the end of the phone sitting in a large office somewhere talking quietly, cupping her phone with the palm of her hand. He imagined her with a nervous tic, pulling her hair behind her ear the way Claire had done since the day she was born if she had ever been in trouble, or Peter's habit of biting his upper lip.

'You have been working on the Logan and Witherspoon rapes. I think there are similarities.' She was more definite now, fortified by his interest.

'Are you working cold case?'

'No.'

There was quiet, he could hear her breathing.

'Not exactly.'

So this was a current case she was working and had searched the database for similarities. She sounded inexperienced. He closed his eyes and let her continue. 'There was an injury to her left shoulder. The computer coughed that up. And of course the rapes. The lack of DNA, the forensic awareness and—'

'The fact he hasn't been caught,' Anderson added. 'What does your boss say? I mean, you shouldn't be looking at this if you are not on a cold case unit?'

'OK, but this is something I am interested in.' A pause.

He didn't respond.

'My DCI doesn't agree with me but he said I could call you.'

'OK, OK,' said Anderson, at least she had ran it past him. 'You see, he will need something to go on, a weight of evidence before he can justify spending time and money on taking the investigation further. There will have been a full investigation at the time. So if no new evidence has come to light it can be difficult to justify . . . Well, it's difficult to justify. That's all.'

Silence. He could almost hear the disappointment as if somebody had physically deflated her at the other end of the phone. No doubt this was exactly what her boss had told her.

He heard a long sigh.

'And has any other evidence come to light?' he asked.

'No.'

'And the computer system has made no other links, no other connections?'

'No. Just your name. And the method. The arm. Women . . .' All her enthusiasm had gone.

'Are you working on something else right now?'

'I'm in the hospital, minding a young man we found on the Bealach Na Ba.'

He had no idea what she was talking about. 'Do you have him handcuffed to the bed?'

She laughed lightly. 'Not that kind of minding. He was dumped up there with a bad head injury, his face has been beaten to a pulp, throat cut. We don't know if he'll pull through, we haven't confirmed an ID yet. It's so sad, but I'm sitting with him, I will be here when he wakes up. If he wakes up. There's a wee flicker every now and again, you know, so I am not risking walking away but I am bored so I was flicking through my notebook. I have been meaning to call you for a while.'

'The best thing you can do is be there. It sounds as though you have your hands full, so why don't you email me the file. And tell your boss that you have done that, make sure it's noted. He can't refuse permission retrospectively,' said Anderson. But he could kick off.

'Oh yes, yes I will.'

'I've just been given a few more days to review these cold cases so I will look at yours as well. If I find any other convergence of the cases, I will get back to you.'

As in: don't call us, we will call you.

'Thank you,' she said, 'thank you so much.'

She sounded so grateful, he felt like a right bastard.

'What was your name again?'

'Morna Taverner.'

'And your DCI?'

'Patrick, Alastair Patrick. He's from Glasgow, that was years ago, he's quite old now.'

Aren't we all? 'OK. Let me have a look, bye for now.'

'Thank you DCI . . . Colin, Mr Anderson, ta.' And the phone clicked off.

After the phone call, Valerie looked at the calendar, counting back and then marking the days when Costello had last been seen. Uncle Archie was concerned about her, her work colleagues didn't seem to be making much of it, so where was she? She didn't know Costello; she had seen her and heard her but had never actually met her, but she had exchanged a few words with a woman called Dali Despande – a name once heard not forgotten – who was also concerned about Costello, but was more concerned about George Haggerty. If Costello had gone off after him, well, more power to her . . .

Val had heard that more than once.

And the question: 'Had she gone rogue?'

Apart from Costello's 'close friendship' with Archie, their only connection was Malcolm. That boy had reached out to Costello, her mobile number had been on the mobile phone that had been found on his bedside table, tucked down the back of a photograph of his parents was her card with her number on it. He had called her, but Archie had said that the call was so short it looked like he had simply called then rung off, the call was not long enough for any conversation to have taken place.

And that hurt. Why did the boy not phone his Auntie Valerie? Because he knew, even at his young age, that she would be pissed?

Valerie tried to put that picture together in her mind. She had been in court more times than she cared to recall in situations like this, especially when she was working with vulnerable children. Was Malcolm vulnerable? She didn't think so. Abigail was a good mother. She could have said anything to her, but how much had her sister changed? Kids very quickly learn to trust, so had Malcolm moved on from Valerie and Abigail and realized he could only trust somebody from outside the family?

Maybe that was the point? He needed to talk to somebody who wouldn't let it get back to . . . George? To Abigail? Who had the boy been frightened of?

Her heart sank, more tears.

She had no money, no job, no carer, no family, everything had gone.

Taken from her

But this Costello had it all. A career, a flat, independence and she seemed as though she had an opinion. She had made her opinion about George quite clear. Was she right?

Had she decided to go after him? Find evidence to bring him down? Was that what was going on in her mind?

Valerie looked around the room, Pippa's style. She could either stay here or she could see what she could do. She knew George. She knew Abigail.

She got out of her bed and, moving quicker than she had for weeks, crossed the room to her handbag, opened her purse and had a good look through her credit cards. They had all been cleared when she sold the flat and there was credit, a lot of it, enough to get up and get out there.

Where would George go? She had been his sister-in-law for thirteen years, she knew him in a way that nobody else did. If Costello could do it, then why couldn't she? She needed to find the truth, whether that meant clearing George's name or not.

Something that Abigail had said that night, that last time she saw her sister at the theatre, had been playing on her mind. Abigail had moved the conversation on so quickly – she must have been wrong, it was something like *George wouldn't let me* or *George wouldn't like it.*

But he had allowed her out to go to the theatre that night. The last time she had seen her sister alive.

Malcolm in bed early as he had a cold. There had been tension in the house that night, nothing spoken but she had been aware of it. She had been wrapped up in her own misery.

Bloody hell, they had sat in that lounge, her thinking about the child that she was about to buy and her sister sitting two feet away, keeping a big secret of her own. Had she grown scared of her own husband? Abigail had mentioned that she suspected George was seeing another woman. He was working away on a new contract, he was going home to Port MacDuff more often, being away from Malcolm more often. Never inviting them to go with him. That had been months ago. She hadn't thought much about it. Abigail was bored and at home too much, she was making up all kinds of stuff about George. He was never home, he was always going back up north to his hometown where Abigail didn't want to go, or was never allowed to go. How odd that Malcolm had never gone north with his dad. He had never been asked.

She had years of expertise as a fiscal; she had investigation skills.

She had nothing, absolutely nothing left to do except drink and she needed something better than that.

But where to start? She lay down on the bed again, her hand wandering to the bedside table where she had secreted the quarter bottle behind her Agatha Christie biography. Just as Malcolm had kept Costello's card, so Valerie kept her vodka. She twisted off the cap; she adored that click of the seal breaking, like the first meeting with a new friend. Then she heard her mobile ring. She could either have a drink, then go into a long and troubled sleep. Or she could look at her phone and see who was calling.

It was a sign. She liked signs. She was beginning to trust them more than her own judgement. Her thumb was trembling as she tapped in her security number.

It was George leaving a voicemail. He wanted to meet her for lunch. Or coffee, for a chat.

Every fibre of her being wanted to refuse.

So she texted back and agreed. A quick coffee at the French Café. The coffee was a legitimate source of caffeine, and it might keep her mind off the vodka.

Valerie knew, felt, she herself had nothing to do with the murders. She knew that anything the police were doing was routine. Valerie couldn't explain where she had been that night, she had no memory she could recall. There was no evidence she had travelled to the house, she was not seen on any CCTV. So why had she felt so relieved when they had told her that?

She had no reason to kill her sister, even drunk, she was

never violent. And there had been no animosity between them. Not really.

But Abigail had opened the door to her killer, the sister who always had the bolt on the door, opening it a crack when the doorbell rang. It was a house isolated in the middle of the city, set back from the road, small windows which were always curtained and barely opened, and the huge monkey puzzle tree that grew at the side of the driveway, shielding the garage and the upper floors of the house.

Everybody looked at Valerie, as if they knew what she was thinking when she had no idea at all. She had no idea what had happened to her sister and the only person that Abigail would have opened the door to was her.

But George had a key, it was his house.

SIX

The rain was starting to ease off, the cloud was lifting giving tantalizing glimpses of the Ben at the head of the loch. By the time the search team arrived, it was almost dry. They were going to walk a couple of metres apart in a band from the north part of the car park, the line of searchers would be following the contour line of the hill. This part of the loch side rose alarmingly, on the water's edge it wasn't very high, a couple of metres. The issue was the rock wall that descended into the water and kept going. The water was very, very deep, yet twenty or so metres south, there was a bay where little friendly waves lapped the shingle, a favourite site for wild camping.

The search team was going to walk, pulling the winter vegetation apart with sticks, looking for anything that might have some evidential value. First of all, the crime scene investigator and his team were going to gather as many blood samples as they could get. There had been pooling and spatter, not easy to see in the grass and the stony ground at the top of the rise, but as the first SOCO pulled up a blade of grass with gloved fingers, she smiled, holding out a small torch. 'There you go, seek and ye shall find. But don't let your big-footed search team stamp all over this. Give us an hour, then it's all yours. We can get it all done and over before it starts pouring again.'

Wyngate closed his own mobile, hoping his poker face was convincing. He had looked at the broken phone, sitting in its plastic evidence bag, shattered. Whoever did this knew the old adage that the way to make something untraceable was to drive a truck over it. He would pass it onto the tech team and see what they could do. But he bet Donnie McCaffrey had recently taken possession of a new Samsung 6 phone.

So Wyngate had asked, 'The owner of the car is missing, and he's a cop from Govan. Do you have a body anywhere?'

'No,' said Mulholland, 'not yet, and I hope we don't. Looks like it's going to be a long day. Hope to God this bloke's not got himself into some drug deal that's gone tits up. Hope to God I am not the one to tell his wife. She'll get no pension if he was on the take. Nothing.'

'Worse than that, we'll need to call in Complaints.'

'I've already heard from Mathieson. Her orders are that when we find what we find, we are to keep it quiet. So let the team know that there is no going home and chatting about it in the pub, otherwise they will be up in front of a disciplinary.' Mulholland thought he delivered this with an adequate sense of poise and authority, he was yielding a very big stick. He now felt like Mathieson's official contact.

A dead cop was something to be kept out of the press, but a dead cop on Loch Lomond was to be kept away from the tourist board.

But Wyngate shrugged as if he had been threatened with a trip to ASDA. 'How long do you think we will have to be here?'

'As long as it takes,' said Mulholland sounding as though he really was in charge now and he had his hands on the budget.

'Well, it's my daughter's birthday party at the soft play this afternoon, and I've been here since before dawn.'

As if on cue, there was a shout from a SOCO, who had been approaching them down the steep part of the path. He was holding something in his hand, strips of paper already in trace evidence sample bags. 'I can tell you straight away that there's a smattering of white powder here, pure cocaine on a presumptive test and a lot of alcohol. Somebody was having a party.'

Mulholland's twisted heart gave a little leap, Mathieson was going to have a field day with this. He could see himself being passed up the chain to the drugs squad. He looked to the sky and smiled. Sometimes there was a God.

Two hours later Valerie walked into the massive atrium of the Queen Elizabeth. She was still shaking slightly. The sight of George, well dressed and friendly, the way he had given her a hug and she had caught a wave of his aftershave, the side of his cheek had rubbed the skin of her face, too close, yet it felt very familiar. Too familiar. She had never enjoyed public displays of affection, but he was holding onto her as if she was all he had left in the world.

Which apart from his dad, she was.

And all the time, the recognition at the back of her mind, why was that scent of him so reminiscent of . . .? She had no idea.

The conversation was about the house and did she want anything. Any of her mother's stuff? The clock? And had she heard from the police, what were they saying?

Her brain had stopped working. She needed a drink in order to cope with any of that, so she had finished her coffee quickly and got a taxi from Byres Road to the Queen Elizabeth, stopping at an off licence on the way. She thought she was being discreet, slugging from the bottle in the back of the cab, but the look the driver gave her suggested he had seen her.

But the vodka had fortified her. Valerie was calm and in control, sucking a Polo mint as she walked into the hospital, looking for a nurse called Hannah. She had told Hannah that she would be wearing a three-quarter-length green coat and a scarf round her neck, clothes she had borrowed from Pippa's wardrobe. Similarly, a pair of Pippa's old specs perched up on her head had aged her twenty years. She hadn't told Archie. His wife's clothes were far too nunty for her, a little too big but they made her look less official, less threatening and more caring. In short, they made her look very unlike herself. She was wearing her own universal black boots, boots made for the weather. They said nothing about her as a failure. She expected the nurse to be nervous, she could get into a lot of trouble for what she had done. She had shown initiative and common sense but that kind of thing was never going to be tolerated in the NHS.

Valerie liked the nurse's thought processes about the identity of the mystery woman they had, especially the fact that the woman had been subject to some kind of violence, and Hannah wasn't going to put the victim back into a situation of jeopardy, so she had gone the circuitous route. That was the kind of thinking Valerie liked. If the woman they had was the woman who had been on the front of the *Daily Record*, then the authorities would know her circumstances. So when Hannah saw the photograph on the front page during the Kissel case, Costello looking sixty, O'Hare looking ninety, she had phoned the mortuary and got through to Jack O'Hare's office, and eventually to the pathologist himself, and he had called Archie at the house getting Valerie, and passing on the number. Valerie had put the phone down and thought this was a sign, if she could get to Costello before anybody else. If it was Costello and that was a big if. So she kept quiet about the message until she had spoken to her. Valerie was justifying it to herself; she was a familial link, her godfather was Costello's part-time boyfriend, or so the gossipmongers would have it. And Valerie would know Costello the minute she set eyes on her; she had looked her up the first time she had heard the rumour about her and Archie. And Valerie was sure Costello would recognize her straight away, depending on how bad the clonk on the head had been.

Valerie stood and looked around the vast white space, her eyes searching for a woman who looked nervous, but one who knew her way around this maze of a hospital. She felt conflicted, she wanted Costello to have resigned because she wanted her to be free to investigate the Monkey House Murders. Not lying in hospital, no use to anybody. Unless . . .

'Theresa?'

Valerie turned. 'Hannah?'

They shook hands. She was younger than Valerie had expected and well, more *common,* a toughness about the hard set of her face, the stink of cigarette smoke that surrounded her like a halo, the long cardigan that had seen better days and was probably an infection risk. After she shook her hand, Valerie covertly wiped her own hand down the outside of Pippa's coat.

'Thank you for coming out,' she said, her accent very broad, harsh to Valerie's ears. 'I didn't really know what to do, and I'd feel stupid if I was wrong. But nobody has reported her missing, we've had two false alarms already.'

'So whoever hit her doesn't want her back.' Valerie nodded

affirmatively, encouraging this chain of thought. 'You are doing
the right thing. I've worked in the domestic abuse unit in
Edinburgh for the last five years and what we need to avoid
is this woman being returned to that environment when she
is so vulnerable.'

They walked towards the lift, keeping their voices low. 'The
police have nobody reported as missing that fits her description at the moment, but when I saw her, I thought I recognized
her, just something about her that was familiar and some of
the injuries she came in with, well they didn't make sense.
She's not been living on the street, no way. I've seen enough
of that in my time.'

'Me too, but what made you think it is my colleague? There
must have been something.'

'Well, she has suffered a psychotic break so she couldn't
tell us anything about herself but it was when I read that
headline that I made the link. Well, I had been following the
Kissel case, the girl who—'

'Killed her child? Yes. I think the whole country was
following that.'

'And earlier today, I was lighting the fire with some old
newspapers and on the front page was a picture of a police
officer and a pathologist.'

'So you phoned Jack?' encouraged Valerie, knowing that
the familiarity of O'Hare's name would encourage confidence.
They were standing in the queue for the lift now, keeping well
back, away from any prying ears.

'So I called his office, they are here in the same building but
he is away, otherwise I could have gone downstairs and got him
myself, but called him and, he must have called you . . .'

'Will he live?' Patrick was curt and precise.

The nurse bustled around the head of the bed, winding a
flex round her hand before forcing it back in the machine,
pulling over a flap and turning a lock.

'Will he live?' asked Morna, repeating the question for
the benefit of the nurse.

'That's not a conversation we tend to have in front of the
patient.'

'Will he live?' repeated DCI Patrick at the other end of Morna's mobile. 'I'm asking for an opinion, not the Gettysburg Address.'

'My boss wants to know what his chances are.'

'I don't get paid enough to speculate.'

'She said she—'

'Yes, I heard. Cheers.' And the phone snipped off.

Morna sat beside the young man. Not so long since she had been in hospital herself, keenly aware of the tubes and tapes. She still had flashbacks to that incident, her right cheekbone still hurt. She looked over at her patient, still intubated, his face swollen and bloody, unrecognizable. His own mum wouldn't know him.

Morna looked at his battered face, and she decided he was lovely. He was a young man, he had on very sensible clothes, stuff that his mum or granny would have bought him. They had cut the clothes from him and she had gone through them, wearing thick gloves, there was so much blood. He had been for a scan and X-rays. They had then taken him down to operate on a slow bleed on his brain. The result was, he *might* make it. He might not, but overall their attitude was a positive one. She had taken his fingerprints and a swab for his DNA; they would process that here. It was very dangerous to do an ID, DCI Patrick had a thing about that. He required proof beyond certainty, probably something to do with his background in the forces, people being blown to bits then having to be identified, she thought. They wouldn't want to get that wrong. Patrick would be insistent, he would want five markers. Both intelligence and confirmatory.

She raised the back of his hand to her nose, seeing the fine dark hair, she breathed in, deeply. Although he had been cleansed and disinfected she could still catch the scent of blood, gentle sweat, patchouli oil and something else? Petrol? She thought she had smelled that on his jumper as well. She turned his hand over and looked at the injuries on the flesh of his palms, scraps and scrapes. He had fallen on concrete at some point, recently.

As she had gone through his clothes, she had noticed there were no designer names on his clothes, all high street brand stuff. Except the Fair Isle jumper, somebody had knitted that for him, with a lot of love. The DCI's wife had made one for Finn, they took a lot of time and skill. She photographed the jumper on her phone and sent the image off to Patrick. Maybe a family member would recognize the intricate pattern and the different colours that wove and danced between themselves. Fawns and browns and creams with a single strand of deep red, well worn. The wool was balled at the armpits and almost transparent at the elbows. A jumper loved so much, it had been worn to its bare threads. She had run her gloved hand round the neck, then down the inside seams, checking there was no label, and that the stitching also looked hand sewn. This was a unique item somebody would be able to identify, unless of course he was a skint student and the jumper had been twenty pence from a charity shop.

She got out her notebook and looked over her list of the items she had photographed before she had replaced them in the brown paper bag before resealing, signing and dating the label.

Now, she was looking at the injuries, the head, the neck, the forearms, the hands, all defence wounds, or those of the attack itself, except those on the palms of his hands. Morna had recognized them, the same pattern covered Finn's knees every summer.

Gravel? So was he running along and he fell? Running along the road at the Bealach Na Ba, running to get away?

But you fall on your knees harder than you'd fall on your hands, surely?

Had he been crouching? Knocked to the ground? Or was he hunched down like he was doing the one hundred metres, down on his hunkers looking for something when he was clubbed on the back of his head, then the knife across his throat?

And why that smell of petrol or engine oil?

What had he been doing?

'I think that is his phone.' Isla McCaffrey passed the plastic bag over to the big male detective, ignoring the small nippy blonde with the bright red lipstick. 'But I can't say for sure. It's in pieces.'

'This may be totally unconnected but do you recognize this jumper?' Bannon showed her his iPad, showing an old beige Fair Isle jumper. The bloodstains down the front were obvious to anybody who had reason to recognize them.

'No, he wouldn't wear something like that.' Isla seemed to relax a little.

'Thank you, so it's quite simple,' said Mathieson through her little red mouth. 'We are trying to understand why your husband's car was up on the lochside on Saturday evening. And we are keen to ascertain his whereabouts now, as I am sure you are,' she added as an afterthought.

'You have phoned about four times asking me where Donnie is and why the car is up there, but I've told you that I don't know. He's a police officer.' Isla shrugged, confused. 'Surely you know?'

'He was off duty. There was no professional reason for him to be there.'

Isla shook her head, her dark curls, unbrushed and tangled, danced round the side of her ears. Dropping her head, she rubbed at her eyes with the palm of her hands. 'I don't know where he is.'

'When did you last see him?'

'Saturday night. He was going to work.'

'But he wasn't, Mrs McCaffrey, he wasn't going to work. He was at Loch Lomond. Can you shed any light why he might have gone there? It would help us a lot.'

'He *was* going out to work,' Isla insisted. 'He wasn't doing anything wrong. Where is he?' She folded herself up on the settee, her sobs racking her body.

Mathieson looked at Bannon, catching the odd choice of words. Isla McCaffrey was harbouring some doubts of her own about what her husband had been up to.

'I'm sorry, Isla, but we do need to know what happened when you last saw him. Do you know why he would be up at Inveruglass?'

She sat up. The precise question concentrating her mind. 'No, I don't, but he was sitting there.' She pointed to the chair that Bannon was sitting on now, a pile of children's clothes, ironed, ready for the drawer were sitting on the arm of the chair beside him. 'Right there and his phone went, his mobile.' She glanced at the plastic evidence bag that lay between them like a traitor. 'And he read the message and said he was going out. That was all that happened.'

'And what time was that?'

'About half past six? Quarter to seven?'

'Leaving his three young children to go out? Was that usual, he got a phone call and just got up and left?'

'It had happened a few times.'

They both caught the slight falter in her tone, she knew now in retrospect that something had gone badly wrong. It had started with that phone call.

'The phone call or the going out?'

'Both. Have you checked the hospitals, he could have had an accident?' She looked up and smiled, her face losing ten years of pain with the one slight hope, somewhere her husband might be.

'We have an alert out, if he's admitted to hospital, then we will know. Who was this phone call from?'

'I can't work out where he might be, it's not like him not to keep in touch.' Despite the heat, she shivered.

Bannon noticed the evasion and spoke again, now his voice very gentle. 'I've never met your husband, Isla, but nobody has a bad word to say about him. So anything you can tell us will help. I look round and I see a young man with three lovely wee children.' Bannon nodded at the photographs of the kids on the sideboard. 'Cases involving other people's children can really get to you when you are a father yourself.'

'Oh it did, it really did. He had been so upset by it, all that baby stuff going on at the Blue Neptune. He had felt restricted in what he was able to do to help. He thought he had read in the newspaper that they had caught the people responsible.'

'That must have given him some comfort?'

She closed her eyes. 'A little, it gets confusing beyond that as Donnie felt he couldn't say anything to me about the cases he was working on. But he wasn't working on that case, so he had a lot to say. The woman who survived?'

'Valerie Abernethy?' guessed Mathieson looking momentarily confused.

'So, she's another live witness to give evidence, and that made two, so that was good. They weren't going to get away with what they did to those women, to that young girl. He was pleased with that.'

'Was he talking to anybody actually involved in that case?' asked Mathieson pointedly, causing Bannon to roll his eyes at the harsh implication of the question.

'He didn't say much, but I can put two and two together. You see he talked a lot about joining the CID. Doing something that he wanted to do, to make a difference. It gave him a warm feeling in his stomach. He wanted to do what he called tough police work. Waiting and watching, ready to do something. He wanted to make a difference, that's all he wanted to do.' She started to sob again. Then sniffed loudly. 'And what kind of police are you? What did you say?'

'We investigate the police,' said Mathieson.

'Issues that the police have,' softened Bannon. 'Because your husband was a police officer we have a special protocol for cases like this.'

'So what was he doing out that night? Practising being a detective?' Mathieson was incredulous. 'Or vigilantism?'

'He wanted to join the CID, he was doing surveillance, he was learning, trying to develop more skills. He said that every-body at work was in a holding pattern waiting for vacancies, that nobody was moving anywhere. Everybody was in this holding pattern,' she repeated as if her repetition made it true, 'and he had applied for a transfer three times, been turned down for numerous training courses. We have three kids, we needed the money. He needed to get on.'

'And what was he doing to get extra money?' fired Mathieson, her mind leaping on the pure cocaine found at the scene.

The slap was quick and vicious; Isla was off the settee and over to Mathieson like a panther, the blow hit her right on the cheek. Bannon was slow to react, trying to reel in Isla's arm where the hand had connected with eye-watering impact.

'How dare you! He wasn't doing anything to get extra money,' she hissed. 'He was doing a job that you should have done, and he was helping to get evidence on somebody.'

Mathieson looked at the palm of her own hand then raised it to her cheek, then checked it for blood. Finding none, she brushed her hands together, her stare fixed on Isla with a condescending look. That was the one line bent cops gave all their dull little wives, stupid women who were kept at home and were far too trusting. But this conversation had gone too far, too quickly. She looked at Bannon.

'Isla, blood was found nearby on the loch side. He might be injured, there was cocaine present, as if he had been taking it.'

'No,' said Isla bluntly. 'Not him.'

'We have to go where the evidence takes us. Maybe Donnie had got wind of a deal and wanted to be present, to make sure before he made it official. He might have been testing the drug,' Bannon suggested.

She shook her head, and then seemed to collapse. 'He's not that stupid.'

Mathieson was losing patience. 'Isla, we need permission to look at your bank accounts, your credit cards, anything your husband—'

'His name was Donnie and you can do what you want. Look around you, we have enough, we don't have an extravagant lifestyle.'

'Some might call a cocaine habit an extravagant lifestyle?' asked Mathieson.

'Donnie doesn't even drink.'

'There was alcohol found at the scene.'

'Doesn't mean he drank it.'

'Can you think why it might be there? If not for Donnie, then who?'

'How the hell should I know?' Isla wrapped her arms round herself. 'You should be out looking for him, he could be in all kinds of trouble. Look at these poor bastards out in Yemen. Just look at the news? Why are you here? Go out and look for him? Please. I need to phone my mum, I'll need help with the kids. This is the worst nightmare, so you can do what you want, look where you want. I really don't care, but leave me and my kids alone.'

'Do you want to be here when we search the house?'

'I don't care.'

'And are you sure it was work that night? The phone call he got?'

'Yes.'

'Why?'

'Because it always was.'

'So this project he was involved in, this evidence he was gathering . . .' Bannon phrased the question carefully. It was the one question that Isla had not answered. 'Had it been happening a lot, these phone calls?'

'Recently, yes,' she sniffed.

'And how long had these calls and texts and night meetings been going on?'

Isla shrugged. 'Not before the Braithwaite case, only after that. He wouldn't, couldn't, tell me what it was about so it must have been a police matter.'

'Or he was having an affair,' suggested Mathieson.

Bannon rolled his eyes in disbelief.

'Do you want another slap?' retorted Isla. She turned to Bannon, obviously seeing him as her ally. 'It was something to do with the Braithwaite case. I've told you Donnie was first on the scene when that wee baby was found.'

'Was there anybody he was talking about, anybody whose name he started mentioning, somebody he hadn't mentioned before?'

'Like some cocaine drug overlord he had started working for on the quiet? Nipping off to Columbia on a Tuesday night to pick up God knows what. My husband is missing so can you please look for him. You are supposed to be looking after him, you . . . people.'

'And that's what we are doing, Isla. We need to know what was going through his mind. Have you heard him mention anybody he didn't speak of before, a strange name dropped in conversation?'

Isla tried to think. 'Well, Colin Anderson for one, because of the baby, Baby Moses. That entire Blue Neptune thing was on his mind, so the Braithwaite name. And then because of that he had been talking to Costello.'

Mathieson nodded. Well, that was two police officers missing.

*   *   *

'Jack called me,' lied Valerie as the lift appeared with a delicate ping. 'He's one of the pathologists. We work together a lot, and he knows Costello and I are friends.'

In mutual unspoken consent they walked along a corridor past the nurses' station, the girl there looked up, smiled at Hannah, gave Valerie a quick once over and no doubt concluded that the woman with the scraped-back hair in the green coat who walked past, throwing her an officious glare, was somebody in authority and she went back to her own paperwork before the woman in the green coat gave her any more.

The unknown woman was in the last room in the corridor, by design or by chance, tucked away from the buzz of the main atrium. Hannah knocked on the door and swung it open; the woman was standing by the window looking across the giant foyer of the hospital watching visitors, nurses and patients walking past or queuing for good coffee, grabbing a takeaway that was more edible than the hospital food, She stayed looking out, taking her time to turn around, and waiting until the two sets of feet had come into her room and stopped moving. Tying her housecoat further round her waist, she slowly turned to face her visitors, her face blackened round the eyes, her expression still wary.

Hannah saw the flicker of recognition on her face when she saw the dark-haired woman beside her. Not a look that encompassed any affection, or any fear, just recognition. A work colleague, just as she had suspected. But not close friends.

'That's great, Hannah, if you can leave us for a couple of minutes,' said Valerie, in a voice that knew it would be obeyed.

'Don't stress her, she's not very strong,' said Hannah, noticing a lack of hello or any type of greeting between them.

'I think she might be a lot stronger than you think,' replied Valerie, looking at the pale face, the grey eyes and the crescent shaped scar on the hairline. It was definitely her.

'Costello?'

The face looked back at her blankly, but the eyes narrowed slightly.

'You know who I am, right?'

The thin lips moved, thinking, searching in her mind for an

answer, more recognition should come, some placement. But she knew.

And Valerie knew she knew.

The patient shook her head. 'I know I don't like you.' It was tempered with a slight smile.

'You know Archie Walker?' Valerie got out her phone and showed her a photograph, Archie looking very neat and dapper in a bow tie at some fiscal's dinner.

Costello took it and looked at the picture for a long time. 'I don't like him either.' She handed the phone back.

'Do you trust me?'

'I don't trust anybody.'

Valerie felt very calm and very in control, she was enjoying the feeling. 'Well, I am your best bet. I have to make something right. I have really fucked up, Costello, I have really fucked it up. And I need help.'

'Join the club.'

'I need your car.'

Morna took another sip of her coffee, how much caffeine could one human being take before their head exploded? Had anybody ever done any research into that? It would be much more interesting than the sex life of fruit flies or transplanting ears from a mouse's head to its bum and then back again. She had been here for nearly ten hours now, not really doing very much apart from musing on bits of information from her notebook, and running the items of clothes through her mind, seeing if there was any more information to be had there. Nothing ever stopped at her, nothing that might be of interest to her or any help in identifying the young man lying in his room. But he was breathing, being attended to, pipes and tubes being changed, readings taken. Their frequency had started at every ten minutes, then twenty, then half an hour, but not any less frequent than that. Morna presumed that any movement in that direction was positive, so she wasn't going to stop being optimistic. He had got through the difficult initial hours. Like those first few breaths of life, they were the most dangerous. As some wag had added, the last few breaths of life were pretty dodgy as well.

Along at the nurses' station the girls were busy, doing their job for their masters. All part of the important chain, but how often did they see the beginning and the middle and the end? How often did they have a good idea and the boss shot them down, even if the suggestion was sensible, they were stupid to have voiced the opinion in the first place. How much worse was it when the boss was a woman?

She was lucky to have Alastair Patrick. He might be a monosyllabic stern-faced bastard, but he was that to everybody, nobody got treated to special sarcasm or an icy glare. They all got it. Except maybe, wee Finn. Alastair and Wilma had given Finn a lovely Christmas present; a light sabre and they never forgot his birthday. The boss never mentioned any family, which always made her wonder.

The girls at the nurses' station had offered her biscuits, a grateful patient had come back with a tray of nuts and dried fruit. They had included Morna in the share-out, made her another coffee, asking if anybody knew who the young man was yet. She answered that they were working on a couple of leads. They had taken that as spiel for 'no' and gone about their business.

She had taken the coffee back to sit outside his room, then as the hours went past and anybody who could give her a row had left, she crept inside to watch him breathe.

She pulled out the brown paper bags with his clothes. It looked increasingly like she was dropping them off, rather than them being picked up. Looking through them, she stopped at the Fair Isle jumper again, thinking who had knitted it for him. His mum? She had an idea, something she had seen on the tele. She got out her mobile phone and, wearing gloves she examined the elbows of the jumper, then the cuffs under the light of her mobile phone with the magnification right up. And saw a few small orange fibres. She looked through the rest of the clothes, only finding a few more round the ankle portion of the socks. Folding the bags back up she tried to think. Then thought she wasn't paid enough to do that and tried to get through to Forensics Services, knowing the significance of cuffs and ankles, places of exposure. Places that could pick up transfer.

She could . . . The door opened. 'Fed up with you bloody cops hanging around here.' The nurse was tired and sounded more than a little angry.

'Try it from my point of view,' said Morna, restacking the brown bag.

'Do you have to be here all the time, do you ever go home? You have been here for hours.'

And she had. Once the nurse had left, Morna got on the phone and tried to explain to Neil that he'd have to get Finn tonight, she was staying at work. As usual, she only got his voicemail. So she phoned Lachlan.

SEVEN

I t was going to be a very long day, a very cold and wet, long, long day.

Wyngate was back on site at first light.

Mulholland had produced a missing person's report that might interest them, only because the report matched something that Ahern had said in his statement, about students coming up and monitoring the loch from the viewpoint. Ahern didn't know any specific times or dates but he recognized the name Kieran Cowan as that of a tall gangly lad who drove an old campervan. He'd seen it a few times but had no idea of the plate number.

The report said Cowan was a student of environmental biology. He was doing a project, a self-styled filming project of nocturnal activity at the loch. It was his preferred hideout that had caught the interest of the station desk staff when it was reported; the viewing site at the north-west bank of the loch.

So why was the only vehicle unaccounted for registered to a cop called Donald McCaffrey? That Mini Clubman had been there for more than thirty-six hours. Mulholland had traced the VW camper that Cowan was known to be driving. It was registered to his dad, a Mr David Cowan. But there was no sign of it around here, which suggested if he left the loch side, it was by his own vehicle. Had he taken the missing police officer with him? Cowan had no criminal record. A quick ring around his family, concerned friends and lecturers, painted a picture of a Corbynite, pint-drinking environmentalist with a passion for wild camping. The type to rant about dead wallabies.

It looked now as though he might have run into trouble himself.

Mulholland addressed the volunteers from the university, friends and colleagues of Kieran Cowan that had assembled on the loch side. They were keen to find out what had happened to him. They were young and fuelled by nervous enthusiasm, although nobody knew what they were looking for. Anything that belonged to him. They needed a much wider search than the police had already carried out and they needed it to be thorough.

Mulholland had heard the mention of a camera more than once. Cowan had not returned it to the university and that was very unlike him.

His camera? Mulholland had queried.

Most of them had seen it or borrowed it themselves. It was a special low light Macro Scub 4. Cowan had probably been wearing a photographer's waistcoat that night, pockets full of batteries and extra memory cards, wipes and brushes. In his bag would be two bars of chocolate, a flask of soup and a packet of hankies. His routine was well known to his friends, he was a young man who was known to stick to his 'routine'.

There was the usual early-morning chaos in Colin Anderson's kitchen, it resembled a café. Again.

Peter looked at his dad, then looked away. Paige even managed a half smile then slid out of her chair, taking a cup of coffee with her and disappeared upstairs. Claire and her boyfriend David had stopped talking, even Moses, still in his basket on the kitchen table, decided to stay stumm and settled for chewing his lip.

'I think you had better sit down,' said Brenda.

'Why, what's happened?'

Brenda gestured that he should sit, then she slid Claire's tablet across the table top to him, through the obstacle course of marmalade and jam jars, and dirty coffee cups. Claire, or more likely David, had a subscription to a daily newspaper. The picture on the screen was one he was familiar with. Costello, coming out of court the day she had given evidence in the Bernadette Kissel case. He read the piece hardly believing what he was reading. They had got it all, her background and who her father was, who her brother was.

'Oh my God, how the hell did they get hold of that?'

Brenda laid a hand across his shoulders, giving him some solace before she sat down and looked at the screen.

'It looks as if the knives are out for her,' consoled Brenda, with no hint of relish in her voice, though there was a time, not so long ago, when she would have taken great pride in reading this.

'It's all here. It more or less says she's responsible for . . . well, for everything but the Vietnam War. A colleague missing, a young family man, Costello forty-two-year-old spinster. And it finishes with a very nasty little line saying she isn't coming forward to defend herself.'

'Which worries me. Why isn't she?' He looked at who wrote it, not surprised at all to see that it was Karen Jones. Bloody bitch. He wondered who her sources were and, as he calmed down, why she had been so one-sided about the piece. She had given a full page spread to the lack of movement on the Monkey House Of Horror, written with the slant of Costello being first on the scene, who her brother was, and the fact that her current whereabouts were unknown.

At the bottom was a picture of George and Valerie, hugging, united in their grief and their search for the murderer. In it, Valerie looked much older, her clothes more suited to a woman twice her age.

Brenda pointed a very clean fingernail to the paragraph stating she remains in contact with a fiscal office. There was a picture of Archie Walker and a picture of George Haggerty, the caption underneath him said that he had been on the receiving end of a *personal vendetta*. And the way it was written, it sounded as if there had indeed been something personal. Especially from DI Costello. The three of them, Haggerty looking young, dark sweeping hair and very handsome. The picture of Costello looked awful, like she was a wrung-out rag.

'Jesus Christ.'

'Colin?' Brenda sat down and placed a cup of steaming black coffee in front of him. 'Calm down. This has nothing to do with you.'

'That wee shit was in this house on Sunday night and he

goes and does this! Bloody hell, it says here that "a source close to the investigation has revealed her involvement with drink and cocaine". What?'

'Did Archie know Valerie was the kind of drunk the papers are making her out to be? No, he didn't, not at the time. Costello is from a family of alcoholics, she deals with scum every day of her life. She found those bodies, who knows what effect that has had on her?'

'I don't believe you just said that,' Anderson snapped at his wife. 'You really think she would have something to do with cocaine?'

'No, but maybe she just can't cope any more. Maybe she's had enough. And when you find her, you should hug her, you owe her a lot.' She kissed him on the top of his head. 'You owe her an awful lot.'

Then his mobile started ringing following by the house phone.

Colin looked at the number on his mobile recognizing at once that it was Mathilda McQueen. Brenda watched as Colin listened. She could hear the chatter but not make out what the forensic scientist was actually saying.

'Are you sure?' he asked, his face pale. He listened again. 'Should you be telling me this? I don't want you to get into trouble. But thanks.'

There was no more chit-chat. He ended the call.

'Well, the police have a leak somewhere. You know that search going on up at the loch. They have found blood, cocaine and some alcohol. There is a mix of blood. A sample from a young police officer called Donnie McCaffrey.'

'The man who found Moses?' Brenda turned to look at the baby; recognizing the name as the man who stayed at the hospital with him when Moses had his breathing trouble.

Colin nodded. 'And another, blood from another person. Only two sources of blood, two sources of DNA. Male and female. The female sample is from Costello.'

'Oh, Colin, I am so, so sorry.'

Archie Walker was the obvious person to have on the scene. The fact that he shouldn't have been allowed due to his relationship with Costello was not mentioned. When he was determined, the chief fiscal was a man you didn't want to cross.

'We have a cop and student reported missing, and another cop we can't find. We were missing one camper van, now located. It appears undamaged. And we have the Mini Clubman also with no signs of damage. And they all have a *last seen* on Saturday night; Cowan's flat mate, McCaffrey's wife and Costello's neighbour. So, did a flying saucer come down and abduct them?'

The camper had been found three miles up the lochside road, tucked into an off-road lay-by. It had been phoned in on the non-emergency number. A van driver for a luggage transfer company, who pulled into that lay-by every day, had seen the vehicle there for three days in a row.

'I'll send Anderson out to have a look at the van, it might hold evidence.' At some point, something terrible had happened. Donnie McCaffrey had suffered some kind of injury that made him bleed and they now knew Costello had been bleeding too.

But there was an outside chance that the situation had been filmed and the camera had caught something of the events that night, witnessed it in some way. One guy, Neil, who ran HikeLite the luggage transfer company, had been out to this site before, and to the Loch Lomond campsite on a weekly basis. He had shown them where Cowan liked to be, up on the highest point of the hill. He had gestured this from the car park. He was pointing exactly to where the most blood had been found. Mulholland and Wyngate had instigated another search, this time for the camera, following all the exit routes from the monument.

Mulholland looked at the motley crew of volunteers, being told to keep in a straight line and go slowly.

They moved off as soon as the light was full although even then they still used torches, the line of twenty bodies advanced steadily and methodically.

A full hour had passed, when somebody on the high part of the land had pointed over to the water. Up until then, every shout had been a false call but the cop was dispatched to go and look anyway.

It was a volunteer. He waded into the shallows, bent over

and picked something out, holding it high above his head with a thumbs-up. A camera.

'That's bloody useful, it's been in the water for nearly two days now,' said Wyngate looking crestfallen.

'It's a marine camera,' muttered Mulholland. 'It's waterproof, you muppet.'

Valerie watched the door close in front of her. Mrs Craig, Costello's neighbour, was away to get the spare key. The old biddy was very picky about who she gave it out to. She thought Valerie was Costello's boss in some way, which Valerie supposed she was.

The little old dear was making a great play of giving Valerie a loan of the key for Costello's flat, leaving Valerie, who had introduced herself as a colleague from the fiscals' office, free rein. The old dear had glanced at the ID and twaddled off to get the keys.

As Valerie waited, she walked over to the window of the flat's hall. A nice flat right down by the riverside. It must have cost her a bob or two, this place. The hallway was carpeted; the window clean and free of bugs, there was a small wooden table under the window adorned by a couple of plants. She placed her hand over one, noting that the tremor in her fingers had gone. It came and went, she supposed as she dried out. Or at least cut her drinking down.

Who was she kidding?

If the tremor ever went away completely, she'd feel odd without it, the shake had been there for so long. The leaf of the plant stayed still as she caressed it, soft and velvety under her fingers. Somebody was making a little home here. Not Costello, not from what Valerie had heard about her; she sounded hard-nosed and career driven. But then she seemed to have a soft side too; Costello looked in on this old woman every morning, making sure she was OK. Mrs Craig had raised the alarm the minute Costello had not returned home. She was the only one who had thought to call the police.

Archie, not Costello, had said Costello's mum and gran had both been drinkers. Costello knew the signs and was very anti-drink, which might explain the disdain with which the

cop had greeted her with at the hospital yesterday. Valerie
hadn't thought much about vodka today, she felt busy and
purposeful.

She leaned forward and pressed her head against the glass,
looking over the city sky, a much flatter city than Edinburgh.
It looked more built up, she could see the cityscape for miles,
flattening away into the distance, the darkness above and the
bright lights down below, distorted into stars by the glass, it
looked like the world had turned upside down.

She felt a tap on her shoulder.

Mrs Craig was dangling a fob with a St Andrews flag on
it. 'Here's the key for you, pet.'

Morna woke, thinking the man had moved, a subtle change
she had caught out the corner of her eye. She sat and watched
him, from her seat in the corner. But now he was still once
more, as if he had been playing statues with her. Overnight
she had received an email; they had found an abandoned
vehicle down near Loch Lomond, Patrick himself was going
down there to oversee any evidence gained from the vehicle
and the local force were securing the locus until he got there.

She pulled her seat over to the bed, and rubbed her eyes,
studying him more closely.

He looked better, he seemed in less pain, as if his head felt
better and the tension had gone, allowing him to breathe a
little easier. The painkillers winning their battle against the
pain receptors in the brain.

She pulled her chair closer still; it was getting light outside.
She took his hand. His skin was warm and clammy. Her own
fingers seemed cold and podgy next to his. He had long slender
fingers covered in fine wiry dark hairs that matched those on his
chest, the little tuft of hair that peeked out from the wires that
crossed his chest and lay on the neck of his hospital gown. The
little pieces of tape on his throat looked like snowflakes.
The bandage round his head looked comical, cartoon-like almost,
wound round and round like he was a mummy.

How would she feel if this was her boy? If this was Finn
a few years on, caught like this, attacked when alone. Somebody
had cut his throat, then battered him with a blunt instrument,

stripped him of his jacket, then stripped him of his identity, only to leave him on top of the most dangerous road in Scotland. So why would somebody do that?

She rubbed the back of his hand gently.

At some point Patrick had woken her with a call and reported that there were now four young men reported missing who fitted this young man's description. Two from Glasgow, one from Aberdeen and one from Sutherland. He was getting further details. Her brief remained the same, sit tight and monitor him. Record anything and everything.

She'd need to call Neil again. Or Lachlan. It seemed DCI Patrick was determined to stop her going home.

She realized she was murmuring out loud. 'So, enough of me. What happened to you?'

He murmured something back, not to her specifically but some words came out, in the ether and to the world.

'Sorry?' she said, not sure if she had heard. 'Did you say something?'

It was quieter and more mumbled the second time. By the end of the word his breath was already tailing off, too much effort.

'You were attacked. You are in hospital, but I guess you have worked that out for yourself by now.'

The breathing changed rhythm slightly. He was waiting on the next bit, a pause between the in breath and gentle exhale.

'Well, you got a whack on the head and a few more on your face—' she left out the bit about the slit throat – 'and then somebody dumped you in the middle of nowhere but—'

He was trying to say something.

Was it Finn?

Was he trying to say Finn?

Did he know her?

Did he know her son?

She tried to halt the palpitations in her chest. Finn had been left with Lachlan, and then her mother would have arrived, and then Neil would have come home. In any case, Lachlan would make sure Finn would be OK. There would be a similar pattern today. Her son was safe, which is more than she could say for the young man lying in front of her. She had heard wrong. 'Don't get stressed. But it was so cold, you didn't bleed the way you should, so you are going to be fine.' She lifted her hand off him for a moment and crossed her fingers hoping she was telling the truth. 'All the vessels contracted, you see, so that prevents blood loss and, on top of that, you have a wee bleed on your brain but they put a wee clip to hold it until it heals properly. My gran had one of them in her head for ages and she did OK.'

'Finn . . .' The word drifted slowly on his outward breath.

'Finn?' she repeated.

'Cam . . .'

'Cam? Is your name Cam? Campbell? Cameron?'

'Cam . . . Finn.' His head rolled a little, flicking backwards and forwards in frustration. Then the hand gripped hers.

'Finn or Cameron?' She felt stupid, she could sense his frustration, see it in the way his eyes stayed closed, but the eyelids kept flickering. This was stressing him.

Then he started to breathe deeply again, fallen asleep, floating back into himself, away to get better where they couldn't chase him anymore. It was up to her now.

'It's OK. I've got that,' she told him, lying into his ear. 'Rest well.'

Morna scrolled through the list of possible matches. Two had been drunk and had left a party at the weekend and not come back yet, Morna knew that was a bit worrying in the city but out here it was a death sentence. There were two missing person reports from Edinburgh and Sutherland. If the Sutherland boy was out in this weather exposed, he'd be dead by now. It wasn't uncommon. Nor was it uncommon to have too much to drink and stagger off a harbour wall into the inky depths.

She scrolled down, looking at the other two; the Glaswegians. One was a cop missing at a crime scene. She had to read that again. Why had that not hit the newspapers? It might have but she had not seen anything other than this room for the last day and a half.

The other one was a student, from Glasgow University. She read the 'last seen', her eyes catching on the fact he had been last seen going out the door of his flat with a film camera. Having had a quick look at the description, the weight and height seemed to match. They matched those of the cop as well, she reminded herself. She closed her phone and rubbed it against her chin. 'Kieran?' She enquired of the body. 'Donnie?'

There was no response to either. He was fast asleep, drifting away in a world of his own.

If she was a betting girl, she'd go for the student. No wife would let her husband out with that ancient jumper.

DCI Patrick walked out the HQ of the Wester Ross Police and took a deep sigh. He glanced at his watch, his face creasing, annoyed at the bloody waste of his life. That was an hour he was never going to get back. ACC Blackward was clear, keep the crime local, get it solved and get it solved quickly. The tourist board marketing people had been pushing the North Coast Five Hundred as an all-year road trip. During the winter months they removed the Bealach Na Ba and sent the route the long way round, but the infamy and the beauty of the road had given it a celebrity status. It was now considered the daredevil way to go; the more weather warnings the better. Blackward had placed in front of him media clippings of the pass; classic cars, hospital beds, you name it, it had tried to go up over the road to Applecross and then to Port MacDuff beyond. And now, all that good will and hard work had gone for nothing. If there was not a quick resolution to this case then the Bealach Na Ba, that golden goose, would forever be tarnished by the memory of a young man, battered and bleeding at the summit.

Patrick had remained silent except to utter three words, 'He's not dead.'

Blackward's reply was swift. 'Yet.'

Patrick had handed over the part of the file he knew the boss liked. Solid evidence. He had a photograph of a unique jumper, and that picture was being shown to a cop's wife and a student's mother. And they were running a trace on the orange fibres, the soil from the soles of the boots. He himself was prioritising the location of the camper. Some result would come of that, even if exculpatory.

And, he closed his eyes thanking God for Morna and her

precision, he pointed to the report about the orange tri-lobar fibres. 'These could be important.'

'And where are they from?'

'Cuffs, socks on the victim. The back of the head. Areas that would have been exposed, if he was rolled in a carpet or something. It's a tough hard-wearing carpet, used in cars, caravans, boats. Not for houses or hotels. The bad news is that Nissan, Volvo and Fiat all use that same material. So do many camper vans, especially conversions.'

'Caravans? Motorhomes?' Blackward had rolled his eyes. 'The tourist board are going to love this. But if we find the vehicle, then we can match it?'

'The dye, yes, the orange dye will be unique for that run.'

Blackward had palmed his hand across his mouth. 'Sometimes I think this place is cursed.'

'It's people, it's only people.'

Blackward had nodded. 'Keep on it and keep focussed. Are we getting anywhere on the coke trail?'

'I think we might be. Too much of it is being moved around too easily. And we have left it, with the knowledge of the surrounding forces, until we get a pattern. The longer we wait, the more we know and we have more chance of getting higher than the monkeys. Would be nice to nail those who are bringing it in.'

'Are we close to doing that?' asked Blackward.

'Maybe.'

'Do you have a good idea who is moving the stuff around, locally?'

'Yes, we do. As you said the tourist board won't like it. But they don't pay my wages.'

'Who found the body?'

'I don't know. You can make that request for information further up the food chain.'

'So who contacted you?'

'No comment.'

Patrick heard gunfire, rapid, assault rifles. The noises went no further than his head. He had heard his own voice report where the body had been found but Blackward looked blank, which showed he had spent too long behind the desk.

So Patrick had excused himself before the boss could ask anything else.

Once out on the street, Patrick breathed in the salted air and watched the seagulls wheel and circle above. He was jealous of their freedom, up and around higher and higher. He phoned Morna to find out how the young man was doing. He was still alive, he was trying to say something, 'Finn' and 'Cam'. He could hear the flicking of the pages of her beloved notebook. She was in love with pens and paper, unlike her colleagues who were very keen on their iPads and electronic notebooks.

Finn? Cam? It meant nothing to him.

Colin Anderson sat down in the blue-carpeted family interview room at the old Partickhill station where Anderson had spent most of his working life. The picture of the flowers on the wall was the same, he could still see a stain on the carpet from a cup of black coffee he remembered going over. So why did he feel so unwelcome on his own turf, being questioned by these two interlopers? It was the summons that did it, the phone call from Complaints that they would like a word with him. The message was clear; get your arse down here. He had left an unusually quiet office, everybody was tiptoeing round him.

They came in, the two of them, Bannon and Mathieson. Anderson knew Bannon, not well but enough to know that he wasn't hated, not the way that some of them were from Complaints and Investigations; the cops who policed the cops. It wasn't an easy job, and Anderson doubted that it was a pleasant one, but he understood the need for the force to be policed. Mathieson, he didn't know. But he presumed she was the small blonde, blanched white, she looked as though she had seen a ghost, her nacreous face highlighted by the dark red of her lips, lips that were firmly closed at the moment, fixed in a tight, thin line. Anderson was a man who noticed women's hair, the way other men noticed curves or legs. He was quick to see that he could look right through hers. It wasn't thick and titan like Brenda's, not curled and blonde like Sally's, not long and auburn like Helena's. Mathieson was almost bald.

Maybe that was why she wasn't a barrel of laughs.

'Sorry, Colin,' she said. 'Not good of us to meet like this but I didn't think I could do this by phone.'

'Do what?' he asked, nodding, shaking hands with them both, acknowledging her apology. He knew that whatever it was; it had nothing to do with him. They were here to get him to spill the beans on a colleague, but he couldn't think who. He had mulled it over in his mind, and hoped it was about Mulholland and his leg, more a matter for HR and occupational health. He would have thought, but who knew with the state of Police Scotland these days, anything to avoid paying an ill health retrial pension.

But he knew, in his bones, it was about Costello.

Mathieson was still smiling slightly, as a look it didn't suit her. Bannon sat down, in the position of the observer. So this was important, this could be serious.

'Your partner DI Costello? Do you have any idea where she is?'

'Costello?' The question had genuinely taken Anderson by surprise.

'Yes Costello, your colleague. You have worked with her for many years. I'm sure you remember her.' The pretence of politeness was gone, now replaced by sharp sarcasm that could have come from Costello herself.

'Yes, I know who she is. I don't know where she is.'

'Nobody does. Do you know this gentleman?'

God they were treating him like a suspect. He knew the next move, to slide a photograph across the table then turn it over at the last moment, increasing the shock value.

Bannon had the grace to look a little sheepish as the 16 by 12 photograph was slid across the table towards him.

Anderson had to cough to hide a smirk.

He looked at it, a fresh-faced young man in a blue jumper – he looked like the sort of man that appears on adverts for formula milk or a new housing development. He would have two small kids and a wife who worked part time, a sandpit in the garden and every house he bought would be another step on the ladder until they started downsizing.

'I don't think I do,' he replied carefully, aware of the sweat of stress around his collar.

'Does the name Donald McCaffrey mean anything to you?'
Something sparked in his mind, but not enough to hold
on to.

'Donnie McCaffrey?' offered Bannon.

'Yes.' The small memory in Anderson's mind caught the spark
and came to life. 'I think he was the first officer on the scene
w-when,' he stuttered realizing he wasn't about to relate an event,
he was about to talk about Moses.

'Yes, when your grandson was discovered in a car, alone.
A Dacia Duster that had been moved from its original parking
spot.'

'In the end that case resulted in two deaths, one fatal
incident and a trial in preparation, so we don't need to discuss
any of that.' Anderson was acting as if he outranked them
now. He did. Talking about the job was OK but they were
talking about his family. 'But don't take my word for it, you
can check the log.'

'We did,' said Bannon.

OK, so that wasn't what they were here for. Anderson waited,
the next move was theirs.

'Colin . . .' It was Bannon's turn to speak, trying to
engage him; he was going to be the matey one, inviting confi-
dences that he wasn't entitled to. 'How well do you know
Costello?'

'As well as any police officer knows another who they have
worked alongside for twenty years. There have been months
on an investigation when we have been in each other's pockets
and other times when we hardly see each other. This is one
of those times – a not seeing each other time,' he clarified for
them. 'Has anything happened to her?'

'We thought you might be able to tell us that.'

'Well no, I haven't heard from her.' Archie Walker had but
he wasn't going to tell them that. An unwelcome thought
floated through his mind at that moment, a text identified a
phone, not the person who sent it.

The two detectives passed a look between them, something that would have gone unnoticed if the person sitting
opposite them hadn't been skilled and experienced in investigation techniques. They were about to change tack.

'I presume that you and Costello have had differences of opinion in the past.'

'Plenty.'

'Do you think she's gone off in the huff?'

'No.'

'So only this time.'

'Only this time, what?'

'For going AWOL. Is she in a relationship?' That was a very focussed question, and the sudden change of direction did not go unnoticed. Was it Archie they were after?

Mathieson caught the hesitation.

'The answer to that is either yes or no.'

'The answer to that question is none of my business. I am her work colleague not her big brother.'

'We are coming to her brother in a moment.'

I bet you are.

'Have you seen the newspaper article? That was very damming.'

'Oh, so the press are the moral guardians of the complaints? God luck with that. And you should be more concerned with finding out who in your team is taking backhanders for dealing that dirt.'

'It was bad,' sympathized Bannon. 'But it wasn't from us, it was from George Haggerty.'

'And who told him? Bloody hell,' Anderson dropped his head into his hands, all those little midnight chats with Haggerty. He'd kill the bastard.

'Anything to tell us?' asked Mathieson.

'Relationships can be very complex. Unless you see the world in black and white, most relationships are shades of grey. My reading of the situation is that she felt very responsible for the death of Malcolm Haggerty—'

'So she was responsible for the death of Malcolm Haggerty?' Mathieson was on it, her eagerness pulling her right into a trap.

'Only as much as you and I are. We should provide a safe society and we don't. Have you never been involved in a case and thought, if only I had done X or Y, they wouldn't have died.' He looked her straight in the eye, she didn't look away. 'Obviously not then. You are very fortunate.'

Bannon decided either he'd had enough, or that they were getting nowhere. He started again with his engaging approach.

'Colin we have a problem, a big problem. Costello has disappeared. So has this young man, under very suspicious circumstances.'

Anderson's eyes narrowed. 'Bloody hell.'

'This young cop was friendly with Costello.' Bannon tapped the photograph.

'I know.'

'His blood was found at the small hill to the rear of the viewing point at Loch Lomond. He may have been stabbed.'

Anderson put his hands up, palms out. 'But he is a police officer, he must have enemies? Why are you talking to me?'

'We have been in touch with the investigating officers and the case is now ours.'

'Why? Because he is a cop?'

'According to his wife, Costello invited him to a meeting somewhere, summoned him, she asked, he jumped.'

'So they were onto something?'

'Onto what?' Mathieson's eyes glinted dangerously.

'Something? I don't know. Wasn't there. Wasn't told.' But he'd bet his bottom dollar that it was to do with George Haggerty. 'Has something happened to her?'

'We have found "significant DNA" on a small sample of blood. And another DNA from a much larger sample of blood.'

'Whose?'

Mathieson hesitated so it was Bannon who spoke. 'McCaffrey and Costello. And you know how we would interpret that. The person with the bigger blood loss was the victim, the other the perp. It's a theory that we are working on.' He upended the pen on his desk letting it drop between his thumb and forefinger. 'It fits the facts as we have them, but that will and can change as the evidence comes in.' He smiled benignly. He didn't believe it either. 'It's just a theory.'

'You think that Costello attacked and wounded McCaffrey? Why the hell would she do that?'

'That is how we would interpret the evidence if there weren't two police officers involved. The problem is that we have no evidence that anybody else was there.'

'Barking, wrong tree and up. Put that in any order you want.' Anderson was scathing in his lack of respect.

'We need to go where the evidence takes us, Colin, and it makes no sense to me,' said Bannon. 'Can you shed any light on it?'

'As I said, it's a theory and being who she is, her family . . .' said Mathieson, staring directly at Anderson. 'Maybe with a little bit of mental instability . . .'

'Hers or yours?' asked Anderson, staring straight at Mathieson.

'We'll see.' She closed the file. 'I presume this interview is over.'

'You presume right.'

EIGHT

The landing of Costello's flat smelled of fried liver and onions, making Valerie feel vaguely homesick yet comforted. She could remember that far back with no problem at all.

'Did you see the newspaper this morning?' The old woman smiled. 'It's terrible what they print nowadays.'

'Don't worry about it, they are just trying to stir up some evidence from the Monkey House of Horror. Costello was very involved in that.'

'And is she all right?'

'Yes, she's fine but we are keeping her out the road, not quite witness protection but that kind of thing.' Valerie was amazed at how easily she lied. Mrs Craig looked like the kind of old dear who would watch *Law and Order*, she'd believe in witness protection.

'Here's my number, you can call me if somebody else wants to borrow the key and you are not sure.' Valerie swapped the key for a small piece of card with the number of her new untraceable mobile number. 'Don't give it to anybody else, please.' Valerie smiled her sweetest smile. 'We need to keep her safe.'

Valerie slipped the key in the lock, opened the door and walked into Costello's life. Costello could not tell the whole story because she didn't know what exactly had happened, but she knew how it had felt when it had happened. And that was far more telling.

Valerie walked into the living room; the huge glass wall that looked over the river was covered by a closed curtain, bathing the room in a dull half-light that suited her purpose and her mood. The subject of her visit was lying on the glass table beside a cup of half-drunk tea, a cold deflated teabag still hanging over the side of the mug. Valerie picked up the laptop and unplugged the power cable. Whatever Costello's brain had forgotten, this laptop would recall perfectly.

She looked around, finding a credit card in the kitchen cupboard above the kettle, as Costello had said. The spare car key in a drawer in the bedroom, her passport in a small case at the bottom of her wardrobe. She looked at the picture, sitting down in front of the mirror, holding her hair up, imaging it blonde.

She didn't look like Costello at all. But she didn't need to.

Walking into the bathroom, she stopped in her tracks. Rivers of red ran down the tiles of the shower cubicle; Costello had been bleeding badly in here. Valerie held onto the wall, looking at the bloodstained towels, the red pooling on the shower tray. She carefully picked up a red piece of cloth, then realized it was the back of a white blouse, bloodstained and cut, slashed through by a very sharp blade. It took Valerie's breath away. Evidence should be bagged, tagged, sterile and contained. It was shocking so close, like Abigail's lilac blouse. She should call somebody, she could call Archie, but that would unravel the whole story and where would that get them?

It could get Costello into a lot of trouble.

No, she had to be a little cleverer than that.

She nipped out to the kitchen and rooted around until she found a pair of marigolds, then went back and bundled up the rest of the bloodstained clothes, grey trousers and a dark cardigan, and stuffed them at the bottom of the washing basket. If they searched the place they would find them. She rinsed out the shower cubicle with bleach and found and wrapped the bloodstained blouse in a roll of cling film, gathered the rest of the stuff on her list and left quickly, locking the door behind her and then giving the key back to Mrs Craig.

Morna had been snoozing in the corner, prodded to wakefulness by a quiet ping. She opened the email, forwarded by DCI Patrick. The attachment showed the student matriculation card of Kieran Cowan, aged twenty-three, student at the College of Sciences where he was studying environmental science, zoology and biology. His classmates said he had left that night to film at the loch as part of a wildlife preservation project. *Film.* And he had his camera with him. There had been an incident, blood had been found. Alastair Patrick was trying to find out details. She'd let him know, but if a DS from Glasgow called Vik Mulholland phoned it was because Patrick had passed on the number.

The jumper had been recognized by Kieran's mother who thought she had knitted it. Patrick wanted more to confirm ID, commenting that when he had shown the picture of the jumper to Wilma, she had given it one glance and said, 'Oh probably,' in reply to his query, 'Did you knit that?' Thus proving to himself that Fair Isle was not singular. Lots of women knitted it, the jumper was years old and no woman would recall that individual colour scheme. The item in question could have been bought in a charity shop last week. It was not an identifying jumper and DCI Patrick was not bringing a woman over two hundred miles only for her to say, 'That's not my boy.'

So Morna phoned Mulholland and left a message, asking him if he could obtain a DNA swab from the parents. But she knew, she just knew, that it was Kieran in the bed in front of her. Then she emailed Patrick with an update on the boy's condition. She held back the fact that they had said he would have sustained brain damage, being so cold for so long with a slow bleed adding to the loss of vital oxygen.

It was a waiting game now. And she didn't want to mention it in case it got back to the mum. Let them enjoy their good news. Their son had been found alive. She read the email again.

Cam finn? Cam ra?

Camera.

She patted him on the back of his hand. 'I have it now.' Before pulling out a notebook and scribbling it down. She'd call Mulholland.

Lachlan and Patrick sat in the corner of the pub, each sipping a whisky, keeping their thoughts to themselves.

'How did it go with Blackward?'

'Usual shite.'

'Ruby McDonald turned up eventually to take wee Finn for the duration, so the boy is over at the farm.' Lachlan shook his head. 'That Neil is a tosser. I knew that Morna would let down her parents one day, such a good wee girl, good at school, good career, then she goes and marries that useless muppet.'

'He might be a useless bastard. He's working a lot of hours though.'

'So I noticed. But then so is she. We need to get Finn back here.'

'You can make that happen, Lachlan. Morna trusts you.'

'He'll be back. Ruby's too busy to deal with the boy. How is Morna getting on? Is she OK? I heard she was at Raigmore babysitting the victim from the Bealach?'

'You heard right,' said Patrick.

'You got any idea who he is yet?'

Patrick shook his head. 'Somebody went to a lot of trouble to kill him, remove him and dump him. I think he's safer where he is. There's more to come.'

Lachlan nodded, settling back in his seat. 'And Abigail Haggerty?'

Patrick nodded. 'Oscar's wife. George's wife.'

'Aye, her. You think that George is going to come back up here for good.'

'I do.'

'Interesting.' Lachlan closed his eyes and took a sip of Talisker. 'And do you think that he will be going up to the lodge? That's what he usually does.'

'I think that will be first place he will be going.' Patrick licked the whisky from his lips. 'But will he go alone?'

'Following his ghosts? Somebody has been phoning the harbour authority asking about the *Jennifer Rhu*, asking about Oscar's drowning. It's the talk of the town.'

'People talk. Let them. I have a smart little DC asking about Jennifer Argyll. And that DC is going to talk the very clever Colin Anderson into having a look around at the Jennifer Argyll case and all that will lead to Sharon Sixsmith and Nicola Barnes. Colin Anderson is not a man who knows when to stop.'

Lachlan let out a long slow breath. 'Are we happy about that?'

'Not bothered, let them find what they can find.'

'What's that line from the film, "fasten your seatbelts. It's going to be a bumpy night".'

They raised a glass to each other, with a sense of closure and contentment.

Anderson was sitting on the settee, waiting for Isla to calm down. He was glad her parents had come to take the children away; one three years old, one two years, the other little more than a baby. Isla's parents were obviously very fond of their son-in-law, a good sign in Anderson's book; dads want good husbands for their daughters. Isla herself was red-eyed and worn out. Her dark hair looked as if she hadn't combed it for a week. She still had some fight in her though.

'So, who are you? Just another bloody cop to talk shite about my husband because he's not here to defend himself? How dare you!'

He had heard about the treatment Isla McCaffrey had given Diane Mathieson, so he retreated into the seat, but she didn't move. She started crying again.

'It's quite simple, Mrs McCaffrey. Your husband is missing, my DI is missing. It's unlikely to be a coincidence given they know each other so well.'

'They were *not* having an affair!' she sobbed.

Anderson couldn't help the smile that curled onto his lips. 'No, I very much doubt they were. The thought had never crossed my mind. And I'm bloody sure the thought had never crossed Donnie's mind either.' That got her interest. She looked up and sniffed, smoothing her curls down around her face, giving her the appearance of a distressed Jane Austin heroine. 'I am not here in any official capacity, but my friend is missing and I am worried about her . . .'

She tilted her head. 'Who are you again?'

'Another bloody cop.'

'Sorry.'

'No offence taken, but we do need to talk.'

'I'm so worried,'

'So am I. Costello knew your husband and thought a lot of him professionally. She thought he was a man of high moral standards and good police instinct.' He felt he was writing

Donnie's obituary. 'They worked together in the case of the baby that went missing.'

Isla's mouth formed a perfect 'O' as the facts fell into place. 'Moses.'

He nodded.

She narrowed her eyes slightly. 'Your son? It was in the paper. You are *that* Anderson.'

'Indeed, my wee grandson.' He felt himself smile; she smiled back.

'With regard to Donnie and Costello, I don't know and am not allowed to know any more than you do, but please don't take any of that shite from Mathieson and Bannon. I think she's a bit power hungry and he's under the point of her stiletto.'

'I guessed that.'

'Costello is out there somewhere, and she's alive. We think. We hope. They might be together. It's a big thing for anybody to kill two police officers. It wouldn't happen in this country, not without what we call "noise" on the intelligence. Somebody would know and somebody would talk. People can't keep their mouths shut.' He looked at her reassuringly. 'When Costello was a new recruit, about two weeks out of Tulliallan, she was called to an incident in a multi-story. A young woman had been run over by a car, deliberately. She was eight months pregnant.'

'Bloody hell.' Isla's hands flew to her chest, still sensitive to feel another's pain. 'That's awful.'

'It was. The baby survived but the mother didn't. Costello was first on the scene. She sat on the concrete, holding that woman's hand until the ambulance came. That baby has grown up to be a powerful lady in . . . well, certain circles of Glasgow society. She's no angel but I think if she heard of anybody killing DI Costello, there would be a shockwave in the Glasgow underworld, and we'd feel it. There has been no such thing. What I'm saying is, you can't kill two cops quietly. Not in this city.' He kept the nagging voice to himself. He was talking about regular police work, and he doubted Costello and McCaffrey were doing something regular, otherwise it would all be logged. It was under the radar of Police Scotland, it might have been under Libby's radar too.

'And you know for definite that nothing bad has happened to him?' she sniffled.

'I'm sorry but I think something very bad has happened. That blood is too much to be, well . . . insignificant. But your husband and my colleague were on the side of the gods. There's no way they were up to criminal activity themselves . . .'

'She was in the paper. Her brother was a murderer. That's what it said.'

'Yes I know. The daggers are out for her and that worries me even more. If there's one thing Costello can't come back from, it's idle gossip. You need to tell me everything you can remember about what Donnie was talking about, thinking about. Anything you can . . . He must have said something to you.'

She seemed to consider this for a moment then sighed. 'He was talking a lot about the Abigail Haggerty case. The one where the boy was killed.'

Anderson felt a little stab of ice in his heart. 'Most of the country was talking about that.'

'He seemed to like Costello, you know, early on when they were working together on the Braithwaite case. She was going to help him get his competencies and get into the CID. That's what he really wanted. He was fed up of being on the outside of where he wanted to be. He had watched Costello, getting things done and making decisions, putting pieces of the puzzle together and being able to think about what was missing, he was doing all that alongside her.'

'She told me that herself, he had a good nose for it.' Anderson hoped that she wouldn't notice his use of the past tense. 'Would he have told you if Costello had asked him to help out unofficially?'

She thought about the question. 'I wouldn't have been keen. It could have damaged his future career. I didn't ask and he didn't tell me. I had some faith that Costello would keep him on the right side of the law.'

'What do you think he was doing up at Loch Lomond on a Saturday night? Or why might his car be there?'

'No idea.'

'And you have no idea where Costello is?'

She shook her head.

'And no idea where her car is. They could have both got into her car and gone somewhere else?'

'Why was there drink? And cocaine? Was she, well, into that kind of thing?'

'No. And that tells me more than anything that the scene was staged. Whoever did this didn't know Costello at all. There was somebody else there, trying to discredit them, hurt them professionally. I'm not sure who that might be?' He left the question hanging, trying not to suggest anything to her.

But Isla looked confused.

'We will get to the bottom of it.'

'It's been three days now, are they going to drag the loch?' she voiced an uncomfortable association of ideas. 'Do you think my husband is at the bottom of the loch?'

'I have no idea. It's not my call to search. They won't tell me but if I find out anything I will call you.'

Anderson walked down the slabbed path of McCaffrey's house. A sandpit in the front garden was closed and tarped against the weather. He guessed the bulky upright was a trampoline. He got in the car and checked his messages. He had missed a call from Mitchum. He called back straight away.

'Anderson, I'll be quick. After they found blood at the lochside I've been under pressure from the fiscals' office to put a trace on Costello's mobile.'

'Good.'

'Well, its battery was put in again this morning and a text message was sent, to Archie as usual. Its activity was very brief.'

'But you got it?'

'We did, bounced off Fearnmore and Skye, vaguely.'

'At the top of the North Coast 500, up north, up near Port MacDuff?'

'And why do you say that? Specifically that?'

Anderson was quiet.

'I need some transparency here, Colin. There's been a young man left for dead at the top of the Bealach Na Ba.'

'Again North Coast 500 to Port MacDuff. George Haggerty grew up there. That's where he went the night of the murders.'

Anderson pulled the phone away from his ear as Mitchum erupted, thinking again about whose fingers were tapping out those texts.

Valerie closed Costello's laptop, lay down and closed her eyes, trying to think she didn't trust herself to remember what she had seen with her own eyes, or more importantly what she had not seen.

She needed to be careful.

Costello and she had both walked round the house in Balcarres Avenue in the same way, following each other's footsteps through that house of murder and bloodshed.

The smell of it being cleaned recently. Costello's instinct had led her upstairs where . . . where somebody had left the CD player repeating that song. 'The Clapping Song'.

That song reminded Valerie of Malcolm.

She ran through the words in her mind, the words about them all going to heaven.

That was a sick joke.

Then George had clapped at Costello at the funeral, Valerie had been too drunk to go. She had intended to go, of course, but had fallen asleep instead of getting dressed, waking up on the sofa with her good black suit crumpled underneath her, still on its hanger.

She could recall times in the garden at Balcarres though; she was sure, happy memories. Could she remember though, her and Malcolm, maybe Mary Jane had been there too, at the bottom of the garden? George at the back door telling them the kettle had boiled, standing in a gap at the back door, the white muslin sheet swirling around him. Then him clapping his hands together to get their attention.

Clap clap.

Did she actually remember that? Or did she think she did simply because it fitted her version of events.

Archie had told her that Costello had already voiced her concerns about Malcolm's safety in the house to some of her colleagues, telling them that he had tried to climb out his own bedroom window to get to her, his dad had interrupted that by appearing at the front door. The single foot, in his trainer, poking out the first-floor window had been quickly retracted. Costello had said the boy had been out, hiding behind the bins, shivering, sick with the cold, dressed only in a Celtic top and leggings. Malcolm had even left a message on Costello's phone, and to give her due, Valerie thought, Costello had brought the matter to the attention of the child protection services.

But Malcolm had slipped through.

There was no evidence that he was a child at risk.

Valerie thought about the minute she had stepped into George's bedroom. Her sister's bedroom. She wanted to see where her sister had fought for her life. The carpet was the same, except for the large hole cut out at the bottom of the bed. The mirrored doors were sparkling and spotless, the duvet was folded up at the bottom of the stripped bed.

She had been quiet, not wanting to interrupt the silence of the ghosts.

These people shouldn't be ghosts, her sister, her little nephew.

The big question was: who had killed them?

The fascist with the lipstick had been murmuring something, 'Yes, of course. Mr Haggerty is devastated at his loss. He has been very helpful.'

Motive? The fascist had shrugged, standing in the doorway watching her every move.

Valerie had shaken her head thinking that maybe her sister had misdiagnosed a patient and they, or their family, had got angry? But folk don't kill over that. They complain to the BMA or the papers, or Facebook.

But Costello had a good theory.

Money.

The life insurance Abigail carried. The life insurance Oscar had carried. The mortgage on the Balcarres Avenue house paid off. That made Valerie stop and think.

Oscar presumed dead. The *Jennifer Rhu* on fire, sinking. No sign of Oscar.

She checked her watch. She was having Costello moved at

that moment. Nobody would know she was there, the strict rules on patient confidentiality would see to that. She had a fractured skull and she was scared, very scared.

Costello had two other questions on her notes.

One comment. Who would Abigail open the door to? What had been said in that phone call?

Valerie tried to recall what she had been told. There had been a fight, verbal, voices raised. The nosey neighbour had called the police three times in the previous eighteen months. Each time Abigail had sent the police away, saying it was nothing. So another episode of shouting had provoked no alarm. It seems George had left, Abigail had texted him while he was on the road then George had called back. They only had George's word for what was said on that call. Or whose finger had pressed send on the text from Abigail's phone. He could have been talking to anybody. It wasn't proof that Abigail was still alive. The estimated time of death was much later, more like five or six a.m. Dead for ten hours when found. Valerie knew how easy it was to confuse a jury about time of death; the musculature of the body, the fat content, the temperature of the room, all that was a movable feast, one that she had dined on in court for the clients of the Crown.

Back at the house Bannon had spoken, standing behind Mathieson, looking over her shoulder. 'Valerie, your sister was very cautious; she had opened her door after one a.m. The time of death was three a.m. Cold night but the heating was on.'

George liked the house to be cool. He didn't like spending money on the heating. And it annoyed his chest. Abigail liked to sneak it on when he was away up north. Was there hell to pay when he came back? She closed her eyes to get her mind back on track. Was Abigail expecting somebody and she had started an argument to get him to leave? Nope, George had a call that summoned him north. So had George told her to expect somebody?

Was that why they were both dressed? No risking going to bed because somebody was going to call.

And who would that be? She had no faith in Mathieson getting anywhere.

Valerie thought back to the house. She had asked to see the boy's bedroom. The minute she stepped onto that grey carpet, she had spotted the gap on his bookcase, where his Millennium Falcon usually sat. She had asked if George had mentioned it. He hadn't.

But it was gone.

Mathieson had dismissed her with a scathing look. Even Archie had shaken his head a little, worrying about a toy at a time like this. It was a big toy, nearly two-feet long. And Costello had been Googling the street map of the area, looking as if she was timing routes in and out.

By foot.

And every route she picked went over the Kelvindale Bridge to the footpath. Valerie shook her head, closed her eyes and tried to concentrate. She could figure this out; she had the skills to do this. That was far behind the house, streets away, a long walk from the front of the house in Balcarres Avenue and Valerie knew from her professional experience how closely that CCTV had been examined. So what was Costello doing, looking at the bridge? A footbridge behind the house, at the far end of the estate.

Looking at the internet history on the laptop and a document Costello had called 'The Sideman', she started tracing the detective's thoughts. The Sideman?

Valerie picked her phone up and Googled that. The feeling of her fingertip on the screen, familiar and comforting. It reminded her of doing her job. The Urban Dictionary said sideman meant an irrelevant and powerless guy. She swiped down reading the more formal definition; an instrumentalist supporting a soloist or a principal performer.

Costello had called this whole file The Sideman. Had she known, or suspected, the presence of another man there? She read on, her brain starting to spark with unanswered questions. Costello's theory was that the sideman had been in the car when George drove in to the garage. George had gone into the house, the sideman had stayed in the garage. George got a phone call to go north, which gave him an unbreakable alibi. The sideman had come out the garage and entered the house. Did he have a key? Or had Abigail been called and told to expect him? Was that what the phone call was about? Valerie thought what that call might sound like. The house was close to the hospital. So X's mum has been admitted to Gartnavel. I've told X he can pop in and get some kip. He'll be exhausted after the drive down from Port MacDuff. Was that what the phone call had said? Then he killed them. According to Costello's route, he had exited via the back garden, a long walk through the streets then over the river. And away.

Had it been that simple?

Had it all really been that simple?

So who was he?

The brown and cream Volkswagen camper was parked in the innermost corner of the long lay-by, hidden by bushes, keeping its secrets to itself. It sat a little out from the verge of wet grass as if somebody in good shoes was going to be getting out the passenger door maybe to stretch their legs or to photograph a lovely sunset over the treetops in the wood behind.

DCI Alastair Patrick paused for a moment looking at the sky, then at his feet, as if there might be some answers there. The younger uniformed cop stood back and left him to it. It had taken him two minutes to judge that the DCI from Port MacDuff was a quiet man and that he was not one to be provoked to idle conversation. He watched as Patrick leaned against the front of the VW and checked the number plate.

'Definitely his car.' Patrick nodded and gestured that whatever silent machinations he had been turning over in his head were now over. He turned as a BMW pulled into the lay-by. The uniformed officer stood, arm out telling the driver that there was nothing to see here and would he kindly drive on. A tall fair-haired man got out the car, already showing his warrant card.

He approached the camper, passing a wry smile to the junior officer. He pulled on a pair of gloves as he passed.

The quiet man turned to greet him, lifting his cap. 'It's Colin Anderson, isn't it?'

'Indeed.' Anderson was at a loss.

'DCI Patrick. Port MacDuff. My DC thinks you are the best thing since sliced bread.'

'He doesn't know me then?' Anderson was finding it hard to read this small, wiry man with his cold stare and purposeful posture. Just looking at him made Anderson feel like a slob.

'She. DC Morna Taverner. She is looking after a young man in Raigmore Hospital. We think he was the driver of this vehicle. We are covering the same ground here.'

'Really.' Anderson wished he had had some more sleep, he wasn't catching on.

'A man with his throat cut and his first words are "camera" and "film". We phoned that in and were told that you already have recovered a Scub from the loch. This man witnessed what went on at the lochside. I'm sure of it.'

'Who is he?'

'Kieran Cowan, student, lives in the west end of Glasgow. No criminal record, nothing untoward about him. Except why did he stop? Why here? To answer his phone? Mechanical failure? To meet somebody? Who slit his throat? How did he get to the summit of the Bealach? It's about 160 miles from here. I asked for an abandoned vehicle check of a twenty-mile radius, it should have been two hundred.'

Anderson looked through the driver's window. 'And who?'

'Whoever.'

'Meeting somebody he knew?' Anderson stood back, trying to find an innocent explanation for the camper being here, abandoned. Why had Cowan walked away? What happened to McCaffrey? And Costello? He couldn't bear to think they were looking for another body. Two bodies. The thought made him chill.

'Family reported him missing. He had been away filming so they left it twenty-four hours plus, thinking he'd got carried away.' Patrick's gloved fingers rattled on the roof of the vehicle.

'Did he tell his friends or family what he was doing?' asked Anderson.

'They said he was looking for criminal activity against the wallabies, he was headed for the car park at Inveruglass. Where McCaffrey's car was found.'

Where their blood had been found.

Patrick's bright blue eyes looked straight through Anderson. *This is nothing to do with wallabies.*

'Your DC?' asked Anderson.

'Morna Taverner? Very good, she was talking about booking you a room at the Exciseman. She suspects you will be coming north, I think she's right.'

'News to me.' Anderson tapped on the window.

'It'll be worth your while.'

'Was Morna the one who called me about the Logan and Witherspoon rapes?'

'She would have phoned you about the Barnes and Sixsmith attacks,' Patrick answered, making his point. 'You two should get together and feed your obsessions. And while you are at it, see if you can cure her of her terminal clumsiness. A car smash and two nasty falls.'

Anderson looked at him puzzled, then went back to looking through the window, holding his hand up against the glass on the back passenger window to protect the glass from the rain to afford him a better view. 'He locked the vehicle before he left it.'

Patrick looked around at the hills, the darkening sky. 'What happened? Did the three of them go away in the missing Fiat?'

'Costello wouldn't drive two bleeding bodies around, and she was injured too. So where is the Fiat and who brought the camper here?'

'Good question. We got hold of the mum, she's bringing spare keys up here, but that will take time. And we need to talk to her about the identity of our young victim.' Patrick hitched up his trouser legs then got down on the ground to look under the car.

The power pendulum had swung again; Anderson was back in charge now. 'And how long does it take to drive from here to the Applecross pass?'

'The Bealach Na Ba?' Patrick wiped his palm over his eyes, trying to see something, then got out his mobile as he was wriggling in the ground, pulling his gloves from his fingers with his teeth. 'Three hours, three and a half from here? Can be five from the city. The roads are good until the last thirty miles or so. Somebody forced him to stop. And abducted him.' The blue eyes narrowed, looking back along the road to the turn off for the loch. 'Agreed?'

'Agreed. So, what do you think? There are no skid marks on the road. It looks like he left the vehicle of his own free will? Did he run out of petrol? Was he flagged down by somebody in trouble?'

'No, he would have pulled the camper in behind the other vehicle. This is parked up at the corner. And why would he take his bag out for that? Why did he leave his camera at the locus? Was he filming and somebody thought he had caught something incriminating on film? So then he got to his car and drove away . . . but then what? Why get out again?' He looked around him, over to the trees. 'He had pine needles on the shoes, his knees and his hair. And gravel in the palms of his hands.'

Anderson looked to the left and the right, and to the forestry commission woods. Then down.

'Morna said his cuffs smelled of oil or something. Was he crouching, feeling under the car? Then what, he ran away? Was chased away?'

'Should we wait for crime scene?' Anderson was looking around the tarmac of the lay-by, which told him nothing, no skid marks, no stains, no tyre marks. But Patrick was now studying it like he was reading the small print of a contract.

'It'll take time for them to get here. It's our force who is dealing with it and Inverness aren't going to stick this on their budget. There's no CCTV cameras out here, are there? I tried to order the footage from the four nearest for the four hours after eight p.m. on Saturday night but you lot have them.'

'There's none at the loch either, the cameras were trained on the shore after the issue with the wallabies but I'll hurry it up for you and see if anybody was giving him aggro on the road,' said Anderson.

'They made him stop. I know how I would do it. If you know beforehand that you want to disable a car. It's a bit like hobbling a donkey. It'll go but it won't get far,' said Patrick with something that resembled a shrug. 'I'm presuming no access to the engine, so it has to be covert.' He walked back to the vehicle and put the torch on his mobile phone back on, then knelt on the ground, swinging the light, making a square of it tracking the outer border of the vehicle's body. 'Over there, the front wheel arch, above that.'

Anderson walked round the car and knelt down, putting his arm up, feeling along the wheel arch, as Patrick told him to move his hand towards the front of the car.

'You're on it.'

'It feels like part of the car.' He tried to pull off the metal box he could feel but it didn't move.

'Try sliding it,' suggested Patrick.

The box gave way with familiar release and repel of a magnet.

It was a small tin, an old tobacco tin. Anderson held it up to Patrick who merely nodded as if it was no more than he would have expected.

'And how does that stop a car?'

'A few heavy ball bearings, fill it with warm candle wax, then stick a magnet on the top, close it and attach that to the bare metal on the inside of the engine casing.' He looked at Anderson, raising an eyebrow. 'Then the heat of the engine melts the wax and the ball bearings start to clatter around, the person stops. It's a much loved old vehicle, he would have stopped. And I think somebody was following. Hector will tell us.'

'Who's Hector, your great crime scene guy? We have a great forensic scientist here, Mathilda McQueen, nothing gets past her.'

Patrick walked back towards the Land Rover. 'Not much gets past Hector, well, not anything edible. He's a very fat spaniel,' said Patrick and Anderson was left to take of that what he could. 'I'll see you at the pub later.'

NINE

Anderson was so tired his headache now would not go away, it pounded incessantly behind his right ear. His eyes were dry, he was hungry but he had no appetite. All because of that wee bundle of peachy loveliness that cried in this basket. Moses had been quiet for an hour between three and four o'clock but apart from that, all Anderson could remember was noise. He had stayed in the kitchen, but he hadn't got as far as sleep when Moses started crying. Claire, her boyfriend David, and the ever-present Paige, had stayed in the front room, watching a documentary about Charles Manson, and eating a Chinese takeaway and Doritos. He had heard Claire and David arguing the toss about why people had followed Manson so blindly. And would it all fade to memory now that he was dead? Unlikely. He might have gone but the memories live on. The horror of it.

As he passed the door, sometime after midnight, on his way to the downstairs toilet, he heard Paige ask, 'So who is Charles Manson anyway?'

Now it was about half four. He walked into the kitchen where Brenda was preparing some milk formula. She was muttering over her shoulder to Moses who was in his basket on the big kitchen table, kicking his legs, wanting his covers away. They had a brief conversation, a weird conversation, like all their engagements nowadays. They now lived together in the same house because of Moses. They couldn't stay together for their own children but they could for a step-grandchild. Brenda was seeing another man, Anderson had met him twice in the passing. He was an accountant called Roger who, being wary kept out of Anderson's way, but he seemed to make Brenda happy – which is more than he himself had managed to do for the last few years.

Brenda turned and smiled. 'I can handle this, I think he has wind.'

'So do I after eating that Chinese. I can't sleep.'

'Well, go and do some work then, that's what you always used to do.'

It was a pointed jab, but mildly delivered. He smiled. 'I'll try to get some sleep before I need to go,' and he went back to his bed and lay there, listening to the noises of people in his house. Like when Claire and Peter were young. Day turns into night and back into day.

He picked up an old Henning Mankell he kept starting but he couldn't get in to it. He took out his tablet and flicked through a few emails, seeing the one from Morna Taverner, with its attachment. The files of a rape – had she said rapes or attacks? – that she wanted him to look at, an enthusiastic rookie. He read on, thinking about them as he looked at his watch; he'd had two hours sleep. She had included Sally Logan in her list, he pondered on the one fact that had always bothered him about her attack. Who would know she was there? On a Scottish hill at six on a summer morning, not somewhere you'd be – unless you had a reason to be there. Or prior knowledge that your victim was going to be there. Anderson decided he'd go into work early. He had a few things of his own he wanted to look up, starting with the employment and human resource history of one Morna Ann Taverner nee MacDonald.

Valerie looked at the red and white brick building, an old house, a big house that had once had a child and a family, kids played in that garden and the trees at the back had swings attached to them in a previous life. But for as long as Valerie could recall, it had been a GPs surgery. Abigail used to say, as they waited in their dad's car at the traffic lights on Crookston Road, that she would work there one day and heal the sick. That was Abigail, she always had grand ideas. Valerie really only ever wanted to go into law and make money. She didn't want to be all holistic, healing people and getting complete strangers to feel better about themselves.

That was Abigail all over; she had worked all during her marriage to Oscar. The bold but unlucky Oscar. Then Abigail had married George and it had all gone a bit . . . well, she had to think of the word. Quiet? Abigail had ceased to be Abigail. She had become George's wife. Valerie had thought at first that it was her sister treading lightly in a new marriage after the tragic loss of her first husband at sea.

Oscar was only presumed dead. Only presumed. The unwelcome thought had been pointed out to her with crystal clarity by Costello and her blackened eyes. They had never found the body, just the *Jennifer Rhu* burning, the painter attaching the dinghy half undone as if Oscar nearly managed to detach it but had failed to escape the flames. What was left of the yacht had still been burning when the coastguard had arrived.

Another one who had gone to heaven in a little rowing boat.

Abigail had been shattered by losing Oscar but had seemed keen to get married again. She wanted a father for Mary Jane. And then she had met George who, like Oscar, came from Port MacDuff. In fact, it might have been at the memorial service for Oscar that Abigail first met George. Valerie had searched for a memory. She must have been there but she could only recall swigging back a good white wine and then doing her teeth in the loo after she had been sick, filling the toilet bowl with sausage rolls and mushroom vol-au-vents. She had a very clear memory of that.

Abigail and George had bonded over the loss of a husband and a friend. At first Valerie thought it was the thrill of the new husband, *George does this* and *George thinks that,* then Valerie came to realize that Abigail had simply changed. She had challenged her about it, of course, and Abigail had said in that way of hers, that in retrospect was slightly nervous, that she was, for the first time in her life, relaxing. George made good money, and there would be a payout from Oscar's life insurance once seven years had passed and he could legally be declared dead. So there was no pressure on her to work, she had loved her adopted daughter, of course, but now she had a son of her own with George and that was special. And that sounded like all the roses in the garden were lovely, with no thorns at all. So why was George disappearing up to Port MacDuff at the slightest opportunity?

Costello wanted to know how much insurance Abigail

carried. The house had already been valued. George was quick to think about getting it on the market.

Was it all about money?

She glanced at her watch now, unfamiliar on her wrist. She had been invited to a meeting at the cop shop tomorrow morning but she was not prepared to face that fascist wee bitch again. Time to dance to a different tune now.

She walked up to the door and opened it; a receptionist looked up, a universal smile. 'Have you got an appointment? We are not actually open yet.'

'Dr Irene Marshall. She is expecting me for a chat, I am not a patient.'

'Oh?'

'I am Abigail's sister, Dr Haggerty's sister.'

'Oh.' The professional face immediately collapsed into one of concern, her eyes began to well up, a manicured hand went up to her mouth. 'I am so, so sorry, you must be Valerie.'

She nodded, thinking that this was the first person who had shown any real emotion about Abigail's death.

'Yes. I can't tell you how bad it has been.'

Then the expression changed slightly as the receptionist recalled the newspaper reports about the alcoholic sister, Valerie, the one who tried to buy a murdered woman's baby.

'Can I get you a cup of tea?' The receptionist waved her hands vaguely over her desk to a door marked 'offices'. 'You have a wee sit down in there and I'll tell her you are here, she's on the phone right now.'

Five minutes later the door opened and Irene Marshall came in, carrying two cups of hot tea. Valerie felt her stomach tighten. She needed a vodka, ProPlus and caffeine. She had a small bottle in her bag, next to the gun still wrapped in a hotel towel. The drink was talking to her, whistling at her for her attention. She pushed the temptation away, she had to try to stay focussed on this. Abigail might have said something. It's impossible to work alongside somebody and not get an idea of their lives no matter how much remained unsaid.

Did she allude to him being abusive? Were they in financial trouble?

'Hi, so sorry to keep you waiting.' Irene smiled an

empathetic smile and handed Val the tea. 'How are you keeping? I saw you at the funeral, but well . . . not the time or the place.' She sat down on the free office chair and she wheeled it towards the table, a ridiculous scurrying motion like a child in primary one. That left Valerie standing where the patients waited. She wasn't being invited into the inner sanctum. She was being politely tolerated. How much had Abigail said about her troubled sister? It had all been in the papers anyway.

'How are you doing?' she said, accompanied by a professional, distant smile.

'I'm fine.'

The next question would be, *have the police got any further forward with their enquiries.* She was close.

'Have they found anything yet? Do they know who did it?' She leaned forward, trying to engage.

Valerie sat down, feeling five years old and somebody was trying to explain to her about the birds and the bees. 'They won't tell me anything, they say that I am too close. It's about George,' said Valerie, the name came out hard, like a ricochet off a cliff face. It stung the silence between them.

'George?' Irene was confused. A phone rang in the distance. They heard the receptionist answer it, a quiet muffled conversation.

'The police never asked us about George. They asked about patients that might have mental health issues, anybody who might have wished her harm.' Irene shook her head. 'But she was doing so few hours, she was really only seeing her own list of patients. Working alongside us, but not part of the team. Which was her choice.'

'Why was that, do you think? Why was she only working those few hours? Was she not happy here?' Valerie looked at her own fingers tapping at the side of the doctor's desk, the skin red and flaking, her nails bitten to the stumps.

Irene Marshall was looking as well, making up her own diagnosis. 'Oh yes, but she wanted to be at home.'

'And that was why she cut her hours down?'

'Yes, Valerie.' Irene had a terrible condescension in her voice. 'She really wanted to be at home, be a housewife. After Oscar died, she threw herself into her work but she wasn't really cut out for it. She wanted a home, and to be at home, and when she married George she took her chance. I don't blame her. This job can be incredibly stressful.'

'But she loved her patients.'

'She did, she did. But the job isn't what it was. Cuts, patients knowing all their rights and none of their responsibilities. It's a highly stressful job, we were glad when she cut her hours, it saved us money. And when your sister got stressed, she wasn't the easiest person to work with.'

'No?'

Irene shook her head. 'I am only trying to help you, Valerie. Your sister could be a little overbearing at times, and I know I shouldn't speak ill of the dead, but she was a different person after Oscar died.'

'After Oscar died or after she married George?'

'One and the same.' Irene avoided the question.

'How is George coping? I've only seen him a few times since it all.' Irene raised an eyebrow, questioning. Was this not in keeping with her happy family internal monologue? Or the photo that had been in the papers.

'At first I was in hospital.' Valerie's fingers went up to the soft wool of the cowl neck of her jumper. 'He was grieving. He comes from Wester Ross, Port MacDuff, so he has been up there mostly. There is nothing down here to keep him.'

'Abigail always spoke as if you were a close family.'

Could she sense a note of sarcasm there? Or was she being oversensitive? 'We are.'

Were. Past tense.

Irene moved to get up, the chat was over.

'Did the police ask anything about Abigail, anything personal?'

Irene gave her a sidelong glance. 'That would be a confidential conversation.'

'I'm desperate, they tell me nothing. She was my sister.'

Irene sighed. 'The police were asking me if Abigail was having an affair but the answer to that is no.' She nodded as if that was the end of it, looking right at Valerie as if she could hear the internal monologue of every justification for every drink she had ever had.

'Did they also ask if Abigail thought George was having an affair?'

'They did, and Abigail did think that George had been unfaithful to her. She had said that to me. She thought she was being betrayed, lied to.'

Valerie took a deep breath, the waft of Ralph Lauren after-shave coming back to her, familiar and sweet, a brush on the cheek. 'Really? Did she ever tell you who it was he was seeing?'

Irene nodded. 'I'm surprised you had to ask. It was you.'

Anderson was having a good think about what Patrick had said. Not a man to waste words, his obsession, her obsession. Morna's, what had he said, 'clumsiness'? A car crash and two nasty falls? Not so much a light bulb moment as a blind man doing a jigsaw with no picture to go on. And no corners to start with. Whatever injuries Morna was sustaining, her boss did not think they were due to clumsiness.

Bannon, though, had been very approachable in a 'if Mathieson asks me I'll deny I ever said it' kind of way.

Anderson had seen the brief phone call as a trade-off. 'I'll tell you what I know of Costello as a human being, and you tell me what you know about Haggerty.' Bannon had been quick to jump on that, repeated the alibi. 'He's innocent, yes. I don't want to know that, I want to know what he does for a living.'

'Something unintelligible with numbers. Project manage-ment with accounts. He's contracted all over the place.'

'Does he have a degree?'

'Yes, business and accounts, computing or something.'

'What university?'

'Is this relevant?'

'Which one?'

'Errr, Strathclyde, I think.' He heard the tap tap on a keyboard.

That made sense. Glasgow was academic but Strathclyde was known for its business school.

'No, I tell a lie.' Anderson could hear Bannon typing. The movement of a mouse being lifted up and put back down again. 'He was at Glasgow.'

'Do you know when?' Anderson was doing a quick calculation of Haggerty's age.

'Nope, they would know though. Why?'

'I'll tell you when I'm sure of something. And you can tell Mathieson that you worked it all out for yourself if it becomes pertinent to the current investigation. How old is Haggerty?'

'Born 7th June 1972.'

'Forty-five. OK thanks.'

Now that wasn't a something, but it also wasn't a nothing. He had a little further down the investigative road to go. Had George Haggerty been at uni at the same time as Sally Logan? The same time as he himself had? So were thousands of other people. Especially as Sally lost that year when she hurt her knee. She was around the uni for five years not four . . . that made an overlap more likely. But how many men are on the outskirts of two rapes?

Himself? Braithwaite? Haggerty?

How much commonality was there really?

As he himself said, it's not a big ocean when the fish swim in the same small circles.

By eleven a.m., Anderson was on his third coffee and had filled three sides of an A4 pad with frenetic scribbling. Despite the serious subject matter, he was totally absorbed in his work this morning, to the extent he was even enjoying it.

Morna was conscientious and methodical, not one to leave any stone unturned. He had logged in to the system to view her access record to the files. She had been off early in the year after suffering injuries after a road traffic incident. Before that she had suffered a head injury after a bad fall. Another fall had left her unconscious for two hours. So she was a good detective with little spacial awareness, guessed Anderson. Apparently it was an ongoing joke in her station although he didn't see Patrick as a comedian. That comment was barbed. Was she a victim of abuse?

It seemed as though Morna had been looking at these cases for four or five years. Before then she seemed to have been on a career break, he checked with HR. That would have been to have her son, Finn. Then she seemed to have gone

back to work and started looking up cold case rapes, searching
the Police Scotland combined database for anything that might
match. But match what?

The top of her list of matches? The cold cases he was
working on were Sally Logan and Gillian Witherspoon, but
the occupant of her number spot was an unknown name to
him but one Patrick had mentioned.

Sharon Sixsmith.

There was no indication that she had been raped, only that
she had been found dead after falling down a crag near
Tornapress. Then he saw it: a badly injured left shoulder. So
what? He could imagine falling down between two sheer rock
faces, you were bound to hit a few bones, injure a few joints
on the way.

But it was the damage to the left glenohumeral joint Morna
had focussed in on, judging by the fact that it was the only
similarity. Then he thought, Sally had been out hillwalking
early morning on her own. This girl had been found, at the
bottom of a crag, her VW camper van . . . Anderson's heart
gave an exited little extra beat and he told himself to calm
down. Retro VW camper vans were a lifestyle choice. It told
you about the person as a consumer, not about them as a victim.
He looked back up. Sharon Sixsmith, twenty-two. The photograph showed a slim, dark-haired girl, she looked very fit, very
bright, she didn't look the sort that would get into trouble
easily. Her eyes glowed with quiet confidence, she looked very
capable. He scrolled around, found the notes on the camper. It
looked as though she had been abducted from it, but it had
taken three months to find the body. Three months? The criminal
connection was not made until afterwards. At the time, she was
just another missing hillwalker. And it would have been too
late for a rape kit.

The boys had a map of Scotland up at the far end of the
office, but Googling was easier, especially as the deposition
site had been so remote. There was no name, just a map refer-
ence and that was too sparsely populated for Google to show
him anything more than a screen of bright green. The satellite
image looked like the face of an evil giant, a black gash for
a smile, wicked in its contortions. The theory was that she

had gone for a walk and got lost, or had been abducted from her VW with no sign of a struggle, or got drunk and was driven away. And she ended up falling down a crag; the investigation at the time went nowhere. A few local troublemakers had been brought in but easily dismissed. This was in April of 1987. Sally had been raped in 1992.

The second on her list was Nicola Barnes. Another rape, although she was still alive. Her car had started to make an odd noise. She had stopped, a good Samaritan had stopped. Anderson's stomach flipped at the name.

George Haggerty.

Anderson let out a long slow breath.

He'd had a quick look at the car then said he'd call a garage. There was no mobile signal, such as the range was in those days. He had driven away and called the garage once he was in range. He had been charming with his lovely smile and big brown eyes. It was while she had been waiting that Nicola had been attacked from the back. Her left shoulder dislocated. No forensics. She had been gagged and blindfolded but had said two things of interest. Her attacker had been wearing something like a boiler suit, and there was a noise that distracted her. Like a slapping sound.

A clapping sound?

George had an alibi, drinking cappuccino in a coffee house where he had told the waitress about the girl he had left with her broken down car.

Another perfect alibi, for him.

Anderson was impressed with Morna.

The third one the electronic intelligence path took him to was much older. This case was a woman called Jennifer Argyll who had vanished into thin air in 1987 on the coast near Port MacDuff. So that was what had sparked Morna's interest, she would have grown up with the case. Anderson knew how these cases became legends in the local stations, everybody would have an opinion. That was as far as Anderson got as Jennifer's file had been transferred to cold case, which he couldn't easily access. But Anderson knew Morna could pluck those connections from thin air just as easily as Jennifer had disappeared into it.

Anderson picked up the phone to call Mitchum, he wanted a meeting to tell him he was going up north. He wanted Morna to book him a room in the Exciseman. There was the added bonus that he couldn't hear Moses crying from up there.

TEN

Erin and Rachel had left Lomondside campsite after a hearty breakfast, cooked outdoors on a single burner Calor gas stove, starting with a knob of butter melting and finishing with the full English swirling in a golden gravy of animal fat and rainwater. It tasted delicious. Then they packed up the tent and repacked their day rucksacks, leaving the bigger rucksacks to be picked up by HikeLite and taken up to the next stop at Bridge Of Orchy.

It was a three-hour walk, to be completed that morning. They hadn't made good progress, the rain and wind had been in their faces every single step of the way.

At half eleven, there was a brief cessation in the onslaught of rain, so they decided to rest before they reached Tyndrum. They were walking cold and tight-legged. The stony path underfoot was puddle after puddle, their waterproof boots had held out for the first thirty miles of the West Highland Way and had then become absorbent. Now it was a question of keeping the water swilling around their feet warm, and keeping out the ice-cold water that lay in wait in the deeper puddles. They walked in silence, the two of them in single file. Changing every so often with one in the lead being battered by the elements, the other sheltering behind. The rain seemed to be changing direction exactly as the path changed, so it was always hitting them in the face. The weather and the conditions underfoot were challenging as the guidebook said it often was when doing winter walking on the west coast. This wasn't pleasant hiking, this was a trial of endurance and character. The beautiful, stunning scenery was clouded, often they were walking through the clouds themselves. And it wasn't quiet, always the splish thud of their boots on the path, the pitter-patter of rain and the squeak of their waterproofs against each other.

They were walking up to Tyndrum to the 'By The Way'

hostel, a hot shower and a cooked meal that was devoid of rainwater. They could dry off their socks, get a rest and, hopefully, a good night's sleep that wouldn't be interrupted by the wind clawing and baying at the door of the tent and the constant irregular flap-flap of battered canvas.

They walked past the River Fillan, flowing high and angry, its grey waters tumbling and rushed. Two gold panners, covered in waders that reached to their armpits, and gloves that melted into a hat showing not one single flash of skin, stood on the calmer parts of the river, ever hopeful of finding a tiny nugget of a darkly glistening stone.

They turned away from the path to the river, heading north towards the hostel. They would be there in half an hour, maybe a little less if the path started to decline, a little more if the wind blew up again. They knew from the map that the lochan was ahead of them and they both wanted to see it. They had hoped the rain would clear, so they could get some photographs taken. They had been discussing it in the pub last night, warm and cosy, and more than a little drunk, looking at the map and trying to get a signal on their mobiles. As was usual in these parts, the barman proved better than Google and was happy to supply the two students of English Literature with the colourful history of the area, despite the fact that he was from the Ukraine. He told the story of Robert the Bruce throwing his sword into the lochan, a fine claymore it had been, about five-feet long and it 'weighed a ton'. The king was being pursued at the time by a couple of armed horseman, probably English, but the details were sketchy. After a few more drams, the defenceless king single-handedly brought down the entire English army before legging it.

They were going to ask if the sword in the lochan was protected by a lady of the lake but they thought the locals might not find that funny and kept their counsel.

Sure enough at the side of the footpath, they came across the stone, a large rectangular rock with the outline of a sword carved into it. 'They used to swing a claymore around their heads you know,' the barman had said, 'hacking bits off anything or anybody too close.'

The lochan nestled in the hills, mist drifting right and left, low on the dark, black surface of the loch. There didn't seem to be any clear border between land and water, no clear line at all, greens and reds and blues, muted black and browns all melting into each other. They stood, looking in silence, catching their breath, before both of them shrugged off their rucksacks, a signal that they were going to rest a while, at least the stone gave them something to sit on.

In silence they sat, the two of them, staring out over the water. Being mesmerized by the mist drifting from left to right, right to left, slowly revealing something on the far bank. Something with legs that floated out in the black water, something with arms up on the grassy bank, somebody with fingers grasping, as if he had reached out and nearly, very nearly, made it.

Anderson closed his eyes and cursed inwardly, his exhilaration of the early morning evaporated in an instant.

They had found Donnie McCaffrey.

There was no doubt it was him. His DNA was on file. They had swabbed the body at the site and the sample had been brought down to Glasgow and processed immediately.

As Anderson was in Mitchum's office, the boss had taken the phone call, his face had turned ashen as he had put the phone down.

Then Mitchum had warned Anderson in no uncertain terms that he was to cooperate with Mathieson and Bannon's investigation. Totally nothing was to override this, no sense of personal loyalty, nothing.

It has to be investigated and it has to look transparent. And where the hell was Costello?

Anderson said he had no idea, as politely as he could, sitting there trying to be calm but thinking where, and when, Costello's body was going to appear.

'Do you think I might do better if I went north? There's a link to my cold case rape enquiry.' He explained about Morna's invite, Patrick had given his consent. The look of relief on Mitchum's face was so joyous, it was as if Santa had existed after all. 'Go, with my blessing. It'll keep you out of Mathieson's claws.'

Anderson excused himself. He went to the toilet where he threw up all the coffee he had drunk that morning, burning acrid in his throat as he wretched again and again. His phone was beeping, as a wave of text messages came in. He leant against the wall of the toilets and took out his mobile, scrolling through, messages from Wyngate, Mulholland, Bannon, another couple of colleagues all wanting to know what was going on. Plus, DCI Mathieson requesting another meeting sooner rather than later. Anderson had been hoping that one would be from Costello saying something, anything. Any kind of explanation for the death of a young man.

Sometimes there is nothing scarier than silence.

Isla McCaffrey sat down on the settee, not speaking, unable to speak.

Mathieson gestured to Bannon that he should put the kettle on. They would have to get on with the investigation and the family liaison officer could do all the handholding she needed to do once they had left.

But PC Donald McCaffrey's wife was sniffling a lot, Mathieson thought she might get further if there were some reinforcements present. 'Do you want a friend with you? Is there somebody we can get for you?'

Isla nodded. 'Can you get Pari, she lives next door?' She shook her head, already worn out and wishing everybody would go away. Maybe she could go back to sleep and wake up again or go back out to Lidl and do her shopping, somehow she needed to rewind the day, rewind the last few days and get back to the point when his phone had beeped and he had looked at it and smiled. He had got up, and left. He had told her not to order too much from the Argos catalogue, don't spend too much on the boys.

Now he was dead.

Gone. Not coming back. Ever.

The female detective was sitting in front of her now, her small pale face all bony and full of contrition. The man had gone out to get her neighbour, her friend. Pari was one of life's calm people. She had been good when Nathan had choked, that was a midnight rush to the hospital. And when she had gone into labour with the youngest and Donnie had been at work.

A policewoman arrived, a beautiful coloured girl and she had muttered a few condolences and then gone into the kitchen to join the tall bloke who had been in the kitchen clattering cutlery. Isla could hear drawers being opened and closed now; they were looking for teaspoons and coffee.

That was one of the last things he had done before he left that night, he had loaded the dishwasher, all the dishes left from that Saturday where her mother had talked about the arrangements for Christmas dinner and he had pulled faces at her over the chicken casserole.

Now he had been killed. She couldn't believe what they were saying now, she put her hands over her ears and kept them there, watching whose stupid red lips that never seemed to stop moving.

When she stopped talking, Isla let her hands fall, she wiped the tears from her eyes, tears of anger not sadness. All of it would hit her later, she was sure of it, but now, here in her own living room, she had a fight on her hands. Somebody had taken her husband's life. And now the police, his colleagues, were ready to attack his reputation.

'I am really sorry to have to go through this with you,' said the torn-faced blonde.

Isla McCaffrey looked at her face and doubted it very much, she looked like a kid who was waiting for the gingerbread to come out the oven.

'Sorry, can you tell me again what happened, I don't think I'm getting this at all.'

'I was saying that we have found Donnie's body at a lochan up near Tyndrum,' said Mathieson. 'Do you know Tyndrum, thirty miles north of here, a few miles further on from Inveruglass?'

'Why? Why was he there?' Isla's face was blank, the news hadn't quite sunk in.

'I'm really sorry, but as yet we do not know, but we are very suspicious of foul play and we are trying to ascertain—'

'Do you think he was murdered? Donnie? My Donnie.'

'Yes, I do. PC McCaffrey had sustained fatal injuries.'

'What injuries? How did he die?' asked Isla giving herself a comforting rub on the arm.

Mathieson bit the side of her lip, ignoring the warning sign from Bannon. 'We are waiting for the post-mortem results. Do you feel you can tell us what he was doing at Inveruglass? What he was doing there that got him killed?'

Bannon had driven Mathieson from Isla's house back to their divisional headquarters at Govan. He had tried to drive legally, with Mathieson snapping at him and swearing at other drivers who had done no wrong other than being in the vehicle in front of Mathieson. They had left Isla with speed that bordered on rudeness the minute Mathieson's tablet had binged and she had glanced at the comments of the email attachment of five photographs. There was one nod to Isla, a brief 'We'll be back' and she had stood up and was out the door, leaving Bannon to apologize, and cast a look at Pari, who caught the meaning and nodded.

'Archie, you know we have found Donnie McCaffrey's body earlier today.' Mathieson sounded tired. 'We are bringing the body down here for a post-mortem, of course, but nobody is telling me bloody anything.'

'Yes, I know. I don't get it. All this is connected somehow, I can't see it. But I'm not going to stop trying. You still think that Costello has got something to do with it? And now these photographs have come to light.' Archie Walker flicked through the photographs feeling sick to his stomach, how a whole life was about to come tumbling down. 'Do you ever think that you never know anybody as well as you think you know them?'

'In my job, all the time,' said Mathieson.

Walker felt sick. He'd been sympathetic and stuck by Valerie during all the chaos that she'd brought upon herself, but there was no way he could help her get over this, indeed he wasn't sure he wanted to. She was having her private life drama. A young police officer had lost his life. No contest. 'I'm struggling to understand these.'

The photographs were so incriminating that even Mathieson was quietly empathetic. 'I'm sorry, Archie, but these put a totally different spin on the situation.' She took the photographs from the procurator fiscal's shaking hand and flicked through them looking for one in particular. The one that showed George Haggerty and Valerie Abernethy in a tight embrace. He had his hands cupping her jaw. It was obvious to anybody that this was not a brother-in-law/sister-in-law saying goodbye. 'Has she ever hinted that she was having an affair with George?'

Archie snorted. 'With George? She always said she couldn't stand the man but I can see it leads you to the conclusion that this was an old-fashioned love triangle, maybe sparked by . . .? Oh, I don't know – how do you justify something like that? Or was she playing at hating him. For Abigail's sake, for my sake?'

'A psychologist would say that Valerie was robbed of one kind of family so she was ready to take on another, one that happened to be her sister's. If you look at what she'd been through, what she was about to go through, the humiliation of the court case. She'd know a decent defence counsel was going to rip her apart. "Miss Abernethy, did you seriously think that you could buy a baby and get away with it?" How emotionally crippled was she going to sound when she answered that? "You were turned down for adoption, Miss Abernethy, would you like to tell the court why, because you were too drunk." Considered too drunk to be a mother . . . and there's Abigail, all sweetness, light and loveliness.'

'So why would she kill the boy?'

'Maybe she didn't mean to, maybe he came in and saw her, maybe that's what sparked the intense rage. Malcolm standing up for his mother. Nobody had ever stood up for her, had they? In her eyes, I mean, addicts always think that everybody is against them.'

Archie shook his head again. 'I really don't believe this.'

'Which is why we are telling you before we put out a warrant for her arrest. That arrest may take place at your house. You need to be prepared for that.'

Archie was speechless for a moment, then said, 'But playing devil's advocate, it does explain what happened to that Star Wars Lego thing she was going on about. That some kind of emotional hook or trophy or whatever you want to call it.'

'We are, of course, going to question George again as he

has lied to us about their relationship, but he has an alibi. It's likely he was trying to protect her – and himself. But we both know that knife was not in his hand.' Bannon had the pictures now, three of them were taken of the couple walking up Great Western Road past the petrol station. He was studying them carefully.

'Can I ask how you got hold of these? The obvious question to me is who took them and why?' said Walker.

It was Mathieson who answered. 'They were sent to me directly from a private detective. He hinted that Abigail had employed him as she didn't trust Valerie and has been waiting for Abigail's lawyer to say it was OK to send these images to me. Believe that if you want. He refused to give his name and we will send the photographs away for forensic examination to make sure they have not been doctored, although they look genuine to me.'

'Is that it?'

'We'll trace who sent them, don't worry.'

They both looked at Bannon, who had coughed meaningfully after swiping through his phone. 'The headlines on that day were . . . yip . . . So this petrol station looks like the one on Great Western Road. You can see the newspapers on the display rack outside. The firestorms in California were front page news, and that corresponds with the date. I think, you could get that enhanced and that would confirm what day it was. The *Evening Times* is there and it's dark so this must be late and I suspect this guy has sent you these photographs and this one in particular because it shows George and Valerie together on the evening Abigail and Malcolm were killed.'

'Which is useful,' understated Mathieson, after a minute of shocked silence.

'Which is very convenient. I'd get them checked out,' said Walker, not able to keep his eyes off them. 'Far too convenient. You have the murder of a young police officer to solve; I suggest you get on with that.'

'And it hasn't gone past me that she's wearing heels in this picture. She's five seven, plus those heels five feet eleven. I don't need to tell you the significance of that,' said Mathieson. 'The height of the spatter shadow at the crime scene. The person who had that knife was five feet ten or eleven, or smaller with heels. I know it's all circumstantial but it's all starting to point the same way.'

Bannon nodded. 'Whatever way it blows, be prepared for the shitstorm.'

Valerie walked out of Judy Plum heading down Mitchell Street. She felt better than she had felt for ages. Liberated, that was the word. She had a plan, something to do with her life. She had bought a blond shoulder-length wig.

Susan, as the woman in the shop had introduced herself, had been empathetic but very matter of fact. It was easy for Val to say what she was looking for. A short blond wig, slightly longer at the back, with a fringe, a longish fringe if possible. She looked around, picking out two she thought would do. Susan held her fixed smile and looked at Valerie's naturally dark hair, such a dark brown it was almost black.

'It might not suit your colouring,' Susan counselled.

'I want something totally different. A totally different look,' said Valerie looking in the mirror and feeling rather joyous.

She walked down the road, thinking about buying a warm jacket and some outdoor boots. She was more than a little fed up with Valerie Abernethy. She didn't know DI Winifred Prudence Costello but she intended to get right under her skin. She knew a bit from what she'd read in the paper. And had guessed that Uncle Archie had a thing going with her and Archie might be old but he was nobody's fool. He didn't like stupid women, so DI Costello was not stupid.

And Costello was going nowhere, she had much more use as a smokescreen, a confusion, an obfuscation. One of Archie's favourite words. That seemed fitting.

She had left the hospital and made a few phone calls, mostly to the Freigate Clinic, a small private hospital that was best known for treating rich people with substance abuse issues, and as such they had three very good psychologists on the staff and two psychiatrists, none of whom had ever set eyes on Winifred Costello.

Valerie had hired a car to take Costello, under an assumed name, from the Queen Elizabeth to the private facility where she would have her own room. And the pay as you go phone that Valerie had just bought for her would be waiting there for her.

She had been lucky that Hannah had been convinced by her story, by her fiscal's ID with her finger covering the name but not the picture. She had told enough lies over the truth to be convincing, and there was the obvious evidence of Costello who had been subject to an attack, and Hannah had to help in their efforts to protect her. Hannah had nodded, but not before asking a few questions about Costello's medical care that proved she was not as gullible as she might appear.

Valerie caught a taxi, directing the driver to Archie's house, checking her phone in the back seat. She saw the breaking newsfeed flash across the screen, the body of the missing police officer had been found. It pulled her up short. She must have squealed as the driver asked her if she was OK. She nodded and examined her phone. Two missed calls from Archie, one from DCI Mathieson. Her mind started to race. She sensed, knew, that she was about to be hauled in to help with enquiries and she knew where that would lead. She adjusted her position in the seat, her mind racing. As she leaned forward she caught sight of the *Daily Record*, lying on the passenger seat. The heads on the picture were tucked under but she knew by the position, Pippa's coat sitting in the window of the French Café. Her and George. He had set her up for the media. Bastard.

As they turned the corner she saw a police car pull into the same street two cars ahead of them. She asked the driver to pull in feigning that she had just remembered she needed to see a neighbour. Did she need anything? She put her hand in her bag; the gun was there, that was all she needed. She paid the driver and walked the rest of the way, staying on the opposite side of the road until she could see, out the corner of her eye, the two cop cars at Archie's house. Without missing a step, she turned right and walked down the side street back into the city. The steps she was taking felt familiar, the gardens she passed, the streets signs, as if she had walked this way before.

*   *   *

Archie was keeping away from his own house. There was a warrant out for Valerie's arrest, there wasn't much more he could do before he could be justifiably accused of perverting the course of justice. Mathieson had decided that Valerie should be brought in and left to stew, and had acquiesced that Walker would supply her with a very good defence brief, Archie had already called Kerr, he was on standby. Walker and Mathieson were both now on very different sides of the fence, but both being experienced they were politely going by the book. Transparency above all else.

Costello? Now Valerie?

Was his life going to get any worse?

So he was now standing watching Mathieson and Bannon search Costello's living room. They had done everything but ask him the question they really wanted to know the answer to, some vestige of professional respect had kicked in. But Walker had no doubt of the arsenal of ammunition Mathieson could bring to bear down on him.

He couldn't appear as concerned about Costello as he really felt; she was a colleague, but over the years she had become so much more. He thought a lot of her, he had total respect for her, but he wasn't in love with her. She was far too annoying for that. It was just . . . he was desperately worried about her.

In response to their indirect question, he had told them he had been in the house a few times, and as far as he knew nothing had been moved or changed. Nothing looked out of place.

'So you don't know where Valerie is and you have no idea where Costello is?' asked Mathieson, her purple Nitrile gloves clashing with the bright red lipstick.

'Or the Holy Grail, or Glenn Miller.'

It was Mathieson that got to him. She was a shady little creature who pouted as she spoke. Was she really so hard and brutal as she looked? Or was it the insecurity of her position, the fact that Bannon would always get a better response from a witness than she ever would. But then maybe that made them an effective team, like Anderson and Costello, the ying and yang.

Her thin blonde hair was sculpted in a wave that kicked out

to rest on her shoulders, a fringe that sat two inches too high was fixed on her forehead with hairspray, the overall effect was that of a blonde helmet on a Stepford wife. She kept talking to Bannon out the corner of her mouth, quietly as if he, as the chief fiscal, was not worthy to hear it, his opinion not worthy to be sought. Bannon, give him his due, was younger and believed more in engagement to get results. Whatever Costello had got herself involved in, it was directly related to what she had seen that October morning six weeks before.

Walker couldn't shake the news about Donnie from his head. 'You don't really suspect her of killing another police officer?' His tone of voice was testimony to just how stupid he thought that idea was.

'At this point I don't really know what to think. I can see her getting angry and lashing out at him, nothing pre-planned, but provoked. Don't you? I've read a fair bit about her. Listened when you and the others are talking about her, I think she'd lash out when she thought she was on the moral high ground.'

Archie could only give a little nod while admitting to himself that Mathieson wasn't too far off the mark.

'And there was the incident when she broke Viktor Mulholland's nose. One single punch. Hardly the act of a professional police officer.' She sighed, looking round the living room, her gloved hand sitting on her hip, a stance that reminded Walker of Costello herself. 'But you know her better. Tell me what you think happened.'

'All this is complicated enough without people starting on hypotheticals.'

'Where would she go, though? Any relatives? She must have somebody.'

'None that I know of, but you might be better asking Colin Anderson.'

Bannon had his hand down the back of the sofa, pulling out a few coins, a remote control, and a crumpled paperback. He looked up and raised an eyebrow, having heard the gossip and possessing enough sensitivity not to point out that it was him here, not Colin Anderson. And his presence spoke volumes.

'What about intimacy?' asked Mathieson.

'Excuse me?'

'Had she mentioned McCaffrey to you or any of the gang of four, in an intimate way?'

'The gang of four?'

'We will be talking to Costello's colleagues, Anderson, Wyngate and Mulholland so we will know if she has mentioned something that maybe you have forgotten.' It was Mathieson's turn to raise an eyebrow, questioning.

Walker answered carefully, 'Not that she told me, but she did know McCaffrey, as a police officer.'

'Off the record, do you have any ideas where she is?'

'And if it's off the record, you shouldn't be asking. But I will answer *on the record*. I do not know where she is.'

'But you know her and we know how well you know her. She has a good police record, mostly,' she added, 'she herself, but when you look back at her family, it's all there. All there for us all to see. So you are here to make sure that we do our job properly, but that is all. Do I think she'd kill a colleague? No. But when I read about her family, about her brother? Then I can think that she has a cop's sense of moral outrage at what happened to Abigail and Malcolm that fits in with her personality. I can see that she might have pulled a young cop like Donnie into her way of thinking . . . and maybe when he realized how far she was prepared to go and he said that he wasn't . . . Then I can picture a scenario that fits what we have here. There could have been a fight, he might have come off worse.'

'I can think as far as that. But she would not be running away. She'd be standing here shouting. And her blood was there.'

'A trickle of her blood, and she is nowhere to be seen, and she has been texting you so she's about somewhere,' said Mathieson.

'But she has gone on the run. She certainly hasn't been back here. That's what I'm thinking. And Donnie McCaffrey is very dead,' added Bannon.

Archie nodded, giving the idea some thought. It wasn't that far away from what he was thinking himself. It was a logical chain of thought that could explain everything and nothing. It would fit the way she had handed in her notice, and left

Mitchum in no doubt about what she had thought of the lack of investigative progress into the deaths of Abigail Haggerty and her son Malcolm. But if she had injured Donnie, she would have taken him to the hospital, not up to Tyndrum to die.

He watched them in silence. Costello's living room was still dark, they hadn't opened the big white curtains that covered the picture window and hid the beautiful view of the Clyde. He lifted his mobile from his pocket, checking it for a message from her, nothing.

He read a few emails from work, looking busy. He didn't want to appear that he was watching them but he couldn't help himself, thinking like a prosecutor. He followed them, seeing what they were seeing and trying to interpret the facts in a different way.

Her car was missing. Her laptop was nowhere to be seen. There was an abandoned cup of tea. Had she left in a hurry?

They went through everything and every room. He followed them out to the linen cupboards, Bannon opened the door allowing Mathieson to look in, have a good search round. Archie could see the white laundry basket on the floor, Mathieson in her haste had missed it and she nodded to Bannon to close the door which he was about to do when Bannon said, 'What's that?' and picked up the bag that was lying in the laundry basket.

'Interesting,' he said as he looked in, avoiding Archie's eyes. 'Bloodstains. On a bath towel. Get all that bagged.'

Mathieson picked it up, suspending it between a gloved finger and thumb, explained it to him as if he was a child. 'Covered in McCaffrey's blood.'

'Somebody's blood. She was bleeding too, remember?'

'There's a pair of trousers and . . . oh no.' She pulled out a jacket and showed them the large slash at the back. 'That looks superficial, that didn't go through. She was well enough to come back here. He lost his blood, and his life at the scene.'

'Well, get it tested and we will find out,' Archie said. 'I can put a rush on it through Matilda McQueen.'

'No, I don't think so. I think, as we basically have the budget from Complaints, then we will get a private lab to run the tests. Not that I suspect McQueen would be underhand in any way but we are going to aim for transparency here. It's time for the truth, whatever that is.'

'Of course. The fiscal's office will support you in any way we can,' Archie said. 'And in my role of chief fiscal, my office is formally requesting a copy of that email, with the photographs attached, of course.'

Mathieson stood up, looking straight at him, trying to figure out what he was thinking. 'Of course, transparency in all things, Mr Walker.'

'Thank you.' This time he gave way to the relief he felt.

Whatever mess Costello was in, she was going to have to get out of it herself.

Walker was wound as tight as a rattlesnake. Brenda had given him a cup of coffee and he was making half-hearted attempts to amuse baby Moses, who was gurgling when he was the centre of attention and scowling when he was not.

Anderson took a long time looking through printouts of the photographs; he placed them on the coffee table in something that approached chronological order. 'You know, Archie, if I was the defence council, I would be asking myself exactly what these photographs show.'

'They show my god-daughter is a lying little piece of shit.'

'Do they? Look at the clothes, three different occasions from the look of them. Valerie is not dressed up, she has no make-up on.'

'She has heels on?'

'She has the shoes on that she was wearing when she was taken to the hospital, that night. She was Valerie Abernethy, the suited, Porsche driving fiscal, on her way to the Blue Neptune; she'd have been in high-heel mode.'

'A woman can borrow clothes, but nobody can wear someone else's shoes,' added Brenda, thinking she had to give some female input.

'And look, she's never kissing him, he is kissing her. Look at this one.' He held one out for Walker to have a better look at. 'In that one, she has her hands up; her palms are on his chest like she is ready to push him away. And it's all a little convenient, isn't it, that these suddenly appear on Mathieson's desk from an anonymous source? So maybe not a little lying piece of shit, maybe she's being manipulated by somebody who is very good at it.'

'Haggerty?'

'I think so, you know what effect those pictures will have on a jury. And Mathieson has moved on them. These pics will get Valerie arrested.'

'I have Kerr booked for her defence, I think she might need somebody good. I will make sure he interviews whoever took the photographs. It's a bit too convenient that it shows Valerie left the hospital and walked in the direction of Balcarres Avenue on the night of the murders. And she has no memory of it.'

'I think Mathieson is too quick. You need to get her to look at that CCTV again, further afield. Find out where Valerie and George went. Don't accept all this at face value.'

Archie Walker looked defeated, he looked crumpled; a sad sight in a man who took great pride in his appearance.

'I've always said the crime was far too controlled for an addict like Valerie.'

'So get hold of Valerie, get her together with the best legal representation and get Mathieson on the back foot. There's holes in her case a bus could get through. You are a lawyer after all. Play the game the way Mathieson plays it.'

'Just one problem.'

'What?'

'I have no idea where Valerie is. Her stuff is in the room at my house, but her handbag has gone.'

'God, it's like that Agatha Christie book when they all disappear one by one.'

Mathieson was cold and wet by the time she got hold of Colin Anderson in the interview room at West End Central at half six at night.

'Right,' she said banging a cup of coffee on the table in front of him. 'Just so you know, we have found bloodstained clothing at Costello's residence.'

'With a slash in it,' added Bannon.

Anderson kept his face straight. 'So a serving police officer who has worked in major cases leaves that kind of forensic evidence lying around her flat? Where did you find it?'

'In her washing basket,' answered Bannon, helpfully before Mathieson could stop him.

'Her washing basket.' Anderson threw his hands up in the air. 'Well, you probably got her right there. I'd say that was the act of a guilty person, putting dirty washing in the washing basket. Jesus, if she had anything to do with this you'd find no evidence at all. She'd have walked down to the river and chucked it in there. It would be floating past Ireland now.'

'People do things by force of habit. Even cops who should know better.'

'I'll give you that,' agreed Anderson sweetly.

His acquiescence unnerved Mathieson slightly, for one single beat she was put off her stride.

'They knew each other; McCaffrey and Costello, so what happened to him? His wife says that Costello texted him, he went out to Inveruglass to meet her. And there was an incident that involved blood, cocaine and alcohol.'

'Crap,' said Anderson.

Mathieson wrote that down.

'Costello wouldn't touch alcohol if you paid her.'

'So he did the drinking and she drove her car, we haven't found it yet.'

'No. Let me put that another way. All evidence is open to interpretation, so I think you are mistaken in your interpretation of the evidence that has been put before you. Do you want to write that down?'

'I know that, Colin.' Bannon was back to first-name terms. His voice was soft and sympathetic which unnerved Anderson more than if he had been scathing and threatening. 'But you can see the uncomfortable position we are in. We have no sign anybody else was there.'

'You didn't know Kieran was there, did you? You don't know who put the tobacco tin in the wing of the camper. No, you don't. Stop bowing to pressure and do your fucking jobs properly. I'd never jump to the conclusions that you have. Unless she was standing there with a smoking gun, covered in an obscene amount of gunshot residue, while standing next to a bleeding McCaffrey who was screaming, "Oh Costello, please don't shoot me again".'

'She was there when the bodies were found at the house, the Haggerty house,' said Mathieson briskly.

'So was Archie Walker. They found the bodies together, full stop.'

'How did she know to go there? There was no inclination, no pointers, she just decided to go round there and hey ho, a twelve-year-old boy and his mother had been stabbed to death.'

'You saying that doesn't change the facts of the case. She went round there in the company of Archie to inform the deceased about the state of her sister, a fiscal called Valerie Abernethy who is—'

'Mr Walker's god-daughter, yes we know. Who is having an affair with George Haggerty? And who we are now looking for in connection with that crime.'

'Again, that's your interpretation.'

'Why did Costello go with him? With Archie to that house? Why?'

'He's a friend, and it was a police matter. Costello had derived the plan to catch the person who had killed Mary Jane Duguid, remember.'

'Your daughter?'

'So it subsequently turned out. And Valerie was nearly killed by Braithwaite. Why shouldn't Costello go?'

'But why with Archie, then, if it was not a family affair.'

'She went because it was a family affair and she's not family. She's a serving police officer.'

'Was, Colin, she *was* a serving police officer.'

'She was at the time and was keeping it all above board.'

'Does she do what Archie suggests? Does she go out with him? Are they having an affair?'

'Well, he took me out for a pint last week, are we having an affair too?' he snapped back.

Bannon was doing his softly, softly thing again.

'I've seen the pictures of that scene, they were pretty horrific. Do you think that could have pushed her over the edge and she might now be planning to take some investigation into her own hands?'

'By killing a fellow police officer? No, I don't think so.' But that was exactly what he thought, Costello and McCaffrey, a two-man tag team. Just like Anderson and Costello had been but Anderson could always rein in Costello, he doubted McCaffrey would attempt to do that.

'What do you think then, Colin? We need some help here.'

It was a textbook ploy to get him to talk but he could see how it might be for them and, he acknowledged to himself, there was the possibility that with pressure from above they might be forced to close the case on the most obvious evidence available in the absence of Costello to give her version of events.

'Well, if you don't hear it from me you would hear it from others. It's a popular theory but I don't think so. She'd be here kicking and punching. I think it broke her and she has gone off to lick her wounds. I think she felt very responsible for the death of Malcolm, the boy had called her on his phone. She had alerted Children's Services. A woman called Dali Despande had placed it on a priority list of some sort but there was no real evidence that the child was in danger. Until somebody stabbed him twelve times, of course.'

'But that person was not a member of the family, so why bring Family Services into it? Surely the tragic outcome of that situation shows that Costello got it wrong, it wasn't his dad that the boy was afraid of. Maybe it was Valerie.'

Of course it was his dad, thought Anderson, of course it was. Whatever else had gone on in there, Malcolm Haggerty had been scared of his own dad. Colin recalled the conversation at Mary Jane's funeral. 'She was very suspicious of George, and wherever she is, I think she still will be.'

'And this?' Mathieson pointed to a picture of the young police officer, a death forgotten in the internecine arguments about a woman who wasn't there.

'I don't know about that. Or him. I haven't heard. I've worked with Costello for years and all I get is titbits of a lot of blood, a bit of cocaine, a lot of alcohol. If you want to give me all the relevant details, I will certainly give you my opinion. If you value it, knowing her as I do.'

'We feel you might be guilty by association, if you assisted her in some way.'

Anderson nearly laughed. 'You have got to be kidding, look at my service record, look at hers . . .'

'Yes, we know,' said Bannon. 'We know that, you and I both know that, but if this goes to court they will argue that if anybody helped Costello, it would have been you.'

'You do know about Costello's family past?' If Mathieson was supposed to edge that question in carefully, she hadn't made a good job of it.

'Yes I do. I know her brother nearly killed her, which is how she got that scar on her forehead. And obviously I know about her brother and father. It's all over the bloody papers.'

'It's in the public domain.'

'The timing is rank.'

'That doesn't change the facts. You do see our problem,'

'If you think she did that—' he tapped his finger on the photograph – 'then I think you are barking well up the wrong tree, she might lash out in anger but not that.'

'So where is she?'

'I have no idea, has there been any movement on her credit cards? Her bank cards? Trace her phone, you're the police you can do what you want.'

'She's taken money out from her account. The transactions started again this morning. And she brought a pay-as-you-go mobile using her credit card. She knows we've been tracing her calls. We will trace the CCTV cameras and then we will bring her in. And we have a White Fiat on CCTV on the A9. Just waiting confirmation.'

Anderson knew that wasn't true, Mathieson was playing him. They'd have confirmation on the car owner immediately, but it made him sit up. 'Really? She's up and moving? She bought another mobile?'

'And headed north. Do you know of any friends or relatives up there?'

Anderson smiled. 'If she turns west off the A9, and joins the North Coast 500 route then you have a connection. She has no relatives up north, she has no relatives at all. But George Haggerty is from that part of the world.'

Mathieson nodded. 'We had worked that out. And you can see how it looks. I'm sorry but Costello is a suspect in this, so as with any suspect, her life, her friends her career, all of it, is under scrutiny. Until we know what happened to McCaffrey, Costello remains a person of interest.'

'And the boy, the one in Raigmore? Cowan?' Anderson directed the question to Bannon who flicked open his folder and ran a finger down an index, then flicked over a few pages. He could hear Mathieson's fingernails tapping in impatience and got the feeling Bannon was winding her up. He would have the information Anderson wanted at the forefront of his mind.

'So preliminary report from the scene of crime, and the tracker dog. Basically, the tyre treads of the camper are at the viewing point car park and he left there at speed.'

'Suggesting that he had done or seen something that he wanted away from?'

'Maybe he drove north for a couple of miles and ended up in a lay-by.' He looked up. 'I think you know about the waxed ball bearings?'

'Two miles, was that enough to melt the wax if they had been put in at Inveruglass, at the viewing site? Or would it have to be warmed by miles of driving?'

'The engine would be hot anyway, he'd driven up from Glasgow remember. And what an easy vehicle to follow. There was no phone or camera in the car, the camera was at the bottom of the loch and the keys were found in a field thirty feet from the lay-by.'

'So he was chased?'

'He stops the van because of the clatter, his assailant comes up behind him, probably friendly as Kieran takes the keys out the engine. There is an incident that involves Kieran being on the ground, then the dogs pick up a scent running towards the trees, over the wire fence, thick trees, running deeper into the forest, he was veering as he ran . . .' He cocked his head. 'That time of night it was dark, keeping in the cover of the tree trunks. Then the dogs found the main site about a hundred yards in. Blood. Disturbance, and then he was dragged out.'

'Why?'

'No idea why. There are signs of blood loss and two things of interest. He seems to have lost his waistcoat, loose, lots of pockets, like a photographer's but the best thing is the few fibres found on a branch, that looks hopeful of something. As if somebody put their hand on a branch and they've left a trace. The lab at Inverness has been sent the sample, so they can be processed alongside the sample from Kieran.'

'So Costello did that, then pulled the body back to a small Fiat and drove 300 miles north to drop it on a remote mountain pass?'

'Something happened. She has not come forward, but she's up and about. You have been on this side of the desk long enough to know what it is like and that there are, very rarely, any surprises,' said Mathieson.

'And if she has gone rogue—' Bannon took a look at the picture of the young cop – 'I can understand her logic. She has a very developed sense of morality and justice which sometimes the police service cannot deliver. And I think she's keeping you and Archie out the loop because she doesn't want to make trouble for you. She is a very loyal friend, she doesn't want to involve you in her . . . well, whatever it is she has planned.' Bannon shrugged. 'That's my thoughts.'

'But she wouldn't do this.' Anderson pointed to the picture of Donnie. 'This guy was one of us.'

The other two sat and did nothing, forcing him to speak. He studied the photograph of the dead young police officer. 'Who has done the forensics on this?'

'Your usual team.'

Anderson nodded slowly. 'OK so O'Hare, McQueen?'

'Yes. Costello's DNA is all over his dead body,' said Bannon.

Mathieson argued, 'I'm a simpler soul. I'm going for the obvious. She killed him. Maybe not intentionally, maybe it was something that got out of hand but . . . Well, you can't argue with the science. Their bloods are mingled. Bloods. Both of them were bleeding. We have one body and the other one is missing. They met in that car park after Costello had summoned him, and something kicked off. There was a fight.'

'Could they have been attacked and she got away?' Anderson asked.

'Away to where? And from what? If that was the case then

why wouldn't she run here so we can help her? Why keep below the radar?'

'Well, you can't have it both ways. If she was keeping below the radar there's no way she'd use her bank card. She's too clever for that, she knows the way we work.' He thought for a moment. 'Was it an auto bank?'

Bannon looked down. 'Yes and a visa card.'

'So you don't know for sure that somebody else isn't using it instead of her? You need to look at the cameras.' He got up to leave.

'It was a female fitting Costello's description that bought the phone. The film does look like her, short blonde hair, anorak.' Mathieson stood up, small and insignificant between the other two detectives. 'And if you hear from her in any way, shape or form, you will tell us.'

He paused. 'I will tell her to get in touch with you, of course.'

'Not quite the same thing, DCI Anderson.'

'It's the best I can do.'

And he left.

ELEVEN

Thursday, 30th of November

Isla had been told to go to bed. Her mum and dad were staying over, and the kids were in the spare bedroom with them. The GP had come out and given her a sleeping tablet, well, five, to get through the next few days.

So she lay alone in the bed she had shared with her husband, as the world went on as normal outside. They had been married seven years, he was her husband, her best friend, dad to her children.

She wondered where Costello was right now. No one seemed to know.

She couldn't get her head round that.

She stared at the ceiling, lying with the light on, her mind not really keeping up with the issues that everybody had brought up, how are you going to cope? She had no option but to cope. Her children would grow up, they would remember their dad. She'd make sure they knew him and the man he was.

And why he had died.

She stared at the ceiling again. There was a spider's web up there, dancing.

She lay in the darkness and then cried her eyes out.

All that did was give her a headache and make her eyes sore. She had no emotion left, except anger. She could hear her mum and dad next door, talking quietly. They still had each other, in their sixties they could still lie in bed entwined in each other's arms.

The pain of that stopped her breathing.

She felt she had nothing to say. She wanted to look after the kids but couldn't look at them with their huge trusting brown eyes, ready to ask where Daddy was. When was Daddy coming home? The questions were bound to start coming and she didn't have the heart to answer them. She didn't have the heart, full stop.

It had been ripped out of her.

Her mum and dad were now settled in the youngest's room and the kids were all piled in together.

Why not use the fourth bedroom? Her mum had asked, and got a dig in the ribs from her father. It was Donnie's room, just for Donnie.

She got up, pulled on her dressing gown, a big fluffy white one that Donnie had bought her when Nathan had been born. He had wrapped it all up in paper, when she opened it in the hospital he'd had to take it back home as it was too bulky to go in any of the cupboards. And she was scared it might get lifted.

She brought it up to her face, smelling the scent of Donnie's aftershave, the times she had lain on the sofa, on a Saturday night; her lying in his arms sipping a Prosecco, him sipping a beer and watching the football while she flicked through a magazine.

Little things, he was never one for the big gestures, but he was always there, always thoughtful.

She went to the next room, the small room that sat next to the box room. She undid the little hook at the top, a simple plain hook sitting in a brass ring. She twisted it round, lifting it off, the door swung open and she closed it behind her very quietly. She turned on the light switch, the tiny room lit up like Wembley Stadium. Books, a laptop, a sound system and one lazy boy easy chair, with a blanket and a pillow on it.

Donnie's den.

He would come in here when he was on night shift and he needed a kip during the day. He'd lie there with his headphones and watch a film on the laptop or listen to his music, a whole wall of his favourite CDs, keeping them away from small sticky hands. And then his vinyl collection, his greatest love: Hotel California, Dark Side of the Moon, Going For The One and every one of David Bowie's thirty-five albums. His adoration of the sidemen, the unsung heroes.

She sat on the arm of the recliner, and reached over to put on the sidelight, then got up to put the overhead light off. The room changed character totally, calming now, relaxing. Lying down on the chair, she pressed the button to drop the back, the footrest coming up under her legs and she pulled the blanket round her.

This was his favourite place, her eyes scanned round at the picture of her and the boys pinned to the corkboard, a list of stuff she wanted him to pick up at Argos for Christmas, before they sold out or it got too busy.

Christmas. How the hell was she supposed to cope with Christmas?

Without Donnie? Two words she could never imagine saying together.

She closed her eyes, she had to be strong. Or she'd fall apart, she didn't really have to do anything, her husband had been killed. She could see herself in the car, him driving the kids squealing in the back, him winding them up and her trying to get them to calm down. They had driven up to Inveruglass many times. The last time the boys had climbed to the viewing point with the Gaelic name.

How do you say that, Daddy?

No bloody idea.

The youngest had climbed up on Donnie's shoulders for a lift, she had taken the eldest by the hand, then had walked up to the top step of the viewing platform where they had a clear view right down the loch. They had sat together. Their hands intertwining automatically, she had had her gloves on, it had been cold. The boys had climbed up and down the steps, the big boy helping the wee boy, punting him up, helping him down. Near the bottom, Donnie had set off to retrieve them.

Donnie had loved the place. Why would he go there, why did he take Costello?

He had liked her, she was still missing. There was still a chance that she would be found alive. At that moment Isla hated her, she was single with no kids: she could die and nobody would notice.

Was she on the run after killing Donnie? She doubted it.

So he had gone there, met her and been murdered. His body taken up the road to Tyndrum, thirty miles north, dumped in a lochan. Thrown away like trash.

By whom? And why?

He wasn't doing anything official, it was something he'd had an idea about. He would have written something down or noted something on his computer. He had a brown notepad somewhere, he was always scribbling here and there.

There would be something in this room.

She was wide awake now.

She looked over at his desk, she could start up his computer, and find nothing. She would do that later. Closing her eyes, she thought of him sitting in his boxers, on the recliner, his mobile in his hand. They had been phoning each other, Donnie and Costello. How often, she had no idea. He had taken the phone out the room, when she had been present, nothing unusual in that, she had no interest in his work, apart from how it affected him.

So he would be in here, on his phone, making notes, even something he typed up on his computer, he would do that while he was on the phone. She glanced over at the bin, it was empty, of course. She had emptied it when things were normal and Donnie was going to walk back in the door.

She closed her eyes and asked Donnie for help. If he was out there in the ether, she needed his help right now. His name was being dragged through the shite and she wasn't going to let that happen. She thought about the last time she saw him, she was going through the Argos catalogue making a list. Why was she thinking of that? She had a nice notebook with flowers on it, that was her Christmas notebook. Donnie had a simple reporter's notebook with a spiral of wire across the top, usually with a blue biro rammed through it.

He had been using it to get the measurements for the new tiles for the bathroom floor, well, that wasn't going to happen now. But he did use that notebook a lot, she had seen him here, on this recliner, phone jammed in between his ear and shoulder, notebook on his thigh, his foot up on the chair, scribbling. She had been telling him that his dinner was ready, he had nodded. It was cold by the time he had come through. When had that been? Last week? The week before?

She didn't know why but she knew now that he had been talking to Costello.

She scanned the small bookcase in the room, and there it was, lying on top of The Godfather DVD collection she had bought him for Christmas last year. She reached over and picked it up. He had written his name on the front page, like a school kid, he had even underlined it and added a doodle of a motorbike.

She flicked it open feeling like a spy, intruding on his life. There was nothing in it. Of course he had torn out the pages with the notes for the bathroom tiles and stuck them on the tiler's business card. There were little fragments of paper at the top, where he had pulled pages out, recently from the fact that the tiny pieces were still trapped in the spiral. Even as she had moved it from the bookcase back to the seat, some had fallen on the carpet, she picked them up carefully and laid them out on top of his keyboard, wary to lose anything that might have been part of him.

Then she looked back at the pad, flicked the top page over, letting it fall in behind the rest. He had been using it, she could see the indents of his writing, the circular doodles that he did when he was bored, or thinking, circles that would pair up and morph into motorbikes.

They had been watching that forensics programme together where the farmer had placed a bomb under his own car, then slashed himself and then shot his neighbour dead making out his neighbour had been targeting him. Donnie had pondered why the farmer didn't move house. But Isla could remember the CSI had held the notepad to an oblique light source and read the indents of the threatening letter that the neighbour was supposed to have written. She went over to the desk and switched on Donnie's desk lamp. She could make out a few letters, see the individual pen grooves of the doodles.

She turned the light out and went back, so the only source of light in the room was the small Ikea desk lamp. She moved the pad back and forth, seeing numbers and cms, that was him making the measurements for the tiles, but there was something else.

A name. It looked as though Donnie had written it and then gone over it again and again, doodling over the letters as he was on the phone. She could make it out, more than a few letters. She fired up the computer, feeling better now that she was doing something, she Googled the name, variations of the same, the search engine brought back a few possibles. Nothing that matched exactly what she had thought she had read. But one entry caught her eye, not the bar at the top but in the two lines of small print underneath.

And then, at the bottom a name she was more familiar with, that was scribbled all over this page. It was just Donnie, being Donnie.

Oscar Duguid, believed drowned, search called off. Leaving a wife Abigail and a daughter Mary Jane. Isla, read that again; Abigail and Mary Jane, Kelvindale Bridge, NC 500, phone land registry, harbour master and Jennifer. Jennifer was common enough but not Abigail or Mary Jane. Neither were particularly common names. Donnie had been ranting about that, the name of the girl Braithwaite had killed though Donnie thought they would have a tough time proving it. Braithwaite, who was arguing it was all his wife's fault, the wife who had conveniently fallen from the top of a high building. Not enough to be not guilty but enough for there to be reasonable doubt in the mind of the jury, he would be a good witness, he might get off.

She couldn't sit here and do nothing.

Anderson sat at his kitchen table, the house was quiet for once, just a steady beat of music from upstairs somewhere and the rasp of Nesbit's snoring. The blank page of his iPad was staring at him. His head was hurting just thinking about what Costello had got herself caught up in. He was concerned about her safety, more concerned than he dared to voice, even to himself. He had seen the worried look on Walker's face, even the fiscal had stopped fooling himself that the texts had been coming from her. They could have been sent by anyone who had got her phone off her. And nobody knew who that was.

But now she had come out of hiding and was back on the road, having purchased a new phone.

He wished he could feel a sense of relief in that, but, and there was a but, it wasn't her.

He called up the map of Loch Lomond, tracing the route

to Tyndrum which followed the West Highland Way. Just as the Bealach followed the 500? Anybody who wanted to be there, had a reason to be there, hiding amongst the tourist traffic.

He thought about the others, the pile of paperwork on the rapes. Mitchum had given him a week. He was so fucked up over this he hadn't given a thought to Sally and to Gillian. Was there a connection as Morna thought?

He tried to put that to the back of his mind, making himself think about the An Ceann Mor viewing point. Somebody had chased the student down. Told him his car was leaking fluid? Maybe Cowan had already stopped due to the noise made by the tin of ball bearings. There must have been some kind of chase, the boy trying to get away and he was pursued through the trees. His attacker caught up with him, battered him in the face then slit his throat. Then what? Why take him so many miles away? A journey that would take over three, maybe four hours and then dump him on a remote mountain pass?

Was it because he was going there anyway? Not out of convenience, but for ease of explanation if their vehicle was spotted en route. Years ago the body should have lain at the pass until the road reopened in the spring but now there was no presumption of isolation. Why roll the body out the car and into a gully? Were they too weak to take it any further? Yet they took the body from the woods to the lay-by two hundred miles north? Tired? Injured? A different person? Or a lack of time? A woman?

Anderson pushed that thought away and looked again at the screen. Or was he pushed for time? Would his tardiness be noticed, and remembered by a third party? There had been many places, better places, to leave the body on the way up. Places where it would not have been found.

It had taken them three months to find Sharon Sixsmith.

So why there?

And found by who?

It was reported a body was found.

He swiped to read the report on the finding of Kieran Cowan, confirming there was a huge part of the story missing. Who had called DCI Patrick? The report said nothing and Patrick said even less. The ones that shall not be spoken of. Small men of few words, short hair and wide necks. Anderson knew who trained in places like the Bealach. Those who needed the bleakest, toughest landscape the British Isles could offer. He knew who and what they were, and he guessed that Alastair Patrick had been one of them. A small lithe Glasgow man with a chip of ice in his eyes, that man would blow your head off and would feel no compunction about doing it.

And that took a certain kind of moral toughness.

Anderson needed Cowan to pull through for him and tell him what happened on that hill, with the blood and the heroin and the alcohol. He had very nearly escaped.

But what of Costello?

He closed his eyes. The music stopped, Nesbitt woke up. A deathly silence fell on the house, just as he had made the decision to go north for some peace. Morna had been pleased of course, Brenda slightly less so.

He opened his eyes wide, startled by the sudden thought that he was leaving his family here, while George Haggerty was still on the loose. At least Mathieson was not taking those photographs at face value and was finding difficulty in tracking the private detective agency who had any records of that assignment. Anderson wondered if it was all an elaborate set-up for George's alibi. He was the only person who really benefitted. Valerie Abernethy was ignoring Mathieson's calls to a meeting, which was a stupid thing to do. Archie thought she was lying drunk in a hotel room somewhere, he was torn between trying to help her, and risking being kicked in the teeth again.

George, of course, had used his charm. Over the phone he admitted he had gone out for a walk the evening before he went up to see his dad in Port MacDuff. He had indeed popped in to see Valerie at the hospital and it was true that she had left the hospital at that time with him. The hospital was less than a mile from the house, so what was so odd about that? The other pictures did not show what they looked like. Just innocent hellos and goodbyes.

Valerie had disappeared now.

George said he had no idea about that.

Anderson thought that George Haggerty was a liar. The wee shitty liar that Archie Walker had been talking about.

His phone rang. He answered it immediately. At first he didn't recognize the voice.

'I need to show you something.' Whoever she was sounded upset.

'Sorry?' He was slow to catch on.

'It's Isla McCaffrey. I need to show you something.'

'Oh Isla, I'm so sorry about Donnie.' He tried to think. 'I was about to go up north tomorrow so I could pop—'

'Were you? Why?'

'On business. I heard about your husband.' To his own ears it sounded beyond futile. He hadn't known the young man. He had hardly given him a thought since he knew that Costello might have broken cover.

'Can you call in here, please?' she interrupted.

'Do you still have your parents there, are you alone?'

'They think I've lost the plot but there's something here I need to show you. Now.'

'There's a name here.' It was three o'clock in the morning and he was studying a single piece of paper under a light, holding it at an angle so he could read the shadows and indentations. He was also trying to ignore the footsteps of Isla's parents in the hall. Three times they had knocked on the door, asking if everything was OK. 'Earl somebody?'

'Earl Slick, he was one of Donnie's heroes. That has nothing to do with it, it's that bit at the top we need to look at. I think he was on the phone to Costello and making those notes at the same time. It must have been important, the way it's scribbled down.'

Anderson sat down on the office chair, the exhausted young woman with red, puffy eyes sat in front of him. She explained where she got the paper from, her grief momentarily lost in her enthusiasm.

'He was on the tail of these guys or something.'

'On the trail of Earl Slick? Who is this Earl Slick? He has underlined that more than once.' He could see himself taking notes on the phone, receiving a lot of information, writing it down then, as the connections were made, his pen would come back to the important point, identifying it so it did not get lost in the page of scribbles. So who was Earl Slick?'

'Well, he's most famous for being David Bowie's sideman but—'

Something jolted in Anderson's mind. 'A sideman? Define a sideman for me, Isla?'

Her tired face creased, thinking. 'Well, it's a guy, a musician who always plays with another guy, usually more famous. The sideman is never a celebrity, but they are always there. Slick has been Bowie's sideman for over twenty years and . . . Roger Pope with Elton and . . .'

'A partnership that last years, one in the open, the other staying well in the shadows?'

'Yes, but they are really good session musicians in their own right. They prefer to be in the background making money and making music, but never in the limelight. They just don't want the fame.' She stopped talking, looking at a signed picture of a spikey haired Earl Slick on the wall. 'That was Donnie's prized possession.'

Anderson let her talk, thinking that George Haggerty had stopped for Nicola Barnes when her car broke down. Somebody had come back to rape her. Had Haggerty called him and told him there was a tasty wee morsel waiting for him. And settled back to give himself a good alibi, while the other man took what pleasure he wanted. And that begged the question, what did George Haggerty get in return? The murder of his wife and child?

He blinked, confused. For some reason Oscar Duguid crossed his mind; the friend of George's who had drowned. No body ever found.

Anderson looked back at the paper in his hand, gratified to see what was in front of him; Donnie and Costello, two police officers had, in some way, got to the same conclusion. 'Interesting. We need every bit of information on this. Jennifer. Jennifer? Somebody has asked me about a Jennifer but not a *Jennifer Rhu.*'

Isla pointed to the computer screen. 'That is, or was, the *Jennifer Rhu.*'

'A yacht? Isla, Donnie would be so proud of you.'

How far had Donnie and Costello got? Definitely suspicious of the main man and the sideman. George and A N Other. Strangers On A Train for the modern age.

But did they have any proof? Or was Costello trying to make sense of all this. He scanned over the indented shadows on the document. NC 500 was an obvious one so his brain latched onto that; the North Coast 500. Where the victims on Morna's list were clustered? Clustered was the wrong word. The victims had been using the same roads, because they were the only roads there. Not the evidence it appeared to be, unless it was written there for another reason that only Costello and McCaffrey knew.

He asked Isla to find Kelvindale Bridge on Google maps.

'Interesting,' said Anderson, looking at the image.

'Is that not near where the woman and the boy were killed?'

'It depends what you mean by near? But yes, within twenty minutes' walk.'

The only people that might know how far these leads went, well, one of them was dead and the other one was missing.

He hoped.

And he needed Mathilda McQueen. He had to get Mathieson on board. He picked up his phone and called Bannon, asking him what CCTV they had requested from Balcarres Avenue and then told him it might be better to get the cameras around Kelvindale Bridge, out of interest. Bannon swore at him for waking him up. Then asked why.

'I'd just do it if I was you.'

'If you are holding back information, Anderson, Mathieson will hit and not miss.'

'I've been mauled by worse than her. Get the CCTV and let me know if you get anything. You can keep the Brownie points.'

By nine a.m. Anderson was packed and keen to start his journey north to meet the clumsy Morna and renew his acquaintance with the quiet man. The weather forecast warned of foul driving conditions but so far his plans for an early start were being thwarted at every turn. He had been summoned to McCaffrey's post-mortem. A copper at Govan had called in to say that he might have a lead on the missing female detective. Anderson dismissed it as he had all the others. Until he saw the contents of the link: an admission report of an unidentified female, taken into the QE 2 hospital early on Monday morning.

Over the next hour, he tried to get hold of a PC Turner, eventually tracking him down in the canteen at Govan. Turner had picked her up while on the night shift after being contacted by the Sally Army. He related the story of her injuries, her location, her lack of ID and lack of memory.

'Really? No memory.'

'Nope.'

'Age?'

'Like in the report, about 60, I'd say. Stinking with drink.'

Anderson's heart fell.

'She has no idea who she is but drinks black tea.'

Anderson spent the next forty minutes on the phone to the hospital, thirty-nine of them on hold, thinking. How injured she had been. Lucky to be alive.

Was it Costello?

The music stopped. 'A friend had come to collect her.'

'What friend? To where?'

The hospital had no idea. She had signed herself out on the basis there would be a private package of care requested by her new consultant, as yet no request had been received.

Anderson wondered if he was getting the runaround. 'Do you have a name?'

'Well, it was a woman.'

'A name?'

'No, try your luck with the ward but you'll get nowhere if you are not a relative.'

'Cheers.'

Costello had no relatives. So who had it been? Another twenty minutes on the phone to the ward and he got a nurse called Hannah. And Hannah had a name, Theresa Neele. He doubted that. Anderson asked Turner to look at a picture he was about attach to a text.

He heard the phone beep. 'No, not her.'

Anderson's heart fell again.

'It could be her mother?'

Anderson put down the phone. And dropped his face into his hands, he had no idea how stressed he had been. He let out a long slow breath. She was out there somewhere, under medical care. Now they knew where to look. She'd lost her memory.

Silly cow. He wiped a tear away.

Thank God. He needed to call Archie but the phone rang instead. He swiped it thinking it would be Turner, or Hannah, with some detail remembered.

It was Morna returning his earlier call. He said he was stuck in Glasgow but would set off as soon as he could, and he'd like to meet straightaway. She told him to come round to the house now that she had been liberated from Kieran's bedside. He was on the mend and would be available for interview soon.

'It looks like he's going to be OK in the long run. His parents are with him now but don't hurry to interview him as he has retrograde amnesia.'

Anderson smiled. 'That's OK.' He then asked exactly where Port MacDuff was. The answer didn't exactly fill him with wonder.

'Port MacDuff? Think Ullapool but with slightly less charm. And more rain.'

That was hard to imagine. He had once heard Ullapool described, with infinite sarcasm, as the entertainment capital of Western Europe.

She had asked if he knew where Fearnmore was. 'Where Loch Torridon meets the Sound. It looks out onto Rona.'

The relief at knowing Costello was around somewhere had lightened his mood, tempting him to say, 'Rona? Never met the woman,' but held his tongue. Morna sounded very earnest, she might not have a sense of humour. 'Port MacDuff, right on the coast. You know Applecross.'

'Well, I know the road by reputation.'

'Yeah, you'd better come the long way round.' she cautioned, 'unless you have a 4 x 4 and even then, we have snow up here already and there's more forecast.'

'Was that not where your young man was found, up on the Bealach . . .?' He made a mess of saying it.

'Bealach? Yes indeed.'

Anderson saw an opportunity, 'Who found him then? If it's inaccessible at this time of year.'

'DCI Patrick.'

'Why was he there?'

'You need to ask him,' was the confusing reply, and she offered to book him a room at the Exciseman for that night. He said that would be very nice and she gave him the address. Then the line went quiet. Then she asked, well stated, 'You've looked at my list, haven't you? Do you think there's something there? That's why you want to come up here.'

'Yes,' he thought, but my reasons are not yours. Then he asked her slowly, what she thought had happened to Sharon Sixsmith.

Her reply startled him. 'You should start with Jennifer Argyll, then Nicola Barnes then think what happened to Gillian Witherspoon. They had the same injuries to their shoulders, and the other one, now that she's dead. Patient confidentiality dies with them. They told me about the shoulder reconstruction she had.'

'What dead one? Gillian?'

'No, Sally Logan. Braithwaite. The one who dived off the top of the building, or was pushed, you know the one who—'

Out of the mouths of babes. Anderson felt his throat go dry, this girl had no idea she was talking about the grandmother of Anderson's grandchild. But she was doing what a good detective would do. He thanked her for the information, he'd explain the rest when he met her. Then he said, for curiosity, testing her, 'Just one more question. Who was Jennifer Rhu?'

'Not a who, a what. That was the boat that went on fire, killed Oscar Duguid.' She said it with the ease of familiarity. Of course she would know, it was a small place. 'He was a pal of George, but you'll know that.'

'Yes. I do, George Haggerty. Do you know him well?'

'Friend of my husband. Why?'

'Just that the name Jennifer Rhu came up, but you solved that mystery. I'll see you later.' He swiped his phone off.

Morna Taverner was on the ball, he'd have to watch himself with that one. She reminded him of Costello.

But now, he had a post-mortem to go to.

Anderson stayed outside of the post-mortem suite, he had been late anyway. On his way into the hospital, he had flashed his card about and eventually tracked down 'Hannah' who was terrified she had done something wrong. It took all of Anderson's charm to get the whole story from her. She had been trying to track down anybody who might know her patient, then she had traced a friend of Jack O'Hare. And she had been called Theresa, Theresa Neele.

The name was vaguely familiar.

Anderson had Googled Theresa Neele, and got Theresa Neale, the name of Agatha Christie's husband's mistress and the name Agatha had used when she had disappeared in 1926, claiming loss of memory.

Sweet.

Hannah gave a brief description, tall, long dark hair tied in a bun, well spoken. From the procurator's fiscal office, she'd had a card.

It was close enough for Anderson; Valerie Abernethy had taken Costello away.

Abernethy had spun a good story, giving Hannah the impression they were going to a private clinic, but had no idea where and Anderson knew that Costello was now behind a big iron curtain called patient confidentiality. She had effectively disappeared again.

And now so had Valerie Abernethy.

By the time he went into the mortuary itself, the post-mortem of Donnie McCaffrey was over.

'I am not repeating it all just for you,' said O'Hare. 'He died of a single stab wound, having suffered five but only one was fatal. Everything else was staged. The cocaine – none in his system. The alcohol – none in his system. He was a clean young man who clearly got involved in a situation. And Mathilda wants you to call her. George Haggerty was stopped for another traffic violation, speeding again.'

'You working for Traffic now?'

'No, but good news travels,' said the pathologist, ticking off boxes on a very long piece of paper. 'She called as she knew you would be here. There was blood found in the boot of his car, it was deer blood so don't get excited. But the sample picked up some orange tri-lobar fibres and that pinged with something the lab in Inverness has found. I hear you are going up there. And if you weren't, you bloody well are now. Fibres in Haggerty's boot match the fibres on the Bealach boy's clothes. Not often Mathilda gets to pass on good news so I thought I'd steal her thunder.'

'He had an offcut of carpet on the floor of his boot,' Anderson remembered. 'Orange.'

'And it will be universally available, I bet. He's giving us the runabout, Colin.'

'They are giving us the runabout.'

O'Hare's pen paused. 'Are you onto something?'

'As you would say, a tentative yes.'

'Did you call Valerie Abernethy about a woman in the QE?'

The pathologist shook his head. 'No, I called Archie's house and she answered the phone. Did she not pass the message on?'

'It's fine,' said Anderson thinking how marvellous it must be to work with the dead, whose capacity to think and be devious was extinct. Just how easy was that?

TWELVE

Anderson made good time, four hours twenty-seven minutes to Port MacDuff. He'd taken the longer but quicker route, up the A9 then across country at Inverness. The air was getting steadily fresher and colder so by the time he was eating a late lunch in Ballinluig it was freezing. By the time he drove past the police station at Port MacDuff, it was freezing and blowing a gale. He thought he might have frostbite. Despite the weather, he decided to stretch his legs after the drive and walk to Morna's house.

He left the car in a public space and got out, making sure his case and laptop were locked in the boot. Pulling on a thick jacket and a woollen hat, he set off along the seafront, letting the sea spray, lifted by the wind, sting his face. Morna lived in Constance House, which was set one street back from the front on Castle Terrace. He stopped to watch the ferry go out, feeling the sea air in his lungs, getting the sense of freedom and of being at one with nature, in all its power. Port MacDuff had a winter population of about two thousand, double that in the summer. The sun took that moment to come out from behind thick cloud to warm his skin. The view over the Inner Sound, the water, the low hills in the distance, dark clouds chasing after the sun, was incredible. And it was so very, very quiet. He could see the attraction of living here, why people came here to escape. No questions asked. Every second person had an English accent, most of the rest were Europeans who had reasons of their own to escape to the arse end of nowhere. Beautiful though it was.

He watched a gang of bikers line up to get on the ferry, their engines roaring. The noise rolled across the bay, at odds with the beauty of the scenery. He turned round, chilled by the wind and keen to keep moving. He saw a thin grey-haired man leaning against the rail further along the harbour. Anderson was sure it was DCI Patrick. Accompanying him was a tall, leanly built man, dark-haired with, from this distance, some grey at the front, maybe even a Mallen streak. They had both been watching him, Anderson was sure of that, but there was no wave of welcome. Nor did they turn and walk away. They just watched. So Anderson waved at them both, then set off towards Castle Terrace, the map memorized from his phone. There were only a few streets in Port MacDuff, it was a small port surrounded by hills on three sides and the very deep water of the Inner Sound on the other.

He kept walking, knowing that Patrick and his friend were still watching. Anderson knew that Patrick might see his being here as a right royal pain in the arse. Patrick could do nothing but acquiesce to his presence; Police Scotland working together and all that crap. But he enjoyed the walk up to the impressive terrace of three-story houses, all painted in different bright colours. His heart was lighter, Costello was alive. He could cope with anything.

Number twelve was bright blue. The five houses in the block had a clear view over the Sound, the buildings in front had been demolished, leaving a flattened area, obviously now used as a temporary car park, a weird assortment of vehicles parked in a very haphazard fashion with no white lines to guide them. He noticed two matching vans parked, a tall young man standing at the open back door of one, clipboard in hand. On the ground were a couple of large bags, easily five-feet long. As Anderson passed, the man read the label on a small rucksack and then placed it in the bigger bag, repeating the process with the next bag, a small holdall; he was moving awkwardly, as if he had a sore neck or a sore shoulder. As he lifted the zippered flap on the long bag, Anderson caught a flash of the orange lining. The man saw him looking and straightened his posture, adjusted the collar of his boiler suit and stared directly back. To his left was another man dressed in a white coat doing something very noisy with white fish boxes, stacking them to left and right then stacking them back the other way. The rear door of his van was open, the refrigerator unit on the top was quiet. He too looked up at Anderson as if they both possessed some sixth sense that had alerted them to his scrutiny. More likely he was a stranger here and they were curious about him. Strangers here should walk along the front, take photographs, buy coffee and get on the ferry, not walk the backstreets looking for number twelve.

Better people than them had tried to psyche out Colin Anderson, so he opened the front gate of the blue house, casually looking over his shoulder to read the side of the van; HikeLite, and a mobile phone number. Anderson tried to gauge the man's height; tall and slim, this was a young man. The fish guy was older, stockier, but was still looking over as Anderson turned to walk up Morna's pathway.

Noted.

Morna opened the door, her face brimming as if he was a long-lost friend. If he had been twenty years younger Anderson thought he would have fallen in love with her there and then. Her red hair streamed down her back, her smile as wide and fresh as a Bavarian milkmaid.

He followed her down the hall listening to her incessant chatter, then into a cold living room. The old blue sofa was covered with a brightly coloured patchwork blanket from the middle of which a crumpled face looked out at him. The blanket was wrapped round a young boy, too obsessed by his X-wing to even look up. From the two posters on the wall, Anderson judged the creased face on the blanket was Hans Solo.

'Somebody a *Star Wars* fan then?' he asked.

'My other half. I think it's genetic.' She nodded at the boy on the sofa. 'Neil's very good on *Star Wars*, *Alien* and *Bladerunner* but can't remember to pick his son up from school. Sorry,' she said, as if he was too important to be interested in her life outside of work. 'I'm DC Morna Taverner. As you might have guessed.'

'Glad to meet you, DC Morna Taverner. DCI Colin Anderson, call me Colin, I work a closed unit so we don't need to be formal.'

'Yes, sir,' she replied, then laughed.

He noticed the swing of her hair, a russet mane.

'And this is Finn, he's a very rude wee boy. I'll put the kettle on.'

Anderson said hello to the boy and got a flicker of a smile

in response. Anderson walked round the back of the settee, taking in the thin carpet, the cold chill in the air, the peeling paint.

Somebody was short of cash here, yet Morna would be on a good salary surely. There was a sense of this house being temporary, nothing in the way of homeliness, a few pictures of Finn on the wall, two years of primary school, proud in a uniform that didn't really fit him. And one wedding photograph, the bride easily recognizable as Morna, the groom just as easily recognized as the man outside with the two vans. HikeLite? Those vans were expensive, Anderson wondered who ran the company. It would be too obvious if he walked back to the window and looked out to see if both vans were still there. Morna was chattering away from the kitchen, asking about his drive up, the roadworks, the weather. All the things you need to know about if you live this far from a good supermarket.

'Is that you then?' he asked Finn, pointing at the school photograph.

'Aye,' said the boy, showing Anderson his X-wing.

'Lovely. The Millennium Falcon is my favourite. Do you have one of them?'

The boy shook his head. 'Death Star, and Imperial Stormtrooper.'

Anderson moved slightly round the back of the sofa, stepping over a dog basket, smiling awkwardly at the boy but the curtains precluded him from seeing the vans in the makeshift car park. All he could see was a fat woman walking past with two Scotties on the same lead. Even she seemed to take a good look at the house as she strolled, oblivious to the weather. He looked beyond her, something trickling into his head, in the car park, in his line of sight, a vehicle pulling away, a small white Fiat car driven by a blonde with a hat on.

He turned back into the room, trying to keep the grin from his face, looking round his eyes saw the picture. It hung on the wall over the fireplace and was a huge photographic print of a beautiful house standing high on a cliff, old and grand. A glassed terrace ran along the front so that anybody sitting there in a comfy Chesterfield enjoying a good malt, could see the waves at low tide and on a clear day, Raasay, Rona and Skye beyond. They were easily recognizable, even to Anderson.

The gold engraving on the bottom of the frame said Le Adare Lodge.

'Is that your house?' Anderson asked the boy, getting a cheery, ridiculous laugh in return.

'Nooooo.'

'Are you sure?'

A huge nod.

'Would you like it to be your house?'

Another big nod.

'Is it your mum's house?' asked Anderson.

Finn shook his head. 'No, my dad's. Chewbacca lives there.'

'Don't you start him going on about that again,' mocked Morna, appearing at the kitchen door with two steaming mugs of coffee and a box of Viennese Whirls in the crook of her elbow. 'Everybody does.'

'Sorry, I didn't mean to stare. It's very impressive. Is it French? The name?'

'The name? It's a corruption of the Gaelic for Dolphin Point. It's the highest point on the coast, over there.' She indicated to the front door, so he presumed, she was talking about the clifftops to the west. She placed the cups on the narrow table on the back wall, a bit rickety.

It dipped when Anderson sat down and leaned on it, spilling a little coffee from both mugs. 'Sorry.'

'No worries, there's normally a bit of paper in there to keep it level.'

They sat facing each other. The table was so small, he could have easily reached out and touched her fingertips, her blue, cracked fingertips he noticed. And he did want to reach out and warm her tiny hand in his. He was glad she had placed a large box between them.

She put the Viennese Whirls right in front of him, still in their box. 'Have you looked at Jennifer Argyll's file yet?'

He was thrown a little at her directness. 'No, not yet.'

'That was where she disappeared.' She pointed up at the picture. 'Last seen walking up to the lodge.'

'Oh right.' It was not that the lodge itself was unimpressive, it was the size of the picture in such a small house. Anderson couldn't think he knew anybody under the age of thirty who would have a picture in their house bigger than their TV screen. 'You son seems to think you own it.'

'He thinks Chewbacca lives up there and he believes Santa lives at Fearnmore Cragg farm and that he snogs Betty Alexander from the post office.'

'The innocence of youth. Are you planning to buy the house when you win the lottery?'

'Aye, that'll be right. I would have to buy a ticket though to give myself a chance, Neil does think of the lodge as his ancestral home. Only because his mum used to clean the floors there and he hung around it a lot as a child. If you are here for a while, you should take a drive up to Dolphin Point, the views are amazing.'

He looked out the window, the view of the car park opposite had been obliterated by a squall of rain. 'And do you see dolphins?'

'That's what we tell the tourists.'

'And what is it now?'

'What's what?'

'The house, is it a hotel or something?'

'Nope,' Morna said, 'it's a heap of bricks. Thank god.' She leaned closer to him, he could see the individual freckles on her nose. 'Bad karma, as if the spirit of Jennifer was making sure it was never going to be a success. Her ghost walks the cliffs, you know. I thought that was why you were looking at it, because of Jennifer.' She sounded disappointed. 'I thought you had read the file.'

'I will, believe me.' He sipped his coffee, breaking that chain of conversation. 'So who looks after the wee guy while you are doing all this? His dad?'

'No, Finn gets the runabout. Neil runs HikeLite, and he is so busy at the moment as he's self-employed and you don't want to turn away any business, do you? He's outside I think, loading up the vans.'

'Neil Taverner?'

'Yes, do you know him?' She smiled, proud of her husband.

'I think he came forward about an abandoned old Dormobile a few days ago.'

Morna didn't flinch. 'Sounds like him, he loves all that old crap. If the owner hadn't claimed it, he'd have tried to buy it.' She shook her head, indulging the vagaries of the man she loved.

'Works all hours, does he? Nights? The 500 is busy.'

'You guessed it.' She was oblivious of the seismic leap Anderson's heart had just made, and the struggle he had not to interrogate her right there and then. 'And for people doing the West Highland Way. Well, that was how it started. He's now getting a lot of business out the 500 as well, it used to be summer-only trade but now the season is all year and he has two assistants, three vans and a larger minivan.'

'What does it entail?' He kept his voice casual, merely making easy chit-chat after a long drive.

Morna looked at Anderson and waved her hands, expansively pulling ideas from thin air. 'Say you want to cycle the 500 on the sixth of December. Well, you would email Neil your route, the hotels you have booked, where your overnight camp is going to be or an agreed pick-up point if you are wild camping,' she warmed to her subject, 'and he will take the heavy bag. That means you only have to carry it from the post office to the camping site. If you leave your bag packed in the morning, Neil picks it up, and when you get to where you are going, your bag will be there for you. It's fifty quid for the West Highland Way, hundred quid for the 500, due to the distance involved. But it's easier now as we can make the vans rendez-vous and swap bags and the vans then go off north, south or west. So, Neil is away less. We also do more remote places off the way, there's a small extra charge to do that but it's worth it, it's getting so busy. Folk are having to take B and Bs and hotels further from the route, in the summer at least. It's so popular, there are mad winter walkers out now. In that!' She nodded at the window.

'I prefer the comfort of the internal combustion engine.' Anderson smiled at her. 'Does he employ anybody?'

'He's very busy.' She evaded the question.

'Just that he has three vans, can't drive them all at the same

time so I presume business is booming as the 500 becomes
more famous. There must be lots of work, I'm not from the
revenue, I don't care if he's moonlighting.'

All Morna said was, 'He works lots of hours,' then she
looked at Finn. She spoke like a woman whose husband was
having an affair; never there, never with their son. A fractured
family.

So,' said Anderson, 'maybe you can you tell me about
Jennifer?'

'Jennifer Argyll?'

'And,' said Anderson, 'the *Jennifer Rhu*. Tell me what
happened there.'

A look of slight shock passed over her face. 'OK,' she said.
'Oh, but you'd be better talking to Lachlan. He was a cop at
the time, he was in charge of it. It was big news. At the time.'
She looked disappointed.

'OK, I'll speak to him. Is this file for me?'

She brightened immediately and opened the lid of the box.
Anderson took out his notebook glancing at his watch. This
could take some time.

Lachlan McRae was indeed the man Patrick had been with,
he was exactly what Anderson had always imagined the inhabitants of Wester Ross should be. He was tall and solid without
carrying an extra ounce of fat although he must have been in
his late sixties, maybe even edging into his seventies. He
seemed to absorb the weather and walked at a speed that had
Anderson struggling for breath trying to keep up with him at,
or maybe that was the wind snatching the breath from him.
Anderson was relieved when they stopped at a set of traffic
lights that had no traffic to control and Lachlan gave him very
scant details of the disappearance of Jennifer Argyll thirty
years before, in November 1987. The older man didn't want
to say very much about it and Anderson didn't ask any more.
It was a debrief. Anderson felt he had the measure of these
two, Lachlan was ex-military and Anderson knew he was being
told enough of the story to tantalize him. The girl had gone
out on a date with an untraced man and had never come home.

'So where was her "last seen"?'

It was then that Lachlan turned and looked at him. 'Up on Dolphin Point, up at the Lodge,' he said, with a shrug that seemed to say, *so what would you expect?*

They walked across the deserted street, a gust of wind blew a sudden squall of rain over the tarmac in front of them, the raindrops bounced up to soak their trousers. Anderson put his hand up to keep the water from his eyes. Once it had passed he turned to Lachlan, who was laughing 'don't worry you get used to it'. But Anderson's eyes fell into the further distance where he caught sight of a woman with her hand also on top of her hood, fighting the force of the weather – but not before he caught a glimpse of short blonde hair. As soon as the woman saw him she turned and walked away, vanishing round the nearest corner.

Anderson stopped walking, causing Lachlan to turn and make sure he was alright. 'Sorry, I thought I saw someone that I used to know.'

'Who?'

'Just a cop I used to work with?'

Lachlan patted him on the back, pushing him on slightly, not letting Anderson entertain any thought of following her. 'Don't worry about it, this place isn't only home to the ghosts of the past, ghosts of the future hang about here as well. She's been around for a few hours. Do you know her?'

'I think I do?'

'Do you have a name?'

'Does she need one?' asked Anderson, feeling a sense of relief, but it was his relief nobody else's. 'Do you know where she's staying?'

'Not without a name.'

'It's OK, I'll track her down.'

The he realized Lachlan had stopped walking.

'The Exciseman's that way.' He indicated down the street and left Anderson to his own thoughts.

'OK,' he said to himself, ignoring the image of Edward Woodward being burned to death.

Checking into the pub was a matter of showing ID and getting a key. His host was curt to the point of being surly. Anderson could cope with that.

He climbed the narrow stairs, his rucksack over his back, laptop in his arms, the wooden tagged key hanging from his finger. Once in the clean, but tiny room, he checked his phone. No signal. Sure that he had seen Costello, he didn't know if he was relieved that she was up and about, or disappointed that she'd felt she couldn't let him in on what she was up to. Or maybe, as Brenda had said to him, it was simply none of his business. He could ask around the hotels but she'd have booked under an assumed name. Any official search would be flagged up immediately and he'd find his remit up here changed to tracking down and bringing in his friend 'to help with enquiries'.

He needed to be careful.

He also tried to ignore the black rolling clouds coming in from the Inner Sound. He was hoping to go out and phone Archie, to tell him that Costello was up and about and that he would try to meet her, and then phone the office for access to the cold case file of Jennifer Argyll. He'd like to see that for himself, not be influenced by the agenda of who was telling him what.

So, he put his phone on charge. The information file tucked under the lamp on his bedside table said the best signal was down at the ferry terminal. He looked out the small window, along the water. The clouds, like his mood, seemed to be getting darker.

On the seafront, his jacket collar rolled up to keep the draft from his neck, his gloved fingers struggled to get Archie's contact on the mobile. The call was answered immediately, Anderson told him that he thought he had seen Costello twice, up in Port MacDuff, sniffing around George Haggerty, or more likely, somebody called Neil Taverner.

All Archie said was 'oh'. Anderson knew there was something else Archie had to tell him, something more important.

'What's happening at your end?'

'I backtracked the CCTV on the night of the murders.' Archie's voice had that clipped quality, he was not happy.

'Should Mathieson's team not have done that?'

'She was checking it for around the time of death, and is

now doing six a.m. through to twelve, and on a wider range of cameras. They have somebody carrying an object that looks like the Millennium Falcon in a bin bag, going across the footbridge. Mathieson missed the exit route, the time, the lot.'

'She's used to investigating cops, this murderer is much cleverer than the average cop.'

'What's that noise?'

'It's a wind tunnel called Port MacDuff. It'd be lovely when, and if, the sun ever shines.'

'Colin? Between you and I, I backtracked the footage from the time George met Valerie at the garage.'

'Did Mathieson not?'

'No, I was more interested in what Valerie was doing.'

'What does she do?' He was trying not to snap at the fiscal but he was beginning to understand the true meaning of the words wind chill factor.

'Nothing. But I go back. You know the off-licence? George was carrying a bag. Easily seen on the footage but not on the images that appeared in the paper. It's a bottle.'

'Alcohol.'

'George had been in earlier that day. He'd bought vodka.'

'OK.' Anderson was trying to piece this together. 'I presume George doesn't drink vodka. Or Abigail?'

'Neither. I think he bought it for Valerie, gave her it, took her somewhere, and left her . . . Last thing on film is them walking into a crowd down near your place.'

'Leaving her with no alibi? You can sanction a request for more footage, but I don't think you need to bother. We have them, Archie, it's a matter of time.'

'He set her up, Colin. He set her up.'

'There's a lot of it about. Don't worry about her, Archie. We are nearly there.'

Anderson sat in the corner of the pub with a coffee and the biggest fruit scone he had ever seen. It was warm, a small tub of fresh butter sat on the side with a small ramekin of strawberry jam, he could see lumps of fruit. He basically enjoyed his work but sometimes it was truly a pleasure. If only the locals would stop looking at him as if they were sizing him up for a wicker cage.

They had all looked round when he had walked in, the seven or eight men, regulars he presumed, from the way they looked fixed onto their seats, the shape of their bodies moulded into the leather.

He gave his order at the bar, the sign clearly said coffee and scones served. If they wanted to think of him as a namby southerner so be it. He hoped they didn't have him pegged as a Christian for his lack of alcohol. He'd know if Britt Eckland put in an appearance. He placed the box file on the table and got out his notebook. They would know why he was here, it would be useful for him to be seen working. As he made himself comfortable, two men got up within a couple of minutes of each other. The taller, younger left by the door that pointed towards the gents and returned a couple of minutes later. The other man, bald, older with a couple of days' stubble on his face went out that same door leaving a trail of Eau De dead fish in his wake, but he failed to return.

Anderson turned back to the file.

Jennifer Argyll had been a truly beautiful seventeen-year-old. She had grown up in Inverness and moved to the port with her parents when she was fifteen. She had worked as a junior clerk in the port authority and on 20th November 1987, she walked up to Dolphin Point and was never seen again. It was that simple.

Nothing else, but he could see how that smile, that face, might have haunted a generation. She had the look of a young Claudia Cardinale. Jennifer had, for some reason, gone off the cliff, or so it was presumed. Her body had never been found despite sea searches, leaving her to walk the clifftops forever in her ghostly form, so the rumours went.

He had Googled the Le Adare Lodge and apart from the many reports of the fire that had flattened the place on 13th of January 1995, there was not much. He looked at a few photographer's shots of Dolphin Point itself, the pictures mostly populated with dolphins. Then he came across a website for Historic Scotland, where people had put their old cine films on line, and he found a treasure trove. He had only been looking for about ten minutes when he struck real gold. There was a film taken in mid-1950s, maybe a bit later, of Le Adare Lodge, a corruption of the old Gaelic of Leumadair, as Morna had said. The scene flickered to life to show the picture of the water, the sea, the waves, then it panned unsteadily round to reveal a man standing on the veranda of the lodge. A set scene Anderson had seen in many of the old postcards of the lodge. The man was dressed in full highland regalia, the kilt, the tartan Glengarry, the sporran, the lot and he was laughing at the camera, saying something a little self-consciously before two ladies appeared, both dressed in their best for the holidays in neat box jackets, high heels and skirts that floated round their knees. They both had hats on, handbags matching their suits dangled over their arms. The man in the kilt greeted them, and two young men also in kilts appeared carrying leather suitcases, one in each hand, and a couple of hat boxes under their arms.

The staff, no doubt.

He Googled the name. Interesting. All the names were interesting.

Were these the wives of the sort of men who would be out shooting anything in sight over the next few days? Anderson nibbled at his scone, it melted in his mouth and he watched the film, enjoying it rather than analyzing what he was seeing. It went on for seven or eight minutes, bits of film tagged together from here and there around the lodge, jaunty figures flickering in black and white, stag heads, the huge open log fire, guns hanging everywhere. He was looking at this when the convivial host turned back to the garden, the camera panned back to the grass that swept down to the cliff steps. He watched with interest as the camera turned indoors to catch a couple of kids running across the terrazzo dance floor. Anderson smiled, that was a piece of history right there. He was still munching his scone, taking a mouthful of coffee when the camera panned back out again, the kilted man stood on the veranda, summoning some other member of staff.

Clap clap.

Clap clap.

*   *   *

Oscar Duguid. Certainly not a common name. A few threats and a quick visit to DCI Patrick had confirmed what Anderson suspected. The kilted man in the cine film was Donal Duguid, the father of Abigail's first husband.

Presumed dead.

His boat had been called the *Jennifer Rhu*.

Rhu was a village in Argyll.

And Jennifer Argyll was also presumed dead.

Anderson was being played, again.

So he did what his instinct told him to, he finished his coffee, nodded goodbye to his watchful companions, left the pub. He drove the Beamer the three miles to Dolphin Point.

In the very last of the light, Anderson stood in the breeze, fresh but no longer howling the way it had been earlier in the day. He could breathe easily. He had parked the Beamer at the south of the overgrown driveway, two huge boulders had been pushed into the middle of the dirt lane creating a natural barrier to prevent any vehicle from going further up the hill towards the cliff. He was a hundred feet or so above sea level already, and the lodge had been at the highpoint of the coast. The road from Port MacDuff had been a long slow steady climb, making the car engine whine and groan, out of its comfort zone.

Anderson had tried to do his homework. He had quickly realized that the Le Adare Lodge was not something that the locals liked speaking about. He had watched the films, seen the exhibition dances of Elenora Haggerty, some relative of George's, Colin presumed, nothing surprised him now. He had watched her dance with a tall handsome man, they did a feature dance, every movement caught on the flickering cine film. He read that she had trained to be a ballet dancer but injured her shoulder. Anderson had hoped it was all going to go a bit Bates Motel after that, Haggerty traumatized by his beautiful mother damaging her shoulder and losing her love of dance and her sanity. But no, she gave up her dreams and settled down to life as hostess and exhibition dancer of the Le Adare Lodge, Dolphin Point, Port MacDuff and had lived a long and content life.

Then Jennifer Argyll had gone missing and the wheel of fortune turned.

It was a long walk, the lane that lead up to where he thought the house had stood was badly overgrown. The lane wound its way up a hill, around a crop of boulders to a tall rock stack right on the headline. Now he had his bearings. He zipped his anorak, and pulled his hat down over his ears, scarf up round his neck, gloves on. He trudged on, weaving his way upward through the thorns and the bushes. Sometimes he found himself walking along a good concrete road, the tarmac only slightly cracked, at other times the tarmac was broken and fractured by the plants growing through. But on the road went, narrowing slightly. He could feel the change in the air, smelling the sea breeze, the scent of salt on his face. It was fresher up here, away from the perfume of the trees and the winter undergrowth, the bare branches that pulled and tugged at him as he pushed his way through.

And suddenly he was at the top of the hill, the great rock stack to the north, the Inner Sound lay in front of him like undulating grey silk. He stood, gathering his breath. The climb had been more strenuous than he had thought, but as he walked into the clearing at the summit, the clouds parted and the sun came out, warming his face once more, letting him breathe and appreciate the crystal clear diamonds of light on the water. The dark grey churn had calmed to a sheet of silver, he could hear the gentle beat and crash of waves on the shore beneath him.

Mother Nature had welcomed him to her world.

He stood and looked around him, pulling the gloves from his hands, feeling his fingers so he could dig around in his pockets for the map. He looked at it again, the small road was there, winding up to the top of the cliff. He walked carefully to the edge, fearing that the breeze which was absent one minute, might gust again and one real blast would push or pull him right over. Was that what had happened to Jennifer Argyll? He looked out over the grey water, where the *Jennifer Rhu* had gone to the depths.

Anderson moved slowly towards the edge and looked down on to another bank of grass, then another below as if the cliff had layered itself, tiered to make it easier to get down to the beach. In the cine film, there had been a wooden stairway attached to the cliff face. He could still see a few wooden uprights clinging onto bare rock. The enclosed beach, a perfect semi-circle of a bay with the cliffs reaching out and high on either side, like arms to protect the pure white sand that looked as though it had been sieved onto the beach. A few cracked slabs of rock forked out into the water, waves cutting over them. Jagged fingers that would be treacherous to any boat wanting to land. Dangerous as they were, Anderson could see how they reduced the power of the waves breaking over them, making the beach itself a much safer place to swim.

He leaned over, seeing, on the face of a cliff with its levels of coarse tufted grass, more bits of the wooden stairway, playing join the dots, he could make out exactly where the steps had been. He looked at the photocopy of the photograph of the lodge, it must have been taken from where he stood. The house had faced right out to sea, from high up on the cliff, far enough back to keep it safe from erosion and the worst of what Mother Nature could fling at it.

He looked up and down, from the height of the rock stack to the beach below. No sign of the house was left, no sign it had ever been.

It was the ghost of a house.

What had he been expecting?

This was where Oscar had played as a child. He had spent his life here and he had been a friend of George's, whose mother had danced so elegantly across the terrazzo dance floor. This was the place that George ran back to, but strangely enough, despite the emotional history he shared, he had never brought his wife or child up here. They had never met his father.

Those boys had been formed by this place. They had married the same woman. Now both children of those unions were dead. As Costello had said, something that is too much of a coincidence tends not to be a coincidence. He walked back towards the road, now he could see some outlines of the brickwork, light grey coloured granite stone, a wall only a foot high that would be solid then vanish in the undergrowth as though it had never been. He walked forward, tracing the footprint of the house. He kept turning round to look at the view, to check it was still there and then find himself doing nothing but standing looking, and looking, the view was beguiling and enchanting.

He continued to trace the outline, his feet getting wet. Looking back he could see his path, the footsteps clear in the wet shiny grass, sidestepping to the left and then wandering to the right like the footsteps of a drunk. Then he climbed over a piece of wall, now trying to find his way through drier winter growth.

Anderson realized he was standing on something solid underfoot, more than the surrounding earth and moss. He scraped the sole of his shoe back and forth, removing the dirt to reveal a white tile, edged with black. He scraped and pulled the branches back with his gloved hand, getting his face scratched and cut as the tiles of the black and white terrazzo floor revealed itself. In his mind's eye, he saw Elenora Haggerty glide across the floor in stiff taffeta and sprung heels, he could almost smell her perfume in the air; hear the small dance band in the noise of the wind as it raced up the cliff face.

He pulled out his phone to photograph the few stones that were still standing, then turned to go back to the edge, a wall a hundred yards or so, mentally mapping out the footprint of the building as it had been the day the photograph over Morna's fireplace was taken. It was a well-known picture of the place, he had seen a few versions on the net, on calendars and postcards.

He paused to look at the grass, his own footprints now almost faded in the rain, the blades of grass he had crushed had sprung back to life – on his footprints only, not on the new footmarks that had closely tracked his. The footsteps walked in a straight line, coming right for him, and then they had pulled away to the side, into the trees that ran down the hillside back to the main road.

'Hello?'

No answer, just a buffering breeze warning him not to make a noise up here. This had been a still and silent place for many years. In his mind's eye, Elenora Haggerty lifted a finger to her ruby red lips as she glided past, keeping the secret.

She was a ghost, the footmarks were real.

Whoever it was didn't want to make themselves known, so Colin Anderson put his phone, the print of the house and the map back in his anorak pocket and made his way down the road, a little more quickly than he had come up.

Halfway down the path, Anderson caught sight of him. Somebody, moving ahead, shambling through the undergrowth. The figure started to speed up, running, pushing aside the dead bracken. Anderson shouted at him but the figure, camouflaged in black and dark green, began to melt into the landscape. Anderson gave chase, nearly catching him at the stream where the wet jacket of the man slipped out the grasp of his outstretched hand, but it was enough to put both of them out of kilter and down they went, down amongst the stones, the darkness and the icy bubbling water.

The water went over Anderson's head. He thought no, not again; he was getting too old for this. But he held onto the man he was chasing, taking in lungfuls of water, writhing and twisting as they both struggled for air. Anderson felt his head scrape against a sharp stone, a blow aimed at his midriff made him pull back. The impact this time was hard and brutal. He still held on, trying to push himself up with his legs so the other guy could pull him free of the water when he tried to stand up. But Anderson rolled and he went under again, feeling his head strike something hard again, and that terrible fear of water filling his nose and this throat. Anderson panicked, his clothes weighing him down, he opened his mouth to scream that this could not be happening to him again. Then he felt a hand grab his jacket and pull him clear, the other man got to his feet quicker, staggering, and barely managing to stay upright. He, an older and balding man, bent over, hands on knees, taking in gasps of breath. He reached out a hand to help Anderson up.

'I'm too old for this, pal.'

'Me too.' Anderson looked at the bald head, the weather-beaten face, the straggly beard and subtracted eighteen years. 'Welcome back from the dead, Mr Duguid.'

They sat on the grass in silence looking out over the Sound, both soaking wet. The smell of dead fish rose steaming from his companion. Anderson was about to change this man's world, he could let him say goodbye.

Anderson regained his breathing, he stood up, looking round at the rock stack, feeling colder than he'd ever felt. He looked up and saw that same woman he had seen before. She took her time looking, keeping her distance, a tranquil figure, unmoving. She turned, walking away quickly, heading towards the road, her hand up over her head, holding her hood up. But again he saw another flicker of familiar blonde hair. And, he thought, just for a moment, that she had a gun in her hand.

'Costello?' he shouted, his fatigue forgotten, he was running in an instant. But she was gone. He repeated her name, 'Costello?' quietly, more to himself than for any other ears. 'Did you see her?' asked Anderson. 'That woman?'

'What woman?'

The file from the Scub camera was now available to view after a huge delay about who was footing the bill for the restoration of a video file that might show nothing. Eventually it had been returned to the Complaints team with an invoice.

Mathieson sat down and clicked a few buttons on the computer. She reached round to retrieve her cup of coffee, took a sip, her eyes off the screen for a full ninety seconds. She glanced at it as she rearranged a file from the left side to the right as it was impinging on her view. She flicked it open to check the date on her timeline of Costello's 'last seen'. She hoped this film would tell them something one way or the other as she wanted some closure on Costello's case, they all needed it. Mathieson, despite her reputation, had a lot of empathy for Costello, but the DI needed to be brought back into the fold, no matter what she had done.

Costello did not have the record of a dodgy cop. In some ways, she had a worse issue; she was moralistic and that was an easier recruit to vigilantism. Mathieson could paint that scenario easily, she could understand it perfectly.

She clicked play and let the screen change, still not paying it much attention, somebody shouted from the opposite side of the room about a sandwich order that was going down to Subway. She asked for a twelve-inch wholemeal with avocado, chicken and all the salad, but no peppers, before adding a packet of Doritos. She could be here all night and she could never work with an empty stomach.

Mathieson turned back to the computer and began to watch,

noting the time the film started with a view of a blade of grass glinting and quivering with perfect spheres of rainwater. It was 21.27. A slight frown appeared on her forehead, both in concentration and concern. She had been expecting the long view clarity of CCTV. Due to the incidents on the loch in the recent weeks, all the CCTV cameras at the car park at Inveruglass had been turned along the shoreline or out onto the islands themselves. This was digital video taken by a camera that had been set to film anything it caught in its sightline.

She was worried about what was coming next, watching with a weird mixture of elation and horror in her stomach. She might be a bitch but she knew to admit when she had been wrong.

The camera had been set to look out over the water, moving slightly when buffeted by the wind or when Kieran adjusted its position. Occasionally a white cloth covered the lens, wiping it clear of rain. For a while the screen was filled with an image of the loch, nothing more, nothing moving but the raindrops pattering on the surface. The camera was being switched on and off, the clock changed, moving on only by a minute or so. Kieran was obviously switching it on when he thought he saw some movement, then he would focus in on something in the water that proved to be imaginary. Then the camera would pull back, going in search of something more promising.

Mathieson was trying to think of Kieran lying on his stomach at the top of the hill, a few metres higher than the viewpoint. Instead of the clear view right down the loch, a famous view often seen on postcards, Kieran had picked this spot for the clear view to the island, looking east rather than south east. From where he was looking, the car park would be behind and below him, over his right shoulder.

Then the camera jerked, as if it had got a fright. Mathieson could imagine Kieran hearing something that made him turn. The camera moved along the ground slightly, blades of grass came close as the camera dropped. Kieran was now closer to the ground. Hiding? It was more of a pull back into cover than a fall. Mathieson frowned. The film of grass getting wet with raindrops continued, with no further movement. Was that it? Kieran had dropped the camera at the first sign of trouble and the film had caught nothing more?

But the camera kept filming, minutes passed. Mathieson was about to sip her coffee when she saw something. She could make out the top of a figure on the right side of the frame, a mound of dark, the head and shoulders swaying from side to side with the effort of climbing the steep hill up from the viewpoint. She wished she had visited that scene herself, then she might have a better idea of the lie of the land. The camera was near the water's edge but in an elevated position, the walker was coming up from the car park, she thought. The figure stood at the top of the hill, looking out over the water with no idea he was being filmed. So that meant the camera had already been abandoned or Kieran was very well hidden. Or this visitor had no notion to look around for a covert cameraman. From the darkness of the film she couldn't make out who it was, but he was well dressed for the weather and didn't really seem bothered about being seen. Then someone else appeared, quickly from the left screen.

The attack was swift and brutal, three low level stabs before the first figure had time to turn around. Mathieson let out an involuntary squeal, and pulled back, her colleagues turned to look at her. The first figure was now on his knees, the camera caught the flash of a blade. She put her coffee down.

Bannon came over, to stand behind her, looking over her shoulder, watching as the knife went in again and again. She pressed pause as the man in the anorak turned towards the camera, trying to get away.

Mathieson took one look at his face.

'Donnie, Donnie. What the hell did you get yourself into?'

Anderson sat on the side of the table, perching himself there, comfortable with the situation. Alastair Patrick was standing in the corner, his legs locked at the knee, arms folded, his jaw tight, unreadable. Anderson was wary where Patrick's allegiance lay. His demeanour was not that of a detective who had just bought into custody a murderer, or a rapist. It was more like the local drunk had been brought in for pissing into the harbour again.

Anderson was keeping his own allegiance neutral. Mathieson had updated him on the contents of the file using the word 'military' to describe the stealth of the fatal assault on Donnie McCaffrey on Loch Lomondside. His eyes swivelled to Patrick as he updated her on the orange carpet and that it might be worth a look at the HikeLite website, he said quietly when Patrick's own mobile had distracted his attention.

Sometimes the better dance was with the devil.

Anderson handed over a mug of soup made by Patrick's wife; Oscar Duguid looked like he needed it.

'So, welcome back from the dead, Oscar. How does it feel?'

'I'm not proud of what I did. But I did need to do it.' He sipped his soup savouring it, his lips making smacking noises. Anderson heard Patrick move behind him, readjusting his position. He could feel the tension from the other man's body. Somebody here had a secret.

Oscar Andrew Duguid, clean, beard trimmed, sat in the small interview room at Port MacDuff, he seemed to have shrunk from the ambling man that rolled out of Anderson's arms, then helped him out the icy waters of the stream.

Anderson was patient, waiting for Oscar to feel comfortable enough to start talking. Starting at the beginning and working his way to the end. Anderson was interested in where Oscar was going to start, suspecting that the story might start much further back than Oscar might be willing to reveal. Maybe as far back as Jennifer.

There was no talk, no eye contact so Anderson thought he had better jumpstart the conversation.

'Whose idea was it to fake your own death?'

Oscar screwed up his face, rubbing his thumbs deep into his eyes and shaking his head. But there was no answer.

'You do remember Mary Jane.'

'Of course I do.' The voice was strong, sounded intelligent and eloquent.

Anderson pushed a picture across the top of the table to him, the picture George had given to him. Oscar didn't look at it before turning it over and pushing it away.

Anderson tapped the back of the photograph. 'That was my daughter, that girl you adopted was my daughter. You going missing sparked off a chain of events that led to her

death, so don't give me any shit about what a hard life you
have had.'

'Sorry for your loss,' said Oscar. 'It's my loss too.'

'Of course, but you did know that she had died.'

He nodded.

'And how do you know that, if you are living in the middle
of nowhere, out of touch with society?' Anderson leaned back
in his seat. 'Who told you? You are no Bear Grylls, so somebody is helping you. Who?'

Oscar Duguid closed his eyes in a very deliberate slow
blink. 'This is a place where people come to run away, they
are very good at hiding you here. Walking around, how many
different accents have you already heard? All those home
counties professionals that couldn't take it anymore and had
to get away.'

'Very few went to the lengths of faking their own deaths.'

'I just wanted to disappear.'

'So how did it go, you bought a small dinghy.'

'No, I didn't.'

'OK, somebody did. Somebody bought one for you, from
somewhere. Might be a bit obvious if they found the *Jennifer
Rhu* burning, the small boat still attached but a second boat
you had just purchased was gone. Nobody had to know about
the second small boat that actually got you off the *Jennifer
Rhu* and back to shore. So who bought you that? Who was
your partner in crime?' Anderson folded his arms. 'And to be
clear, it was a crime.'

It was a guess but he knew he had struck gold. There was
a mastermind in this and it wasn't Oscar Duguid. His gut
feeling was that Oscar was a man in search of nothing more
but a quiet life.

'It's all nothing to do with me. I'm happy sitting in the
corner of the pub, or in the back room, eating the leftovers,
having a shower, moving around but mostly living up there
near the lodge. It's fine in the summer, not best in the winter.
The winters are tough,' he said, touching the reddened
skin of his cheek, as if it was still tender. 'I have a hut. It's
fine.'

A look passed from Oscar to Patrick. All he got back was

a brief nod. It was not returned. Anderson made a note to search the hut.

'Who bought the second boat? We need a name?'

It came as no surprise when Oscar Dugiud's lips opened to form the name. 'It was George Haggerty.'

The story that Oscar Duguid told was frightening in its simplicity. He had a boat and he was a good sailor. George Haggerty had bought a small boat with an onboard motor months before in Glasgow. Nothing that could be traced back to either of them. Oscar sailed out, set his boat on fire before returning to shore on George's boat. Then he tied it back up again behind the yacht George had owned at that time. He left his own dinghy tied to the burning remains of the *Jennifer Rhu*.

'The *Jennifer Rhu*?' asked Anderson, 'Named after?'

'Jennifer Argyll,' he said through a painful smile. 'She was a crush of mine. She needed to be remembered.'

'More than Abigail?'

'Yes. Oh yes. If I had stayed married I would have died. My life was managed from the minute I got up to when my head hit the pillow. The life of being a husband and father wasn't for me. I had to bail out. Nobody's fault, I'm just no good with four walls, pension schemes and thirty-five hour weeks. At the time, nobody said anything apart from how sorry they were. We got away with it.'

Oscar was used to sailing off on his own, it raised no suspicions. They found the boat still burning and the presence of the dinghy alongside suggested he had tried to free it but had fallen overboard. Search and rescue found nothing. There was nothing to find.

'Who insured your life for two million pounds?' asked Anderson, and saw Patrick's eyes narrow and flicker. He hadn't been expecting that.

'I did.'

'Who advised you to do that?'

'A friend.'

'A particular friend?'

Patrick was paying a lot of attention now.

'George Haggerty.'

'Of course it was. And what did you think when Abigail

was insured for two million and she was then murdered, with all that money going to . . . oh yes, her husband. George Haggerty.'

'I didn't get a penny.' Oscar looked a little confused.

And looking at him, Anderson believed him. 'Of course you didn't, you were dead. Abigail got it, and now George has it.'

He had escaped the madness of his married nine-to-five life to escape to a different madness of this life up here. This was where he wanted to be, where he was born. And then he started mumbling about wanting to be here with Jennifer.

He heard Patrick sigh, Anderson felt that he was kicking a puppy. This man needed help.

'Do you want to rebuild the lodge, Oscar?' he asked gently.

And then Oscar began to cry.

Patrick tapped Anderson on the shoulder, time to call it a day.

'Was it all back to bricks and mortar?' he muttered as Oscar was taken away.

'Life's loss but I bet the money will be useful, though not to him,' said Patrick in response. 'Not bricks and mortar. Cocaine.'

'What?'

Patrick's voice was low. 'Look, the North Coast 500 is a gift to a dealing network. The place floods with tourists. Then consider that anybody who builds on land on that route is on the gravy train for life. Somebody couldn't see a way of bridging that gap between what they had and what they needed. So they killed until they got what they wanted. The oldest motive in the book. Money. Pure greed.'

'They killed Abigail and Malcolm for that?' Anderson sat back down.

'Looks like it.'

'Do you know who they are? Anything to do with a company that might be driving luggage around the North Coast 500, specifically?'

Patrick gave a short sad smile, 'Yes, but it will break some-body's heart.'

*   *   *

One of the men looked right into the camera. The camera jumped, and rolled to the side, the world tumbled making Bannon and Mathieson both twist their heads as they tried to make out what they were seeing. A dark figure moving toward it very quickly, and then veered off to the right.

'I think that's where the boy makes a run for it. He gets chased and we know what happens next.'

The camera was still moving, sliding to the left towards the drop to the water where it was found. There was a jerky image of the female figure walking backwards, then dropping to the ground, and clumsily getting to her feet again. Then the screen filled with movement of limbs and shadows, that image was lost as the camera became airborne and started to film grass and sky. Then the screen filled with dark, murky water.

'Bloody hell, what was that about? What were they doing there?'

'Diane, you need to get that middle section slowed and analyzed.' Bannon realized that the DCI was shaking. It wasn't easy to watch the death of a colleague, unable to do anything about it. Except catch the man who had used that knife.

'Why don't you go and put the kettle on? I'll get a note of the timings, there's one bit where the second attacker looks right at the camera. The tech boys will be able to catch that and work it up. We've got one of them, Diane. He's on a shoogily peg, it's a matter of time.'

'They might be able to do something, but the lower part of his face is covered. Don't get your hopes up. They killed McCaffrey. That student was very lucky to survive and I don't think Costello, if that was Costello, would have been able to get out of there alive.'

They were settled down for a second viewing of the film, fortified with black coffee and the knowledge of what they were about to see, they hoped they could watch it this time with more analysis and less emotion.

'That look like McCaffrey to you?' asked Mathieson.

They watched as the guy on the ground tried to get back up before they saw the blade again. The guy on the ground then stopped moving.

'Was he dealing? That looks like an organized take down,' offered Bannon.

'There's no evidence of that anywhere in his life, he was a normal young man with a wife and kids. How the hell did he get into this? Shit! Who is that?'

Another figure appeared.

'That's a female. What the hell is she doing?'

'Walking backwards? There's somebody behind her, she's talking to them, hands up trying to appease them. The camera has moved to follow, showing that Kieran was still filming. He got the murder on film.' Only seven minutes had passed. They both leaned forwards, watching carefully as the smaller figure turned to the camera and seemed to fly through the air with such force that her body juddered as she impacted the ground. The bigger figure, walking up behind her, was still bringing his arm down, following through from the strike to the back of her head.

The enhanced film moved frame by frame showing two dark figures started moving, pulling at clothes. They took their time, confident that they would not be seen, unaware of the low light camera watching from the undergrowth. They had on gloves, their faces covered, clearly very forensically aware. They were wearing something like black boiler suits.

'What is going on here?'

'Mixing the blood, the DNA? I don't know. So we have Donnie, two assailants and one other unidentified . . . victim? He's pouring the contents of a bottle. Do you think that's cheap whisky? And what's he doing?' One of them had pulled back Donnie's face and was tapping something in it. The taller one kicked the prostate small figure with his foot, the hat slid slightly to reveal some short blonde hair. Mathieson groaned.

'Well we know what happened,' said Bannon over her shoulder. 'We need to know who those two are? Any ideas?'

'Too clean to be regular drug take downs. That looks military to me.'

'Let's go through the file again. And you'd better phone Anderson and tell him, I'm sure he'd like to know.'

THIRTEEN

Friday, 1st of December

Morna got up, thinking how cold and damp the house was. She walked into the shower, letting hot water run over her, wondering if they had enough bread left to make toast for breakfast. Neil had forgotten to get any shopping. She needed to feed Finn before she delivered him to her mother's so she could get to work.

When she got dressed, she walked into her son's room to start the difficult task of waking up her six-year-old. The room was very cold, the air damp, the curtains at the window billowing, lifting the hem from the carpet. She turned round, looking at the bed, the shape of the duvet, ruffled up on the bed like a small log. Before she reached out to it, she knew her hand would go right down until it reached the mattress. The bed was empty.

Morna looked at the curtain, still shifting with the wind and rushed out the room to get her mobile. She phoned Neil, left a message and then called Patrick who answered immediately, and told her to keep calm. He mentioned an amber alert, told her to keep her mobile phone with her.

She said she had to get out and search, she wasn't staying here.

He said he would get a team organized when he thought it was pertinent to do so.

What?

'He might have climbed out the window, Morna. We have to be sensible here. Go round, ask Lachlan, check Finn's friends, phone round, be logical and don't panic. Everybody round here knows Finn. He'll have gone off on a Star Wars adventure. They will spot him, don't you worry.'

And with that the phone was cut off leaving her staring at the screen.

*　　*　　*

Patrick looked around, standing on top of the hill, watching the lie of the land, binoculars at his eyes. He was close into the side of the wall, a small cliff face, scanning the horizon down towards the water, watching. He checked his watch; it was half past three. Finn had been missing for eight hours. People were predictable and he was sure Morna was no different. She had spent most of the day with Lachlan, being driven around, leaving her mother at Constance House to watch the phone in case there were any sightings. Patrick knew that wasn't going to happen. The lack of sightings would drive her to look round Dolphin Point eventually, within the next hour, he reckoned. People really could be that predictable.

Ten minutes later he saw Morna walk along, hearing her shouting for Finn, on her own. No Neil with her, that suited Patrick fine. That useless piece of crap would be out doing his own dirty business. He had been worried that Anderson might get involved but Patrick had made sure the city boy was where he belonged, wrapped up in the office, dissecting the video from the loch.

He took no pleasure in watching Morna, listening to her hoarse voice shouting, the heartbreak she had been going through that day. In every way, she was on her own. Slowly, he lifted the phone and called a number and gave a set of coordinates. She was on form, she wasn't going to be going anywhere fast, the guys would move in and take her, easy.

He waited, motionless. He was a man who could wait for a long time. Occasionally pulling back into the shadows when he thought Morna might be looking up his way. How pathetic she was, how programmable. One word from Lachlan about how the boy had believed Chewbacca lived up here, that the boy believed Neil when he told him the tall stories of this magical place and this might be the place a boy would run to. Morna had really accepted their reasoning. She had checked everywhere else, and now she had been brought to where her son might be. So she thought.

It had been easy to take the boy.

Taking the mother would be easier.

He waited until he saw the man approach, forty degrees behind the target, downwind, so she wouldn't catch the stink of dead fish. It was going to be a simple take down. Patrick didn't stop and watch, he didn't need to. Seen too much of that in his time.

He slipped his binoculars into his pocket and walked away.

Morna was looking for her son, meandering over Dolphin Point, no plan to her search. Neil was going round the town, asking in pubs, like that would help. She was walking south out towards the lodge. It wasn't like the wee boy to wander away, but her mind didn't want to think past that possibility. She'd had eight hours of tears and screaming and doubt.

DCI Patrick had taken charge. He was organizing the search teams. The helicopter would get called out, the dogs, everything for wee Finn. Patrick adored her wee boy. She couldn't work out why she had heard nothing so far, the sky was quiet. Even Anderson had given her nothing but platitudes, leave it to Patrick, he knows what he's doing.

She checked her watch, it was mid-afternoon. Where was a search team? What was holding them up? She should have brought the dog, but she didn't want to interfere with the search dogs. But she couldn't sit at home doing nothing. Morna turned, thinking she heard somebody coming through the hedgerow behind her. She called out, shone her torch around for a bit of extra light, but it was just the bushes waving, only the wind. She shouted, calling out again and again, the breeze catching her words and taking them out to sea.

Then she stood very still for a moment, in windblown rain; she pulled her jumper round her, zipped up her jacket. There were sounds out here in the half-darkness; she shouted her husband's name louder, then quietly. Then she called for her son.

She tried to ease the beating in her heart. There *was* somebody up here with her.

She stood very still, very still indeed. Listening. Then the thought struck her that now Finn was gone, they might be after her. But why?

Her car was down at the road so she turned and started to walk, then ran, her arms pumping. The sound of her throat rasping for air, she heard her footfall, but nothing following them. But she felt she was running for her life. She believed in the instinct of danger, she needed to find Finn and she needed to be alive to do that.

She ran through the undergrowth. It was getting thicker, holding her back. She thought she was running down to the road but looking back she couldn't see the rock stack. She couldn't see it against the darkening sky. Had she come down the wrong way? Her wet red hair was straggling behind after her. She stumbled as she ran, her arms windmilling to stop her falling. There was somebody there now, she could hear their feet behind her, they were getting closer. She was being chased down. She risked a quick look over her shoulder, managing to run forwards while looking back.

She ran straight into his arms, a fist to her stomach. She was down, winded.

Morna lay in the undergrowth, sleeping in a nest, comfortable and still. They circled round her, people like vultures. She lay in the middle, a tiny form in a big spinning wheel. The man looked down at her and smiled.

Easy.

'What do you mean, you let him go?'

'Nothing to hold him on,' said Patrick, tapping angrily at the enter button on his laptop.

'Well, fraud for a start, he defrauded his insurance company out of millions of pounds. If we don't get Haggerty for the murders or for facilitating those rapes, we could at least hold him for fraud.'

'DCI Anderson,' Patrick began, ready for a speech, 'in the whole scheme of things, of life and death and the universe and the glory of a sunrise, nobody cares. Joe Bloggs out on the street would clap at that fraud, bravo they would say. Sometimes better to go with that, eh? What good would it do? Ask yourself, what good would it do? Let Oscar be. Anything else would be cruel. And Morna's boy is missing. Did you know that? And now we can't find her either. I'm worried, DCI Anderson.'

'Sorry. Surely Finn's just wandered off and got lost? Morna is a trained police officer, any idea where she has gone?'

'Do you?'

'No. Has she just upped and left?'

Patrick had his chin on his hands, deep in thought. 'Her son was abducted, she has been abducted.'

'So why are you not out there looking for them. Get an incident room set up, call in the squad for a house to house.' He was appalled. 'If that's what you think why are we doing nothing?'

Patrick raised an eyebrow. 'Just as you are turning over every leaf to find Costello and Abernethy?' He gave a trite nod. 'We have the situation in hand, believe me.'

It sounded like a slight threat. This was Port MacDuff. Anderson needed to be careful, he wasn't going to be burned in a wicker pyre. He had missing people of his own to look for so he excused himself and went to phone Mathieson for an update. 'Fine,' he said, as he went out the office door, 'your turf, your rules.'

FOURTEEN

Saturday, 2nd of December

Morna woke up, slowly. Looking at a ceiling she didn't recognize, a wooden slatted roof with the cross beams stuffed full of some yellow packing stuff that looked like fluffy clouds or dandelion heads. She was under a warm duvet, she was fully dressed, except her boots that she could see paired neatly on the floor beside the bed. Her head hurt but she wasn't injured. She eased her limbs one by one. And she could smell dead fish.

She had been found by somebody and brought here; she slid out from under the duvet thinking about finding Finn, and finding a toilet. She looked around, she had her anorak on when she'd been outside, and in the pocket was her mobile phone. She looked out the window, nothing there just trees and brown ferns, no sign of the cliffs, no sign of the rock stack. She pulled back the curtain that served as a door, it covered nothing more than a fire and a chair, an ancient chair piled up with dirty cushions. There was a radio on a shelf, some electric equipment, and a pile of blankets on the floor. She recognized it immediately as a dog bed. There was a Calor gas cooker in the corner, a plastic bag from the local co-op.

This was somebody's secret hideaway? Or did they live here? Her anorak was on the back of the chair and her mobile was on a shelf. She grabbed at it but it felt too light, somebody had taken the battery out.

She looked around; there was no sign of life, nothing.

Morna wasn't staying, so she slipped her boots on. She opened the door and pulled her hood up, the wind had got up but it had stopped raining. She made her way round the back of the hut and squatted to empty her bladder, hoping the relief would help her think clearly.

Looking at the sky, the cloud cover had lifted a little so she could see the flat peak of the rock stack, and from that, she knew roughly where she was, inland to the south of the stack, so the coast road would be right in front of her as she stood here. She needed to make her way down there. But she didn't, she turned round and went back in, switching on the radio, being careful not to untune it to the station it was already on. She knew it would be local, for the weather if nothing else. She listen for a few minutes, realizing the time, hearing the news, the local news. Nothing about Finn, nothing about her boy.

She felt sick. She was on her own, there was some conspiracy going on. DCI Patrick and his little smiles. He had done nothing. She was a cop and she had been abducted, just to get her out the way? Why? To get Finn out the village?

She looked round, searching for clues, opening bags, looking under the bed, the person that lived here led a very simple life. There was an old bookcase, shackled together, stuff that a charity shop would throw out; there were a few tattered books, a couple of candles. A battery-powered lamp, a good torch. And at the bottom, yellowed and musty was a curled page on a pile of old newspapers. She bent down and looked at them, thinking she might see a headline of other children that had gone missing, children she knew nothing about. Other victims. These papers were old.

She lifted the top one, Jennifer Argyll, November 1987. A beautiful photograph of Jennifer, on the front page, curled and fragile with time. It was a familiar picture for her, the official press photograph. And a clipping, the name of the newspaper cut off the top. An attack on a mystery woman, raped, a twenty-three-year old. The following newspaper carried the same story; a story that went nowhere. Then Sharon Sixsmith, the one found at the bottom of the gorge and then one she didn't recognize, Patricia Sandyman. The article was cut out. No date. Morna looked round until she saw a small army knife on top of the pile of books.

It would do. She slipped it in her pocket and ran.

There is some comfort in knowing that today is the last day of your life.

No better player than a woman with nothing to lose.

There had been a lovely item on the news that morning, a still from CCTV six weeks before, on the Kelvindale walk. A picture of a person, walking, probably a man, just a person the police hoped might be able to assist them with their enquiries as they might have seen something pertaining to the murders of Abigail and Malcolm Haggerty. To anybody else watching it looked like a bloke walking home with a package under his arm. Thirty-three inches long, twenty-two inches wide, carried on its side so it fitted under his arm.

She recognized it, she had built it.

Valerie had paused the TV screen, and looked closely. She knew that shape: the Millennium Falcon.

She had known that she had to move and move fast, Mathieson was close to the truth, but she was closer, so she rolled the white Fiat into the trees and down into the thick bracken. There was only dense undergrowth in sheltered places, and there was little shelter on the headland, up near the lodge. She'd do the last bit by foot. But she had her boots, her jacket and her gun.

She was going to end it now. She'd been following Haggerty for a couple of days now. He had been doing nothing but lazing around, drinking, meeting his friends and socializing, constantly on his mobile to somebody. The one place he had not been was the care home where his dad was. This morning was different though. Haggerty had been up, ready and was moving quickly. She could sense things were coming to a head. He would have seen that footage from the bridge and she was going to get him before he boarded a ferry and slipped away.

Her decision was made.

Valerie Abernethy felt the happiest she had felt for ages.

DCI Alastair Patrick was back at the rock stack, standing in the shadows, as motionless as the standing stones. His utter stillness made him invisible, the way an aboriginal standing can be mistaken for a tree. His background of grey rock matched the pallor of his face.

'Is this where Oscar lives? Up here at Dolphin Point?' asked Anderson, sotto voce.

'Be quiet and keep your eyes open. And don't move, if you move you will be seen.'

'But is this where—'

'Quiet.'

He had got a similar answer when he asked, 'What are we doing up here?'

They had been there for two hours, at Dolphin Point, on the far side where the outer limits of the house used to be. Anderson was in awe of Patrick's ability to remain motionless. He tried to amuse himself, keep himself warm, closed his eyes and tried to keep standing up, got cold and numb. He wanted a hot coffee and his bed, a cooked breakfast, anything but to be here. But he didn't really trust Alastair Patrick. Not one bit.

'Hear that?' whispered Patrick.

'What?'

'Vehicle coming.'

'You can hear that?'

'I can if you don't speak.' Patrick's head was down, looking at his feet, as if he was concentrating on his ears.

'We should be out looking for Morna and the boy. Abigail and her boy were killed, now Morna and her boy have gone missing.' It was the fourth time he had said it.

Patrick said, 'Huge difference between being missing and being dead.' Then he ignored him.

The noise of the engine stopped. To Anderson it only sounded like the wind dropping a little. Patrick held his hand up, telling him to wait. And pointed to the Sound, where the land flattened off. In the cine film this had been where the tennis courts were, flat all the way to the cliff with a gentle seaward fall. Anderson suddenly got a very bad feeling about this, he watched where Patrick had indicated to look, and saw a disturbance in the trees. He dropped down a little to stay out of sight as they walked into view. The two of them.

'Who is that?' he whispered.

'If there is a god it will be Haggerty and Taverner,' whispered Patrick, then turned to look straight at Anderson. 'Why? Who were you expecting?'

'The Argyll and Sutherland Pipe Band for all I know.'

Anderson grew silent, fascinated as he watched the two men; Haggerty, the smaller figure out in front, walking through a plain flat field of grass but following a definite path. Neil Taverner, taller, at the back was less certain, he kept turning round, checking the horizon. Alastair Patrick didn't move, he stayed very still against the rock face. Neil Taverner's eyes passed right over them. Anderson wondered how often Patrick had stood here, watching.

'Who is that?' asked Anderson as a smaller figure came walking over the hill, from behind the rock stack. They too, were heading towards the sea.

'I have no bloody idea,' replied Patrick, almost in admiration that something was going on that was unexpected.

'I think I do, I think that's my DI.'

'The untraceable Ms Costello? Well, she's come ready for the party. That's a firearm in her right hand.' Patrick raised his binoculars. 'Bloody hell.'

'She can't be allowed to do this, she can't risk everything to take Haggerty out. We have enough on him.'

'She doesn't know that though.'

Patrick remained immobile so Anderson made a decision and ran, slipping out from his hiding place and moving fast across the ground, losing height with every forward stride, gaining on the two men from behind. They both took off at the sound of footfall without looking round, but they had seen the woman with the firearm. They were caught in a pincer movement. Both ran towards the edge of the cliff, trying to outrun them before they ran out of land.

Anderson could hear Patrick behind him, shouting, and then the woman held the gun up as if to fire it. She took aim and seemed to pull the trigger. Anderson yelled at her, holding his arm out.

It all happened in perfect slow motion.

Absolutely nothing.

The woman tried to pull the trigger again.

Nothing.

Anderson was still shouting Costello's name. *He's not worth it.*

She didn't seem to hear, but he had no idea if she could

hear him. Then she was running, still holding the gun, making for the smaller of the men. She was going for Haggerty, getting closer before she tried firing again. Anderson saw Patrick cut off to his left, blocking any escape that Neil Taverner might think he had.

The two men backed up, Anderson noticed how much land they had covered, how little grass was left between them and the cliff top. Then he saw the hand rise again, gun perfectly level, this time in a double-handed stance, like a police officer. She stood firm, and pulled the trigger, nothing happened.

Haggerty stopped and turned towards her. Facing her, he brought the palms of his two hands together.

Clap clap.

Then he turned, resuming his flight.

Patrick was running up fast behind her, reaching for the gun. The woman screamed as it was wrestled from her hand, she twisted free and started running, running as if the devil himself was after her. The look on her face was one of intense concentration, beyond human, she was a killing machine.

And she ran. Heading for Haggerty.

Anderson stopped, watching in horror as she kept moving, grabbing Haggerty round the waist. He had been expecting a punch or a blow but not to be held, so low, her arms round his waist, her shoulder pushing him off balance. She was light, but quick, and she had the momentum of the roll of the land to carry them both stumbling towards the edge of the cliff. He saw Haggerty's heels dig into the soft ground, his hands trying to prise himself free from her, but she had her prey. She wasn't letting go now. Anderson thought he saw Haggerty manage to force up her head, forcing her to choose between releasing him or having her neck broken.

Anderson didn't know if they went over the edge together or apart. He saw, he thought, blue sky and grey sea between them, before they hung in mid-air for the briefest of moments. Then they plummeted from his view.

Anderson stood shocked, blinking, thinking about running forward to make sure, but his legs didn't move. He heard the waves, somebody screaming and somebody shouting. He turned. Patrick was pointing it at him, right at his forehead.

'Drop! Drop.'

Anderson opened his mouth but dropped to his knees, this had all been so, so wrong. He heard the gun fire once, a bang so loud even the wind stopped in shock. Anderson felt himself fall. Face down into the grass, it was wet on his skin. He heard another blast then another two. He felt the rain fall on the back of his neck, a dribble leaked from the corner of his mouth. He heard Patrick approach. He thought there might be another bullet in the chamber; the muzzle would be cold against the back of his head. Military precision, Mathieson had said that. Why had he not listened?

He thought about Moses, about Claire and . . . then he felt a hand on his collar, pulling him up.

'Silly bastard. That piece of shit was right behind you.'

Anderson raised himself up on his elbows and looked behind him. Neil Taverner, lying with bits of him missing, staring at the sky. Glinting in the grass was a knife, with a long thin blade. He was less than two feet away. Anderson had seen the damage that knife could do.

So very close.

Anderson put his head back on the grass, He wasn't going anywhere for a wee while yet.

Anderson had to crawl the first few yards before he was up on his feet, walking towards the edge. His shoes slipped on the damp grass as he neared the precipice. Slowing, he stepped carefully, the edge was unstable, broken, land slips, mini cliffs, bites taken out here and there. He got back on his knees, hearing a warning shout from somebody behind him. He crawled to the edge, looking, his dirty fingers clawing through the mud then over at the waves crashing on the rocks below. Down near the narrow band of soft white sand lay the body of George Haggerty spread-eagled on the waterline. His head in the water being buffeted, rolling back and forth with the advance and retreat of the smallest waves like a nodding puppet. If the fall, over a hundred feet, had not killed him, then the sea surely would.

Anderson steeled himself to look along the water's edge. Nothing. Then he moved closer, looking directly down,

scanning the cliff, then he saw her, caught on a ledge. He
shouted down but there was no reply, no response at all.
He looked past her to the mass of blonde hair caught on a
grassy ledge further down.

Not Costello.

Back at the Exciseman, Anderson had spent a long time in a
hot bath thinking about Costello and where she was. As Valerie
had been lifted from her narrow grassy hammock on the side
of the cliff onto a cradle and winched up the cliff face, her
eyes had sought out Anderson. They suspected a spinal fracture
and a few broken limbs but as they carried her past she had
weakly pointed a finger at him. He had lifted her oxygen mask
just enough for him to hear, 'Costello's fine. She did good.'

He whispered in her ear, 'And so did you.' He replaced the
mask, her eyes closed with a sense of peace. Mission
accomplished.

He had felt like crying, Patrick had stood back, giving him
a moment.

At the Exciseman bar, the owner was now very friendly,
telling Anderson to get his jacket, there was a double measure
of eighteen-year-old Glendronach waiting outside.

'Outside?'

Beyond prying ears.

Alastair Patrick was sitting alone, on a bench on the seafront,
two crystal glasses cradled in his gloved fingers. Without
looking, he passed one over to Anderson and for a moment
they sat in silence, the wind had died, the rain had stopped.
They looked out over the dark water of the Sound, it merged
into the darker sky somewhere beyond the horizon. Patrick
seemed hypnotized by the rhythmic sweep of the beam of the
Rua Riedh lighthouse.

Anderson felt comforted by it. How many sailors out there
in the unseen darkness, were watching.

'So, what are you SO14? SO15? Any other number we mere
mortals are not allowed to know about?' asked Anderson,
sipping the malt. It warmed his heart.

'SO 15? Do I look like a tosser?' Patrick whispered.
'Anyway, all this almost makes you believe in the Good Lord,

now that the demons have been chased, the resident evil is no longer . . . resident.'

'That was some shooting you did.'

'Not that difficult. I wasn't caring if I hit you.' Patrick kept his eyes on the water.

'You a weapons man, somewhere?'

'Some might say.'

'Was Valerie trying to fire that gun? Did it jam? How did you know it would fire?'

'Ruger. It fires OK if you release the safety.'

Anderson smiled.

Patrick continued, 'And for your paperwork, you need to know that Kieran Cowan was never left alone after he was discovered. The chain of evidence was kept intact, your little orange fibres are safe evidence. And he's alive to testify that it was Haggerty who attacked him.'

'Would I regret asking who was watching over Cowan on the Bealach that morning, if I needed a statement?'

'No, you wouldn't regret it. But you wouldn't get an answer.'

'OK. Is something going on up here? Something important?'

'Some folk might say that. Preparation. Exercises. You've seen the news.'

'The Yemen? Are they going to—'

'I wouldn't know.'

Another silence felt between then.

'You saved my life, Neil Taverner was going to slit my throat.'

'You would have survived. He's watched too many Hollywood films to do it properly.'

'You knew for a while though. About them both.'

'They were clever but it was a house of cards. We needed a catalyst, after we found Cowan, I knew it was game on. It was stepping stones after that. The McCaffrey boy. Then the Abernethy woman came here, stuck out like a sore thing. We were watching, of course, waiting. And she was following him. He wasn't expecting that so his guard was down. Sneaky woman, Abernethy, surprised me.'

'He thought he had killed the woman who had been

following him. Haggerty must have thought they got away with it.'

'Feeling secure made them sloppy.'

'Why did you take Finn?'

'For his own safety. Morna said she was doing her sergeant's exams. Neil immediately increased her life insurance. Then there were a couple of accidents, incidents? Nothing was going to happen to Morna on my watch. Easier to lift them and contain them. She'll forgive me when she calms down. She has more to concern her.'

'It was not lawful. And what happened to Neil Taverner wasn't lawful.'

'It was quick, better than he deserved,' Patrick's voice was hard.

'What happened to his body?'

A shrug.

'I thought you might have an idea.'

Patrick ignored him. 'The Millennium Falcon is in Taverner's garage. Abernethy's fingerprints are on the inside which is perfectly natural as she's on record as saying she built it with Malcolm last Christmas.'

Anderson nodded, glad of solid evidence.

Patrick said quietly, 'Did you not see Neil Taverner roll down that hill? I think his body got washed out to sea.'

'I saw him lying . . .'

'You saw nothing, you were chewing the grass.' Patrick looked along the water, watching the light sweep. 'Aye well. They'll be a wee hiatus in the efficiency of drug running for a while. Hope the drug squad try to capitalize on that. Slip in someone undercover, somebody good.'

'Sounds like you fancy the job yourself?'

'Twenty, thirty years ago nae bother.' Patrick took a large slug, smiling. 'It's always the same. You need balls to do that kind of job.'

'Who dares wins?'

And Anderson thought that Alastair Patrick might have winked at him.

FIFTEEN

Sunday, 3rd of December

C ostello was in her hospital bed, sitting up like a posed doll, stiff against the pillows. The bruising around her eyes had blackened. Her hair was sticking up. She looked like a drunk raccoon.

She was wondering when the pain would cease when the door opened. A tall blond man walked in followed by a small man, better dressed, with salt and pepper hair. OK, maybe not better dressed but he carried his clothes better, as if he owned them. With the taller man, it was the other way round.

'So here you are,' DCI Colin Anderson said, not keeping the bite of anger from his voice. Just because she wasn't fit enough to hear it, didn't mean that he wasn't going to say it.

'How's Valerie?'

'Three vertebral fractures, both femurs broken. She's in Raigmore.'

'Did you really think it was me?' asked Costello.

'I hoped,' answered Anderson. 'Especially when she went over the cliff.' He resisted the urge to lean forward and pat her on the head. The fracture at the rear of her skull was covered by a dressing. He had seen the film now, Costello running forward to help a fatally wounded McCaffrey. Not hearing the second man, Taverner, arm raised ready to bring a tyre lever down on her head. O'Hare said she had been lucky. She had her hood up and a hat on under that. The cushioning had saved her life.

Costello's eyes looked at Anderson then to Walker, back to Anderson. 'And who are you, exactly?' She wasn't laughing; there was no sarcastic humour in her face.

Now it was Anderson and Walker's turn to look at each other.

'You two are so easy to wind up.' She smiled. 'Getting a bit of memory back every day.'

'I've brought you some grapes,' said Walker, pulling up another seat.

'How long have we worked together?'

'Must be about twenty years, maybe more,' said Anderson. 'It seems like a life sentence.' Injecting a sense of their normal relationship into a conversation. 'How is your memory really? Do you remember resigning?'

Costello tried to shake her head, then stopped as it hurt so much.

'You told the big boss to stick his job up his arse.' Anderson said gleefully. 'But Mitchum didn't process it as he thought you . . .'

'Weren't serious?'

'No, he thought you were barking mad. There will be an investigation but I think Police Scotland will have you back. So how is the memory really?'

She shrugged. 'Patchy. It's not so bad, living in this world in my head. Things are very clear, very cut and dry, I know the essence of somebody, nothing else. It's useful.' She chewed on her lip, looking out the window, a slow smile formed on her lips. 'So Valerie got him. Our plan worked.' She closed her eyes now, as if with that knowledge, she could sleep more easily. 'She's paying for me to be here you know.'

'Well she can afford it, she's going to inherit the house.'

Her eyes flashed open. 'You were with me.' Her forefinger drifted towards Walker's face, seeing a small nod of agreement. 'When we found the bodies. Haggerty killed them both.'

'He couldn't have, he was on the A9 at the time. He got his sideman to do it for him. Haggerty helped Taverner with the rapes. Taverner did Haggerty's murders for him. As you guessed, he was in the garage all along.'

'Bastard. I knew Haggerty was behind it. You lot were doing bugger all about it. So I did something myself. Poor Abigail, targeted by George after Oscar disappeared.'

'You were very sure, on very little evidence.'

'I was on the receiving end of his taunts. I have a very clear memory of that. I have a clear memory that he had persuaded you lot not to listen to me, he wanted to discredit me. Though I doubt he thought I'd get suspected of murdering Donnie.

He must have loved that. You can't protect yourself against gossip and lies, so in that way, he got me. And he got me good.'

'Why were you there at the lochside? Whatever it was, you could have come to us,' said Walker delicately. 'We would have listened.'

'You didn't. You told me to get lost. All anybody could talk about was his alibi. Donnie was the only one who listened to me. And that got him killed.' She blinked back a tear. 'George was tailing me at times after Abigail's death, I did tell you that. And what did you do? You told George.'

Anderson closed his eyes. Had he really done that?

'George was off his work after the murders, he had all day to annoy me, and you lot were happy to stand aside and let him. I was following him as much as he was following me. Donnie and I were nowhere near careful enough. It had become comical almost, it made us forget how dangerous he was, and I will never forgive myself for that. But we had no choice. But you know . . .' She was getting angry. 'It took us ten minutes looking into George's life up north to come to Neil Taverner as the man with the opportunity. Donnie and his love of the sidemen, he almost profiled Taverner before we got near him. An adoring wife who earns more than he does, whose value goes up as a mother, yet the father is not close to the child. You do my crime and I will do yours, not an uncommon thing when there is a long-term bond between two people. The bond between Taverner and Haggerty was much stronger than the bond between Taverner and his wife, or Haggerty and his wife.'

'Costello? What were you doing at the lochside?' Anderson asked again.

'We met to go to the campsite, it's only four miles up the road, and wait for Taverner to do his pick-up of the luggage. That was all. We met at the loch so we were only in one car, to look less conspicuous. But we didn't think they were following us, we didn't think.'

In hindsight, Anderson had thought it through. They hadn't been as careful as they should have been. Costello had believed that Haggerty thought she would accept his warning off, but Haggerty had realized that she had taken it as a sign to freelance her investigation. He had made her more dangerous. Anderson might have told Haggerty that himself. Donnie had thought Cowan was Taverner and had followed him up to the viewing point. Cowan had been in the wrong place, wrong time.

Walker filled up the gaps. 'So Taverner and Haggerty realized there were three of you and only two of them, so they placed a stop box on each vehicle in the car park. They came prepared to clean up the situation. As you were left alone, they presumed you were dead. Haggerty goes after Kieran, and waits for him to pull over. Taverner takes Donnie away from the scene and drives up north, as he was scheduled to do. You were in the grass bleeding. Haggerty had to retrieve your phones, mix the blood, spill a little cocaine, pour some drink around the scene. They wanted to destroy your reputation. Cowan made them panic, it made them careless.'

Costello settled back into the pillow on her chair. She closed her eyes, her eyelids pink islands in the bruised patches around her eye sockets. 'I think I can see Donnie on the ground, I was coming up the hill, my thighs are sore because of the climb. I remember trying to get away. I ran forward to help but . . . Then I don't remember. I was on the ground at one point. I tried to get up, I remember wet hands round my neck. There was a blow on the back of my head, not sure what happened then. I don't recall much but being in here.'

'You crawled away, through the undergrowth. You got out.'

Walker said, 'The doctor explained your thinking brain shut off, your deep brain was looking for patterns, for safety. People do the weirdest things. So by the time you were picked up in the middle of Glasgow, you had changed, showered and gone back out. You left your car at Lochmaben Road.'

'Where my grandmother used to live.'

'You drove it there, ignoring the clatter of the ball bearings. You sat in the park then ran off when the police were called. Then you walked home, then out to Buchannan Street, we have you on CCTV. Do you know why you did that?'

She shook her head. 'I have no idea.'

'You could have come to me,' said Anderson.

'George was at your house, so what good would that have
done me?'

And it was true, he'd lost count of how many times George
asked him if he'd seen Costello.

And George had known she was onto him. He knew they
could be intercepted and caught red-handed at a baggage pick
up or drop and the one closest to Glasgow seemed most logical.
He wondered how many times they had watched Costello and
she had not moved, but when she did they were ready. She
had been arrogant and stupid, and because of her, three wee
boys would grow up without a dad.

'Taverner was picking up and distributing drugs, mostly
cocaine. The big bags, like a golf flight bag, well they contained
the luggage for transportation to the different sites, and they
were lined with old carpet, orange tri-lobular fibres. That puts
a lot of connections together.'

'So George wasn't the rapist,' asked Costello.

'He wasn't. He was the facilitator of the rapes. There's a team
on it now. They have already proven he knew Sally and that
Haggerty and Taverner were in Glasgow when she was raped.'

'But it was very useful for him to have us pursue him on
something he was innocent of. The "Clapping Song" playing.
He clapped at me at the funeral. So no I did not work it out,
he told me. The clapping is in Sally's notes, it's in the case
file of Gillian Witherspoon as well, and there will be more,
there will be more out there. Haggerty clapped, Taverner raped,
Haggerty probably watched.' Costello thought about shaking
her head again.

'We think Taverner had a bad shoulder, there's anecdotal
evidence of a young woman throwing him at karate, breaking
his shoulder. That might have annoyed him a bit.'

'Easy for Taverner to drive around, early morning, late at
night. He had a right to be everywhere. Woman walking,
hiking, camping on their own.'

'So it was all for money, and the nice little line they had
running cocaine about the country. I wonder how many of
their hikers are extremely regular. And sniff a lot.'

'All small fry compared to the murder of Malcolm and
Abigail.'

'You were right about the MO. Haggerty came home the previous evening and drove in to the garage. I think Taverner was in the boot. Taverner stayed in the garage, then walked in the back door, killed them. The guy on the CCTV on Kelvindale path is the right height for Taverner, not for Haggerty. There is no DNA because of that outfit he wears, it's like a boiler suit, with the name of the company on it. He killed them, slipped a jacket over his easily recognizable suit and left. Walked back to wherever he left his car. It wasn't sophisticated, it wasn't even that clever. It was merely effective.'

'Haggerty had been using that path for years, he was a secretive man and the path had been closed from his end, so it's likely that he "allowed" naughty Malcolm to open the path again knowing that it would give Taverner a way out in the early hours of that morning largely unseen. Nobody else knew about the path at the back, Haggerty would deny it. Mathieson and her team missed it, they didn't know where to look, a small gap in an overgrown hedge. Heads will roll that the search team missed that.'

'And Oscar Duguid? The first husband? What's his role in all this?' asked Costello.

'I think something happened to Oscar Duguid when he heard about Mary Jane's death. Her murder shocked him, just because he walked away from the marriage doesn't mean he stopped loving his daughter, my daughter,' said Anderson. 'He thought he had left them comfortable and safe, his friend moved in as role of father and protector. He knew about the attacks on women, that was his insurance to keep them quiet about his disappearing act. They didn't stop the attacks. Haggerty is a man of intense cruelty, Oscar was OK with faking his own death, but he must have had a serious rethink when Abigail was murdered. And maybe when he worked out what might have happened to Jennifer Argyll up at Dolphin Point. His Jennifer, thirty years before. That's still under investigation. Lachlan McRae was the SIO on her disappearance.'

'Where is he now? Oscar?'

'DCI Patrick is saying nothing. You can attach electrodes to his testicles and you'll get nothing out of him,' said Anderson smiling.

'Reading the reports. I fail to understand why Taverner's body was washed out to sea,' said Walker.

'You had to be there,' said Anderson blithely. 'I'm more interested in the psychological hold that house held over them, it became a focus for memories. That's why people have cenotaphs set in stone, I suppose, so their memories are also set in stone. Happy days at the lodge, the three boys growing up there. Then Jennifer Argyll went missing, Oscar's heart was broken and from then on, it was all downhill.'

'Memories, eh? Powerful but untrustworthy.'

'They are useful,' added Costello.

'Well, I had better get home before I get forgotten about,' said Anderson.

'And I'm going to visit my sober god-daughter,' Walker shrugged, 'now that she's therapeutically plastered.'

'Oh very good,' laughed Anderson. 'I'm going home to a kitchen which is slightly busier than Sauchiehall Street in the Boxing Day sales.'

'And does that not make you yearn for the ruggedly beautiful isolation of Dolphin Point?' asked Walker.

Anderson appeared to consider it carefully. 'Nope.'